POLITICS AND PHILOSOPHY IN PLATO'S *MENEXENUS*

Menexenus is one of the least studied among Plato's works, mostly because of the puzzling nature of the text, which has led many scholars either to reject the dialogue as spurious or to consider it as a mocking parody of Athenian funeral rhetoric. In this book, Pappas and Zelcer provide a persuasive alternative reading of the text, one that contributes in many ways to our understanding of Plato, and specifically to our understanding of his political thought.

The book is organized into two parts. In the first part the authors offer a synopsis of the dialogue, address the setting and its background in terms of the Athenian funeral speech, and discuss the alternative readings of the dialogue, showing their weaknesses and strengths. In the second part, the authors offer their positive interpretation of the dialogue, taking particular care to explain and ground their interpretive criteria and method, which considers Plato's text not simply as a de-contextualized collection of philosophical arguments but offers a theoretically informed reading of the text that situates it firmly within its historical context.

This book will become a reference point in the debate about the *Menexenus* and Plato's political philosophy more generally and marks an important contribution to our understanding of ancient thought and classical Athenian society.

Nickolas Pappas is Professor of Philosophy at City College and the Graduate Center, City University of New York, USA.

Mark Zelcer is Visiting Assistant Professor of Philosophy at the State University of New York, Oswego, USA.

POLITICS AND PHILOSOPHY IN PLATO'S *MENEXENUS*

Education and Rhetoric, Myth and History

*Nickolas Pappas and
Mark Zelcer*

Routledge
Taylor & Francis Group

LONDON AND NEW YORK

First published 2015 by Routledge

2 Park Square, Milton Park, Abingdon, Oxfordshire OX14 4RN
52 Vanderbilt Avenue, New York, NY 10017

Routledge is an imprint of the Taylor & Francis Group, an informa business

First issued in paperback 2019

British Library Cataloguing in Publication Data
A catalogue record for this book is available from the British Library

Library of Congress Cataloging in Publication Data
Pappas, Nickolas, 1960- author.
Politics and philosophy in Plato's Menexenus : education and rhetoric, myth and
history / Nickolas Pappas and Mark Zelcer.
pages cm
Includes bibliographical references and index.
1. Plato. Menexenus. 2. Rhetoric, Ancient. 3. Rhetoric--Philosophy. I. Zelcer, Mark,
author. II. Title.
B376.P37 2015
184--dc23
2014029207

ISBN: 978-1-844-65820-6 (hbk)
ISBN: 978-0-367-25613-5 (pbk)

Typeset in Times New Roman
by Taylor & Francis Books

CONTENTS

Acknowledgements   vii

Introduction   1
An eccentric dialogue   *1*
The question of parody   *4*
If not parody   *7*

PART I
The *Menexenus*, its persons, its problems   13

1   Synopsis of the dialogue   15
Opening dialogue (234a–236d)   *15*
Funeral speech (236d–249c)   *16*
Closing dialogue (249d–e)   *19*

2   Persons and dates of the dialogue   20
Socrates   *20*
Aspasia   *31*
Other tutors: Connus, Antiphon and Lamprus   *37*
Archinus and Dion   *40*
Menexenus   *42*
Pericles   *45*

3   The Athenian funeral speech   58
The genre: three cautions   *58*
The Menexenus *against the backdrop of its genre*   *67*
The funeral speech in Loraux   *71*

4   The *Menexenus* as parody, as improvement   77
The relationship between the two funeral speeches   *77*
Positive arguments: the Menexenus *speech as improvement*   *82*
Positive argument from precedent   *85*
Negative arguments: against the Menexenus *speech as parody*   *88*

CONTENTS

PART II
Education and rhetoric   **95**

5 Scenes of instruction; Pericles' missed opportunities   **97**
   Education and rhetoric   97
   Pericles and moral education   99
   Scenes of instruction in the Menexenus   *103*
   Instruction as intrusion   111

6 Philosophical rhetoric   **116**
   Logos *and* ergon   *116*
   Praise   121
   Improvisation   132

PART III
Myth and history   **141**

7 Myth   **143**
   Stories of Athens   143
   Mythic passages in the Menexenus   *146*
   Plato's myths   150
   Autochthony in Athens   157
   Autochthony in Plato   162
   Autochthony and nature in the Menexenus   *166*
   Autochthony and human difference in the Menexenus   *169*
   The meanings of autochthony   174

8 History   **182**
   Philosophical history   182
   Omissions and other distortions of history   183
   The Menexenus *and the historians   195*
   Order in history   199
   Soul, city, world   201
   A parody of history?   206

Conclusion: Buried in philosophy   **214**
   The Menexenus*'s improvements to the funeral speech   214*
   The Menexenus *and other dialogues   215*
   The Phaedrus   *218*

   Bibliography   222
   Index   231

ACKNOWLEDGEMENTS

Although the *Menexenus* is a short dialogue and the scholarly literature on it small compared with every other Platonic work, a book of this kind incurs many debts. Its ideas arose out of a broad range of research and benefited from contributions to that research along the way.

Several scholars helped our research in correspondence, often giving us looks at unpublished material and providing useful specific advice. We gratefully acknowledge J. E. Lendon, Peter Liddel, Christopher Long, Bruce Rosenstock, Ed Sanders and Kendall Sharp. M. M. McBride offered generous comments on earlier versions of this material.

Some parts of this book were presented as lectures. We are happy for this chance to thank audiences at the Ancient Philosophy Society, at City College and at Stony Brook University. Heidi Northwood's comments at the APS added much of value to the argument now developed in Chapter 8.

We are also grateful to the students at City College, Baruch College and the Graduate Center, to whom we taught the *Menexenus* and whose enthusiasm convinced us to move forward with this project.

From M. Z.: Work on this book often was interrupted, by teaching, a dissertation, a wedding, a war and fatherhood. I only made it through because of the support of family and friends. It is a relief, if a small one, that I can thank them publicly. My parents, siblings and their families, whose respect for scholarship is unparalleled, have been a great font of generosity and support. Alex and Rachel Kozlowsky have been extremely encouraging throughout the whole time I have known them and I am grateful for their presence in my life. Finally, *aharon aharon haviv*, Dahlia, *sine qua non*.

From N. P.: The *Menexenus* has long been an object of interest. Of the many teachers I have to thank, William McCulloh is especially relevant. How telling that he taught Greek at Kenyon College not only to me but also to another recent scholar of the *Menexenus*. I am happy to thank Burt Hopkins and Brian Seitz for many kinds of philosophical help and encouragement. As for my wife Barbara's help to me, I can only describe it justly in hyperbolic terms. I thank her again.

Nickolas Pappas
Mark Zelcer

INTRODUCTION

An eccentric dialogue

One line from the *Menexenus* has the sound of a proverb: "It is not hard to praise Athens among the Athenians"; and Aristotle quotes the sentiment in his *Rhetoric* as he might quote a proverb.[1] He could not have known that this act of citation would provide the telling evidence to later centuries that the *Menexenus* is a genuine Platonic dialogue, maybe the only conclusive evidence. For in the absence of this reference in Aristotle, the unusual character of the *Menexenus* would have led most scholars to classify it as spurious.

As things stand, and despite its assured status among the authentic works, the *Menexenus* has not found a place in the modern Platonic canon. Although it has lately been the subject of some discussion by classicists, that discussion focuses either on the *Menexenus*'s contribution to the genre of the Athenian *epitaphios logos* "funeral oration, funeral speech",[2] or on the information it offers about the intriguing figure Aspasia of Miletus.[3] Notwithstanding Charles Kahn's invaluable exploration of the *Menexenus* half a century ago,[4] the time since then has found few philosophers studying the dialogue.[5]

Why the inattention and the suspicion? The *Menexenus* may be Plato's most eccentric work. It contains very little argumentative back-and-forth; the voice it represents is that of a shadowy woman; the framing dialogue around its main speech is a playful tease; and most distinctive, the dialogue orients itself against another text, whether in parody, homage or intended improvement. Aside from the brief opening dialogue between Socrates and this character Menexenus, and a mere breath of closing conversation between them, the *Menexenus* amounts to a speech suitable for recitation at public funerals during wartime and reminiscent of the great speech that Pericles had delivered early in the Peloponnesian War.[6] Socrates has made fun of existing Athenian funeral rhetoric – at least, Menexenus understands him to be mocking that rhetoric – and he recites the kind of speech that he says he would give on the occasion of a public funeral. He claims that his tutor Aspasia composed this speech, and her credentials are impeccable, she also having (as Socrates says) written the speech that people attribute to Pericles.

1

The *Menexenus* already stands out for being so nearly a single stretch of prose, and not the short-questioning, quick-answering exchanges that typify Platonic dialogues. It is true that other dialogues contain long speeches too, and enigmatic ones: think of some long unbroken sections of Plato's *Phaedrus*, *Protagoras* and *Symposium*. The *Apology* is almost entirely a monologue, while the *Timaeus* and *Critias* come as close as the *Menexenus* does to being one straight speech speedily introduced by prefatory conversations.

Indeed, many of those other long speeches in the dialogues claim to be the words of other voices, often voices as exotic as Aspasia's. Plato ventriloquizes in the *Phaedrus* composing a speech about love in the style of the orator Lysias, in the *Symposium* with the medical–cosmological speech of Eryximachus and the tender encomium to love from Agathon. Timaeus in Plato's *Timaeus* is a non-Athenian bringing new cosmologies to town; the *Critias*'s Critias a discredited oligarch; Hermocrates (had Plato ever written the dialogue in which *he* speaks) a general from the Sicilian city of Syracuse.

As a platform for an unexpected authority's voice the closest dialogue to the *Menexenus* might be Plato's *Symposium*, in which Socrates introduces a view of *erôs* "love" as the teaching of the priestess Diotima. Diotima, like Aspasia, is a woman Socrates speaks of as impressive. Nothing is known about her today, as next to nothing is known about Aspasia. Diotima might be a Platonic concoction and therefore even less available to historians than Aspasia is, and yet this unknown woman delivers a philosophically ambitious discourse on love.[7]

But the *Symposium*, the *Apology* and the *Timaeus* are among Plato's most widely read dialogues. Even that unfinished mythic history the *Critias* has earned a special place in cultural history as the account of the island nation Atlantis. What makes the *Menexenus* any more eccentric than those specimens? And does its singularity account for its greater obscurity?

There is this, that the *Menexenus* revisits and rewrites an existing text. Even more than it is about Athenian history or about patriotic sentiment it is *about another speech*. In this sense, and it is a very specific sense, the *Menexenus* possesses a literary quality the other dialogues do not. It needs to be emphasized that this is a very specific sense of "literary quality". The literariness in question is not a matter of beautiful language or appeals to human emotions, although some treatments of the dialogues as literary understand what is literary in those terms, and moments in Plato's critique of poetry understand the poetic in the same way. Nor does the *Menexenus*'s literariness much resemble that aspect of the dialogues that many literarily minded readings seize on and turn on, namely their being dialogues among concrete characters set in particular places. The *Menexenus* does contain particular characters, and it refers to others worth bearing in mind (Aspasia, Pericles); but what distinguishes it is the entirely different writing-effect, sometimes called intertextuality, in which one work rewrites what has already been written, making its assertions in resistance to a preceding voice.

From a modern perspective this feature of the *Menexenus* makes it precisely more literary than any other dialogue, which is to say literary in a precise sense of that word. "Literature" today, largely *un*like what Plato's times called poetry, implies works that exist in written form, mainly reaching an audience by being read (silently and individually). The poetry that the *Republic* censors is recited by its authors or performed at dramatic festivals, sung by adolescent choruses or retold to children by their nurses. But Plato lived at a time that saw oral transmission being replaced by writing and reading. In *Frogs*, performed a few years before the trial of Socrates (performed when Plato would have been in his mid-twenties), even the god Dionysus enjoys Euripidean tragedies by reading them. Closer to home – as far as the *Menexenus* is concerned – Thucydides takes pains to distinguish the history he wrote from those ostensible rivals composed for recitation before a crowd. His own history, presumably not delivered orally, is built to last, a *ktêma* "possession" *es aiei* "forever".[8]

The new pre-eminence of writing as the standard way to disseminate a work, with reading as the standard way to experience it, makes one work's incorporation of another possible as it had not been before. There is no denying that Euripides revisits Aeschylean tragedy in numerous ways. Aristophanes takes over Euripidean scenes to complex effect. But the audiences of Aristophanes and Euripides typically did not go through two passages side-by-side as Plato's readers could do with the speech in the *Menexenus*, whose precedent was available for comparison in written form. As close reading becomes possible when writing is common, so does intimate and specific rewriting that can now announce itself as such.

In another way the revisitation of an earlier work can be seen as producing an effect contrary to the effect that Plato's dialogues achieve with characters' conversations. For what typically happens in a Platonic dialogue is that its participants set aside the contexts in which ideas are born. Whether a questioner (usually Socrates) cross-examines someone else's beliefs, or the leader develops a new theory (be it Socrates, the Athenian Stranger, the Stranger from Elea, Timaeus or Parmenides leading), claims are tested as if they had fallen from the sky. These claims often begin with what the interlocutor says right now in conversation. A verse from Homer might give Socrates an idea, or something from Protagoras that he heard someone talking about, but the integrity of the texts he quotes from does not concern him.[9] Rarely does Socrates dig into a written work to unearth what it is saying. Even from a distance of millennia it seems possible to glimpse the unfairness in his reading of Anaxagoras.[10]

Outside the *Menexenus* there is one scene above all that finds Socrates engaged in reading someone else's composition. Protagoras challenges him to explicate a bit of Simonides; Socrates tangles with the poem but then declares the activity impossible. Responding to poems means speaking in the poets' absence as one should be speaking in their presence. The only philosophical method that Socrates acknowledges is back-and-forth conversation with a live interlocutor. Certainly his dismissal of the poets' wisdom in the *Apology* implies that he questioned them. The task they failed at was that of explaining their own verse. And an enigmatic passage from Diogenes Laërtius' life of Plato says that Plato, then an aspiring young tragedian, burned his poems *pro tou Dionusiakou theatrou Sôkratous akousas* "having heard Socrates in front of the theatre of Dionysus". Does this only mean that Plato heard Socrates talking and put his childish poetry aside to follow him; or does it refer to Socrates' cross-examining Plato about the poems he'd written?[11] In that case Socrates is again seeking out poets to examine and not their poems.

If you colour-code philosophical methods as Nietzsche does, the practices depicted in the dialogues are "blue" philosophy to be contrasted with "grey" reading. The preface to *On the Genealogy of Morals* contrasts the grey hue of Nietzsche's own genealogy with the *Hypothesewesen in's Blaue* "hypothesizing out of the blue" that characterizes philosophical essentialism, or conceptual philosophizing. Grey is the colour of the "hard-to-decipher hieroglyphic writing [*Hieroglyphenschrift*] of humanity's moral history" – which makes grey the colour of reading, especially when the writing was produced so far away that black marks on white paper blur into grey.[12] In these terms the typical Socratic conversation, treating everything people say as if it had arrived out of the blue, defines itself as a setting in which one does not read much in order to do philosophy.

Compare those exchanges among Plato's people present to one another with the "exchange of ideas" that takes place in the *Menexenus*. To read the speech in the *Menexenus* is to read with constant reference to the Periclean speech in Thucydides, as well as with reference to the larger historical narrative in which Thucydides embeds that speech. What the funeral speech says, it says with and against the text of Thucydides. It talks by talking back, and hearing what it says calls for a variety of overhearing that Plato's dialogues have mostly shut out of philosophical communication. More than any other work of Plato's, this one philosophizes not by inventing something new to say where no one yet had said anything – or *as if* no one had said anything yet – but presupposing what was said before, and so deliberately reducing the vocabulary it will be able to speak with. This means that the challenge the *Menexenus* takes on is the challenge of seeing how much it can say in that antecedently existing vocabulary.

The question of parody

The word "literary" can signal a type of anxiety among philosophical readers, when they use the word for what philosophers have written. Sometimes a literary quality is even taken to distinguish some works by a philosopher from others by the same author that are more recognizably philosophical – *Repetition* from the *Concluding Unscientific Postscript*, in Kierkegaard's case, or Rousseau's *Promenades* from his *Social Contract*.[13]The anxiety concerns how the reader might find philosophical content in the work. Is *Thus Spoke Zarathustra* philosophical in the full sense of containing assertions about philosophical questions and reasons for accepting them? Or (instead) does its narrative enact philosophical ideas? And what is the (philosophical) content of such enactment?

If the *Menexenus* is literary in a way that no other Platonic dialogue is, and if its literariness explains why philosophers do not read it more than they do, the particular species of literariness most often attributed to this work is *parody*. Understood as parody, this revisitation of the famous speech by Pericles is a mockery of the original. Plato writes his own funeral speech, magnifying the flaws endemic to the genre of such speeches, as a joke at the expense of all self-important public speakers; but especially a joke at the expense of Pericles, the legendary democrat and regrettable influence on Athens.[14]

The prefatory conversation between Socrates and young Menexenus is one reason readers cite for taking the speech to be a parody, in our opinion a disproportionately influential cause of this interpretation. Already Plutarch comments that *meta paidias ta prôta gegraptai* "the first part was written playfully".[15] It is telling, and it should serve as a caution to modern readers, that Plutarch does not treat this playfulness as cause to take the funeral speech as a joke. Apparently the first part of the dialogue can have fun without spoiling the seriousness of what follows. Even with respect to the opening dialogue, that word that Plutarch uses, *paidia* "play", says less than "joke" would about the sentiments Socrates expresses in the conversation. (Plutarch's word picks up on one of the *Republic*'s and *Sophist*'s condemnations of *mimêsis*, that it is *paidia* and not serious.[16]) Because of the way Plato writes, Plutarch worries that he should not trust this part for historical information about Aspasia, namely the claims that she wrote the speech of Pericles and then tutored Socrates in rhetoric. That Plato might be saying something in a contrary spirit, condemning Aspasia, does not occur to him. Speaking playfully might mean that what is said could be exaggerated, wishful, or disengaged from bitter reality; evidently not (as far as one can tell from Plutarch's few words) that what is said is sarcastic and a way of condemning Aspasia.

Aspasia is the second great reason for the lingering fear that Plato cannot be serious. Patriotic oratory associated with Athens's leading citizens turns out to have come from a non-Athenian and a woman – not just any foreign woman, but one who is known in some sources as a prostitute or madam. If more information of a reliable kind had been preserved about Aspasia, this reason for dismissing "her" speech would carry the day. In fact, though, such summary judgements about Aspasia are both more unequivocal and more decided than the actual evidence warrants.[17]

Finally parody is suggested by the long stretch of historical narrative that takes up most of the *Menexenus* speech, a military history that reviews "the Athenian century" from the city's arrival on the world stage at Marathon, holding back Persia's first invasion (490), until the peace that ended the

Corinthian War (386), a peace brokered by Persia and signalling Persia's *de facto* hegemonic control over Greece, Persia winning through diplomacy and money what it could not take by force. Do the distortions and omissions in this narrative reveal Plato's facetiousness about patriotic history? If not, there ought to be some order to the speech that leaves it not simply false and incomplete, when it is, but false and incomplete in the interests of besting a more accurate traditional (or Thucydidean) narrative.

After all, tone is hard to prove. Ancient anecdotes prefaced by "He said a funny thing" now bring a weak smile or bafflement. Indeed – and this familiar fact seems not to have affected those who call the *Menexenus* a parody – the general rule regarding ancient witticisms is that their humorousness was perceived then rather than now, or then much more than now, *not* that ancient audiences failed to detect humour that modern ones all pick up. Almost as a rule jokes lose their punch (which is why we say you had to be there); almost never do they become funny much later after having been originally heard as serious. We will address the question of parody by asking not whether the *Menexenus* is serious or funny,[18] but whether its speech is intended to improve upon the original in Thucydides. A defensible answer to that question will speak to the question of parody, since a parody points to faults in its original by exaggerating and worsening those faults. If Plato puts this funeral speech forward as something better than the speech attributed to Pericles, he is not also spoofing Pericles or the funeral speech tradition. Parodies are not written that way.

Suppose someone objects that a work can parody some other work and also be a superior example of the same genre as the original work, *and* in fact be intended by its author as superior to the original. This would be a minority view of parody, if only because one normally sorts parodies into different genres from their objects. The parody of a love song is a joke-song or a novelty, not another love song. Spoofs on adventure tales are not adventure tales. And as a rule parodies do possess those amplified failings.

Rather than quarrel over the meanings of critical terms, the interpretation in this book will focus on seeing the speech in Plato as intended to improve on the speech in Thucydides. This reading is denied by every interpreter who calls the *Menexenus* a parody. If some readers share our conclusion about the Platonic speech's intended superiority, but they still want to call it a parody on some new understanding of that term, they are welcome to do so.

The question of intended superiority speaks more directly to Plato's purpose in writing. Light touch and jokey tone do not prove that he either did or did not envision this speech delivered in Athens; they do not settle whether he thought the speech showed how much more a philosopher could accomplish with public rhetoric than even the best public speakers. Cicero appears to report that in his (Cicero's) day Plato's funeral speech was read aloud annually in Athens, evidently to a popular audience. The point of this passage is narrow, arguing for the excellence of Plato's prose style, but notwithstanding the dispute over how to read Cicero in this passage, he does seem to call the *Menexenus* a superior piece of public oratory.[19] In similar spirit Dionysius of Halicarnassus, who lived in the generation after Cicero's, praised the beauty of a sentence from the *Menexenus* speech in his *On Literary Composition*, while his essay *On Demosthenes* celebrates the dialogue as a whole – treating it not only as something serious or earnest, in other words, but as a good example of oratory.[20]

Two centuries after Cicero, during the period now called the Second Sophistic, the rhetorician Hermogenes of Tarsus comments on the *Menexenus* amid his general flattering assessments of Plato, whom he judges to possess the most beautiful panegyric style of all prose authors. Hermogenes quotes the funeral speech approvingly for the solemnity with which it opens. He does not address the question whether Plato meant the speech as a joke – that question seems not to have occurred to him – but it would be harder to get further from a joking speech than one that exemplifies solemnity.[21]

Already the testimony from Cicero, if it is his and it can be trusted, makes the hypothesis of a parody perverse, comparable with learning that the Irish Parliament had passed Swift's "Modest Proposal" into law. What blindness would the later Athenians have to have been afflicted with to recite a mockery of the city on patriotic occasions? More to the point, both Cicero and Dionysius read the speech as a good work of rhetoric, thereby making it easier to see it as written that way, which is to say written *well*, hence not as parody. Even Robert Clavaud, for whom this is counter-evidence against his own view, seems to concede that Aristotle's quote from the *Menexenus* communicates no hint that Aristotle sees the dialogue as ironic. In fact Clavaud turns to Dionysius for a judgement about how well the speech is written but does not trust Dionysius' sense that it is not written ironically (nor Proclus' sense for that matter).[22]

This book will develop the argument against reading the *Menexenus* as parody, not mainly on the basis of praise for the speech from other authors, rather on the grounds that too many elements in the speech and in the framing dialogue make more sense, from a Platonic point of view, as intended improvements upon the speech of Pericles than as parodic exaggerations of that earlier speech's failings.[23]

If not parody

Deciding whether or not the speech is parody does not bring the discussion to an end. Quite the contrary: "Does Plato mean it?" invites important further questions, such as: "What does he mean when he means it?"

Take the considerable praise in this speech. Socrates finds every good word to say about Athens and Athenians. Reading the speech as a parody implies that it gushes with praise in order to mock the patriotic praise generally found in funeral speeches. If the speech is *not* a parody, what does its hyperbole imply about how to use language of praise? Can it be that excessive praise is really the correct amount – or to put the point conversely, can the speech be saying that praise rightly calibrated to avoid excess will fall short?

Or consider the abundant Socratic references to education that do not correspond to anything in the original speech, except insofar as they contradict Pericles' contempt for Sparta's tradition of endless training. Pericles depicts an Athens whose example teaches other Greek cities but that never had to do any learning to achieve its excellence. If the *Menexenus* speech should be seen as better than Pericles', what is the speech telling its imaginary audience when it harps on education? That education is a good thing, to be sure; also no doubt that Pericles neglected to educate; but maybe also something more specific about the uses and the possibility of moral education within a democratic culture.

Above all there is the historical narrative that dominates the speech, which constitutes Plato's reply not only to Pericles (and perhaps, through him, to the funeral speech genre) but also to the entire work of history that contains his speech, the *History of the Peloponnesian War*. Thucydides presumed to teach the world how one writes history, and to a remarkable degree he established standards of exposition, evidence and explanation. Picture Plato, whose dialogues rarely talk about history, witnessing the influence Thucydides had begun to have. What if Plato wished he could curb that influence from the start? What if he saw some fundamental difference in method between how Thucydides narrated events and how a philosopher would tell the same story?

The difference in methods of historical narrative rests on the kind of difference that Bernard Williams identifies between Plato (together with other philosophers) and Thucydides (along with Sophocles), Thucydides finding the world indifferent to virtue.[24] The Thucydidean narrative treads onward driven by error and chance as much as by the insight of a few remarkable leaders; by some cities' grand ambition and restless need to dominate, other cities' fear and their self-interested machinations to prevent being dominated. Moral psychology only rarely accounts for historical change, and then only under serendipitous circumstances.

The alternative to a Thucydidean narrative does not have to involve rewriting history so that it forcibly reaches a happy ending. Plato is hardly committed to optimism about human events; anyway there is only so far that he could distort Athenian history before losing credibility with the readers who knew what had happened. But even a sad tale can be told in more than one way. On some tellings, missed opportunities and misjudgement send history down one path when it could have gone another way. Other stories make the trip to the bad end the only way possible. Thus for Plato the preceding century displays the same psychological forces at work that determine the good city's slide through worse forms of government in *Republic* Books 8 and 9, and that cause the soul to deteriorate from virtue into the basest vice. In Plato's city and soul, happiness issues from the wisest participant's education of the others; increasing vice and misery occur when the other players rebel against that oversight. So too on the world stage, where history becomes explicable, as Plato must have found the version told in Thucydides confusing and devoid of purpose.

Again, reading the *Menexenus* speech as a paradigm of philosophical history requires *not* reading it as a parody that magnifies the faults of the work it rewrites. The *Menexenus*'s history would have to be Plato's proposal for new and better history.

Amid these teachings about praise, education and history, philosophers might also glimpse what example the *Menexenus* speech is supposed to set for them. By showing how a philosopher would refashion the political performance known as the funeral speech, Plato is showing not only what rhetoric is but also part of who the philosopher is: a speaker who educates in a certain way, praises in a certain inflated way, worships in a certain way, recounts history in a certain psychologizing way. On this reading Plato sees that you will not grasp everything about what philosophers are like when you watch them officially philosophizing. You should also see how philosophers do the things that non-philosophers do: philosophers when they're at home. (One of Plato's words for the most capacious home humans have is "cave". The *Republic* makes clear that what philosophers do inside the cave is no small part of who they are.) So the *Symposium* makes Socrates not just a philosopher but also a lover and a fighter, albeit a lover the world never saw before and a kind of soldier almost as unprecedented. In the same spirit the *Menexenus* puts the philosopher up on the speaker's platform to say, "Here is the philosopher doing what only democratically chosen leaders have done before now". This is perhaps a first motion towards making philosophers into kings.

Some of the claims about the *Menexenus* in the coming chapters will sound straightforward. They might be obvious to anyone who reads the dialogue carefully. Other claims need to be developed against the backdrop of historical contexts that the general reader does not know. Besides its overall obscurity of purpose, the greatest barrier to reading the *Menexenus*, the reason it remains so unknown within Plato's hyperfamiliar corpus, is that it is the most time-bound of his dialogues. The *Apology* presupposes ancient Greek judicial standards and expectations, but any modern reader can see what it means that Socrates is on trial for his life. The *Symposium*'s model of courtship between adults and adolescents is not the model in use today, and the *Euthyphro* equates religion with a now-alien polytheism, but people do still fall in love and religion does claim to justify morality, and it can be easy for readers to see continuities between those dialogues' concerns and their own. (Sometimes too easy.) The *Menexenus* and its funeral speech operate within such a specific setting that the dialogue's dominating concern can be hard to glimpse. Aspasia, the tradition of the funeral speech, the speech of Pericles: these were familiar to Plato's contemporaries but hardly known today. So more than most of the other dialogues this one requires stage-setting, some explanation of the names that appear in the *Menexenus* and of the genre that its funeral speech belongs to. These preliminaries will take up the first part of this book (Chapters 1–4). Many readers will not need those chapters. But they might help the *Menexenus* reach an audience it has failed to speak to before now.

Notes

1 This sentence, from *Menexenus* 235d, appears twice in the *Rhetoric*: 1.9 1267b8, 3.14 1415b30.
2 Thus Loraux (1986). In this connection also see Dean-Jones (1995), Frangeskou (1999), Poulakos (1990), Pownall (2004), Stern (1974).
3 Henry (1995).
4 Kahn (1963); also see Huby (1957).
5 The exceptions are worth citing: Clavaud (1980); Coventry (1989); Long (2003); Monoson (1992); Rosenstock (1994); Salkever (1993); Wickkiser (1999).
6 The speech of Pericles, commonly referred to as his Funeral Oration, was apparently delivered in 430. *N.B.: Unless otherwise indicated or where it is obviously* CE *(e.g. a reference to 1989), all dates are* BCE. The reader should bear in mind that this speech is known only through the version that Thucydides relates in *History of the Peloponnesian War* 2.35.1–2.46.2. There is no other surviving record of the speech, nor even a surviving reference to any source for the speech besides Thucydides. Thucydides may have compiled several witnesses' recollections of the speech, combined more than one speech, or otherwise rewritten what Pericles said. Plato had not been born in 430, so he must have known the speech through the text of Thucydides' *History.*
7 It has even been speculated that Diotima *is* Aspasia, a fictional character based so closely on Aspasia as to have been transparent to Plato's contemporaries. David Halperin, one proponent of this reading, calls Diotima a non-erotic "surrogate for Aspasia": Halperin (1990: 129); cf. Clavaud (1980: 59n.131).
8 Aristophanes *Frogs*: Dionysus reading tragedies in script, 53–54; each spectator has a *biblion* "book", 1114. On rival historians see Thucydides *History* 1.22.4.
9 Plato: line from Homer, *Lysis* 214a; something from Protagoras, *Theaetetus* 152a. In this latter dialogue Socrates discounts the act of reading Protagoras without having done so. The man must possess an esoteric doctrine that he communicates only to his students, so it is no use reading his book: *Theaetetus* 152c.
10 Plato *Phaedo* 98b–99c. On one reconstruction of Anaxagoras that shows the flaws in Socrates' reading, see Sedley (2008: 8–12).
11 Plato *Protagoras*: Socrates reading Simonides, 338c–348a; speaking in poets' absence, 347e. Socrates dismisses the wisdom of poets, *Apology* 22b. Diogenes Laërtius, *Lives of the Eminent Philosophers*: life of Plato, iii; Plato aspiring poet, iii.5; "having heard Socrates", iii.6. On Socrates as interpreter of poetry in *Protagoras* see Carson (1992); Pappas (1989).
12 Nietzsche *On the Genealogy of Morals* Preface §7.
13 Stanley Cavell comments on these and other works – works by philosophers but not quite in philosophy – with special reference to Wittgenstein's *Philosophical Investigations*: Cavell (2005: 193).
14 Arguments for reading the speech as ironic or parodic have a long history among modern scholars. Chapter 4 will take up this question in detail; among recent relevant articles see Long (2003), Salkever (1993), Trivigno (2009). For an overview of the modern issue see Clavaud (1980: 45–74). Clavaud himself, while

reading the *Menexenus* as parody, takes the object of that parody to be not just Pericles' funeral speech but all the funeral speeches of democratic Athens.

15 Plutarch *Pericles* 24.4.

16 Imitation *paidia*: *Republic* 10.602b, *Sophist* 234b. In the *Phaedrus* it seems all writing is *paidia*: 278b. The *Timaeus* calls the study of nature *paidia*: 52d. See Nehamas (1982: 53–54).

17 Chapter 2 will weigh the ancient testimony concerning Aspasia and its implications for reading the *Menexenus*.

18 When Clavaud reviews the literature on the *Menexenus* he sorts its opposing sides into "*les partisans du sérieux*" and "*les partisans du comique*". We find that procedure unpromising because it invites subjectivist assessments of exactly the kind we are trying to avoid. For a discussion of a strikingly incomprehensible joke from antiquity see Borthwick (2001: 494) on a passage from Plutarch's *Laconian Apophthegms* (*Moralia* 233a).

19 Cicero *Orator ad M. Brutum* 151. Cicero speaks of the circumstances that an author has to face *in populari oratione* "in a public speech". Some modern authors cite Cicero in favour of the view that Plato meant the speech as good political oratory: Kahn (1963: 229); Huby (1957: 105–6). The sentence that claims an annual reading for the *Menexenus* has been questioned for over a century, on the grounds that Athens with its "degenerate citizens" under Roman rule would not have been permitted to voice patriotic sentiments: Sandys (1885: 162–63). The reasoning is dubious. Precisely because Athens no longer posed a risk, it could be permitted a nostalgic voicing of past glories. See Trivigno (2009: 49n.2). Not surprisingly, Clavaud (1980: 251) joins those who doubt Cicero's testimony.

20 Dionysius of Halicarnassus: on a sentence from *Menexenus* 236d, *De compositione verborum* 18; on the dialogue generally *Demosthenes* 23–30. Dionysius makes clear what he considers the shortcomings of Plato's rhetorical style, but mainly by comparison with the high standard set by Demosthenes.

21 Hermogenes of Tarsus *Peri Ideôn* "On Types of Style": Plato the most beautiful panegyric stylist, 389; *Menexenus* 236d example of best solemnity, 250.

22 Clavaud (1980): no sign Aristotle perceived the speech as ironic, 21; grants that other ancient sources accept the speech as serious, though he finds them wanting as a result, 34–35; turns to Dionysius, 183.

23 See George Grote: "The funeral harangue in the *Menexenus* proves that, whatever he [Plato] thought about Rhetoric generally, he was anxious to establish his title as a competent rhetorical composer" (Grote 1865: 9). John Cooper, in brief introductory remarks to the *Menexenus* for his anthology of Plato, records the view that the dialogue is parody as one common interpretation, but he replies: "better, since Socrates' speech is in fact a highly skilled oration of the genre … is to think that it may show (as indeed the *Phaedrus* claims) how very much better a skilled philosopher is at the composition of speeches than the usual rhetorical 'expert'" (Cooper 1997: 950). Given his role, in his compilation, of introducing each dialogue quickly, Cooper cannot say much more; but this book as a whole spells out the justification for a reading essentially like his.

24 See Williams (1993: 163–64): "Plato, Aristotle, Kant, Hegel are all on the same side, all believing in one way or another that the universe or history or the structure of human reason can, when properly understood, yield a pattern that makes sense of human life and human aspirations. Sophocles and Thucydides, by contrast, are alike in leaving us with no such sense. Each of them represents human beings as dealing sensibly, foolishly, sometimes catastrophically, sometimes nobly, with a world that is only partially intelligible to human agency and in itself is not necessarily well adjusted to ethical aspirations".

Part I

THE *MENEXENUS*, ITS PERSONS, ITS PROBLEMS

1

SYNOPSIS OF THE DIALOGUE

The *Menexenus* divides obviously into two parts of unequal length: the frame, which consists in the opening and closing dialogues between Socrates and Menexenus, and the speech attributed to Aspasia sandwiched between them. The speech itself can be further divided into numerous sections, but for a useful first look it is worth identifying three: a history of Athens, an exhortation to virtue and a consolation for the living.

Opening dialogue (234a–236d)

The dialogue opens when Socrates encounters the young Menexenus, who wants to be chosen to deliver the coming funeral oration for the war dead. Socrates and Menexenus engage in atypical Socratic banter, in which Socrates describes how noble the orators can make anyone who died in battle seem to have been. Menexenus treats this as Socratic mockery. He laments the performance that the Athenians are likely to hear this time, given that the council will be making its decision at the last minute, leaving speechwriters very little time to compose.

But the speeches are generally prepared well in advance, Socrates says; and anyway, how hard could it be to praise Athenians in front of an Athenian audience? He speaks so breezily about the oratorical art that Menexenus asks whether Socrates could manage a funeral speech were *he* to be chosen. (One of the atypical touches in this exchange is the sight of Menexenus as questioner challenging Socrates' claim to knowledge and ability – though Socrates does not crumple under questioning as his interlocutors tend to do.)

Yes, Socrates says, he could manage. He has a tutor in rhetoric, Aspasia, whom he just heard preparing a funeral speech. She has taught him what needs to be in such speeches, such as the one she composed for Pericles to deliver. After his training, Socrates could recite a funeral speech on the spot. He is or pretends to be reluctant, not wanting Aspasia to discover that he is giving her speeches away. But Menexenus insists and Socrates begins to recite.

Funeral speech (236d–249c)

The praise for Athens begins with a mythical prehistory that elides into a century's worth of Greek history told from Athens's point of view.

Praise of the dead via Athenian prehistory (236d–239c)

The speech as a whole begins with self-consciousness about its own role in the praise of heroes. The praise in this speech will cite the good lineage of the dead, their education and finally their deeds.

The dead soldiers boasted a pure lineage. Their ancestors did not immigrate from elsewhere; rather, Athenians sprang from and were nourished by the same earth to which they now return. Thus honouring the Athenian land honours the men. Athens itself deserves praise first because it is loved by the gods, and second because Athens bore men while all the other lands bore animals. As a proof, says Socrates, realize that Athens alone at the time produced the ideal food to nourish humans; and a true mother innately possesses and provides the resources to feed her offspring. The earth then introduced unnamed gods to educate her Athenian youth in the basic arts of life and weaponry.

The first Athenians created a good regime – also worth mentioning, inasmuch as good regimes make men good and bad ones ruin them. Thus praise for the dead soldiers should also include mention of the regime that educated them. The first Athenians established a constitution under which all Athenians since their time have lived, which is to say an aristocracy, regardless of the different names that subsequent generations gave to their form of government. For even when Athenian governance goes by the name "democracy" it consists in the multitude's approving the best man to rule – which is to say that it amounts to aristocracy. The Athenian people are willing to put their best citizens into positions of authority because of their fundamental equality. Once upon a time all Athenians were born equal, so no one will be anyone else's master or slave.

The poets have already hymned the accomplishments of those mythical first generations of Athenians: fending off the Amazons, protecting the Argives against the Cadmeians and then the Heracleidae against the Argives. No speech can match the poets' versions of these great deeds; so why not devote the speech to the story still untold or unsung, the story of what Athens has done in recent years and within the community's memory.

Athenian history (239d–246a)

The bulk of the speech follows; it is a history of Athens that mainly lists battles and wars, beginning on the eve of the first Persian invasion. Persia expanded under Cyrus the Great, first freeing the Persians from the Medes and then enslaving the Medes in turn.[1] Cambyses enlarged the empire into

Egypt and Libya; his successor Darius added Scythia and took control of the sea.

Then Darius accused Athens and Eritrea of plotting against Sardis. He sent an army into Greece that the Athenians repelled at Marathon, while the rest of the Greeks refused to participate. Even without joining in, though, those other Greeks learned from the Athenians' victory that the Persians were not invincible. By teaching that lesson to the rest of Greece, the Athenians of Marathon became the fathers of Athenian freedom and continue to deserve the highest praise. Second only to them are the victors at Salamis and Artemisium. Those victories at sea were notable for liberating Greeks at large from their fear of superior naval forces. And third in the praise they deserve are those participants in the Persian War who secured the joint victory over Persia – Athenian and Spartan forces fighting together – at Plataea.

Socrates' history continues with more engagements between Greece and Persia: the final blows against the Empire at Eurymedon, Cyprus, and Crete. Athens and its Greek allies frightened the Persian king away by defeating Persia and Egypt at sea. The other Greek cities first wanted to emulate Athens and then were overcome by envy, and the result of this envy was warfare among Greeks.

First Athens fought on behalf of Boeotian freedom at Tanagra and Oenophyta, prevailing when the Spartans abandoned the battle. Then all Greece took up arms against Athens. The Athenians won again, defeating the Greeks and their Spartan leaders in sea battles at Sphagia, but refrained from destroying their vanquished enemies outright. Athenians consider it wrong to destroy fellow Greeks as one destroys barbarians, so they spared the lives of the Spartans at Sphagia.

In a third war, Athens fought in Sicily on behalf of freedom for the Leontinians. Treacherous Greek cities imposed heavy losses on Athens in land battles. Many cities also joined in naval warfare in the Hellespont, where Athens won a ruinous sea battle over an alliance of Greeks. Those other cities' treachery took the form of secret alliances with the same barbarians that a unified Greece had once expelled. Nevertheless Athens showed its strength at Mytilene, in the battle of Arginusae, defeating Sparta and Persia at sea in a disastrous battle.

By now Athens had earned a reputation for being undefeatable; what conquered the city was no outside enemy but internal strife. Even so, this civil unrest in Athens was the kind that all cities ought to wish for, if they had to endure civil divisions. Everyone was amicable, thanks to the kinship that began with Athenians' collective birth from earth; today they have forgiven one another for a conflict that began in misfortune rather than in malice.

But Athens did not forgive the other Greek cities, which repaid the generous treatment they had received from Athens first by joining the Persians and confiscating Athenian ships, then by taking down the city walls. The Athenians decided not to go on fighting against the enslavement of Greeks, whether by barbarians or by other Greeks. Sparta took this inaction as an opportunity to reduce the rest of Greece to slavery, and soon Argos, Boeotia, Corinth and even Persia came to Athens seeking help. Prone to pity as usual, Athens liberated the Greeks; and indirectly saved Persia too, by permitting exiles and volunteers to help the Empire.

After being forced into the war Athens fought Sparta so successfully that the Persian king sought a quick resolution. He offered to side with Athens in exchange for recognition of his rights over the Greek cities in Asia Minor; but Athens, purely Greek that it is, refused the bargain. In the end Athens managed to keep its fleet, its walls and its allied cities, and bring the war to a close. Nevertheless the city lost good men, forced into defeat by rough terrain at Corinth and treachery at Lechaeum. For that matter those Athenians who freed the Persian king and drove the Spartans from the sea were also good men, and also deserving praise and honour.

Exhortation (246a–247c)

Socrates promises to keep reminding the audience of the praise that has gone to brave Athenian soldiers who died for their city. He links the dead with the living. As the soldiers now being mourned did not leave their posts in battle, the living must not abandon their virtue. He speaks in the first person on behalf of the fallen soldiers, fashioning a "speech from the dead" out of the kinds of things they had said while still alive. Here is what they would be saying to their family members now if they could.

Regardless of how they lived (the dead say), they died nobly. They did not disgrace their descendants. Their children ought to follow suit, for such other good possessions as wealth, physical beauty and knowledge lose their value, or even make the one who has them look worse, if they are not accompanied by virtue, and particularly by the virtue of courage. The dead ask of their children only that their children surpass them in virtue.[2]

Consolation (247c–249c)

The speech ends by consoling the dead soldiers' family members. They in turn ought to console their parents, urging them to bear up under this misfortune. No further laments: what all parents wish is for their children to grow up to be virtuous and respected, and their dead sons now are both. It will only dishonour the fallen soldiers if their parents now indulge in grieving them. What the dead really want and need is that their families be cared for, and Athens has seen to this responsibility, with institutions to protect both the parents and the children of the war dead. In particular the city will nurture the orphans as a father does and arm them for battle when they are grown.

Socrates now dismisses his fictitious audience. They have discharged their duty to mourn and they should depart.

Closing dialogue (249d–e)

Socrates and Menexenus exchange a few words before parting. Menexenus says he has met Aspasia and knows what kind of woman she is. He doubts that she wrote the speech. Anyway he thanks Socrates for reporting the speech and promises not to tell anyone that he heard it; to which Socrates replies with the promise to deliver more fine speeches.

Notes

1 Although Persians and Medes were two different peoples, the classical Greeks seemed to have used the two names for them interchangeably. Thus one who adopted Persian customs and clothing was said to *mēdizein* "mede-ize", to become a Mede. The biblical Book of Esther combines them too, never referring to Persia alone but rather to "Persia and Media" (Esther 1:3, 14, 18; 10:2).
2 For an insightful summation of this passage (which we will not spend much time discussing) see J. T. Roberts (2012: 142–44).

2

PERSONS AND DATES OF THE DIALOGUE

Readers can take the dialogue form of Plato's works too far. He was not writing modern biography. Nor does the dialogue form have to mean that everything said in the dialogues, said by Socrates for example, must be understood *strategically*, as a claim being pitched to a particular person on one occasion with some concrete aim in view; or *contextually*, as a claim whose meaning always returns to its being meaningful for the person who espouses it. Accordingly, this book will try to base its claims about the funeral speech in the *Menexenus* on what that speech says about education, rhetoric, myth and history; not on what the speech must be saying about Socrates or Aspasia.

And yet there is no point in denying that the conversations in Plato take place among specific people. And unlike the characters in epic and tragedy (though significantly *like* some of the characters in Old Comedy), these speakers are actually existing Athenians, together with some non-Athenian Greeks, both famous ones and also obscure citizens who happened to know Socrates. Modern scholarship knows a few things about these people independently of what Plato says about them. So, it makes sense to ask, what does Plato think it means that this person in particular is defending patriotism, or relativism, or materialism? Surveying the names that appear in the *Menexenus* is probably the best way to insert the modern reader into the conversation that Plato has written – attaching bodies to those names – and sketch out what might be at stake for its participants.

Socrates

Because he dominates any list of Platonic characters, but mainly because he dominates Western culture, Socrates can be talked about without the usual introductions. Still it is worth observing how the *Menexenus*'s depiction of Socrates differs from other testimony about him. Here and probably nowhere else Socrates is trained in rhetoric[1] and almost intimate with the man who ran Athens. As only a few other Platonic works do, the *Menexenus* casts Socrates as authority rather than interrogator. And it portrays him as dead – not in the sense in which the *Phaedo*'s last page describes his cold and lifeless body, but with an exceeding anachronism that seems to suggest this is not Socrates speaking with Menexenus but his ghost.

Socrates as authority

The Socratic pose of ignorance, making no claims but only challenging other people's puffed-up claims to knowledge, is partly a characterization found in some of Plato's and Xenophon's writings about him and partly an easy exaggeration based on that portrayal. This one-dimensional figure never asserting, only quizzing, is memorable and a delight, but untrue to many of Plato's greatest works, in which Socrates propounds and defends theories about politics, psychology, poetry and other substantive topics. Plato's Socrates is quite capable of claiming intellectual authority for himself, as he does in the *Menexenus*.

In one way the *Menexenus* shows what it might have been, a dialogue in which Socrates the negative spirit attacks the interlocutor's pretensions to knowledge without advancing a position of his own. For a second that old familiar Socrates appears, when Menexenus tells him he has nominated himself to deliver the speech at a military funeral. In the *Euthyphro* or *Ion* such pretensions lead to Socrates' burning away every scrap of confidence the pretender has. But here Socrates merely raises an eyebrow at Menexenus before shifting the conversation to what *he*, Socrates, is able to do with oratory; and where he learned it; and what a fine speech at a public funeral would sound like if he were to deliver it. Socrates passes up the opportunity to deflate someone else's claim to knowledge so that he can present his own.

The departure from familiar Socratic interrogation is marked formally by a departure from even the grammatical pretext of Socratic questioning. The opening conversation is very short as Platonic back-and-forth exchanges go. Yet it contains an unusual number of questions aimed at Socrates by his interlocutor instead of the other way around. Menexenus asks Socrates what he knows about rhetoric and how he knows it, and what kind of speech he would give if he were so lucky as to find himself in Menexenus' place. Plato seems to abandon the pretence that Socrates only questions, as if questioning had ceased mattering to a characterization of Socrates.

Socrates as public speaker

Socrates calls his rhetorical ability the result of tutoring. He studied with Aspasia of Miletus.[2] Even a reader who is not surprised to find Socrates claiming expertise about something would not expect the topic to be rhetoric. Rhetoric is the activity of Sophists (as the *teaching* of rhetoric also is), and amoral people like Thrasymachus. In the *Gorgias* Socrates denies rhetoric the status of knowledgeable skill or profession. A better word for it is *empeiria* "knack, know-how, practice", because rhetoric belongs among such shady occupations as pastry-cookery. Socrates is more conciliatory in the *Phaedrus*, the other dialogue that examines rhetoric, holding out the possibility of a sound rhetoric grounded in philosophical understanding of the soul. But this is a concession to what rhetoric could become not what it is. Its actual practitioners steam ahead ignorantly, and even this Socrates who finds potential in philosophical rhetoric would not brag about having studied the business with a practitioner.[3] Why is the Socrates in the *Menexenus* bent on advertising the trouble he went to to study rhetoric?

That question points towards the most significant question about the Socrates in Plato's dialogues and probably also the unanswerable one. To what extent does Plato use this recurring figure to tell of the person he knew who lived in fifth-century Athens; and to what extent does he make the name a fluid character, a synecdoche for the philosopher as such? The two possibilities are not mutually exclusive. To a great extent Plato's friend really did represent the realization of human beings' philosophical possibilities, not only for Plato but for many Athenians of his time. To them Socrates was a walking synecdoche, and describing him amounted to describing "the philosopher". This only makes the question that much harder to handle. As a portrait, a dialogue containing Socrates will contain information about the historical person. But to the extent that the portrait idealizes Socrates it inclines towards being a vision of the philosopher as such as instantiated by Socrates.

Not every event can belong unambiguously to either the general or the particular. Plato says that Socrates faced capital charges and was convicted and put to death, and presumably says all this because it happened, not because a true philosopher must suffer such misfortunes. And indeed the figure who really existed is often relevant to how one reads Plato.[4] It matters to a reading of Plato's *Theaetetus*, in which Socrates says his mother was a midwife, whether this unique remark reports something true about the Socrates of history or symbolizes something about the Socrates who belongs to philosophy as such. That is to say, does Plato report the midwifery as biography or only as part of his definition of the philosophical genus? And when Socrates says in the *Menexenus* that Connus taught him music, it matters whether this datum is biographically true or rather exists in the text to show what kind of philosopher/spokesman Plato is constructing, one who – perhaps in contradistinction to the historical figure – both learned and practised music.[5]

Finally, it matters to ask, as the *Menexenus* forces its reader to wonder, whether Socrates really studied rhetoric with Aspasia. If not, does Plato wish he had? That is not a preposterous idea, considering the failure Socrates made of his one attempt at public speaking, when he faced the Athenian jury and turned them against him. A little good rhetoric might have made that trial come out the opposite way; Plato can be indulging in "what if" thinking.

At a more global level, contemplating not the Socrates who existed but the philosophical type for which "Socrates" is a useful name, Plato might see some value in philosophers' acquiring skill at rhetoric. If their rhetoric is not the manipulative kind, unchecked by reference to the truth, that becomes soul candy without the accompanying nourishment of truth, it could work as legitimate persuasion to the truth. And Plato must have looked back on the beginnings of the Peloponnesian War, as many Athenians did, with poignancy and regret. When the ruinous war began, Athens had nothing better than a demagogue to speak at the military funeral and articulate the city's misguided values. If only a philosopher had stood before the citizens instead of a politician! The speaker would not have to have been Socrates, any more than Socrates has to serve as philosopher-king in the *Republic*'s imagined city.

To put this question another way, without answering it now or even pretending it will find a definitive answer: does the *Menexenus*'s opening conversation attribute rhetorical and musical training to Socrates in order to tell the reader something about Socrates (something that verges on embarrassing: the bit that does not fit into a simplistic characterization of him; Socrates as odd individual); or is it in order to tell the reader about what philosophers do, that when they want to they know perfectly well how to pour out the magicked patriotic oratory?

Both options are available if the speech is a parody, and also if it is not. Call the speech an earnest bid to one-up Pericles, as this book will do, and a philosopher's capacity to produce such a thing shows that philosophy knows how to reintroduce its understanding of principle back into the workings of ordinary politics. Indeed this is close to Wilamowitz's description of the *Menexenus*, over a century ago.[6] But the idealized philosopher does not have to be the one who now and then reveals a masked rhetorical gift. Alternatively, if you call the speech in the *Menexenus* a parody of political rhetoric, the dialogue is proving that the philosopher swears off rhetoric and mocks it not out of stereotypical naivety but as a laudable choice. Real philosophers could write flag-waving speeches if they wanted to. They fail to because they choose not to.[7]

The two readings of the *Menexenus*, jest and earnest, are also both compatible with a biographical reading of this remark about his tutors. The opening dialogue in which Socrates announces that Aspasia taught him rhetoric either shows him to have possessed an expertise he claimed not to have, or even to want, on all the famous occasions on which he cross-examined pompous Athenians; or it portrays him as the type of man who would pretend to have taken such lessons from Aspasia. If the speech is a parody he can be pretending to have studied rhetoric. If he really intends to put the speech forward then it makes sense that he studied with Aspasia (and note his insistence on keeping this fact a secret, as if in acknowledgement that people otherwise had no way of knowing about his rhetorical expertise).[8]

Socrates among the powerful

Could Socrates have known the woman Pericles lived with after divorcing his first wife? The popular image of Socrates has him humble and barefoot, a poor man at home in cobblers' shops or out in the streets of Athens, not the type who would be familiar with the city's first citizens in the halls of power.

To be sure, the popular image contains exaggerations. Socrates fought for Athens as a hoplite, a soldier in armour with a heavy shield, and to belong among the hoplites and own his personal armour, a man needed more property than poor Athenians had. Socrates probably seemed poor to those friends of his with real money, Plato and Xenophon for instance. (The very rich were not always skilled at distinguishing between degrees of not being wealthy; they are not always adept at those distinctions today.) And the modest wardrobe may have been more symbolic than financially necessary. Plato depicts Socrates barefoot in a *tribôn* but does not tell his readers what the original readers would have known, that this was Spartan dress. Athenians who admired the Spartan way of life wore the Spartans' simplified and masculinized clothing, and not because poverty forced them to.[9]

Even without being poor, Socrates could have been an obscure private citizen lacking access to Athenian luminaries; and some of the evidence suggests that he was. Thucydides brings his story of Athens down to 411, when Socrates would have been almost sixty, but the *History* never mentions him. In Plato's *Apology* Socrates tells the jury he had mostly avoided public life, and the exceptions are sufficiently unknown that he has to explain them. Socrates refers to Pericles several times in the dialogues, but usually in the way one refers to a public figure, a personage one knows, or knows of, at a distance. The lone exception is the *Gorgias*, in which Socrates tells Polus it would not be hard to find Athenian witnesses against the position Socrates is defending. "If you wish to bring witnesses against me … there is the whole household [*oikia*] of Pericles". This has the sound of an unexplained inside joke, certainly not requiring that Pericles knew Socrates.[10]

Against such signs of the obscurity that Socrates lived in, the main counter-evidence comes from Aristophanes. A mention here or there is one thing; *Clouds* made Socrates the great object of Aristophanic satire in 423, presumably because the audience had already heard his name. Plato and Xenophon, who would write at such length about Socrates later, were still little boys, and Athens knew about Socrates. Later the comedies *Birds* and *Frogs* direct jokes against Socrates too.[11] The modern word "celebrity" does not apply to the ancient world with any exactness, but if part of the concept of celebrity is that people might have heard of someone without knowing anything about that person, then Socrates played the Athenian celebrity at least to that degree.

And if Plato's dialogues contain no evidence that Socrates knew either Pericles or Pericles' friend Anaxagoras, they leave no doubt as to the intimate relationship between Socrates and Alcibiades, who was a foster son to

24

Pericles and (part of the time at least) a member of his household. Besides Anaxagoras the other intellectual known as friend to Pericles was Protagoras, and the dialogue named after that Sophist is premised on the fact of a long meeting between him and Socrates. For that matter Socrates says in the *Protagoras* that he met the Sophist at a meeting that Paralus and Xanthippus were also present for. They were the sons of Pericles by his first marriage, and Socrates mentions their presence as if he already knew them. The other son of Pericles, the one also named Pericles whose mother was Aspasia (Pericles the Younger), converses with Socrates in Xenophon's dialogues.[12]

Poor or not, obscure or not, if Socrates could have Alcibiades for a close friend or lover, know the younger Pericles well enough to talk to and his half-brothers by sight; and if Protagoras could recognize Socrates when they met; then he travelled close enough to Pericles to have met Aspasia.[13]

But even if Socrates did not meet Aspasia through those other family members, there is an additional grim connection that would have guaranteed some familiarity, maybe some acquaintance, between him and Aspasia. As Plato's *Apology* recalls the trial of the Athenian generals after Arginusae, and more specifically in Xenophon's retelling of the case, Socrates had stood alone against the mass call for a collective trial and execution of six Athenian generals in 406, near the end of the Peloponnesian War. One of those six was Pericles the son of Pericles and Aspasia. Socrates demanded but failed to get separate trials for the officers, who were already blaming one another (and their crews) for having failed to recover the survivors in the storm that followed that battle. A separate trial seemed to be each man's legal right.[14]

One has to imagine Aspasia following the developments closely with her only child on trial for his life, and hoping that Socrates would prevail. Given such an interest in the case she could not have failed to know the role Socrates played. Even if they had never met, she would know him thereafter as the man who wanted to save her son.

Socrates as dead man

The last point to make about the Socrates of the *Menexenus* involves more speculation. The speculation will not shape the general line of interpretation in this book, but the textual facts are too striking not to comment on.

The *Menexenus* contains a sizeable anachronism. Other Platonic dialogues have anachronisms in them too, but nothing that is anywhere near this egregious. Socrates recites a funeral speech to Menexenus that contains a lengthy history of Athens. One hundred years go by in this history, beginning with the Persian Wars (490) and continuing to the King's Peace or Common Peace (386); and the last thirteen years of this chronology *come after the death of Socrates* in 399. Aspasia has also been dead, though the year of her death is not known with the specificity that Socrates' death is. In any case the anachronism would not be remarkable as it affects Aspasia. If Plato did not know Aspasia intimately himself he may well not have borne in mind, while summarizing recent history, which of the events he specified Aspasia would have been alive to see. But Socrates had been his close friend; the execution of Socrates divided Plato's life into *before* and *after* in that way that leaves people aware, when thinking of any event, which of the two periods it belongs in. ("My father was still alive when I got this job".) When Plato set about summarizing local history, it would have been impossible for him to forget that his friend had been dead for a decade.

To say "The Greeks did not have a modern sense of anachronism" is irrelevant. This is not historical fussiness, it is the awareness of a friend's death. One would have to say that the Greeks lacked an understanding that the dead do not continue to walk the earth. Modern ideas of anachronism have nothing to do with it. Plato could not have neglected to notice that Socrates hadn't lived to see these fresh humiliations to befall Athens; nor could he have failed to realize that his dialogue portrayed Socrates still speaking after the date of his death.

The anachronism leads back to the difference between Plato's writing about the man Socrates he knew who really lived, and his elucidation of the philosopher as a type, someone who *could* live – a human possibility – whether or not he had existed thus far. For what the anachronism in the *Menexenus* means, the one that leaves this character "Socrates" speaking of events the real Socrates could not have seen, depends on how Plato has conceived this character in this particular dialogue. On one reading Plato includes the anachronism because Socrates matters to him as a token of the philosophical type rather than as a figure from history, and this dialogue will show how that type delivers a funeral speech.

The other alternative reads Socrates as the historical figure who faced an Athenian jury and was executed. If Plato wants *that* man to be his speaker in this dialogue set clearly after his death, then he may mean for the *Menexenus*'s "Socrates" to be speaking after his own death: in other words for him to be a ghost, a being summoned from the grave. Bruce Rosenstock[15] has developed the proposal that Menexenus is speaking not to the eccentric Athenian gadabout who occupies most of Plato's dialogues but to that man's shade; "Socrates" is a revenant, a ghost that haunts the world.

Rosenstock's reading solves the anachronism, though he has to disrupt readers' expectations about Platonic dialogues to do so. Plato sets conversations in everyday places: private homes, a walk through Crete, the king's porch in the agora, a wrestling room at the gymnasium. In real life these are not places where the dead speak and the long-gone present themselves, and such things do not happen in the dialogues either. (In the *Phaedo* Socrates seems to believe that the spirits of some dead can haunt monuments and tombs, but those are the souls of the vicious, still too attached to their bodily desires.[16]) The "revenant" reading calls for more than a new way to see the

Menexenus; the Platonic corpus would have to be seen in a new way as well, now becoming a genre that can swerve into ghost stories.

How decisive is this consideration of what is possible in Plato's dialogues? It matters; but as a criterion for reading Plato it has to be used judiciously. The *Menexenus* stands alone in other ways too, depicting Socrates as a trained orator and letting the demonstration speech he delivers take over the dialogue. If your test for what is possible in Plato becomes the genre as its central examples define it, then it is as easy to say Plato did not write the *Menexenus* as to grant that he wrote it and deny he could make one character in it a ghost. Maybe odder things happen in the odder members of a genre.

The positive argument for Rosenstock's reading is more specific than that negative consideration. The reading harmonizes with a theme that recurs in the *Menexenus*, of souls traversing the border between life and death. Socrates says funeral speeches make him think he has travelled to the Isles of the Blessed; Menexenus calls Aspasia *makaria* "blessed", a word used of the dead. The funeral speech closes with a report of the words and sentiments of the dead soldiers, as if Socrates – or Aspasia, who is presumably dead alongside him – had heard their shades talking.[17]

Because of such resonances with the dialogue's themes, the interpretation is not just tacked on to handle the anachronism but works with the *Menexenus* as a whole. A dialogue that looks into funeral rhetoric and proposes an authoritative example of such rhetoric takes on added resonance if Socrates derives the authority he speaks with from having already died. And when the speech's final section purports to tell the thoughts of Athens's dead soldiers to their surviving families, the possibility that the speech began on the other side of death's divide gives that peroration a credibility that no living speechmaker could boast. Pericles closed his funeral oration with sparing words to the Athenians who mourned their dead, including the instruction to the widows that they remain quiet, neither heard nor heard about; but the funeral speech genre more typically closes with some reassurance about mortality.[18] The *Menexenus* resurrects the dead soldiers as no other funeral speech does, practically delivering the mail from the audience's lost sons and fathers.

This book will advance other reasons for seeing the *Menexenus*'s speech as an intended improvement upon its original. Those arguments are intended to stand on textual grounds without the need of any such more mysterious questions. But if Socrates is indeed functioning as a ghost who revisits Menexenus from beyond the grave, that reading would work together with the others to make this speech superior to its unphilosophical model. By speaking from the side of the living Pericles could only speak politically or ideologically, confining himself to the matter of what the city of the living does next. Socrates' shade, having just conversed with the shade of Aspasia (which is much what Socrates' closing words in the *Apology* had looked ahead to doing[19]), can reincorporate the dead into the assembly of Athenians that came together at the funeral for the sake of the dead.

27

A rival account of the anachronism

This is as good a place as any to stay with the anachronism and ask what else a reader can do with it. If in fact the framing dialogue is as mundane as it first looks to be, and this is the same old Socrates breathing air with Menexenus, how can the speech that he recites travel so far into the future? Is there no better explanation than an incredible word about those anachronizing Greeks?

Debra Nails argues with as much boldness as Rosenstock. Plato did not write the anachronistic section of the funeral speech at all. Someone else did, a member of Plato's Academy who added this history after Plato's death.[20] Not a ghost, but that more familiar figure the ghostwriter, accounts for the *Menexenus*'s anomaly. Plato's text becomes consistent upon the removal of its inconsistent false elements.

As Nails knows, one needs more reason to attribute 244b–246a to a later hand than the bare fact that this attribution removes the anachronism. She offers a reason, pointing out that such emendations took place in the Academy, "much writing of dialogues and editing of works that had varying degrees of Platonic core; and it is no special feat to add a couple of pages in the style of the existing *Menexenus* speech, to bring the work up to date".[21]

It would indeed have been no great feat for one of Plato's young associates to fill out the speech. But why add only a dozen years to the history? Plato lived for forty years or so after the end of the Corinthian War. The speech could have gone on much longer than it does and still only speak of events he would have known. Better still, the hypothetical later author could have taken the *Menexenus*'s history of Athens only one decade beyond Plato's death to finish the story with the Battle of Chaeronea, when after all its efforts to unify Greece Athens found itself and its allies defeated by Philip of Macedon. That battle brings the end of the autonomous Greek *polis* and the end of any alliances that matter among cities – one for the history books, it is a fitting conclusion for a funeral speech. Certainly Demosthenes found it fitting: his funeral speech came after Chaeronea. Plato's surviving student could have made that the apt final moment in the *Menexenus*'s history. If Plato's heirs had added to the funeral speech it is surprising that they could not do a better job of it.

Nails' main argument is the best kind of argument to make in support of her claim. The shorter version of the history hangs together as a whole better than the long anachronistic version does. Without the interpolated pages, she says, the narrative moves from "the furthermost to the closest", from gods and then heroes to wars against barbarians, closer to home with the wars against other Greek cities and finally at the doorstep to witness the Athenians' civil war. "To move ... *backward* to war with other Greeks again before ending is a rhetorical lapse that need not be attributed to Plato himself".[22]

Arguing in this way takes Nails' proposal out of the realm of speculations and makes it possible to disagree with her reasonably. If a rival reading to hers makes the existing history ordered and compelling, her proposal for a later co-author loses some credibility. But if the shorter history that Nails calls the genuine one is more coherent as it stands than the longer version, there is some reason to envision Plato's heir having rewritten what the master left behind.

Chapter 8 will argue for a rival reading of the speech's history and a coherent form to its existing story. Closing with the political triumph of Persia does not amount to moving backwards, as Nails alleges, but if anything all too Platonically *forward*, from bad to worse as Plato always depicts history's movements. For the first appearance of the Persians shows them losing at Marathon, while in their last appearance they broker the peace that ends the Corinthian War.

There are two problems with Nails' argument even in the absence of a good rival. First, she does not give a reason for the narrative to move from the far to the near.[23] Why *should* Plato recount history as a progression from the distant and divine to the close-at-hand and ordinary? The analytical history of a city in *Republic* 8 does not follow that path. When the *Timaeus* and the *Critias* together describe an original Athens that defended the world from the predations of Atlantis, that narrative (however incomplete) establishes Athens first before voyaging to the west for a look at the enemy, it does not swoop in from far horizons to survey the Athenian homeland.

Finally it is a problem for Nails that if Plato does want to move his story in towards Athens, he spoils that progress himself at a crucial point. Persia and extra-Hellenic negotiations do not enter the story only after Socrates' death. The speech itself depicts the last days of the Peloponnesian War (however much it sugar-coats the chaos and desperation of those days) as a time when the other Greek cities allied themselves with Persia.[24] Only then could they defeat Athens. But this means Persia has re-entered Greek history even before the swerve in that history away from its focus on Athens. If Plato did mean to move history in one direction (for whatever reason) he would have ended it still earlier.

The full reply to Nails requires an alternative to her reading of the historical narrative, and that will have to wait until a discussion of the *Menexenus*'s historical narrative. For now it is enough to note that the burden of proof remains on her proposal for resolving the anachronism in this dialogue. The anachronism between the framing dialogue and the speech within persists as a problem, and perhaps a flaw in the dialogue.

What would account for such a flaw, assuming that Plato did not forget that Socrates had died? Any answer must be an invented one, going beyond all possible evidence. But here is a proposal that one can entertain without straining. Suppose Plato wrote the speech in the *Menexenus* as free-standing oratory, a prose monologue demonstrating that a philosopher could outdo Athenian orators even at their own job – and while he was at it to outdo Thucydides too. The motive is not far-fetched; nor is the exercise. Plato sometimes wrote such free-standing speeches suitable for public delivery, if ancient testimony about his lecture "On the Good" is to be trusted.[25] After having written the funeral speech he enclosed it in a framing dialogue, because a framing dialogue would let him ascribe this speech (and the famous earlier speech too) to Aspasia, thus subverting the place of Pericles in Athenian history. The framing dialogue had Socrates in it,[26] which created an obvious inconsistency. But Plato could not go back and change the speech, whose history ended where the laws of history required it to. He left the speech and its frame together, ill fit as they were, rather than give up either the frame's references to Athenian politics or the speech's philosophically significant reconstruction of history. Chronological consistency is desirable but not a *summum bonum*.

Imagining Plato's construction of the dialogue, even with unprovable hypotheses, brings this discussion from the dramatic date to the date of the *Menexenus*'s composition. If Plato wrote all of the *Menexenus*, he must have finished it in or after 386. But how long after? Did he write a speech whose history of Athens ended on the morning that he was writing, or did he look back after decades and compose a history that ended with the momentous events of 386 because of their importance? A later date of composition would at least have the advantage of excusing some of the mistakes in the history – time plays tricks on even Plato's memory – but it calls for some substantial integrity on the part of the history, enough to make 386 the right endpoint and not just the date that Plato had reached.

Conversely, the more integrity the history possesses, and the more orderly its governing structure is, the less reason readers have to date the dialogue to or near 386. In this sense, a persuasive interpretation of the historical narrative may well leave the date of composition as unclear as ever – except with the provision of course that Plato did not write the *Menexenus* before 386.

Two last comments are worth making. First, this book will find resonances between the *Menexenus* and other dialogues, but especially connections with the *Republic*. To the extent that theories of Plato's development are sustainable, the *Menexenus* makes most sense as a rough contemporary of the *Republic*. Aside from being short it does not fit among the ostensibly "early" dialogues. Socrates never interrogates Menexenus; does not claim ignorance; does not wish for analyses of vague moral language; does not finish the conversation amid *aporia*. He does, as this book ought to show, embed education in the workings of a good state; deploy language of self-conscious extravagance; found a city in a tale of autochthonous birth; analyse historical events in psychodynamic terms. Whether written before or after the *Republic*, the *Menexenus* attests to philosophical commitments that are closer to that dialogue's commitments than to those of any single other work.

Finally, the peculiar content of the *Menexenus* makes it the hardest dialogue to date with traditional stylometric analyses. It has almost as little back-and-forth conversation in it as the *Timaeus* and the *Apology*, so that like those dialogues its uses of certain interlocutory answers ("Of course, Socrates"; etc.)

are not available to be counted and compared. Moreover the funeral speech orients itself to a much earlier model, as those other two monologic dialogues do not. The language in the *Menexenus* has too much to do with the language of Pericles and Thucydides to permit straightforward comparison with other dialogues.[27] Those who find the chronological ordering of the dialogues a nuisance or worse will be just as glad to see that some standard techniques for calculating that chronology do not work as well with the *Menexenus*. Those who value and rely upon chronology will have to adjust themselves to knowing less about the *Menexenus*, in this respect as well, than they know about the more canonical works of Plato.

Aspasia

What makes Aspasia surpassingly difficult for readers of the *Menexenus* goes beyond the usual difficulties caused by fragmentary evidence and untrustworthy sources. Those are problematic enough. The best-known names from ancient Greece, from Pericles to Socrates to Plato and Demosthenes, present more challenges than our long familiarity with them would seem to promise. Lesser figures threaten to disappear altogether to become mere tokens spoken of contradictorily by different authorities.

What makes Aspasia's case different is the disproportionate place of the *Menexenus* in the tradition of reports about her. If one decides that hostile literary sources in antiquity combined to smother what otherwise would have been a positive message about marriage and virtue, that is because the *Menexenus* participates in the scurrilous attacks on her that were led by comic poets. If the classical sources seem trustworthy and capable of joining in some consensus statement about Aspasia, that conclusion follows from a reading of the *Menexenus* that understands the funeral speech as positive and valuable, and that takes Socrates' ascription of the speech to Aspasia as a nod to her genuine rhetorical skills. The *Menexenus* tips the balance of ancient sources.

It often happens that the reputations of secondary characters from antiquity hang on a single text. Certain names appear only in Herodotus or only in Thucydides, and what those historians have to say about those names shapes what the subsequent centuries thought of them. The present case is tricky in that Aspasia is as important to determining the meaning and tone of the *Menexenus* as determining the meaning and tone is to one's sense of Aspasia.

Madeleine Henry's book-length discussion of the information available about Aspasia has become the standard treatment of her.[28] Both imaginative and critical, Henry sifts through the mentions of Aspasia in Old Comedy's plays and quoted fragments, and then through the unstable evidence that derives from philosophical works by "Socratics", if one may still use that word without bias to characterize all those who associated with Socrates.

Henry correctly hears Old Comedy as mockery of Aspasia, "invariably sexual, sexualized, and sexualizing".[29] Fragments of comedies by the playwrights

Cratinus and Eupolis contain the kinds of obscene insults that Athenian comedy of the fifth century thrived on.[30] Aspasia comes in for stock accusations of sexual shamelessness, concubinage and pandering.[31] An uncertain attestation from Plutarch involves another comic poet, Hermippus, who allegedly brought impiety charges against Aspasia.[32] It is hard to guess what kernel of truth might lie deep within this claim. That Hermippus abused Aspasia in a comedy of his? That she represented Athenian new thinking? Socrates certainly did undergo prosecution for impiety, but the references to other such prosecutions that come down from later antiquity might all have been inspired by that one factual case, impiety charges coming to mean that someone had been a controversial intellectual.

At least in the case of Aristophanes the mention of Aspasia survives in a full-length work and there is less guesswork involved. It is his first extant comedy, *Acharnians*, produced in 425. Already sick of the war with Sparta, an Athenian country boy Dikaiopolis tells his version of how the hostilities began. Independent of Aristophanes it is known that some sort of Athenian embargo against the city of Megara, a declaration known as the Megarian Decree, ignited an already volatile situation among the Greek cities to bring Sparta and Athens into open fighting. The real story behind the Megarian Decree is obscure, involving Corinth and Sparta in balance-of-power considerations; Dikaiopolis boils it down to Athenian pranksters' kidnapping a prostitute from Megara and the Megarians' retributive theft of two of Aspasia's prostitutes. *Acharnians* contains nearly the only mention of the decree by a contemporary author.[33]

What political reality lay behind this tale of a drunken romp? Quite likely no more than a law that Pericles introduced for reasons that most Athenians could not understand or did not fully trust; so Aristophanes puts the power behind the throne, with Aspasia, and then compounds the joke in the tried-and-true Old Comic way of making her a brothel keeper.[34]

What rings true about the passage is the honest citizen's sense of exclusion from power. Dikaiopolis will end the play negotiating his own peace with Sparta, a move that shows the extent of corruption he perceives in Athens. If you want a reasonable truce you have to make it yourself. A private citizen so marginalized can only imagine what prompts political leaders to act as they do, and when citizens try to understand political processes they often find bedroom stories psychologically satisfying substitutes for real explanations. Aristophanes does not have to embody misogyny to put this story in his character's mouth.[35] Dikaiopolis lives outside the city walls and far outside its centres of power, and he can only speculate about contemporary affairs in his coarse way. Subtract the obscenities and the juvenile whoring and the passage implies that Aspasia was a public figure with influence over Pericles.

Aristophanes wrote for an audience that, while understanding the complex issues of the day, did not find them as funny unless they had been distorted one way or another.[36] Nor should one have to add that Aristophanes habitually

32

took liberties with the Athenians he wrote about. Socrates is only the most famous example. That Aristophanes turns Aspasia into a madam and retells the Megarian Decree as a misadventure among prostitutes only goes to show that he treats Aspasia in the same way he will later treat Socrates.

Against the evidence from Aspasia from contemporary comedy there are the nearly contemporary writings by Socratic authors and the *Life of Pericles* that Plutarch wrote centuries later. Plutarch's *Pericles* assists the historian with basic facts about Aspasia's life: partly because of him it is known that she must have been born around 470 in Miletus and moved to Athens in 450. She may have been related, through marriage, to Athenian aristocrats. And she must have begun her involvement with Pericles before 440, because their son Pericles the Younger could not have been born after that date.

Pericles and Aspasia could not have been husband and wife in the full legal sense, because she was not an Athenian citizen. Perhaps they lived in the kind of domestic partnership in which she was the acknowledged *pallakê* – what used to be translated "concubine", but today that word is both dated and prurient-sounding and does not acknowledge the range of the word's meanings, from a man's sexual relations with his slave to his cohabitation with a woman who had not been made his wife through formal betrothal (perhaps, to use another modern phrase that risks anachronism, like a common-law wife).[37] Her year of death is unknown, although she could not have survived Socrates, or not by much.[38]

Pericles, the son of Pericles and Aspasia, could not have been born an Athenian citizen, thanks to legislation his own father had written and supported in 450 or 451; ironically, before meeting Aspasia. But whether through a special waiver that his father pleaded for or by some other means, the son must have been made a citizen, because he went on to be elected *stratêgos* "general". He was one of the Athenian generals tried *en masse* and executed after the battle of Arginusae, and only citizens could be elected to that position.

Plutarch had access to countless sources that have since been lost. But despite his good sense in reading those sources he does not subject them to the direct criticism that is now standard practice.[39] He typically does not *name* his sources, either. The unwary reader takes away vivid novelistic details of the least trustworthy sort. Did Pericles really (and, it seems, uncharacteristically for an ancient Greek man greeting his wife) kiss Aspasia every day?[40] Unless Pericles or Aspasia personally announced such a thing there could be no source for the story, and a motive strong enough to make them tell the world would be a strong enough motive to induce them to lie.

The historical uncertainty is too bad, because Aspasia's relationship with Pericles matters more than as gossip for readers of the *Menexenus*. The dialogue says she taught Pericles rhetoric. Does that statement rest on a genuine intellectual and emotional closeness between them? The speech in the *Menexenus* that Socrates attributes to Aspasia manipulates the metaphors of parentage, legitimacy and true Athenian citizenship. What does it mean that by law she could only bear a bastard?

It may also have come time to stop calling Aspasia a *hetaira* "courtesan". The word might appear to offer a compromise between comic playwrights who made her a prostitute and the sources for whom she was practically a wife. But the Greek category *hetaira* is nowhere near as well attested as this usage implies. A *hetaira* may have been a *pornê* "prostitute" and nothing more.[41] Though desirous of avoiding the tendentious insult, the word *hetaira* perpetuates it.

Tellingly, the remaining testimony about Aspasia, the only references from authors who might have known her (and who surely knew people who did know her), does not make her either *hetaira* or *pornê*. It is possible to read the *Menexenus* as some obscure variety of attack or mockery: Menexenus says "I know Aspasia" with what may be a wink.[42] Even so no one calls her a prostitute in that dialogue. And the testimony from other friends of Socrates has even less to do with whores and courtesans.

Plato's age-mate Xenophon, for instance, brings Aspasia's name up in two works: the *Memorabilia* or *Reminiscences* of Socrates and the *Oeconomicus*.[43] Both times it is Socrates who speaks of Aspasia. One major subject of the *Oeconomicus* is the training of a new wife, and Socrates offers to introduce his interlocutor to Aspasia who will "explain everything" about such training.[44] Aspasia might be the source for marital principles that all newlyweds should learn in order to create and sustain a good marriage.

Married love is the subject again when Socrates appeals to Aspasia in Xenophon's *Memorabilia*. He quotes her directly on the subject of match-making, appealing to her as an expert.[45] Aspasia says, according to Socrates, that matchmaking is spoiled by false praise. False praise leads to disappointment; so instead of praising indiscriminately, matchmakers ought to describe potential spouses with the most accuracy they can.[46]

The emphasis on marriage, and specifically this emphasis on marriage in moral education – heterosexual desire conducive to developing virtue – is a theme that Xenophon's Aspasia shares with the Aspasia represented in the earlier Socratic author Aeschines, and one reason for seeing Aeschines as the source for Xenophon's portrayal.[47] Aeschines wrote a dialogue *Aspasia* that Cicero quoted from[48] and that Barbara Ehlers has reconstructed.[49] In this dialogue Xenophon and his wife become characters, and Aspasia interrogates each in turn about envying someone else's wife or husband. "You would rather have your neighbour's house than your own if it were better; doesn't it follow that you'd rather have your neighbour's spouse as well?" Xenophon and his wife are both embarrassed when the argument leads them to say yes. Aspasia has presumably brought them to see a conflict between choosing the best possible wife or husband (or continuing to yearn for that impossible ideal) and respecting the one they have.

The shrewd assessment of spouses, and the training of them, might appear to be pedestrian domestic topics for the *Menexenus*'s master rhetorician to occupy herself with. Did she captivate the intelligentsia of fifth-century Athens with commonplaces about matchmakers' reports and men's imperfections?

On Henry's reading of Aeschines, his special merit consists exactly in preserving the "Aspasian" philosophy as a theory of married life. "Aeschines' Aspasia had observed that heterosexual eros could be a path to *arete* [virtue] and had demonstrated that within marriage such a possibility was manifested in each spouse's wish to be the other's best possible mate".[50] The *Menexenus* does not speak of erotic attachment. It even seems unable to identify a place for such attachment in an Athenian's life. If anything the founding myth for Athens has its people springing up from the ground instead of from any reproductive impulse. The city will not need *erôs* when it can generate its people in a new kind of lone motherhood.[51]

But if celebrating true Athenians makes the *Menexenus* a masochistic obsession (assuming this is Aspasia speaking its words) in the mouth of a homeless non-Athenian and permanent illegitimate, she is just as likely to feel inadequate by going on about glorious matrimony, considering that no relationship she entered into in Athens could be a publicly recognized marriage. This advocate of the virtue that grows in heterosexual marriage would be declaring herself shut out of the pursuit of virtue in Aeschines' dialogue, just as Henry says she is shutting herself out of Athenian public life in Plato's. Henry cannot make Aeschines a champion of Aspasia's wisdom and read Plato as abusing her.

And after all, while courtship and marriage are the subject matter of all these excerpts from Aeschines and Xenophon,[52] unifying those philosophical treatments of Aspasia *and* differentiating them from Plato's, the available evidence from those Socratics also shares the themes of *teaching* and *praise*. In Xenophon's *Memorabilia* Aspasia represents the right calibration of praise and in the *Oeconomicus* she is the authority on educating a man's young bride. Aeschines represents her questioning husband and wife about prizing the best spouse, the one worthiest of highest praise, as well as performing a crash course in dialectical education.[53] These subjects praise and pedagogy dominate the *Menexenus*.

For one thing, the talk of teaching and learning between Socrates and Menexenus alerts the reader to the role that education will play within the funeral speech. Part II of this book will argue that education, and in particular education in virtue, pervades the speech. Socrates will call the speech educational when he introduces it, and use the same language about the speech-within-the-speech that he claims to report from the underworld. He will insert education into the version of the Athenian autochthony myth that he tells, even though such stories traditionally did not speak of the gods' teaching humans.[54] The *Menexenus* depicts the city of Athens as a teacher to other Greek cities, not in trivialities but in the virtue of courage. Pericles himself, despite having called Athens "the school of Greece", treated courage as a trait that was best when not taught but only spontaneous.[55] Aspasia informs this substantial motif of the *Menexenus* not as a matchmaker but as an educator whom Socrates represents.

As for praise and exaggeration, which can blur into one another in Plato, again the Aspasia glimpsed in these other authors resembles the character that Aspasia would have had to be to write the *Menexenus*'s funeral speech, but not insofar as she represents heterosexual virtue. Understanding the rhetoric of the funeral speech, which will be the principal goal of Part II, entails scrutinizing the ways in which it praises Athens, especially in one passage that piles praise on top of praise. As there is a difference between the street-savvy teaching that Aspasia passes along in other authors' works, and the teaching that the *Menexenus* credits her with, so too there is a parallel difference between the Aspasia who assumes that everyone knows what overvaluation amounts to, and this Aspasia, behind the *Menexenus* speech, who forces her audience to wonder what praise really is and how to calibrate it, and what degree of praise suits the greatest and highest objects. Plato may be bringing forward potentialities in Aspasia that Aeschines and Xenophon left unexplored; he may be the author who best recognizes the significance of her talk of praise and overvaluation in a marriage. The others, however sympathetic they are, hear that talk of praise in marriage and assume that its real subject is marriage. Plato understands that what Aspasia says will find its full significance (as her model of how to cross-examine does) when applied to a subject larger than marriage. Her real concern is praise. Examining the praise and pedagogy at work in the *Menexenus* speech will reveal the specific dimensions along which Plato extrapolates from what Aspasia said to what she must have really been saying.

Far from demeaning Aspasia, Plato may be said to liberate her concerns from the focus on courtship and marriage that existing conceptions of woman imposed on everything a woman said. Such liberation resembles what the *Republic* promises to talented women in Kallipolis, de-domesticating them so that the intelligence they had wasted on gossip about romance and betrothals can serve the city. Plato sees, as Aeschines and Xenophon fail to see, that Aspasia merely uses womanly subjects to communicate philosophical teaching.

The test for the claim that Plato depicts Aspasia respectfully will be the test of this interpretation as a whole. If the *Menexenus* can come to look like a worthy candidate for improving upon the original speech by Pericles, then attributing that speech to Aspasia is some kind of compliment. It might even be the substantial compliment that she was indeed, as Socrates says, the one who taught Pericles all the rhetoric he knew.

The point can be put more narrowly. The *Menexenus* raises questions about teaching and about praise. The most philosophical evidence available about Aspasia concurs with the *Menexenus* in associating those themes with her name. Far from subverting other philosophical representations of Aspasia, Plato sublimes them. The famous funeral speech known as Pericles' own resists its own ambitions either to praise or to teach. If the *Menexenus* speech proves to treat praise and education seriously in response to Pericles, then it will make sense to say that Aspasia, its author, is being taken seriously, by a philosopher, as another philosopher. If (again) the speech is a mockery of rhetorical praise and of the possibility of moral education, then Aspasia will have functioned only as a way to mock rhetoric in general.

***

There is a story about the Spartan woman Cynisca whose brother, King Agesilaus, encouraged her to breed horses. Late in Socrates' life Cynisca entered some of her horses in the Olympics as a chariot team; for only in this way could women participate in the Games. Cynisca's team even won, and Agesilaus then said he put her up to entering, wanting to show how little value an Olympic crown must have if even a woman could win it.[56]

Is that also Plato's strategy in the *Menexenus*? If even Aspasia can write a funeral speech, has Plato delivered the most stinging criticism possible against rhetoric? But Diotima differentiates univocal from equivocal predication in the *Symposium*, and that dialogue's readers do not conclude that metaphysics must be a pretty easy pastime if girls can figure it out. To be a real insult the funeral speech will have to be a bad speech, and parodically bad. Aspasia's participation by itself does not make it a parody.

Other tutors: Connus, Antiphon and Lamprus

Several of the minor names in the *Menexenus* occur within a dozen lines of text. They are not names of participants in the dialogue, but they add a backdrop to Socrates' claim that he studied rhetoric with Aspasia.

Shortly after crediting Aspasia with having tutored both him and Pericles, Socrates adds that he had studied music with Connus the son of Metrobius; and that "even the student of much worse teachers – someone who learned music from Lamprus and rhetoric from Antiphon of Rhamnus – might distinguish himself praising Athens in front of Athenians" as most public speakers content themselves with doing.[57]

Lamprus is scarcely mentioned in Plato's corpus or anywhere else before later antiquity. But he matters the least of these three for comparison with Aspasia, considering that he shares neither a student nor a discipline with her.

Connus the son of Metrobius was a figure of somewhat greater fame, even though the attention that is known to have come to him was mostly cruel.[58] In Plato's dialogues his name appears twice as tutor to Socrates, here and also in the *Euthydemus*, where he is said to be still alive and teaching. The dramatic date of the *Euthydemus* must be late in Socrates' life, inasmuch as tutoring him earns Connus the nickname *gerontodidaskalos* "the old men's teacher", so the reference might be a small anachronism.[59] The non-Platonic mentions of Connus are clustered around the year 423, when he was already being spoken of as over the hill. He would have to have been highly superannuated another twenty years after that.

Those non-Platonic references come from Athenian comedy. At least one comic playwright, Ameipsias, wrote a comedy titled *Connus*.[60] Connus must have enjoyed some kind of reputation. But not enough remains to tell what that reputation was. Comedy about a music teacher? Why did it have a chorus of *phrontistôn* "thinkers"? One can only guess.

The surviving comedies of Aristophanes contain two jokes involving Connus. In *Knights* (dated to 424) he is a man past his prime; rather he is the proverbial man past his prime, the basis for comparison that other old-timers resemble.[61] He is a standard for shabby treatment two years later in *Wasps* when Bdelycleon tells his father that no one values the old jury men of Athens, any more than they value "the vote of Connus".[62] The *Wasps* merely testifies to the low esteem in which Connus is held; the context in *Knights* puts him in the company of has-beens, contrasting that low status with some greater repute he once enjoyed. "How are the mighty fallen". In both cases the man was sufficiently prominent that he could be ridiculed on stage.

Thus far nothing definite follows about Aspasia. Pairing her name with Connus suggests more that Socrates had two famous teachers than anything else. He was taught by the best.

If Connus is a colleague to Aspasia, Socrates cites Antiphon[63] as her opposite. This is Antiphon of Rhamnus, a necessary qualifier, as many ancient figures have the same name, even others in Plato's dialogues.[64] The Antiphon that Socrates speaks of in these unflattering words appears in other classical works. He taught rhetoric and wrote sample speeches, as Socrates says Aspasia did. Clement of Alexandria later called him the first to accept pay for writing forensic speeches. Probably because of his practice in rhetoric, he is called a Sophist by Xenophon in his own recollections of Socrates, in which Antiphon plays a sybarite and hostile rival trying to poach Socrates' students. But Thucydides, emphasizing the man's character over his way with words, makes him a reserved figure not given to public speaking but a natural leader. After the oligarchic revolution failed, Antiphon defended himself "the best of anyone up to my time". The restored democracy executed Antiphon, who responded to the death sentence, according to Aristotle, with philosophical greatness of soul.[65]

But here is Socrates, portrayed in conversation at least a decade later (maybe two or three), sneering at Antiphon's abilities and associating him with the rhetoric that truckles to its audience. What could be the motive behind this swipe at a man long dead? More importantly for the reader, what is its point? Not only anti-democratic enough to represent the oligarchs, Antiphon even refused to address the Athenian assembly. To Thucydides his reticence shows his seriousness; a democratic thinker could read it as contempt for fellow citizens; neither one would expect this type to pander to the public. And how to explain the contrast with Aspasia? If she becomes the anti-Antiphon, does

38

that make her a democrat? But this speech that Socrates credits her with, while conciliatory towards democratic institutions, hardly repudiates the oligarchs' slogan about rule by the best.[66] Plato does sometimes distance Socrates from prominent oligarchs, as if in an ongoing effort to clear his name: Socrates does not belong among the Thirty Tyrants and therefore did not corrupt the youth. The Tyrants were on the verge of executing him when they were forced out of office; and he never slept with Alcibiades.[67] But the setting and the purpose of the *Menexenus* speech do not make this a natural occasion for such distancing.

One part of the explanation is that Antiphon represents professional persuasion in a kind of opposition that is familiar to Plato's readers. If Xenophon bears witness to genuine rivalry between Antiphon and the Socratics,[68] then Socrates stands for philosophy as it would refashion public rhetoric. By invoking Aspasia as his teacher he supplies the new philosophical rhetoric with an old pedigree. This is rhetoric that, being philosophical, cares for the city's welfare and orates in agreement with sound reasoning. Meanwhile Antiphon's competitiveness with Socrates leaves him vulnerable to being classified with all other professional rhetoricians. Not seeking truth as philosophers do, those speechmakers must be basing their craft on appeals to the crowd. It is an occupational hazard of both writing and teaching[69] for money, activities that Plato and other Socratics routinely contrast with the unpaid philosophizing of Socrates.[70]

Seen as one more persuader for hire, Antiphon threatens to blend into the crowd of Sophists whom Plato routinely contrasts with Socrates. There is something generic about the opposition – not trivial, only not specific. One fact about Antiphon that might enhance the contrast is a claim, credited to him, that goes to the heart of the *Menexenus*: Antiphon said that Greeks and barbarians are alike by nature. Socrates will tell a story of Athens in this funeral speech that is organized around the difference between the ethnicities, and it may be that he mentions Antiphon by name to bring the issue of Greek and barbarian into the dialogue.[71]

Another reading of Antiphon rests on shakier ancient testimony, but it would add a meaning to his name if that testimony can be trusted. Hermogenes, writing in the second century of the present era, says, "I hear from many that Thucydides was the pupil of Antiphon of Rhamnus".[72] Hermogenes does not believe this tradition; nevertheless a book probably dating to the same time as his, the section of pseudo-Plutarch's *Lives of the Ten Orators* on Antiphon, attributes the same claim to Caecilius.[73] The two passages seem to refer to more than one another. Evidently a tradition existed that made Thucydides the pupil of Antiphon.

If the report is true, it adds an edge to Socrates' mention of Antiphon. Now the opposition between Antiphon and Aspasia makes their students into opposites, Socrates on one side (with Plato behind him) and Thucydides on the other. This would immediately mean that Plato is treating Thucydides as the *de facto* author of the speech of Pericles. Moreover, setting Thucydides against the Socratics draws attention to the historical narrative in the *Menexenus*. For the largest most obvious difference between the *Menexenus* speech and the speech it answers is the chronicle of Athens that Plato inserts into his memorial. It is a history to rival the one that Thucydides tells, tucked into the speech where the historian tucked his great speech into his chronicle; as if to draw attention to the rhetorical nature of Thucydidean history as a whole.

Archinus and Dion

Menexenus tells Socrates that either Archinus or Dion is likely to be chosen as funeral speaker.[74] On at least one interpretation of the *Menexenus*, these names tell us how to take the funeral speech. Archinus and Dion were both unacceptable speakers, the one too brutal and the other not a citizen. So the mentions of their names, being as they are not factual references to funeral speakers, must in some other way describe the parameters within which Socrates/Aspasia will be speaking.[75]

Even if this reasoning is sound, it proceeds from a combination of clear and contestable claims about the two names. Perhaps the phrase "Archinus and Dion" carried immediate significance in Plato's time; today the allusions threaten to remain opaque.

A scattering of information survives about Archinus.[76] The difficulty lies in determining which facts typify his place in Athenian politics and which are anomalous. A speech by Demosthenes calls Archinus *meta ge tous theous aitiôtatou* "the one most responsible, after the gods", for the restoration of Athenian democracy after the Tyranny of the Thirty.[77] In the same spirit the Aristotelian *Constitution of Athens* classifies Archinus approvingly among non-extremists who opposed the Tyrants.[78] It was presumably as a moderate that on the one hand Archinus worked to prevent the oligarchy's sympathizers from emigrating to Eleusis – effectively punishing them – but also enforced the post-Tyranny amnesty that protected both the Thirty and their supporters, and also opposed dramatic expansions of the Athenian citizenry to include the non-citizens and slaves who had fought on behalf of democracy.[79] Perhaps this means that Archinus represented constitutional stability and lawful democracy.

Archinus was capable of acting with violence. He not only supported the amnesty under which the Thirty Tyrants stepped down, he had someone who violated that amnesty executed without trial. But one doesn't need to get into the business of excusing Athenian violence to question whether his name in the *Menexenus* must function as the name of a bloodthirsty politician. Archinus also proposed a decree reducing the comic poets' pay.[80] What makes his murderous enforcement of the amnesty (an amnesty that protected Socrates) the salient trait that his name refers to, and not one of his other public deeds, above all his effort to restore democracy? Especially considering that Archinus' name does not appear elsewhere in Plato, the reference resists definite interpretation.

More to the point, there are some respects in which Archinus' actions in Athenian politics bear on the content of the *Menexenus*. If it is striking that his violent enforcement of the amnesty clashes with the funeral speech's claim that Athens ended its civil war with gentle reconciliation,[81] it is equally worth noting that his fight against expanding the citizenry – his insistence on a sharp distinction between Athenians and non-Athenians – squares with the funeral speech's use of that same distinction. If Archinus appears at the start of the dialogue as a comment on internal relations in Athens, he may just as easily appear to remind Plato's reader of the salient fact about relations between Athens and other Greek cities.

The question of relevance also applies to friendship or collegiality between Archinus and Anytus of Euonymon. The two evidently represented similar political sensibilities and perhaps worked as allies;[82] but Anytus would soon prosecute Socrates.[83] That fact about Archinus' political bedfellows could also be called the salient piece of information about him; but there are no grounds for singling that fact out as the significance of Archinus' name in the *Menexenus*.

Much less is known about Dion, at least about the Dion that Menexenus is likely to be referring to. The name has inspired controversy thanks to the famous Dion, Plato's friend from Syracuse, who embroiled Plato in Syracusan politics and died fighting the tyrant Dionysius II. That is the first Dion that a reader of Plato's would think of; but if he were the Dion being referred to in the *Menexenus*, the mention of his name would have to be a joke. Dion's status as a non-Athenian would have disqualified him from speaking. Did Plato identify a foreigner as a likely funeral speaker by way of a sly observation that the issues at hand transcend any individual city's interests?[84]

More probably the *Menexenus*'s Dion is one whom Xenophon mentioned in *Hellenica*, a Dion who served as ambassador for Athens to Persia in 392.[85] The very existence of another Dion suggests that Plato is not alluding to his friend from Syracuse. If the name "Dion" had a natural Athenian referent, a joke about internationalism would have been so understated as to go unnoticed. Plato is probably naming a political figure who participated in the negotiations that led to the "King's Peace", that treaty brokered by Persia that concludes the *Menexenus*'s history.

The Athenian Dion also makes sense as the reference of this sentence inasmuch as he offers a contrast to the young Menexenus. For if Archinus more than anyone else saw Athens back to democratic functioning after the Thirty Tyrants, and Dion's name belongs in the story of how Athens reached the endgame that led to the King's Peace, then both of these potential speakers are active political figures who participated in the events that the *Menexenus*'s history tells about.[86] Maybe Menexenus ought to take a hint from them and involve himself in Athenian politics and accomplish something on the city's behalf, as these other men had to do before anyone considered them for funeral speakers.

The figure of Socrates, however, stands as a reproach to both Archinus and Dion. He is a funeral speaker too, after all; and compared with the service *he* provided to Athens, the efforts of Archinus and Dion are trivial and wrongly directed. Flurries of activity in the assembly and on diplomatic voyages to Persia, barely a moment (as far as the historical record shows) spent on improving the people of Athens.[87]

Menexenus

Aspasia speaks to the reader of the *Menexenus* from backstage: Socrates delivers her part. Menexenus has much less to say in this dialogue, but he gets to speak his own lines.

The obvious reading of this Menexenus is that he is the same young man Plato put into two other dialogues: the *Lysis*, in which he appears as such a close friend of the title character that Socrates examines them both hoping to detect the nature of "the friend"; and the *Phaedo*, which is a significant appearance for the character despite Menexenus' not saying anything, because belonging to the group that witnessed Socrates' death puts him among the circle of Socratic insiders. If the Menexenus that Socrates runs into who is now coming out of the council meeting is the same one as in those other dialogues, the *Phaedo* confirms that he will be an intimate friend to Socrates, while the *Lysis* leads one to expect an enthusiastic young man, quick to answer if not always good at answering.

Leslie Dean-Jones has argued for another Menexenus. Socrates is known to have had a son by that name; and Dean-Jones makes the case that Menexenus in the dialogue bearing his name is this son.[88] The Menexenus who appears in the *Lysis* is addressed by Socrates as "son of Demophon",[89] but Demophon's name is not mentioned in the *Menexenus*.

Too many considerations weigh against the hypothesis. Menexenus and Socrates engage in banter that hardly sounds like what we would expect from an Athenian father and son. Would a father offer to strip naked and dance for his son's pleasure, even sarcastically? Maybe under the right circumstances. Would a son call his father by name? Not likely. Could an Athenian child get away with openly doubting his father's honesty?[90]

The substance of what Socrates tells Menexenus also suggests he is not talking to his son. He tells Menexenus that he studied with Aspasia and Connus, which is autobiographical information that his son surely would have known by this time.[91] But beyond such specifics, the tone of the conversation is unsuitable for father and son. Menexenus acts as if he were as qualified as Socrates to speak in public – overt disrespect for an Athenian son. (And one wonders how he could have prepared a text and presented himself to the council without his father's having learned of the plan.)

One reason it is difficult to pin down Menexenus' identity is his tender age. Whether Socrates' son or just a young man Socrates knows, he is junior enough to invite condescension and a show of indulgence from Socrates, who inclines towards reacting that way towards everyone. Does Menexenus sound big and brash about speaking at the funeral despite his youth because he is talking to his father, or because he is so self-aggrandizing that he talks that way to everyone?

In an important respect the answer does not matter. Menexenus has such a high opinion of his own talents as to have presented himself to the *boulê* as one qualified to speak for the city at a military funeral. Son or not, he has the uneducated confidence of the interlocutors that Socrates undoes through interrogation: Ion, Euthyphro, Callicles and the well-known rest of them. Menexenus even thinks highly enough of himself to question Socrates. And here is something singular about the *Menexenus* and a reason to entertain Dean-Jones' reading in addition to the reasons she gives: Socrates positively indulges Menexenus. Shyness or not he will recite a stirring patriotic speech at the boy's behest (with an offer of naked dancing thrown in for good measure).[92] Menexenus asks what kind of speech Socrates would give and Socrates uses none of his dialogical judo on him but answers the question. He learned a fine example from Aspasia, he says, and delivers the funeral oration.

Menexenus' mocking spirit creates a problem for readers who deduce from the opening dialogue that the speech is a parody of public rhetoric. The greatest support for that reading comes from the opening and closing conversations, barely if at all from the speech itself. And within the conversation it is Menexenus, not Socrates, who represents this position. Menexenus is the one who thinks Socrates is joking and actually hates all rhetoric; it is Menexenus who believes that Aspasia could not have written the speech. Socrates by contrast keeps claiming that Aspasia is a skilled rhetorician, and does not change his story. When readers of the *Menexenus* say they hear the joke and the mockery in the speech, they are sounding like the brash and cocky interlocutor rather than resembling the philosopher.

The reader who wants to link philosophical views to the Platonic characters who espouse them ought to do so here, and ask: which character thinks Socrates is mocking public speakers? Which one thinks the speech is a joke? The unseasoned boy talks that way, the one who knows less than he should; the one who at the end of a fine speech (a speech he acknowledges to be fine) still thinks the important question is "Who wrote it?" If you really want to read Plato as an author who keeps claims sorted by the characters of those who put those claims forward, then you should associate the interpretation of this speech as ironic with the type of auditor who is young and self-absorbed, and prone not to detect the merit of another person's accomplishment.

Even more relevantly, Menexenus offers Plato the chance to begin this dialogue with a tailor-made opportunity to satirize rhetoric. Menexenus sounds something like Ion in the dialogue named after him; but Socrates is relentless with Ion and what he knows, until Ion admits his incompetence. Why does Socrates not put Menexenus to the same test? There is any number of concepts that Menexenus could be shown not to grasp. Even better, given that Menexenus wants to be the city's speaker, Socrates can have him give his speech right now. *That* would show the failings of his rhetoric, as the failings of rhetoric show in the "Lysias" speech in the *Phaedrus*. A hapless sample speech from Menexenus would shut the boy up and parody Pericles both at once. That Plato elects to have Socrates deliver a speech instead of a wrongheaded speech by Menexenus suggests that the speech given here has philosophical value.

One last thought about Menexenus as the son of Socrates. Although deciding either way on this question does not affect this book's reading of the funeral speech, Dean-Jones' proposal works in a fascinating way together with the suggestion, already raised, that Socrates is a shade returned from Hades. If Rosenstock and Dean-Jones are *both* correct, the Socrates who speaks in the *Menexenus* is a shade appearing in the presence of his son, as part of the process of humbling the son. And the historical background to this time suggests a meaning to such an appearance. The Peace of Corinth that marked the end of the Corinthian War in 386 was (as implied by one other name it had: the King's Peace) a treaty brokered by Persia to quiet the fights among Greece's cities. While bringing peace[93] the treaty had the effect, and revealed the motive, of consolidating Persia's influence over Greece. In particular this treaty recognized Persia's control over those Ionian cities along the coast of Asia Minor (including Miletus, home town to Aspasia) that had revolted early in the preceding century. At that time Athens had supported their revolt, and Persia's first march into Greece, until it was stopped at Marathon, had been planned as a punishment for Athens. Ceding the same Ionian cities to Persia constituted a final acknowledgement by Athens that its struggle had been in vain. One hundred years after Marathon, Persia won the war with Greece – or rather won in the Peace what it had lost at war.

Meanwhile 386 was the year in which Athenians first included revivals in their annual dramatic festivals. Until then all tragedies performed in Athens were new plays, written for that occasion and never played again, at least not performed again in Athens. In 386 the Athenians first dipped back into their dramatic history and reperformed a tragedy by Aeschylus. As the fourth century proceeded they made tragic repertory an ever more common occurrence.[94]

It is not known what play by Aeschylus the Athenians revived in 386. But even if it was not *Persians*, the city would have been alerted to Aeschylus (who had been dead a lifetime by then) more than it had for years, and alerted to allusions to his plays. And if both interpretive suggestions about the *Menexenus* quoted here are true, that Socrates is dead and therefore present as a ghost and Menexenus is the son he appears to, then their conversation re-enacts the scene in *Persians* in which the ghost of Darius appears to Xerxes.[95]

In the *Persians* Xerxes sees his father after having returned to Persia, defeated by the Greeks at Salamis. In the *Menexenus* it is the Greeks who are lost, defeated in the peace brokered by the Persian King. Xerxes has just met with the Persian elders. Menexenus just met with the Athenian *boulê*. His father's ghost appears and surveys the loss – the father of Xerxes but also the father of Menexenus. Darius' elegy for his empire includes a recapitulation of Persia's glorious history; Socrates recounts the glorious past of Athens.

Again, this proposal rests on two suggestions, both of which have to be true for this interpretation to be. Then too the relationship between the *Menexenus* and other literary works has more to do with Thucydides than with Aeschylus. Both the funeral speech of Pericles and the historical narrative it is embedded in are assessed and rewritten in the funeral speech of Socrates and the historical narrative embedded within that. But rewriting Thucydides is not inconsistent with also rewriting Aeschylus. On the contrary, in one respect the two appropriations of earlier works reinforce each other. For as a response to Pericles' speech the *Menexenus* puts Socrates in the place of the man who, during Socrates' lifetime, wielded more power than any other Athenian. Socrates as Aspasia's favoured student, the one she told her real speech to, for a moment becomes the man who runs Athens. The allusion to the *Persians* puts Socrates in the place of Darius, the most successful of the dynasty of successful Persian monarchs. Either way you read the dialogue, this is what rhetoric would sound like if Socrates ruled the world.

Of course Socrates did not rule. He lived a private life and died an unenviable death, and for all Plato knew that was the end of him. Even so, Plato seems to remember Socrates drawing the same comparison at his trial, when he wondered if his coming death might feel like a dreamless sleep. The king of Persia himself doesn't sleep so well! – Socrates saying that as if a comparison between him and the great king were the most obvious pairing in the world.[96]

And to the extent that Socrates represents more than Socrates alone, to the extent that he also carries the meaning of "the philosopher" with him everywhere, the sight of him addressing Athens as a man of power brings the change to mind that Plato will register in other words in another place, when he has Socrates conceive the day that either kings turn to philosophy or philosophers turn into kings.

Pericles

The historical person of Pericles, the author of the most famous funeral oration in the ancient world, is named only twice in the *Menexenus*, but in some form his voice is heard throughout the dialogue; and in a way (so goes the argument of this book) his ear is present too, Pericles being part of the target audience for the *Menexenus* speech. His own funeral speech defines

Pericles for later ages, and to a great respect it had already defined him in ancient Athens. Readers of the speech since his time or a little later took it to exhibit the height of his rhetorical abilities and to display the power of his personality and his thought. And that speech, more than anything else is, is the subject of the *Menexenus*.

In numerous unmistakable ways the *Menexenus* harks back to the Periclean speech, with Plato expecting his reader to compare the speech Socrates gives with Thucydides' version of the speech by Pericles. To remove all doubt Socrates ascribes the entire speech he delivers to Aspasia. Plato suggests that Aspasia wrote the original funeral speech for Pericles, just as she wrote the speech Socrates delivers in the *Menexenus*, maintaining the old slander that Aspasia taught Pericles how to speak.[97] But the connection between the speeches does not have to depend on Aspasia's relationship to them when the speeches are as structurally similar as they are. The *Menexenus* speech ultimately comes out of Pericles' mouth and talks back to his speech, whether to silence that first speech and all the rhetoric it stands for (if it works as parodies do) or to improve upon it (if it is meant as an improvement).

Given his importance to the *Menexenus* even from a position outside the dialogue, Pericles needs a few words of introduction of the sort that Plato's contemporaries would have taken as too obvious to mention – not an attempt at a summary of his life, for which many sources are available,[98] but an encapsulation of those aspects of his life and public persona that are most relevant to the *Menexenus*.

The ancient evidence about Pericles is sparse for someone who must rank as the most famous statesman to emerge from classical Greece. Pericles left no memoirs, correspondence, or other writings.[99] Some of his speeches were reported by Thucydides, and statements attributed to him were handed down by contemporaneous authors. But as a rule the authors of his own time record only satirical fragments in the plays of Aristophanes and other comic poets, a story in Herodotus about the birth of Pericles.[100]

In an indirect sense Herodotus might be speaking of Pericles elsewhere too, in disguised form. Perhaps the comments of the *Histories* on the origins of Athens[101] are motivated by the wish to correct the patriotic version of those origins as propounded by Pericles.[102] But such allusive references are a long way from usable biographical evidence.

Much more detail exists in such later sources as Plutarch's *Life of Pericles* (together with his *Life of Cimon*) and the Byzantine *Suda*. These were written many centuries after the time of Pericles: their authors had access to earlier sources now lost, but it can be hard to sift out what is reliable in their reports on those earlier sources.[103]

The main sources for a study of Pericles date to the century between his death and the death of Alexander the Great. *The Constitution of Athens* comes from around the end of that period: it is an Aristotelian document, traditionally credited to Aristotle himself but now sometimes attributed to a member of his school. That portrait of the Athenian democracy includes information about the early life and career of Pericles.[104]

The most significant source is Thucydides. His *History* loses some of its claim to impartiality when its narrative repeatedly endorses the policies and tactics of Pericles. But no one can doubt Thucydides' access to information about the prominent figures of Athens, nor his scrupulousness in gathering and presenting that information. Born into a world that lacked traditions of scholarly method, Thucydides invented his own rules and then followed them.

Most relevantly to the present topic, the *History* preserves an account of the funeral oration Pericles delivered after the first year of the war. It is likely that Thucydides was present when Pericles spoke; and considering Pericles' fame and the fame of this speech he must have felt constrained to repeat Pericles' own words, for otherwise too many people could have spotted errors in his version, errors of the sort that he was most dedicated to avoiding. For his part Plato not only responded to Pericles through the funeral speech as Thucydides reported it, but also must have read the *History* in its entirety;[105] presumably he expected his reader to be familiar both with the speeches of Pericles and with the man's entire political legacy, as Thucydides presents that legacy.[106]

Plato himself supplies different evidence about Pericles. Pericles is a recurring topic in Plato's *Protagoras* and *Gorgias*, while in other dialogues he comes in for glancing criticisms, occasionally damned with faint praise. Once Plato does have Socrates compliment the man: *pantôn teleôtatos eis tên rhêtorikên genesthai* "the most perfect at rhetoric of anyone alive".[107] Most generally one can say that Plato looks at Pericles as a parent, an educator, a statesman and an orator; and one reason for seeing the *Menexenus* as a significant Platonic work is that it connects with all these more isolated comments about Pericles.

As for the life itself: Pericles, born around 495, died in 429 of the plague that killed a considerable fraction of Athens. On his mother's side he belonged to the powerful and sometimes scandalous Alcmaeonid family. He married as a young man and had two sons, Xanthippus and Paralus, who are sometimes mentioned together in Plato.[108] He divorced this wife, and some years after the divorce he took up with Aspasia.

Pericles probably made his first mark in political life when he was in his early thirties and brought a prosecution against the Athenian statesman Cimon. Cimon had been the hero of the battle of the Eurymedon, at which – more than a decade after the Persian War – Athens led Greek forces to a primarily naval victory over Persia. Thanks to Cimon, Persia ceased to be a threat on the Greek seas, and the alliance of Greek cities led by Athens became a notable military force. But back in Athens, Cimon's main rival was Ephialtes, political mentor to Pericles. No doubt because of his association with Ephialtes, Pericles prosecuted Cimon for taking bribes after an audit of Cimon's term as *stratêgos* "general" found a discrepancy in the official accounts. Cimon was acquitted, but Pericles' action had proved that he could be defeated politically. Within a couple of years Cimon had been ostracized.[109]

Pericles did not emerge from complete obscurity to bring legal charges against Cimon. Sometime before the trial, in 472, he served as *chorêgos* "chorus leader, producer" of a trilogy by Aeschylus that included *Persians*.[110] A *chorêgos* spent his own time and money organizing a dramatic production. This seems to have been (and seems to have been seen as) an aristocratic institution surviving into democratic culture,[111] and Pericles may have taken on the production to establish himself as a public figure. In any case he went beyond merely being known to operating within Athenian politics when he initiated the prosecution.

His mentor Ephialtes was assassinated within a year of the ostracism of Cimon, and Pericles soon moved into the position of greatest prominence and power in Athens. From 454 until his death in 429, he was annually elected, almost without fail, to the position of *stratêgos*. Although officially the *stratêgoi* were military leaders, in practice they wielded authority in the Athenian assembly as well, with the right to speak first on proposed legislation. Pericles seems to have taken advantage of these privileges. In practice he ruled Athens without effective rivals; so a famous passage from Thucydides can sum up his political career: "He was not led by the multitude [*plêthos*] but rather led it"; and Athens "became democracy in word [*logôi*], but in fact [*ergôi*] rule by the pre-eminent man [*hupo tou prôtou andros archê*]".[112] The *Menexenus* might be acknowledging the same domination of Athenian politics by a single person when it says that some call Athens a democracy, others by another name, but it is really an *aristokratia* in which the populace approves rule by the best.[113]

Beyond literal politics, Pericles represented the new ideas that characterized Athenian culture after the Persian Wars. He associated with the sophist Protagoras and the Parmenidean philosopher Zeno. Above all he was influenced by Anaxagoras. How close such connections were is impossible to estimate. These men may simply have dined and talked together, or Pericles may have studied with them, as Plutarch says he studied music with Damon.[114]

As *de facto* leader of Athens Pericles pursued and expanded the democratic agenda of Ephialtes. Domestically this agenda consisted in transforming the Athenian constitution to put more power than ever in the hands of its citizens. Pericles also expanded the policy of paying citizens for performing public service, above all for jury duty. This controversial move[115] democratized the city more than any official restructuring of the constitution could do, because it meant that people could afford to take days off work to judge criminal cases and lawsuits and perhaps to fill other public offices. Even that is putting the point weakly. The working poor (and the non-working poor) not only had an obstacle removed to their participation in public life, they had a substantial positive reason to involve themselves in politics when they otherwise would not have bothered to.

It was also Pericles who championed and oversaw the remarkable building project that created most of the ancient Athens that today's tourists flock to. Drawing on the funds of the Athenian-run alliance the Delian League, Pericles saw to the extravagant reconstruction of the city's Acropolis, including the Parthenon.

A democratic agenda informed Athenian foreign policy under Pericles, inasmuch as he emphasized the construction of new ships and the presence of the Athenian fleet in the Aegean. Citizens of the lowest economic ranks could not afford the armour that a hoplite warrior wore into battle. On land they served as auxiliary lightly armed archers or not at all. But they could all row in Athens's ships, and the navy came to be identified (by both proponents and detractors) with democracy and the poor. To enhance democracy was to enlarge the fleet; in this sense it was the democratization of Athens that led to the city's overwhelming power in the Aegean Sea, a growth of power that contributed greatly to the other Greek cities' fear and resentment of Athens and therefore (as Thucydides saw it) made the Peloponnesian War inescapable.[116]

The war between Athens and Sparta had plenty of specific and more immediate causes besides the existence of the navy. Most of those involved Pericles as well. He formed alliances with strong states long opposed to Sparta and fostered the spread of democratic constitutions throughout Greece. In general he seemed, if not bent on inciting a war with Sparta, at least aware that open warfare between the two cities was bound to develop, and concerned to prepare for a fight. He shaped the military strategy that Athens followed as long as he was alive and commanding the city. Conscious of Sparta's infantry superiority, Pericles gathered the Athenians who lived in the countryside to move within the city walls so that Sparta would find no one to attack when they marched against Athens. Meanwhile Athens could use its ships both to strike against other cities and to protect the imports that sustained its population when all the local farmers were living inside the walls and left their fields untended. The goal was a war of attrition that would ultimately discourage Sparta.

The war had begun in 431 when Pericles delivered the funeral speech that Thucydides records in his *History*. Whether or not the strategy Pericles envisioned was the best one to follow is a moot point, for within two years he had died of the plague, and Athens subsequently followed a different strategy for the twenty-five remaining years that ended in Sparta's victory.

This much about Pericles is enough to identify several points over which Plato would have opposed him. In general Plato most takes issue with the democratic innovations that Pericles brought to Athens and the credibility that his name and charisma lent to democracy. Plato is notorious today for his opposition to democracy, though the issue does not figure prominently in the *Menexenus*. The *Menexenus* even appears to have made its peace with this unruly form of governance, except insofar as democratic culture obstructs education.

49

Also vague, or only indirect, are references in the *Menexenus* to the friends of Pericles who represent the new ideas afoot in Athens. Glamorous and compelling rhetoric was part of the new era that included sophistry and tragedy; and broadly speaking, to the degree that the *Menexenus* directs itself against Pericles' rhetoric it has reason to suspect his intellectual attachments as well. Nevertheless Plato's attacks on the associates of Pericles are more explicit in other dialogues, scarcely surfacing here.[117]

As a political leader, however, Pericles is everywhere in Plato's funeral speech even if his name is not. Pericles constructed the empire that inspired countless battles and ruined Athens; so the *Menexenus*'s story of the city is a story of his effects as a leader. Beginning almost at once after the Persian War, that story recounts the shifting alliances and exhausting wars that Pericles either led Athens into himself or left behind him as the legacy of his foreign policy and military strategy. Whatever Plato's attitude towards Athenian history is in the end, it begins with the political reality that Pericles created, either criticizing that reality, trying to accept a redescribed version of it, or – the subtlest transformation, one to watch for throughout – willing away Pericles' role in history in favour of larger, impersonal forces that are comprehensible only to a philosopher.

Finally, a word about the occasion that history preserves as the first appearance Pericles made before the public, his work as *chorêgos* "chorus sponsor, producer" for *Persians* (and other plays by Aeschylus, now lost). This last thought develops comments made above: Dean-Jones' proposal that Menexenus is the son of Socrates; the argument from Rosenstock that Socrates is a ghost; our own suggestion that the conversation between the two reprises the "séance" scene in *Persians*. Suppose Plato planned the *Menexenus* as a reply to Pericles along another dimension. First his dialogue rewrites the most famous speech that Pericles gave, and then it rewrites the play he famously produced. What an optimist (and ignoramus) Pericles had been to imagine Salamis as the end of Persia's empire. Socrates now contemplates the end of Athens's empire at the hands of Persia. And where the *Persians* may have functioned as a political message from its *chorêgos* endorsing the work of Themistocles in routing Persian ships,[118] the *Menexenus* makes its image of imperial decline the indictment of Periclean policies.

Even without summoning Aeschylus, the *Menexenus* comes at Pericles from several directions at once. In this respect, even if not in any others, it belongs in the centre of a discussion, informing and deepening all the comments about Pericles that other dialogues make in passing.

Notes

1 But note that the remark that Connus is his tutor in music is also found in the *Euthydemus* 272c, 295d. See below on Connus.

2 See below on Aspasia. Socrates also speaks of his tutor in music, Connus the son of Metrobius, a much lesser figure than Aspasia; nevertheless see below on Connus.

3 Plato: Socrates learned rhetoric from Aspasia, *Menexenus* 235e; rhetoric an *empeiria* like pastry-cooking, *Gorgias* 462d–e; rhetoric based on understanding the soul, *Phaedrus* 270b–c; its actual practitioners, *Phaedrus* 272d–273a. See the Conclusion on the relationship between the *Menexenus* and Plato's criticisms of rhetoric.

4 The *Symposium* offers an example along these lines. For obvious reasons the *Symposium* has invited updated versions, reinterpretations, in fiction and on the stage. Plato peopled it with a comic and tragic playwright, physician, politician and the rest, and for the most part these can be replaced with stock characters from other cultures. But replacing Socrates with another philosopher – whether real, fictional or archetypal – puts out the *Symposium*'s fire. Thus an otherwise successful production in June 2007, *The Dinner Party*, directed by David Herskovits (with dramaturg Kathleen Kennedy Tobin), at the Kitchen in New York City. See Isherwood (2007). What made that production fizzle? Simply that one great reason for Socrates to tell what love is, is discovering the love that might have motivated *him*, Socrates, the philosopher people wanted to understand in ancient Athens and would still like to understand today – not "the philosopher", but this peculiar example not yet duplicated.

5 Plato: mother of Socrates a midwife, *Theaetetus* 149a; Socrates' never practising music, *Phaedo* 60e–61a. On the historical status of the midwife–mother story see Burnyeat (1977).

6 As Pamela M. Huby puts his position (not far from her own): "Wilamowitz thinks that the speech was an attempt to show that Plato could do as well as the orators if he chose … The jesting dialogue was added as a screen for the fact that it was the writer of the *Gorgias* who was now trying to write a speech". Huby cites *Platon* I, pp. 265–67 and II, p. 142. Huby (1957: 104n.2). Other readers have held variants on this view. Clavaud cites Croiset and Kennedy, who called the opening dialogue comical but the speech within serious, while Hude thinks that as Plato writes he passes from being ironical to being serious. See Clavaud (1980: 49–50, 56).

7 According to a memorable anecdote that Aristotle tells – memorable because it sounds as unlikely today as it did in his time – Thales proved the practical potential of philosophers by cornering the market on olive presses one year when he foresaw a bumper crop of olives: *Politics* 1259a6–23. If the *Menexenus* were out to prove the rhetorical abilities of philosophers, it would belong in the same tradition of philosophers' demonstrating pragmatic knowledge.

8 *Menexenus* 249e.

9 See A. G. Geddes (1987: 320). Plato portrays Socrates in *tribôn*: *Protagoras* 335d, *Symposium* 219b.

10 Plato: Socrates in public life, *Apology* 32b–d; the household of Pericles, *Gorgias* 427a–b. On other references to Pericles in the dialogues see the section on Pericles below.

11 Aristophanes: jokes about Socrates, *Birds* 1280–83; *Frogs* 1492.

12 Plato: Socrates not acquainted with Anaxagoras, see *Apology* 26d, *Phaedo* 97b–d; Socrates and Alcibiades, *Symposium* 213b–223a; "in love with" Alcibiades, *Gorgias* 481d, *Protagoras* 309a, *Symposium* 213d; Paralus and Xanthippus, *Protagoras* 315a. Socrates and Pericles the Younger, Xenophon *Memorabilia* 3.5.

13 Plato *Protagoras*: Protagoras recognized Socrates, 316c.

14 Nails (2002: 79–82). For ancient descriptions of the case see Plato *Apology* 32b–c, Xenophon *Hellenica* 1.7; see Xenophon's direct reference in *Memorabilia* 1.1.18 and the more oblique allusion at 4.4.2.

15 Rosenstock (1994).

16 Plato *Phaedo* 81c–d.

17 *Menexenus*: Socrates *eis makarôn nêsois* "on the Isles of the Blessed", 235c; Aspasia *makaria*, 249d; speech from beyond the grave, 246d–248d.

18 Thucydides *History*: Pericles to survivors, 2.45.2. On the genre of funeral speeches see Chapter 3 below. For reflections on mortality in those speeches see Lysias 2.77–78; Demosthenes 60.37; Hyperides 6.42–43.

19 *Apology* 41a–c.

20 Nails (2002: 319–20).

21 *Ibid*: 319.

22 *Ibid*: 319. Emphasis in original.

23 Another problem is that "far" and "near" are sometimes literal terms in this description, sometimes metaphors. Persia is literally further away than Sparta; but the gods' role in the history takes place right at home, when the first Athenians sprout from the earth. This is far away only in a conceptual sense. And then the tales of Athenian heroes sometimes take place in Greece, further from Athens but still nearer than Persia is.

24 See *Menexenus* 243b.

25 On the lecture see Aristoxenus, *Harmonics* 30.10–31. Gaiser (1980) collects the relevant evidence on this much-anecdoted speech. Whether or not that lecture points the way to an esoteric Platonic doctrine lies beyond the scope of this chapter; it is enough if Plato wrote a lecture.

26 With only cautious appeal to the dialogues' chronology, one can still observe that the works in which Socrates is not the main speaker are all dialogues thought to have been written later than the rest. Whatever his reasons, Plato first made Socrates his exclusive protagonist and only later introduced other speakers in that role. So, if the *Menexenus* is not a late work (see below), Plato would have put Socrates in it as a matter of course, even though his purpose was to connect the speech with Aspasia.

27 For a summary and assessment of stylometric and other methods of dating the dialogues see Brandwood (1992).

28 Henry (1995).

29 *Ibid*: 19.

30 For a succinct contrast between "Old" and "New" Comedy see Aristotle, *Nicomachean Ethics* 8.4 1128a21–24. Aristotle might not be using the words "old" and "new" in consciousness of two distinct comic genres (Irwin 2000: 226). Nevertheless his word *aischrologia* "shameful language; obscenity" captures Old Comedy in the technical sense as that is known today.

31 Henry (1995: 20–25). See especially two fragments of Cratinus from his *Cheirons*: Kassel and Austin (1998: fragments 258, 259). Eupolis' *Demes* has Pericles the Younger, Aspasia's son, ashamed to have a whore for a mother: Kassel and Austin (1998: fragment 110).

32 Plutarch *Pericles* 32.1.

33 Aristophanes *Acharnians*: "Some young guys drunk from playing cottabus [a game with wine-dregs] go to Megara and steal the whore Simaitha. And the Megarians all worked up stole two of Aspasia's whores in turn ... Then Pericles the furied Olympian shook Greece with his lightning bolts", passing the decrees that barred imports from Megara, and that prompted the Megarians to seek help from Sparta: 524–34. See Henry (1995: 25–26) for

discussion. For a passing reference to the Megarian Decree see Thucydides *History* 1.139.

34 See Sansone (1985) on parallels between this putative explanation in *Acharnians* and the opening sections of Herodotus' *Histories*, which mock the Greek penchant for tracing wars back to abductions of women (starting of course with the Trojan War).

35 Sometimes Henry identifies misogyny too freely: Colakis (1998). Henry's assessment of the testimony about Aspasia suffers the most from her tendentious reading of Old Comedy as a genre – for example, women can't govern in Old Comedy and "their attempts to do so … must always be considered an inversion of the norm" (Henry 1995: 21). This is an uncharacteristically inattentive response on Henry's part to *Lysistrata*, whose title character is both sage and savvy; or to *Ecclesiazusae*, which celebrates its feminist utopia at almost as many points as it mocks the idea. It would be fair to complain about this play's ambiguity, but Henry does not. She is right that women in the assembly represent "an inversion of the norm". It would not be the premise for a comedy otherwise. But inverting the norm is not a problem when the norm is diseased, as Aristophanes often pictures the Athenian norm. If rule by women inverts the norm, all the better for rule by women.

36 The audience that saw *Wasps* knew that Athenian litigiousness and widespread criminal prosecution were really about finding a balance between democracy and demagoguery. But what worked on stage was an inverted battle between generations that involved a reasonable if supercilious son and his randy, uncontrollable old father.

37 See Roy (1997) for a fuller discussion of the available variations on marriage. "A *pallakê* seems to have been any woman living with a man over an extended period but not married to him by *engye* [formal betrothal]. The term *pallakê* could cover women of very different standing" (*ibid.*: 17).

38 For a reasonable summary of evidence see Henry (1995: 10–17). Also see Nails (2002: 58–62). Nails comes to different conclusions on some particulars. For archaeological evidence that helps to confirm Aspasia's relations with the family of Alcibiades see Bicknell (1982).

39 But Henry (1995: 70–74) argues that Plutarch cannily withholds agreement from most of what he reports about Aspasia. Also see Ginsburg (1997).

40 Plutarch *Pericles* 24.6. Athenaeus tells the same story: *Deipnosophistai* 13.589e.

41 On the difficulty of maintaining a clear distinction between the terms see Cohen (2006: 96–99).

42 *Menexenus* 249d.

43 On Xenophon's Aspasia see Henry (1995: 45–52).

44 Xenophon *Oeconomicus* 3.14.

45 Socrates calls himself a metaphorical matchmaker in the *Theaetetus*'s "midwifery" passage, in which he speaks of his mother the midwife and himself as midwife of philosophical thoughts. The analogy takes a surprising turn when Socrates claims that midwives also introduce men and women to each other, planting the seed they will harvest later. He too makes matches, joining fertile souls to the teachers most likely to impregnate them with philosophy. There is no evidence that Athenian midwives played a role in arranging marriages; significantly, Socrates does not pretend that his mother ever did any matchmaking. Wherever the midwifing analogy comes from – whether or not the mother of Socrates ever served as midwife at a birth – the matchmaking could therefore have been inspired by either what Aspasia really did around Athens or what she was reputed to do; reputed widely enough that Xenophon would have reported and

assumed the truth of the claim. Also see *Republic* 8.546a–d on the beginning of the good city's decline. The city begins its downward slide because of failures in matchmaking. "When the guardians give brides in marriage to bridegrooms [*sunoikizôsin numphas numphiois*] at the wrong time [*para kairon*], their children will be neither well-born nor fortunate" (*ibid.*: 546d).

46 Xenophon *Memorabilia* 2.6.36. Once again Socrates speaks as if he knew Aspasia personally. So when he says in the *Menexenus* that he studied rhetoric under Aspasia, that is not an automatic signal of parody. On this last point see Pomeroy (1996). Pomeroy points out that during the Peloponnesian War, "the luxury of secluding respectable women had to yield to harsh necessity"; she concludes that "the traditions that Aspasia lived in the same household with Pericles' married sons and their wives and that she conversed with married women are believable" (*ibid.*: 649). In the same spirit we might point to associations in Greek authors between wartime and women's freedom: Aristophanes *Lysistrata*, in which Greek women rise up against male militarism; or Herodotus *Histories* 5.87, in which Athenian women use their broaches to stab a man to death after a ruinous battle against Aegina. The less secluded a life Aspasia had to have lived, the likelier it is that she would have talked to Socrates, whether about funeral speeches or about the best way to sell a husband to a potential wife.

47 Barbara Ehlers proposes Aeschines as the source for Xenophon's portrayal of Aspasia. See her reconstruction of Aeschines' dialogue *Aspasia* in Ehlers (1966: 101–3). Henry seems to adopt Ehlers' proposal with enthusiasm – see Henry (1995: 52, 56) – although her notes call it a "plausible but unprovable view" (*ibid.*: 151n.53).

48 Cicero *De Inventione* 1.31.51–52.

49 Ehlers (1966). Henry takes issue with Ehlers' proposal that the dialogue cast Aspasia as a courtesan – how (she asks relevantly) could a young man's father send him to a courtesan for lessons in rhetoric? – but generally accepts and relies on the reconstruction: Henry (1995: 40–45). On this see Ginsburg (1997: 191).

50 Henry (1995: 50). Henry sees the enticing presentation of Aspasia in Aeschines as the path not taken by philosophy. "For a moment, philosophical discourse allowed a woman to advocate that women and men, connected by eros, search together for the good" (*ibid.*: 56).

51 Discussing the myth in Part III we will remark on its even repressing the traditional story behind Athenian autochthony, a story that retains erotic impulse in the form of Hephaestus' attempted rape of Athena, hence his ejaculation that wound up on the fecund earth. Not very satisfying as images of *erôs* go; but even this is missing from the spontaneous birth of Athenians when Plato's *Menexenus* retells the story.

52 The same is true for a passage in Athenaeus, writing about a century after Plutarch. In *Deipnosophistai* 5.219e a character tells of the love advice Aspasia gave to Socrates when he fell in love with Alcibiades.

53 Cicero appreciated the exchange that Aeschines reports, and not because it pleads for marital harmony. According to Cicero's Aeschines, Aspasia invented induction, the form of cross-examination in which an interlocutor responds to several uncontroversial examples and the questioner finds a general principle fitting all the responses. The principle will then undermine what the interlocutor had said or claimed to believe about the contentious subject at hand. That the subject for Aspasia is wanting someone else's wife or husband might distract you from noticing that Aspasia's method is the strongest crowbar in Socrates' elenchtic toolbox. If he learned this from her then she was his teacher in the full sense of that word. Cicero *De Inventione* 1.31.51–52.

54 Autochthony is identified explicitly at Lysias 2.17, Demosthenes 60.4–5 and Hyperides 6.7–8; in every case, when those other speechwriters mention education, they keep that subject sequestered from autochthony.
55 Thucydides *History* 2.39: Pericles contrasts Athenians' automatic courage with the kind Spartans exercise.
56 Kyle (2003). See Xenophon *Agesilaus* 9.6; also Plutarch *Agesilaus* 20.1; on Cynisca's victory, Pausanias *Description of Greece* 3.8.
57 *Menexenus*: Socrates studied with Connus, 235e; "even the student", 236a; most speakers content to flatter, 235d.
58 On Connus see Nails (2002: 103–4).
59 Plato *Euthydemus*: "He is teaching me to play the lyre even now [*eti kai nun*]", 272c; Socrates in present tense again saying that Connus "gives me trouble when I don't obey him", 295d; Connus as *gerontodidaskalos*, 272c.
60 Athenaeus *Deipnosophistai* 5.218c on the play *Connus*, which seems to have been another attack on intellectuals produced in the same year as *Clouds*.
61 The chorus of *Knights* brings Connus up when speaking of the Old Comic playwright Cratinus, neglected by his former fans and wandering around Athens angling for a free dinner – "like Connus", 534.
62 Aristophanes *Wasps* 675. Nails (2002: 104) renders this line differently, as if it called Connus himself one of the old jurors, and the salt fish and so on were gifts that the state bribed them with to gain votes. But the gifts in question are supposed to indicate luxuries that old jurors are *not* getting. Bdelycleon is telling them all they have been duped.
63 On Antiphon see Gagarin (2002); also Nails (2002: 32–34).
64 The *Parmenides* as a whole is a conversation remembered by one Antiphon who is said to have a grandfather of the same name, 126a–c. An Antiphon who is neither of those, Antiphon of Cephisia, is present at Socrates' trial: *Apology* 33e. Avery (1982: 145n.1).
65 Antiphon: took money for speeches, Clement *Stromata* 1.79; Sophist, Xenophon *Memorabilia* 1.6.1–15 (cf. Nails 2002: 33); public figure, Thucydides *History* 8.68.1–2; executed by the restored democracy, *History* 8.90–91; accepted sentence with greatness, Aristotle *Eudemian Ethics* 1232b6–9. Avery (1982: 157–58).
66 The theme of education that pervades the speech already distinguishes its politics from democratic ones. On this subject generally see Part II below. Also consider the *Menexenus*'s reworking of something Pericles says about the word "democracy" (Thucydides *History* 2.37.1) to yield the claim that what looks like democracy nevertheless behaves like an aristocracy: *Menexenus* 238c–d.
67 Plato: the Thirty Tyrants and Socrates, *Apology* 32c–d; on Alcibiades, *Symposium* 219c–d; also see *Charmides* for Socrates' ways of distancing himself from this young man who would grow up to be one of the Thirty.
68 Xenophon's judgement of Antiphon has proved controversial. Was the Sophist and teacher in his works this same Antiphon of Rhamnus? Avery (1982) identifies the two; Pendrick (1987) distinguishes them. Most recently Gagarin (2002: 41) has defended Xenophon's credibility.
69 Pendrick (1987: 49) says there is "no evidence" that Antiphon of Rhamnus taught, but then he has to explain away the testimony of *Menexenus* 236a. Avery (1982: 156) reads *Menexenus* 236a as proof that the orator was a teacher; this naturally becomes part of his argument that the orator was the Sophist. See Gagarin (2002: 41).
70 Blank (1985).
71 On this claim about Antiphon and its political implications – how could this egalitarian have been an oligarch? – see Avery (1982: 147–49).

72 Hermogenes *Peri Ideôn* [*On Types of Style*] 400. Wooten (1987: 122).

73 "Plutarch" *Lives of the Ten Orators* 832e.

74 *Menexenus* 234b.

75 Monoson (2000: 184n.7).

76 See Nails (2002: 43–44) for all ancient mentions and a summary of known material.

77 Demosthenes *Against Timocrates* 24.135. Archinus participated in the uprising in the deme of Phyle, and his name appears on stele fragments honouring those participants. For discussion of epigraphical evidence see Raubitschek (1941). The name *Archino[s]* appears at *ibid.*: 288, line 55.

78 "Aristotle" *Constitution of Athens* 34.3.

79 *Ibid.*: 40.

80 Nails (2002: 43).

81 The citizens of the city and of Piraeus *hasmenôs kai oikeiôs allêlois sunemeixan* "gladly and appropriately mingled with one another", *Menexenus* 243e–244a.

82 "Aristotle" *Constitution of Athens* 34.3.

83 Plato *Apology* 18b.

84 This too is part of Monoson's reading.

85 Xenophon *Hellenica* 4.8.13. This reading is proposed by Herrman (2004: 46n.9).

86 Incidentally, a reference to Dion in Xenophon tells *against* readings of the *Menexenus* that see some parts of the dialogue's history of Athens as interpolations by later hands, for if the Dion who might be selected to speak is being rewarded for his public service, the allusion must date to 392 at the earliest. More likely, since Dion's negotiations with Persia were ultimately related to the King's Peace of 386, his opportunity to speak at a public funeral may well show that the treaty had already been agreed to. Thus the opening frame of the *Menexenus* would reinforce the substance of its historical narrative in pointing to a date of composition of around 386 – unless, unbelievably, the later editors who inserted historical information bringing Socrates' narrative to 386 also then thought to go back to the dialogue's opening and insert Dion's name there in the interests of historical consistency.

87 If Archinus proposed reducing the pay for comic poets, Plato would have to acknowledge his participation in the moral improvement of Athenians, however small and indirect that contribution was. Archinus is also said to have proposed a decree specifying the 24 letters of the Greek alphabet in what became their standard form: in a very literal sense (though insufficiently Platonic) this bears on Athenian education too.

88 Dean-Jones (1995).

89 Plato *Lysis* 207b.

90 Socrates' offer to strip naked and dance, *Menexenus* 236d; call Socrates by name, *Menexenus* 234a, 234b, 235c, 235e, 236c, 249d; doubt Socrates' honesty, *Menexenus* 249e. Aristophanes *Clouds* is just one text indicating that Athenian young men called their fathers "father": Pheidippides addresses Strepsiades as *pater* at 35, 81 and 93, for example, and even at 1326, the closing scene of his greatest rebelliousness.

91 We are grateful to the anonymous reader who pressed this point.

92 Dancing naked, *Menexenus* 236d.

93 The ancient world had seen truces for centuries before this one; this treaty seems to envision not just the cessation of open killing but a way of pre-empting future warfare (Tritle 2007: 180–81).

94 Pickard-Cambridge *et al.* (1988: 99–100).

95 Aeschylus *Persians* 629–842. Commenting on another passage in the dialogue Clavaud asks rhetorically and with heavy irony, Does Plato mean to supplant

Persians? See Clavaud (1980: 138). Our answer: yes. A more general version of this point, connecting the *Menexenus* with the revenants of Athenian drama, appears in Petre (2009), although Petre does not include the possibility that Menexenus is the son of Socrates.

96 Plato *Apology* 40d–e.

97 Henry (1995: 27–28).

98 Recent examples include Kagan (1991); Tracy (2009).

99 Kagan (1991: xi). Plutarch *Pericles* 8.5: Pericles left behind nothing *eggraphon* "written" except for *psêphismata* "proposals approved by the assembly".

100 A story about the birth of Pericles and the dream that came to his mother Agariste before she gave birth to him appears in Herodotus *Histories* 6.131; the same story is found in Plutarch *Pericles* 3.

101 Herodotus *Histories* 1.56–57.

102 Gray (1997); see Moles (1996: 268–69).

103 On ancient sources for the life of Pericles see Kagan (1991: xii).

104 "Aristotle" *Constitution of Athens* 26.3–28.3.

105 Yunis (1996: 137n.4).

106 In addition, the discussion of the *Menexenus*'s historical narrative in Chapter 8 below will argue that it responds to the Thucydidean history as a whole, and to the spirit of Thucydides' historiography, not merely to anything in the funeral speech that Thucydides reports.

107 Plato: glancing criticism or faint praise for Pericles, *Symposium* 215e, 221c, *Meno* 94a–b; "the most perfect", *Phaedrus* 269e.

108 Plato: Paralus and Xanthus, *Protagoras* 315a, *Meno* 94b.

109 On Pericles: Eurymedon, Thucydides *History* 1.100, Plato *Menexenus* 241e, Plutarch *Cimon* 13; Cimon's rival Ephialtes, "Aristotle" *Constitution of Athens* 26; Pericles prosecuting Cimon, "Aristotle" *Constitution of Athens* 25, Plutarch *Cimon* 14.2.

110 Kagan (1991: 36).

111 On the details of the institution and also on its political significance see Wilson (2000).

112 Thucydides *History*: Pericles leading rather than led, 2.65.8; nominal democracy led by one, 2.65.9. This characterization of Pericles as *prôtos anêr* is hard to translate. The literal English "first man" is not idiomatic. Some translations say "first citizen" but "citizen" is not in the Greek. Perhaps the nearest connotation that remains true to Thucydides' Greek is "number-one man", informal to the brink of slang but correct in its overtones.

113 *Menexenus* 238c–d.

114 Plutarch *Pericles*: Pericles and Zeno, 4.3; influence of Anaxagoras, 4.4–5.1 (see Plato *Phaedrus* 270a); music lessons with Damon, 4.1–4.2. For discussions of Pericles and his intellectual circle (some more persuasive than others) see Podlecki (1998).

115 Aristophanes *Wasps* hints at the enmity that Pericles aroused among some Athenians for his policy of paying people to perform their duty to the state.

116 Thucydides *History* 1.23. On the fleet, see Hale (2009) for engaging overview; more discussion in Chapter 8, in connection with the navy's role in history.

117 *Protagoras* and *Theaetetus* criticize Protagoras; *Phaedo* 95a–100a ascribes mindless materialism to Anaxagoras.

118 Some historians read Pericles' staging of the *Persians* as a political act by which he allied himself with Themistocles; most recently Podlecki (1998: 11). But see Balot (1999), who objects that as *chorêgos* Pericles would have had little influence over the content of a play.

3

THE ATHENIAN FUNERAL SPEECH

The genre: three cautions

Some features of the Athenian funeral speech genre remain fixed over time, and for obvious reasons. A speech that belittled the dead would be hard to recognize as a funeral speech at all; one that made no comments about the city's values and continuing needs would not register as a military funeral. But these persistent features are very broad characteristics. To be more specific about the *Menexenus* either meeting or defeating expectations will require a more detailed sense of the genre within which Plato is writing.

It would be anachronistic to speak of "literary genre" in Plato's time.[1] But he would have understood the impulse behind grouping certain types of speeches together and identifying their common properties, and the opening conversation of the *Menexenus* is enough to show that these funeral speeches were regarded as a type when Plato was writing.

An Athenian *epitaphios logos*[2] was a speech delivered at a collective military funeral; the Athenians seem to have held one such funeral each year.[3] The custom began early in the fifth century, estimates of its origin going from 508 to 460; it continued until late in the following century. Some form of the observance may have persisted into Hellenistic times and later, well after Athens ceased being an independent state with its own army and wars.

Developing over a century and a half, and representing more than a hundred authors, the genre must have exhibited a wide range of possibilities. In fact the surviving speeches, as different as they are, still share a basic outline or internal structure and a set of topics to touch on. This does not mean that all the topics appear in every speech; but every speech contains some of them, and the elements are ordered by all the existing speeches in more or less the same structure.

To speak of "surviving speeches" can be misleading, however. At some point late in the fifth century some funeral speeches began to exist in written form, and some of these are known today. But the reader of the

Menexenus who begins with these works would do well to keep *three cautions* in mind:

1 The funeral speech tradition existed for a generation, maybe longer, before ever taking written form.
2 The extant speeches are mostly not what they appear to be (i.e. records of speeches delivered). Indeed the group contains no canonical members of the genre.
3 Despite the value of looking at the genre as a whole before reading the *Menexenus*, the speech attributed to Pericles is overwhelmingly the most relevant one for Plato; it is the one that the speech in the *Menexenus* enters into conversation with, as no other speech is.

First a few words elaborating these cautions; then a few words about what the tradition of the funeral speech can and cannot reveal about the *Menexenus*.

A cryptic remark in the late encyclopedic *Suda* says that Pericles was the first who "spoke a written speech in a law court, those before him having improvised [*prôtos grapton logon en dikastêriôi eipe, tôn pro autou schediazontôn*]".[4] If this report reflects some historical reality, the one thing it will *not* mean is what it appears to, that Pericles brought texts of his speeches with him into court and spoke from a scroll or tablet. First of all his oratory (aside from funeral speeches) took place in the assembly, not in court. His authority and his reputation rested on what Pericles said to the collected public of Athens on a regular basis for decades, not what he occasionally said to jurors. As a frequently elected *stratêgos* "general" he enjoyed speaking privileges during assembly meetings, and he is known to have pushed hard for the passage of certain bills. Plutarch says Pericles left behind nothing *eggraphon* "written" except for *psêphismata* "legislative proposals".[5] He did find himself entangled in legal actions, first when he brought charges against Cimon, then again as a defendant when he was convicted of embezzlement.[6] He would have had to speak in court on both of those famous occasions. Also, in Plutarch's story about Aspasia's trial for impiety, Pericles explicitly speaks in her defence, moved to tears. If that trial never took place then neither did his tearful plea.[7] And needless to say if the trial did take place, Pericles did not choose that occasion to introduce the practice of reading a prepared speech. The other two trials did take place, but they both would have been odd occasions for Pericles to innovate with formally prepared speeches, in the first case because he was making his name as a public figure and in the second because his integrity had been impugned and he needed to re-establish his credibility.

The *Suda* also does not have to be reporting that Pericles arrived at the speaker's platform – whether in court, in the assembly, or at a state funeral – holding the written form of his speech to read from. The entry says not that he read his speech from a written text, using a verb like *anagignôskô*, but that *eipe* "he spoke" a speech that was already *grapton* "written", by contrast with his predecessors' *schediazontôn* "improvising".[8] The sentence is clearly consistent with the meaning that Pericles memorized previously composed speeches before delivering them. If there is some kernel of truth in that claim, minus the connection with court cases, the *Suda* could be saying that funeral speeches before Pericles were composed on the spot, but that he for the first time prepared a speech in advance.[9]

It is hard to get much further with this bit of testimony. It may originate in a stilted delivery that Pericles had, or the formality of his speeches compared with more conversational rhetoric that politicians used before him. Formality and stilted delivery would work well with Platonic passages about Pericles, here and in other dialogues, to flesh out what Plato found worrisome about political rhetoric of his day. On the other hand the report might be doing nothing more than preserving in confused fashion the fact that Pericles' funeral speech and others after it existed in written form, but no speeches did before it. As a set of written speeches the genre began when Thucydides, writing his history of the Peloponnesian War, included in it the funeral speech that Pericles delivered early in the war.

The evanescence of earlier speeches does not make them irrelevant to the developing rhetorical form. Most of the surviving texts make some reference to what speeches before them have said. Pericles distinguishes his own wariness about speeches at funerals with his predecessors' enthusiasm for the custom; he declines to tell all the details of recent Athenian military history, perhaps in contradistinction with what other funeral speeches have done. Other extant funeral speeches from Athens likewise refer back to the models they follow and will try to surpass.[10] Such clues will not reconstruct the lost speeches, but they do suggest that the general form of the speech already existed before Pericles.

With Pericles comes the written speech, then – but here again there is a caution (number 2 above). The six surviving examples of funeral speeches (discussed below) constitute a nearly incommensurable bunch. In no sense are they six comparable specimens ready to be assigned to a single species. If one were to attach an asterisk to each speech whose membership in the genre was problematic for one reason or another, each of these six would be asterisked, though for different reasons.

For starters, the speech of Pericles purports to be a summary or presentation of what he said in public; but it found its written form in a work of history composed years later, by an author who does not pretend to transcribe speakers' actual words, and in a style of Greek much closer to the rest of that author's *History* than to what most audiences would expect from a public oration. Thucydides makes clear that he is not writing to impress a listening audience. Early in his history he outlines the methods he used; the result of patient research may be dry, he says, lacking the mythic elements that season other people's stories. But readers who want an accurate chronicle of the war will find this form more useful than the entertaining alternatives. "It is composed as a permanent possession [*ktêma … es aieî*] rather than as a competition-piece [*agônisma*] to be heard right now [*es to parachrêma akouein*]".[11] He could hardly be saying more plainly that the words in his *History* are not words of public proclamation.

This form of writing that does not resemble the winning language of public address will be the history's governing voice. Thucydides will not write in different styles when presenting what people said. The many speeches he includes in his account will not contain the words people actually speak. It was too hard to bear in mind *tên akribeian autên tôn lechthentôn* "the very exactness of what was said", the words of the speeches verbatim.[12]

In short, the genre of the written funeral speech began not with a text produced by an orator to be delivered publicly, but with an after-the-fact reconstruction of what that orator said by a historian who was unconcerned with verisimilitude in transcription (to a great extent, unconcerned with what Plato will call *mimêsis*). This leaves the later written speeches in the curious position of joining and often emulating a speech that was made into writing accidentally – a particularly curious position in light of the fact that several of the genre's other members never existed *except* as written speeches that no one planned to deliver.

The speech in the *Menexenus*, for instance, is not even put forward within the fiction of the dialogue as an actual speech. That is, Plato does not write a dialogue in which Socrates, Aspasia or anyone else delivers this funeral speech. Socrates does not even tell the speech to Menexenus in the thought that Menexenus will deliver it if he is chosen as this year's speaker. Even within the fiction of the dialogue, the performance by Socrates is meant as a secret: Socrates tells the speech for Menexenus alone.

Of course the speech in the *Menexenus* is the oddest case of the six. There is no point deciding in advance how it is related to the other examples when this book as a whole is engaged in determining what its purpose and function are. It is only safe to say that if any of the six speeches are parasitic upon the genre this one is, as much a comment on public rhetoric as an example of that rhetoric.

But two of the remaining four speeches, both of which lie chronologically between the one by Pericles and the one in the *Menexenus*, were also written without being intended for public delivery. Gorgias of Leontini and Lysias the son of Cephalus, who were both professional orators, evidently wrote those speeches as professional samples of their work.

From the time that Socrates was still alive until after the death of Plato, professional rhetoric-experts in Athens wrote sample speeches – samples of a defendant's or plaintiff's speech in court, for instance, to show how persuasively they could assemble the facts in a legal case to favour one side or the other. Presumably the public read these samples to gauge the speechwriters' skill, and people who found themselves involved in a legal case would then hire the writer whose speeches had impressed them. But speeches for demonstration were not restricted to courtroom rhetoric. Gorgias, the expert in rhetoric best known from the dialogue that Plato named after him, was famous for self-advertisement. The *Encomium to Helen* first sets itself the supreme oratorical challenge of exonerating Helen from the charge of having caused the Trojan War; then piles on more self-advertisement with the argument that powerful rhetoric from Paris left her helpless to refuse his seductions.

As it happens, Gorgias was one of the authors of a surviving sample of a funeral speech. This speech exists only in fragments quoted by other later authors.[13] Enough of it survives to communicate Gorgias' signature style: a sensation in his own time but stilted today, when the symmetry in his sentences feels more mechanical than prestidigitatious, and turns of phrase are memorable as preposterous rather than as *mots justes*. Already the great work of literary criticism from later antiquity, *On the Sublime*, mocks Gorgias' language in the funeral speech as characteristically overblown for effect and senseless at heart: "Xerxes the Zeus of the Persians" indeed![14]

In fairness to Gorgias, his rhetoric was no joke in Athens when he first arrived and demonstrated what he could do with a speech. Even Plato, for all his suspicions about the influence that rhetoric could exercise over the masses, paid grudging tribute by making Gorgias the spokesman of this new nihilism. For Plato it is Gorgias and the power of persuasive language that usher in a new kind of politicking, one that is capable of accomplishing anything it wants in a democracy, and that is coolly careless about what ought to be accomplished, as long as one keeps winning public support.

Although some of the funeral speech of Gorgias survives only as short phrases, one stretch of continuous prose identifies it as an *epitaphios logos* suited to Athenian public funerals. The context does not let Gorgias' readers determine what his purpose may have been in writing the speech, aside from showcasing his rhetorical talents. One problem is that a funeral speech written as a demonstration needs to leave out specifying details. Imagine an all-purpose eulogy today, written to guide members of the clergy in composing their remarks for a funeral. The sample eulogy will propose an order of topics and maybe comments about the family members' grief, the nature of mortality, and so on. But to the degree that it can adapt to fit any deceased person the sample will not contain specifics about an individual.[15] Almost like such a eulogy, the funeral speech by Gorgias does not comment on a particular war or battle that Athens is engaged in at the moment or on an enemy it is fighting. The relative ahistoricity of the speech lets it display the general form of the genre better than it would do otherwise, but not the tactical political function of political rhetoric.

Lysias wrote the other speech that was apparently produced as a demonstration. Lysias was a speechwriter and a friend of Socrates. One anecdotal tradition holds that when Socrates was indicted on the charges for which he would be convicted and executed, Lysias offered to write his defence speech

(Socrates refused). And Plato writes as if he knew Lysias and his writings. The *Republic* is set in the house of Cephalus, a wealthy Athenian resident alien, with his sons Polemarchus and Lysias present. Although Lysias only receives a mention in the *Republic*, in the *Phaedrus* it becomes his turn to represent Athenian rhetoric. Socrates uses a speech about love purportedly written by Lysias as a springboard for investigating both the nature of love and the nature of rhetoric.[16]

Lysias has the same incentive Gorgias does for producing a demonstration speech. Aside from the difference that his sample survives whole, it should resemble Gorgias' in exhibiting the general features of a funeral speech while omitting the political details that show where a speaker tailors civic traditions to fit a particular situation.

Lysias does not omit all such details. The Athens of his speech is embroiled in the Corinthian War, that war that ended with the "King's Peace" that the *Menexenus* finishes its history with. And yet the war, and the Peloponnesian War too, receive only cursory treatment in this funeral speech. Lysias reviews the mythic wars that Athens played a part in, and dwells on the Persian War, to produce a historical backdrop that would suit nearly any period of the Athenian democracy.

Lysias resembles Gorgias in another crucial respect. Neither author was an Athenian citizen. Where Gorgias as itinerant teacher came and went, Lysias belonged to a family that had settled in Athens permanently; during the rule of the Thirty Tyrants the sons of Cephalus did not affect a non-citizen's neutrality but committed themselves to seeing democracy reinstated. But their commitment underscored their non-citizen status. The Tyrants had Polemarchus killed, and Lysias escaped death only thanks to paying heavy bribes.[17] As a non-citizen he was vulnerable regardless of his family's long residency in Athens and their wealth.[18] No matter how long his family had lived in Athens, Lysias was bound to experience its laws and customs as an outsider. And there is no possibility that Lysias either delivered his speech or wrote it for delivery at a funeral. Such patriotic occasions called for the speakers' own words, and those speakers had to be citizens. The speech of Lysias, like that of Gorgias, could never have been spoken.

The remaining two speeches are attributed to Demosthenes and Hyperides, though some scholars challenge the attribution to Demosthenes and speak of "Demosthenes" or pseudo-Demosthenes when referring to that speech. Apparently both of these works were written for specific occasions and actually delivered. They are Athenian funeral orations in the complete sense. The authors were Athenian citizens, and the existing text came from their hands. No doubt it is for this reason that the speeches attempt to explain recent events – Demosthenes recounts the Athenian loss to Philip of Macedon at the Battle of Chaeronea – instead of describing the more eternalized city of the demonstration speeches.

When Socrates jokes with Menexenus about funeral rhetoric early in the *Menexenus*, he is plainly talking about speeches delivered in public at military funerals. In this sense, these last two members of the genre should be the ones most relevant as background to the *Menexenus*. The problem with taking the speeches by Demosthenes and Hyperides to define the genre is simply that they join the group late, having been composed and delivered in 338/337 and 322 respectively. As regards what the genre does and says, these late dates mean that the speeches come from a time long after the end of the Athenian empire, even after the end of the city's restored fortunes in the fourth century. How well Athens fared after losing the Peloponnesian War can be debated indefinitely. Its legal institutions were sound and it remained economically dominant well after giving up imperial ambitions. But that is Athens in the time that we refer back to as "the fourth century", or rather the first two generations of that century. Despite the continuing strengths of Athens before 338, it lost its independence as a freestanding *polis* for good upon losing to Philip at Chaeronea, even if there was a brief time after the death of Alexander – a time celebrated by Hyperides – when it seemed that Athens might throw off the Macedonian yoke and return to its old self-sufficiency. Demosthenes and Hyperides could only write elegiacally and nostalgically about Athens as a culture and a form of government, and those topics had helped to define the genre of the funeral speech. Their funeral speeches only pretend to cover the main topics of the genre.

The late date for the last two speeches also matters because it means they were written after the *Menexenus* and after Plato had died. They speak of a political reality unlike any that Plato knows or can guess at. The *Menexenus* speech sees Persia's re-established influence over Greece as the permanent new unpleasantness, never imagining that soon after Plato's death Persia would crumple before Macedonian and Greek attack and Athens would find its wings clipped by a new Greek-speaking empire.

The most obvious implication of these two speeches' late dates needs acknowledging too, and emphasizing. Plato could not have read them preparatory to writing the *Menexenus*. They will not be part of his conversation with the funeral speech, except in the indirect respect in which they reflect features of that genre that may have existed in now-lost speeches. By this indirect reasoning, examples of the genre even much later than its other members can suggest the parameters of the genre; its lingering assumptions. Then Plato might be responding to speeches that, although they themselves have not survived, still exercised some influence over the later speeches that did. The late speeches are certainly worth studying, in other words, as indicators of how Plato's audience might have received the *Menexenus*. But in no sense will they explain the speech in that dialogue.

In fact, if some agreement between Plato's version of a funeral speech and the version by Demosthenes or Hyperides appears too close for coincidence, then unless some unknown speech served as influence and source for both of them, the later speech may well be following Plato's lead. The possibility is not to be ruled out. The last two speeches in the group cannot be said to reveal generic causes for what the *Menexenus* says when they too might be effects of that speech.

Proof does not exist for an influence that the speech in the *Menexenus* had on either Demosthenes or Hyperides. Although it seems likely, given what has survived of the Athenian funeral speech, that its available examples included the *Menexenus* along with the speech of Pericles – meaning examples that were available to Athenian orators: written, known – nevertheless this does not constitute evidence that Demosthenes and Hyperides drew on those surviving examples as models for their own speeches. But there is an issue here of locating the burden of proof. Our point is that the speeches of Demosthenes and Hyperides cannot be cited as evidence for the funeral speech genre as it existed before Plato, the genre independent of Plato's contribution, for the simple reason that they wrote after he did. The burden of proof falls on anyone who wants to use these later speeches as separate evidence for the genre, because using them as such evidence requires showing that Demosthenes and Hyperides *did not* read the speech in the *Menexenus*. And how would you show that?

The group of funeral speeches now seems to contain no full-fledged members. The tradition of the written speech starts with one whose author did not write it and whose written form does not aim at duplicating the speech that people heard. The sample speeches by Lysias and Gorgias stand outside the tradition they presuppose; and the authentic speeches by Hyperides and Demosthenes arrive too late to contribute to the genre they are joining.[19]

The *Menexenus* stands further outside the imagined heart of the genre than any of the other cases do in ways that go without saying. The fact that its readers continue to debate whether or not it is a parody, a question that does not come up about any of the other speeches, already marks off the distance between the *Menexenus* and a typical funeral speech. At the same time, and curiously enough, the speech in the *Menexenus* inserts itself into the centre of the genre.

1 It is structured as a response to the speech of Pericles, which is the example that continues to found the written genre.
2 It details the relationship between Athens and other cities and nations as do the later speeches (by Demosthenes and Hyperides) that were actually delivered.
3 It follows the speeches of Gorgias and Lysias in presenting itself as a sample funeral speech, not to be presented, and authored by the non-citizen Aspasia.

It can be fairly paired together with any of the other members of the group. Indeed the surest proof that this genre is a motley is that an example as perpendicular to the group as the *Menexenus* speech is can be ensconced within the group as it is. This might be the *Menexenus* speech's self-consciousness at work. A self-conscious member of a genre in one respect belongs outside the genre (not arising "spontaneously" or "naturally" among the other members) and in another way has to be in the genre, willing itself to be exemplary.

That the *Menexenus* is self-conscious is evinced by how often readers call it a parody. A certain kind of audience interprets all self-consciousness as parody, perhaps in the well-intentioned wish to save the self-conscious work from being considered mannered or stylized.

The point of dissecting the genre's surviving members is not to serve a flippant scepticism that denies the existence of the genre. Funeral speeches did exist. Athenians wrote and delivered such speeches and they took a recognizable form. But for all the value of studying this aspect of the historical background to the *Menexenus*, the patchwork quality of the genre as it has survived shows that the funeral speech tradition does not determine and fix the funeral speech that Plato writes. One will not be able to buy an explanation of the *Menexenus* on the cheap by deriving its features from those of the genre, if the genre lacks canonical members that could display those features.

Turning away from the genre as a coherent group leads back to the speech of Pericles and the third caution, that none of the other speeches matters to a reading of the *Menexenus* anywhere nearly as much as the Pericles speech does. The speech in the *Menexenus* hones its points by contrasting itself with the speech it seeks to undo, the one that Socrates calls the speech of Pericles.

This word "undo" is the vaguest one available. It is consistent with the dominant judgement of the *Menexenus* as a parody of the Periclean speech, for one does undo an earlier work by mocking it. But you can also undo the predecessor by supplanting it and robbing it of the place it had once had. The point now is that if Plato has written a parody it parodies the speech by Pericles and not funeral speeches as such; if Plato's speech purports to best its rivals it does so by besting Pericles' speech.

To the extent that the speech that Pericles delivered, as it exists in written form in Thucydides, founds the tradition of written funeral speeches, the *Menexenus*'s orientation to that one predecessor locates the *Menexenus* within the genre in a striking additional way. Socrates reports the speech of Aspasia's as in effect the same one she had taught to Pericles. He does not specify whether Pericles botched his speech in the telling with inept delivery or whether the fault lay in his intentional tampering with the speech Aspasia had taught him. Whatever went wrong between Aspasia's composition and Pericles' delivery, Socrates promises to right that wrong by going back to the source and origin of all written funeral speeches. In this sense *he is not adding a speech to the genre* and following after the speeches that other authors contributed, but retrojecting his speech back into a place that precedes the written genre. Hijacking history, Plato restates what the genre had been.

He makes the predecessors to his speech into its copies. This may be the best new *epitaphios logos*, this unknown speech that Socrates is giving Menexenus, but as Aspasia's composition it is older than all the others. It is the model that had been followed by the speech that became a model for later speeches. Thanks to Aspasia's influence over Pericles, this new funeral speech refuses to be measured against the others but establishes itself after the fact as the measure for all the others.

The *Menexenus* against the backdrop of its genre

All cautions about the genre of funeral speeches would add up to a half-truth without the acknowledgement that the surviving examples share a general structure. They do fit together in some ways.[20]

First of all, the speeches that survive as wholes begin with an introduction, traditionally called the *prooimion*. The *prooimion* announces the occasion and comments on the fact of the speech: that a speech has been mandated, that it will be no easy task, that these fallen soldiers already distinguished themselves more than enough by fighting and dying for Athens.

Beyond saying "A speech is coming", the funeral speech *prooimion* revisits the justification for such a speech, and it traditionally reproblematizes that justification. What are these words for? Is such a thing even possible? Pericles begins his speech by denying that any words belong in a tribute to the dead. Words are the wrong currency for paying back these soldiers whose excellence consisted in their actions. Lysias imitates Pericles with friendly hyperbole. An eternally long speech would still not suit these fine men's deeds. Multiply these words' value by infinity, and they will still not be worth enough. Again Demosthenes: the brave men's virtue exceeds what any speech can tell. Even the speech of Hyperides, the very start of which has been lost, sounds a note of worry about its poor words and the rich deeds of the fallen soldiers.[21] Whether Pericles legislates the form of introduction for subsequent speeches, or he too follows in the steps of a tradition that effaces its own words' worth, the *prooimion* that questions the value of mere words is a condition of the genre if anything is.[22]

So when Socrates begins his own idea of a speech, the introductory comments will either lose some of their force, to the extent that they harmonize with the generic *prooimion*, or gain force by cutting against the genre's grain. Socrates says the law commands a speech, in addition to the deed constituted by this funeral, as tribute to the city's dead soldiers; and it is right to deliver such a speech given the many fine functions of speech: to praise and honour the dead, to console and exhort the living.[23] Plato's introduction speaks to the justification for a funeral speech as much as the others do. It acknowledges the dead soldiers' sacrifices as piously as they do. That it interprets piety as calling for a speech rather than providing a reason not to speak, surprises the conditions of this rhetorical form enough to be a Platonic assertion about the functions of public language. Especially in light of what the speech goes on to say about those functions of language, praise and moral education and consolation – all in need of scrutiny, and all of them laid out for scrutiny in the *Menexenus* – Socrates' embrace of good words for the dead neither reduces to formula (for it would be a peculiar formula that contradicted the genre's tradition) nor winks as parody (unless praise and exhortation are being set up as laughable).

Third and fourth in every complete speech come the consolation and conclusion. These are closely similar too but not as simply as the introductions are. The *epilogos* "conclusion" rounds off every speech: "Now I have spoken": "You are dismissed". The part just preceding it, known as the *paramuthia* "consolation", varies more than the conclusion does, but its possibilities are bound to be limited. In the consolation the speaker addresses the dead soldiers' families, and there are only a limited number of socially acceptable ways to speak of the dead to the ones mourning them.

For the most part, these speeches do not identify the dead by name. They are a citizens' collective and they died collectively.[24] The rhetoric of democracy might account for this anonymity, but democracy is not the only explanation when non-democratic cultures also submerged their individuals into a band of equals – the Spartans for example calling their male Spartan citizens *homoioi* "equals" or "peers". The Spartans too, without being democratic, saw one another as equals. Therefore, when Plato follows this tradition in his own consolatory section and speaks of the soldiers as an anonymous crowd, he does not have to be taking on the values of democracy, whether seriously or in jest. Nor is he necessarily subverting democracy with collectivist fantasies of *esprit de corps*. The nameless condition of its dead comes with the genre and may be perpetuated for different reasons in different speeches.

Another aspect of the *Menexenus* speech's *paramuthia* makes it stand out from the other speeches. The funeral speeches tend to acknowledge the soldiers' mortality, offering as compensation for their death in battle not eternal life in a different realm but eternal tributes to the dead in this realm. Living forever is not an option for any human being, the speeches say; the fact makes the loss of these family members easier to bear, for they did not surrender immortality when they fought for Athens.[25] The speeches promise an endless remembrance of the kind that people do not receive in death after long and safe lives.[26]

The two speeches written after the *Menexenus* try to have things both ways, pledging eternal glory for the dead in the memories of their compatriots while still holding open the possibility of continued personal existence after death. Demosthenes treats this possibility as a reasonable expectation in spite of human ignorance on the subject. After him Hyperides goes further to imagine which Greek heroes the general Leosthenes will meet in the underworld.[27]

It would strike a harsh and tasteless note if the *Menexenus* speech did not anticipate endless tribute to the wartime dead by their survivors. But along with that general desire to honour the fallen soldiers it also speaks of specific institutions to be perpetuated in their honour. The finest memorial for the dead is extensive publicly funded education and training for their children.[28] As for the afterlife, a subject on which one might expect emphatic assertions by Plato, there the *Menexenus* seems inclined to follow the tradition. Death sounds thoroughly other than life, not its continuation.[29] At most, more tentatively than Demosthenes will do, this speech nods at the possibility that the dead might retain some sensation or awareness of the living.[30] This hypothetical hope is slender enough not to contravene what earlier speeches said, as if it might sound disrespectful to surviving family members to proclaim their sons' and fathers' afterlife; as if dwelling on their lucky being-whisked-away to blessed rewards could diminish the recognition of their achievement and sacrifice.

But the *Menexenus* speech's doctrinal agreement with the rest of the genre, that the dead are dead and only these memorials to them remain alive, combines with a passage that is unmatched by the consolation sections of the other speeches. In an extended speech-within-the-speech Socrates reports what the dead soldiers had said and thought while they were still alive, and what they would say to their families now if they could. He speaks on the dead men's behalf, knowing what they want to say. Their sons should try to exceed them in virtue; their parents should restrain themselves from excessive lamentation. Because they died virtuously these Athenian soldiers enjoy the right to urge their families on to greater virtue even from beyond the grave.[31]

Without actually asserting the existence of life after death, this voice from the grave carries the moral authority of a resurrected soldier. Because it keeps itself from contradicting the other speeches' treatments of death and remembrance and yet invents a new section for the funeral speech that (as far as the evidence indicates) seems not to have existed before, this speech reads as a careful interpolation. The speech-within-a-speech is as it were the nearest thing to a Platonic myth about the afterlife in a setting that does not permit explicit talk of immortality.

Even in light of this Platonic variation on the *paramuthia*, the first, third and fourth sections of the speeches still tend more towards uniformity than towards diversity – that is to say their introduction, consolation and conclusion. In the part of every speech that comes second, though, a wide array of topics becomes available. Moreover this part, the *epainos* "praise" section, accounts for most of the length of all the existing speeches.[32] In each case it is longer than the other three parts combined. Praise can speak of the dead soldiers' origins; the city's mythical accomplishments; its brave and benevolent victories in more recent history; the Athenian constitution; the customs that characterize the city, such as its ten tribes. Finally the customs might lead the speech to meditate on how Athens preserves and transmits its culture.

Some speeches' *epainos* section includes all possible topics. More often they omit one or more. Thus the speeches by Pericles and Hyperides leave out the usual history of Athens. When two speeches do both contain all the same elements in their *epainos*, they can differ in how much space they allot to each one and in how they treat the subject.

Consider the references to *freedom* (as the meaning of democracy), *history* and *education* in the *epainos* of the speech in the *Menexenus* as that compares to the *epainos* sections of other speeches.

When Socrates associates the Athenian people with freedom, the freedom he recognizes is independence from foreign rule, not a liberty within and recognized by the state, as the freedom of speech would be. But when other speeches praise Athenian civic culture they equate democracy with freedom and precisely with the freedom of speech.[33] Socrates' failure to mention free speech when he characterizes democracy therefore takes on an edge it would not have showed except against the backdrop of the funeral speech genre.

The tradition does not speak as clearly about history. Some *epainos* sections recount no history at all. Lysias emphasizes the mythic history of Athens and almost completely skips over the Peloponnesian War. Demosthenes prefers the legendary origins of the ten Athenian tribes, mythic material attached to present social institutions.[34] If it is only being compared with the speech by Pericles, the one in the *Menexenus* might appear to be more obsessed with Athenian history than it looks alongside Lysias and Demosthenes. Socrates includes both mythic and human history and harps on the benevolence of Athens, just as Lysias and Demosthenes do. On the other hand he sounds nothing like any of the other speakers in diagnosing the Greek enemies of Athens, let alone when he blames their enmity towards Athens on their ethnic impurity. Pericles sets Athenians apart from Spartans and above them, but he does not call the Spartans half-Greek or Sparta no better than their stepmother. This tripartition of humanity – Greek, half-Greek, barbarian – belongs to the *Menexenus* alone.[35]

As for education, the most wide-sprawling of these examples, Socrates makes it both a purpose of his funeral speech and the main undertaking for which a state is responsible.[36] In this case the conventions of the genre do not help modern readers. Pericles finds the subject barely worth mentioning. Athens is a "school for Greece" and its constitution is imitated by other cities, but Athenians themselves seem not to stand in need of learning anything. Spartan training in particular is too onerous.[37] Gorgias appears to credit soldiers' excellence to some sort of training but there is not enough in this passage to say clearly. Lysias announces that his speech will bring a pedagogical effect; but at points when it would have been easy for him to equate Athenian battle virtue with training he praises the Athenians' nature, that which does not come of training. The writers after Plato foreground education Platonically, or in language close enough to Plato's that one cannot rule out the *Menexenus* as an influence on their speeches.[38]

The *Menexenus* stands alone among the speeches in one detail. Perhaps in keeping with classical prejudices rooted in aristocracy, or in agrarian culture, none of the other speeches mentions *technai* "skills, professions". If they acknowledge education, that does not encompass training in a productive and marketable skill. But in the *Menexenus* education precedes even culture, for after giving birth to the first Athenians the Attic earth brought gods to them to teach the aboriginal people the *technai* essential to both war and peace.[39] Training in *technê* is education in a precise and literal sense, comprising teachers and factual knowledge and measurable results.

It may be that Demosthenes and Hyperides speak of education as they do for the reason that the funeral speech in the *Menexenus* had already done so. That would be the strongest reading, that Plato introduced education so forcibly into his speech that it became a part of the convention for the *epitaphios logos* as it had not been before him. The historical record is too incomplete to prove such claims of influence. The weaker lesson to draw from the variety in how the speeches treat education is that the genre, or the tradition, taken as a whole, offers no useful context explaining Plato's statements on education. The comparison should be made specifically to the speech of Pericles.

These have been glances at topics that call for deeper examination and that stand up under the scrutiny to reveal more about Plato's purposes in writing his speech. Later chapters will expand these comments about education to show how persistently the *Menexenus* returns to the subject. Education also connects back to Plato's introductory reference to *ergon* "deed, action" and *logos* "word, speech"; for the opposition between *ergon* and *logos* famously runs through and organizes the entire speech of Pericles, with word always deferring to deed. The subservient *logos* comes to be associated on one side with *nomos* "law, custom", on the other side with any training or discipline superadded to natural human action. Even in elevating the *logos* to a status compatible with battlefield action, as the *Menexenus* does, by no means to a rank above action but now belonging in its company, the Platonic speech seeks to return pedagogy to a productive contributing role in culture. Education no longer opposes the natural excellence of Athenians but helps to create that excellence.

History too needs to be explored at length. Here the uniqueness of the *Menexenus* in dividing humanity three ways will bear fruit in the history it tells. What sounds like a crude insult about other Greeks' bastardy lets Plato describe history as a dynamically evolving process akin to the process by which souls and cities decline in *Republic* 8 and 9. Athenian policy becomes a story freed from the haphazardness that history had seemed to possess, in which one event follows another. History is now rendered as the outcome of psychological forces as surely and as scientifically as one soul or city becomes another.

The funeral speech in Loraux

Nicole Loraux is the pre-eminent commentator on Athenian funeral oratory. Her book *The Invention of Athens* collects and analyses the members of this group synoptically and sheds much light on the funeral speeches.[40] Loraux's argument contains too many elements to be summarized here, and most of those elements while helpful to anyone who wants to understand Athenian democracy lie outside a study of the *Menexenus*. Loraux's work bears on the present study mainly insofar as it argues that:

1 Athenian funeral speeches promulgate an ideological but unstable "theory" that enlists aristocratic values in the defence of democracy.
2 Plato's *Menexenus* is an ironic funeral speech, a parody of the genre aimed at exposing the falseness in the other speeches' salutes to democracy.

The two points go together. Loraux is attributing not just loose-gun irony to Plato that mocks everything about funeral rhetoric, but the particular pointed mockery of the democracy's attempt to understand itself.

For Loraux to be right about the compound point, the funeral speeches of Athens have to be playing an ideological role of the sort she describes; and the *Menexenus* must be criticizing that role – criticizing the speeches not just any way, but by means of the ironic hypertrophy of their ideological elements. The first claim is dubious or still unproven;[41] the second must be wrong if any of the guiding ideas in this book are right.

Some of the ideological features that Loraux claims to discover in the funeral speeches are no more than one would expect to find in any public rhetoric. The orations constitute "hegemonic speech" that sees history from Athens's point of view and with Athens always a benevolent power. "Athens is always in the forefront; this is both necessary and good". But this is a very general point. Even if you deplore patriotism you will not be shocked to hear about patriotic language at soldiers' funerals, any more than readers are shocked at Loraux's claim that Pericles represses mention of the Athenian empire.[42]

The point becomes more specific when Loraux characterizes the funeral speeches as maladept attempts at democratic theory. According to her, Athenian funeral rhetoric has an aristocratic genealogy. This does not mean that funeral speeches attack democratic institutions, but it does leave the democracy bereft of its own democratic language in which to defend, or even to describe, its way of life. The imbalance in articulateness between aristocratic and democratic values forces the funeral speakers to defend democracy on aristocratic grounds. Thus the funeral speeches say nothing about such concrete democratic practices as the drawing of lots and wages for public service; they make democracy a government *for* the people, as if from above, not government *of* the people.[43]

Democracy appears to have always possessed a false consciousness. In this spirit Loraux even takes M. I. Finley to task for his scepticism about alienation in ancient Athens.[44] But with her evocation of alienation and her divide between mutually uncomprehending aristocracy and democracy, Loraux begins to sound anachronistic. The Marxian analysis attaches an ideological function to the funeral speeches that is difficult to sustain on the basis of what the speeches say. And to the extent that a claim about the speeches' ideology is unconvincing, so is Loraux's reading of the *Menexenus* as a critique of that specific ideology.

There is nothing wrong with seeing the *Menexenus* as a critique of Athenian public rhetoric. But critique does not have to mean parody. The speech in the *Menexenus* can also criticize other funeral speeches by offering an alternative to them, as this book will argue that it does. Loraux does not leave room for that kind of critique. "It would be pointless to try to see the Platonic epitaphios as a 'reasonable' funeral oration", she writes, despite the interpretive tradition to the contrary. The existing funeral speeches "must have attracted the irony" of Plato, who enacted his pastiche by overstating the incoherence about democratic ideals that Pericles and others tried to make work.[45]

If the funeral speeches are not obfuscatory aristocratisms to begin with, the Platonic parody of course cannot operate as Loraux says it does, exaggerating distortions of democracy. More generally Loraux needs to recognize, as she seems to have inoculated herself from doing, that Plato can mark his own speech off from the tradition he inserted it into without making it the ludicrous version of that tradition; and absolutely without that tradition's having pro-pagandized for Athenian democracy in the half-powerful and half-clumsy way that she finds it doing.

One of the readings that Loraux cites (with disagreement) is Victor Cousin's, whose preface to an 1827 edition of the *Menexenus* called it a reasonable version of the Athenian funeral oration. "For Cousin, the dialogue is 'both a criticism of the ordinary funeral orations and an attempt at a better manner, the accepted genre'". Loraux does not say enough to rule out this approach to the *Menexenus*, that it stands as a proposal for how funeral speeches ought to look from now on and always should have looked.[46] As such a proposal the *Menexenus* would be a reproach to past members of its genre without mocking them or itself; not in the least satirical, it would correct the genre by offering a better example of a funeral speech, not an example so bad it defames all the others.

But to see just how the *Menexenus* speech might be a serious alternative to Athenian funeral, it will be necessary to learn more about the topics that have done no more than cross the stage so far: education and rhetoric, myth and history. Once the speech in the *Menexenus* can be seen as containing viable proposals on these subjects, it will no longer be a bare logical possibility that this speech is a serious alternative to other funeral speeches, but the most natural description of it.

Notes

1 The main problem with speaking of literature to Plato's Athenians is that the nearest concept they had was *poiêsis* "poetry"; and for them as for most people

today poetry meant verse. It would take Aristotle's *Poetics*, written in Plato's wake, even to begin challenging that association of poetry with verse, and to challenge the association of literature with poetry: 1447a29–b24.

2 English-language references to the famous speech by Pericles call it his "Funeral Oration". There is nothing inaccurate about "oration" but then there is nothing inaccurate about "speech" either. Indeed, just because it is so much broader "speech" translates *logos* better than "oration" does. But mainly for the sake of plain-spokenness this book will tend to say "speech". In Greek a speech like this one, delivered at a funeral, was called an *epitaphios logos*, and some discussions today use the Greek phrase in emphasizing the genre as a whole and an idealized object, in contradistinction to this or that speech that serves as its example. We do not feel the same need to keep genre and examples strictly distinguishable, above all because Plato's speech has much more to do with the single example of *epitaphios logos* that Pericles made famous than with the genre that claimed him as its founder.

3 According to common estimates, classical Athens engaged in battles in two out of every three years. But this figure seems not to include smaller border clashes, raids and ongoing sieges by Athenian garrisons; add those and the average Athenian citizen could be felled in armed conflict in more than two out of every three years.

4 *Suda* "Pericles", Adler pi 1180. The *Suda* is a late Byzantine source, dating to the tenth or possibly the eleventh century CE. For that reason among others it is often unreliable. Yet it does draw on sources that are otherwise lost, and cannot be ignored across the board.

5 Plutarch *Pericles* 8.5.

6 Plato and Thucydides report the embezzlement trial from very different perspectives on Pericles, which confirms that it took place: *Gorgias* 515e–516a; *History* 2.65.2–4.

7 Plutarch *Pericles* 32.3. Some argue that this is not just a garbled recollection of a comic playwright's attack on Aspasia, because impiety was an offence too grave to be thrown around in comedy; thus Bauman (1990: 38).

8 Because this verb for "improvise" *schediazô* appears in the *Menexenus*, and because improvisation is a topic in later chapters of this book, the passage from the *Suda* will come up again later.

9 Lysias 2.1, written about the same time as the *Menexenus*, says that speakers only had a few days to prepare their speeches. It seems the *boulê* chose a speaker only days before the funeral. Menexenus remarks on the short notice (*Menexenus* 235c), and explicitly concludes from this fact that the speaker will have to *auto-schediazein* "improvise". The short notice further supports the belief that speakers before Pericles did not write their speeches down at all.

10 Thucydides *History*: Pericles on his predecessors, 2.35.1; on not reviewing all known history, 2.36.4. Other references to predecessors: Lysias 2.2, Demosthenes 60.1.

11 Thucydides *History*: method, 1.22.1–3; permanent work not contest winner, 1.22.4. This remark may be a dig at Herodotus, who is said to have read sections of his *Histories* aloud at the Olympics (i.e. in a competitive context).

12 Thucydides *History* 1.22.1. These methodological remarks have inspired much debate. How close to historical fact did Thucydides aim when quoting public speeches, and how close did he hit? Here what matters is that Athenians knew the speech that they called "the speech of Pericles" in the form relayed by Thucydides, which may have hewn close to the content of the original speech or wandered quite far away from it, but was never meant to reproduce the rousing effect of the man's public performance.

13 Herrman (2004) gathers together new translations of all the speeches under discussion in this section.

14 "Longinus" *On the Sublime* 3.2. Why is "the Zeus of the Persians" risible? Pseudo-Longinus does not seem to find it blasphemous, except insofar as the comparison comes from a domain too far above the thing compared with it; like calling your wallet pocket "the Fort Knox of my trousers". Note that the inverse figure, in which Fort Knox becomes America's wallet pocket, sounds unobjectionable, as it would have been acceptable in ancient days to call Zeus the Xerxes of heaven.

15 Such models exist online; see Keefer (2011) who calls them "sad libs".

16 On Lysias: offered to write for Socrates, Cicero *De Oratore* 1.231; speech attributed to him, Plato *Phaedrus* 230e–234c. This speech must be Plato's own concoction; but inventing a speech to represent an author takes more intimacy with the author's work, not less, than it takes to quote something the person did write. Plato must have been deeply familiar with the real Lysian rhetoric in order to pass off a fake like this one.

17 Lysias 12 *Against Eratosthenes* gives a synopsis of his arrest and narrow escape. If an Athenian drachma is one day's pay for a labourer, the amount Lysias paid in bribes (12.11), three talents or 18,000 drachmas (besides other properties, and quantities of other cities' currency) comes to what a labourer could expect to earn in fifty years.

18 See, for example, 12.6 on the Tyrants' targeting wealthy metics to seize their money. Lysias survived the Thirty Tyrants and saw the reinstatement of the democracy, though later certain specifics of his history become obscure. He requested Athenian citizenship in return for services to the democracy, but if he was granted full citizenship he may have had that converted to a secondary protected status.

19 Loraux (1986: 134) summarizes the problem of the evidence perfectly: "lacking any epitaphios dating from the Pentecontaetia [the fifty years between the end of the Persian War and beginning of the Peloponnesian War], historians of the oration find themselves … forced to deduce the model from its imitations".

20 For the broad four-part outline given here see most recently Herrman (2004: 6).

21 Thucydides *History* 2.35.1–2; Lysias 2.1; Demosthenes 60.1; Hyperides 6.1–2. The opening of Gorgias' speech might be read as the suggestion of words' inadequacy as such, but that is a stretch; anyway in its fragmentary condition this speech may be missing its introduction.

22 Again, Demosthenes and Hyperides write after Plato, and very plausibly conscious of him. But if they do know the *Menexenus* and they nevertheless revert to an effacement of oratorical language despite the different stance in that dialogue, their doing so speaks to the standing power of the genre in this particular.

23 *Menexenus* 236d–e. Needless to say this is a first look at a cluster of topics to be considered separately and extensively in the later parts of this book.

24 The remarkable exception is Hyperides, who surrenders his entire speech to the Greek general Leosthenes (despite the protestation that in honouring Leosthenes he is honouring all the soldiers, 6.15).

25 Lysias 2.78 makes this point explicitly; also see Thucydides *History* 2.43, Gorgias 6.

26 Eternal memory: Thucydides *History* 2.43.2–3; Gorgias 6; Lysias 2.79–80; Demosthenes 60.32; Hyperides 6.41–42. This sentiment while possibly in tension with the troops' anonymity – how will they be remembered forever if no one says their names? – does square with what is known of Spartan burial customs, according to which graves were unmarked unless they held a man who died in battle or a woman who died giving birth.

27 Demosthenes 60.33–34; Hyperides 6.35–39. This mythic imagining by Hyperides should not be taken too literally, for in a later fragment of the same speech he refrains from asserting the soul's existence after death, contenting himself with an either–or reminiscent of Plato's *Apology*: either death is the end, or it is followed by a further existence in Hades, 6.43.

28 Plato *Menexenus* 249a–c. Pamela Huby (1957: 104–14) reads this section as the historically specific reaction to a proposal that Athens stop caring for the orphans of the war dead. Whether or not Huby is right about this historical point, she has spotted the centrality of education to the *Menexenus*; she should be more widely cited for having made a point of that theme.

29 Plato *Menexenus*: dying bravely as opposed to continuing in a cowardly life, 246d; the parents of these soldiers did not expect immortality for their sons, and by implication did not get it, 247d.

30 *Menexenus* 248b–c.

31 *Ibid.*: 246d–248d.

32 Ziolkowski (1981: 57, 95) begins with the general four-part structure for all these speeches but then examines the *epainos* sections in further detail.

33 *Menexenus* 238d. See Thucydides *History* 2.37.2, 2.39.1; Lysias 2.18; Demosthenes 60.26.

34 Lysias: history, 2.4–70; mythic accomplishments, 2.4–16, Persian War 2.21–47; battles of the Peloponnesian War, 2.58–60. Demosthenes: history, 60.7–11 and 60.27–31; the ten tribes, 60.27–31.

35 Demosthenes blames the Theban commanders who led combined Athenian and Theban troops to defeat against Philip, 60.22. But he does not blame the Theban rank and file for the loss, let alone their ethnic origin.

36 Plato *Menexenus*: education in funeral speech, 236e; as the main undertaking of the state, 237a, 238b, 238c, 241b.

37 Thucydides *History*: school for Greece, 2.41.1; constitution imitated (never imitating in turn), 2.37.1; no need for Spartan training, 2.39.1.

38 Gorgias on training: 6. They exercised both body and mind. Lysis: pedagogical effect of the speech, 2.3; battle-virtue natural, 2.50–51, 2.61. Writers after Plato: Demosthenes 60.16; Hyperides 6.8.

39 Plato *Menexenus* 238b. Loraux (1986: 212–13) also points out the absence of *technai* from the other speeches. But she draws different conclusions about Plato's purpose in introducing *technê* when he does.

40 Loraux (1986).

41 At least one reviewer emphasizes the distance between Loraux's interpretation of the funeral speeches and the available information: Loraux's "specific arguments ... sometime stray from the actual evidence", rendering the result "provocative but not always convincing" (W. C. West 1988: 396).

42 Loraux (1986): "hegemonic speech", 133; "Athens ... in the forefront", 191; Pericles represses mention of empire, 88. On this last claim see Tompkins (1988: 308).

43 Loraux (1986): democracy defended on aristocratic grounds, 219–78 (e.g. 274–75); lots and wages not mentioned, 223; government for the people, 231.

44 *Ibid.*: 347. The reference is to Finley (1973: 64–68).

45 Loraux (1986): "would be pointless", 404; on ancient readers who took the speech as serious, 521n.176; modern readings to the same effect and Loraux's comments on them, 225, 476n.27, 521n.175; "must have attracted the irony", 198–99; Plato overstating words of Pericles to expose "what the epitaphios merely hinted at", 239–40.

46 *Ibid.*: 521n.175. Paula Winsor Sage (1989: 67) is one reviewer who finds unsupported Loraux's claim that Plato writes ironically.

4

THE *MENEXENUS* AS PARODY,
AS IMPROVEMENT

The relationship between the two funeral speeches

Speaking of other Athenian funeral speeches, and especially the one ascribed to Pericles, raises the inevitable first question, or rather a meta-question, about the *Menexenus*. Like other meta-questions this one feels as if it ought to come before anything else, while in another sense it is the kind of issue that can only be settled after working through the entirety of the dialogue: *is this dialogue's funeral speech a parody, a joke, and a condemnation of public rhetoric? Or can Plato really mean this as a worthy funeral address and right political speech?*

Certainly the *Menexenus* is sometimes read as a joke or satire. The funeral speech presents itself so patently as a *version* or a *rewriting* of the speech by Pericles (to choose two deadpan nouns) that one can hardly describe or summarize the *Menexenus* without saying something about the tone of the rewriting. At the broadest level one can classify all readings of this dialogue on the basis of whether or not they take the speech to be a parody.[1]

The question of parody as we are treating it is a question about the *Menexenus* alone. A general discussion of how to read Plato's dialogues would derail this scrutiny of a single work. This is not to disparage the larger debate and the value of recent contributions to it,[2] only to acknowledge the space it would take to respond to the general questions. What follows will neither draw on global claims about Plato as author of dialogues (whether he does or does not endorse the statements made by Socrates, the Eleatic Stranger and so on) nor seek to support one global claim over another. The answer to the question "Is the *Menexenus* a parody?" will be independent of whether or not all Plato's dialogues are parodic; and it will turn on the characteristics of this dialogue, not on characteristics that all the dialogues share.[3]

Regarding the *Menexenus*, the main problem with casting the question in terms of "parody" is specifying the alternative. What else could the funeral speech be, and how else could it relate itself to the speech made by Pericles? The commonest alternatives – that the speech is *serious* or *in earnest*, or *straightforward* – invite objections of false dichotomy. "The speech can be ironic and in earnest at the same time", someone might say, or it can be both playful and serious, and so on. And where every description of the dialogue can merge into its ostensible opposite, this debate seems doomed to have no resolution.

Franco V. Trivigno (2009) directly attacks the dichotomy between seriousness and parody. "Adherents on both sides seem to think that the options [parodic or comical, serious] are mutually exclusive". Reading Aristophanes' *Frogs* as an example of what would have been recognized as parody in classical Athens, Trivigno points to the "serious purpose" that parody can have. He is unsatisfied with would-be compromises that parcel the *Menexenus* up into some funny parts and some that are not. On his view the funeral speech is parodic throughout and serious throughout – serious in that it is seriously engaged in attacking Pericles and Periclean Athens. Martial virtue is inadequate; Athens has not cared for its citizens properly; overpowering praise in public rhetoric is a dangerous thing; Athenian imperialism betrayed the city's principles. These are deadly serious charges and they all come sheathed in the merriment of parody.[4]

Trivigno's discussion attributes a number of specific positions to the *Menexenus*, some of them more plausible than others. But his programmatic account of parody is separate from any specific parodies he identifies and the serious import that might lie behind them. To begin with, transcending the gulf between comical and serious as easily as this should not count as a resolution. If the existence of some serious intention at all suffices to make a parody serious, then even the intention to show how good you are at parodying should satisfy. You find a song insipid so you write a spoof of it. By Trivigno's criterion that assertion you would make in all seriousness "The song is insipid" brings your spoof into a complex middle state, simultaneously comical and serious.

The problem begins in Trivigno's definition of parody as "an imitation that distorts a target text, author, or genre". Trivigno calls this description "intentionally broad" and it is in fact broad enough to illuminate numerous examples.[5] But in one respect it narrows the field, for the word "distorts" must mean that a parody imposes changes on its target *for the worse*. You do not seek out cosmetic surgery that promises to distort your ears or nose. When the writer tells the critic "You distorted what I wrote", that is never a way of saying "Thank you". The other words in Trivigno's definition are neutral, but "distorts" implies that the parody amplifies the target's flaws or absurdities.

But then, when Trivigno focuses on the parodies in *Frogs*, he identifies "two techniques of parodic distortion, *inversion* and *amplification*".[6] These two can be techniques for improving a work as much as for demeaning it. Now parody would seem to be capable of changing its target for the better.

In one of the first examples of parody that Trivigno identifies, Socrates opens his speech with an antithesis between *logos* and *ergon* that recalls the opening of Pericles' speech, but elevates *logos* to parity with *ergon* where Pericles made *ergon* the clearly superior term.[7] The allusion has been noticed and treated as a critique of what Pericles said.[8] But for Trivigno, because the change from Pericles to Socrates inverts the original, it counts as a passage in which "Plato seems clearly to be parodying Pericles".[9] That is an unconventional understanding of parody that runs parody together with homage, devotion and variation on a theme. Parody of this new kind might indeed be serious in many ways, but it does not bring the bite normally associated with parody. The parody that ridicules its target will not go that easily into the same category as "serious" and "earnest".

The distorting effect of parody suggests a different way to put the question that might arrive more successfully at what people are asking about with the word "parody". This is the approach already described in the Introduction. Suppose that instead of wondering how ironical, comical or satirical the funeral speech is (or the opposite: how solemn or serious) the question asks: *is this speech meant to be better than the speech that Pericles gave?* Does Plato intend to improve and correct the speech that his peers regarded as the greatest of all funeral orations? Or has he made a worse speech than Pericles' was, to demonstrate the faults of the original through magnified versions of those same faults?

By and large the readings invested in calling the speech parodic find the speech presented as flawed and failing, neither a better production than Pericles' nor meant to be, though probably resembling his speech enough so that their shared errors can be made visible. And the readings that call the speech serious, as ours does, say that Plato wrote it to be a better funeral speech than the funeral speech of Pericles.

The new cast to the question does not reorient the discussion completely, only provides more manageable terms. For all that it is a better specimen of rhetoric the *Menexenus* speech may have humorous passages in it, just as on the opposed reading one might want to call the speech a serious object, for all that it is not meant to correct and improve upon the speech of Pericles. What makes a speech appear to have been "intended as better" is still not a trivial question, let alone what makes it one that Plato (who is often given to idiosyncratic literary preferences) would consider a better speech.

Interestingly, two recent articles on the *Menexenus* that most successfully avoid unproductive talk of parody and seriousness do so by asking whether and how the dialogue's version of a funeral speech is better than the speech of Pericles.

Stephen Salkever tries to bridge the divide between opposed readings by speaking of the *Menexenus*'s "playfulness". Conceived as a third way between irony and earnestness, this playfulness is unsatisfying. It suggests too much of a light touch for readers who want Plato to be proposing this funeral speech as legitimate rhetoric; it is not committed enough to comedy for those who smell a joke seeping throughout the *Menexenus*. Salkever starts with a strong conception of irony, possibly too strong to satisfy the second group: "Most of those who characterize the *Menexenus* as ironic … characterize that irony either as a rambunctious parody ... or as bitter satire". Meanwhile the "serious" statement has to be very serious. Salkever says "there is no clear political program or set of principles to be found in the dialogue", as if only a political statement so fully elaborated could qualify as a serious statement.[10]

Salkever's reading of the *Menexenus* makes the funeral speech into a wise contribution to political philosophy, a voice against inflated political ambitions and in favour of modest ethical life for individuals. Salkever's "playfulness" means not one more calibration of tone between the poles of dogmatism and sarcasm but rather a resistance to political formulas. It bespeaks a combination of frankness and humility on the part of the statesman. In the end the word "playfulness" is misleading, because the value of Salkever's interpretation does not inhere in its having found the right name for the tone of the *Menexenus*, but in the way he sifts through the speech to find its points of improvement over Periclean rhetoric. Here the merits of his approach reveal themselves. The mythical origin of Athenians out of the Attic ground "makes the greatness of Athens depend on the good fortune of her natural origin and on divine favour, not on the special bravery of Athenian men of war" to which Pericles had given the credit. The myth elevates the character of public rhetoric; and elsewhere Salkever points to examples of "Plato's aspiration to match and exceed the scope of Pericles' oration".[11] What makes Salkever's investigation into the *Menexenus* so valuable to other readers, even when they disagree with specific conclusions that he comes to, is this very focus on the dialogue's attempts to outdo Pericles. References to its ironical or comical features merely lead Salkever's discussion towards that goal.

Christopher Long is the other recent commentator who finds a useful fresh way to cast the problem of parody. Long emphasizes the *Menexenus*'s ambiguities and free play as Salkever did. His reading envisions a dialogue between two speeches. Plato composes the Aspasian oration as a complement to the speech of Pericles, overstating where that speech does, *not* because Plato really wants to assert such extreme claims about democracy, governance and military virtue; instead because these one-sided pronouncements talk back to the one-sided argument in Pericles. The readers who can let both political voices sound in their heads will move towards a fuller understanding of what the city is and should be. "The two voices, when heard together, give rise to a broader, more complete picture of politics than either provides in isolation".[12] Plato supplied the counterpoint to what had been, until his *Menexenus*, a song sung solo that let its hearers believe it was the only music in town.

This Platonic reply to Pericles has a sceptical effect. Hearing both sides, one comes to trust neither side blindly. The Aspasian oration dissolves "the aura of authority on which such political ideologies depend". At this abstract level Long's assessment resembles Loraux's, and he acknowledges the resemblance. Undermining alone can be the effect of irony, mockery and humour, and at times Long accordingly emphasizes the parodic aspects of the *Menexenus*, as when he dwells on an alleged "unwillingness to laugh" in young Menexenus.[13]

But Long has less need to insist on the dialogue's comical or parodic elements than Salkever does. His image of an implicit dialogue between the two speeches does not require the *Menexenus* to be ironical. Long identifies freedom as the governing value of the speech of Pericles, and he sets that freedom against the care and communal justice that inform the speech Socrates attributes to Aspasia. Where Pericles relates the citizens to their city as lovers to a love object, Aspasia connects them with a different species of love, *her* citizens now being children of the motherland; the individualistic ethos of courtship and reciprocity yields to an ethic of care. Or rather, as Long emphasizes, the ethos does *not* yield. The most philosophical reader's task is now neither to stay with the values of Pericles, nor to abandon them in favour of the values of Aspasia, but to recognize that an ongoing exchange between the two sets of values belongs in all serious thinking about politics, thinking that seeks "the self-reflective path between spellbound patriotism and deaf disengagement, between a politics of freedom and one of justice".[14]

Long forces the relevant question to be not how playfully or ironically Socrates speaks in the *Menexenus*, but how good his speech is supposed to sound compared with the speech of Pericles. His reading marks out a midpoint among answers to the question "Is this speech supposed to be better or worse than the speech of Pericles?" inasmuch as Long sets the two up as peers. To a degree Salkever aims at a similar resolution, as his reading pictures the dialogue's readers forced to negotiate between two compelling sets of values in the two speeches. Salkever and Long are both worth looking at in this much detail because neither of them takes barbed or humorous remarks to gainsay philosophical merits in the funeral speech; they both try to hear what positive contribution to political discourse the *Menexenus* is putting forward.

It is striking that neither Salkever nor Long makes much of the theme of pedagogy, despite their both dwelling on care and nurturance as the public values that the *Menexenus* extols. One might expect Plato to make educating people an important part of *any* process of caring for them. Salkever takes the response to Pericles to consist in attention to personal virtue, "living the life we have as well as possible".[15] Long finds an ethic of care and familial cooperation resisting what is otherwise a distorting attention to freedom. Surely it helps both approaches, when setting the two speeches up as one another's peers, that both sides of the dichotomies they examine are valuable. Freedom has its merits as an ethic of care also does, and the best political philosophizing can be said to give voice to both. For Salkever the play engages several oppositions, though the opposition between personal virtue and political greatness dominates; and when these are the terms Salkever's own position does sound like the most sensible one, that true statesmanship has to recognize both sides.[16]

What happens in another type of case, when the difference between the *Menexenus* speech and the one that Pericles delivered consists in attention to education (see Part II of this book), or in the discovery of intelligible forces at work in world history (see Part III)? Then it is harder to see the outcome of the two speeches' dialogue with one another as a playful active tension in which judicious philosophers take heed to find history both coherent *and* meaningless; or in which wise thinking about the *polis* consists in both pursuing and slighting the moral education of its citizens. Readings like Long's and Salkever's lose some of the appeal to a tension between the two peer speeches to the degree that the *Menexenus* can be seen as embodying political positions whose contraries – the neglect of education; history understood as meaningless – have no serious standing in political discourse. The *Menexenus*'s views about education and historiography are two of this book's main subjects, so we will not be able to equate the *Menexenus* with its predecessor.

Positive arguments: the *Menexenus* speech as improvement

Put in general terms, the argument for seeing the *Menexenus* speech as better than Pericles' might sound dogmatic. That argument can only be spelled out over the length of this entire interpretation. But even a rough itemization of the dialogue's parts shows how the argument will go. Consider the *Menexenus* divided into sections as follows:

1   A *dialogue* between Socrates and Menexenus in which Socrates mocks rhetoric but also claims to know a funeral speech superior to the one attributed to Pericles.
2   An *introduction* that juxtaposes *ergon* "work, deed, action" with *logos* "word, speech, argument", opposing those concepts but also seeking a balance between them, where Pericles had opposed them to elevate *ergon* above *logos.*
3   A mythic *prehistory* of Athens in which its first citizens are born out of the earth and educated by gods.
4   A *history* of Athens, covering the preceding hundred years, full of omissions and misrepresentations.
5   A *speech within a speech* that represents the beliefs and wishes of dead Athenian soldiers, now repeated to their survivors as moral exhortation.
6   Menexenus and Socrates again in a *closing dialogue* that jokes about Aspasia's authorship of the speech.

Take it as uncontroversial that (1) and (6) speak in a joking spirit. But put those sections aside and look at (2)–(5), comprising the funeral speech. This book will read those passages not so that parody becomes impossible, but along lines that make coherent sense of all these parts of the funeral speech without the need to appeal to parody as explanation. What follows here is a thumbnail sketch of the interpretations in later chapters.

First, (2) can be shown to be consistently Platonic. Even without reference to other dialogues' uses of *ergon* and *logos*, this harmonizing of the two only needs to be compared with analogous passages in the speech by Pericles, to appear as an intended improvement over the original rather than a parody. A parody would more likely exaggerate and mimic the original's habit of championing *ergon* over *logos*; the speech in the *Menexenus* resists that habit.

Also, (2) addresses the challenge of praising Athens and the Athenians. Again the Socratic speech is more thoughtful than its predecessor. Where Pericles asked rhetorically "How can a speaker praise to the right degree?" to imply that no speaker can, that the funeral speech *nomos* "custom" laid a burden on all would-be orators,[17] Socrates treats the question as one that has an answer. The question about rhetoric is no longer a rhetorical question. What *is* the right degree of praise? A speaker should determine what it is and deliver praise to that degree. Pericles sees praise, being *logos*, as an adornment always prone to going wrong. The answering speech assumes that the *logos*, therefore also the *logos* of praise, can be calibrated to suit its subject.

The prehistory in (3) includes an autochthony myth about the first people which, in one form or another, was a common enough story in classical Athens. Section (3) adds an uncommon epilogue to that myth in which Olympian gods teach survival skills to those ignorant newborns. This section might be the most overtly Platonic. The *Republic*'s noble lie celebrates autochthony, but other dialogues also find Plato endorsing the self-sufficient patriotism that autochthony means to underwrite. Birth from the soil together makes all Athenians siblings, too. No mythic belief could be more salutary in Plato's eyes.

Meanwhile, the addition of gods and lessons to this version of the myth, by inserting education into a time even before organized society, validates an emphasis on training and acculturation that Plato could not imaginably make the object of parody.

The last part of the speech (5) might appear in some critique or parody, but only one in the worst taste, a speech that was willing to mock dead soldiers in the interests of scoring a hit against a political opponent. (The Athenians would really have had grounds for convicting Socrates if he'd voiced such sentiments.) The speech that Socrates reports as coming from the fallen soldiers to their families and children is full of pieties; but those are the pieties about courage and self-sacrifice that Plato's dialogues never criticize and often repeat. As Salkever writes, "the living are urged to do better than the dead and to do so in a truly extraordinary but thoroughly Platonic way".[18]

So far sections (2), (3) and (5) all make more sense as improvements upon Periclean rhetoric than as the funny exaggeration of it that they would have to be to qualify as parody. Pericles says nothing about autochthony despite that concept's pre-eminence in Athenian life; Socrates insists on it. Pericles hardly mentions the death of the soldiers being honoured at the funeral, but Socrates brings them into the public gathering with their own speech to add to the conversation. This is the stuff of reformation not lampoon.

In the case of (4), the *Menexenus*'s dry, long and only occasionally accurate survey of Athenian history, it is again true that Plato answers a silence from Pericles with a superabundance of talk. Pericles declines to review the Athenian history that he says his audience already knows. The speech in the *Menexenus* dwells on the city's history, some of it so recent that Plato's readers would have known all this and much more about the events recounted.

But such a simplified contrast will not settle the question of parody. Section (4) contains too many worrisome details for that. It tells the history of Athens far from comprehensively, omitting events that even modern readers know about, and distorting others. Some events are identified by the names of the battle sites; others appear only in circumlocution. The ironic reading of the speech as a whole fits this section (which is the *Menexenus*'s longest part by far) much more plausibly than it fits any other section.

Any good assessment of such a passage needs to begin with a patient study that attends both *externally* to its departures from known events, and *internally* to the patterns within the narrative, such as its alternation between naval and infantry battles. Existing discussions have accomplished the first of these tasks, contrasting the *Menexenus* chronicle with what happened, how it came out and how Plato's contemporaries must have interpreted those events.[19] But a narrative's departures from historical fact will not always reveal the narrative's own shape or structure. Looking for the omissions can even distract from the narrative's commission, which is to tell a certain intelligible kind of history – to tell a familiar story in a newly intelligible way.

Looking for internal integrity in this history brings to light a desire to find order in a historical sequence that could otherwise resemble a chaos of events. Somewhat as Plato's *Timaeus* seeks to tame the universe into a natural history organized around a few abstract principles, the *Menexenus* sketches out an organized political history. It simplifies and omits not to show that all local histories are propagandas, but because a philosophical history will be one that does not replicate the confusion of actual events.

More specifically, as Part III of this book argues, historiography in the *Menexenus* parallels the psychological and political narratives in *Republic* 8 and 9. This parallel does not make the history true or even more plausible than it had been, but it does make (4) look less like a way of ridiculing the writing of history as such, and more like a first stab at scientific coherence in a practice that had been an unscientific jumble. If an interpretation along these lines is possible, then even (4), *prima facie* the most troubling part of the *Menexenus*, no longer has to demonstrate irony at work in the speech.

Clavaud (1980) makes the astonishing claim, more than once in his study of the *Menexenus*, that only section (5), the moralizing finish of the speech, reads as serious and reflective. For this reason, according to him, adherents to the "serious" reading of the *Menexenus* focus on that passage.[20] A position like Clavaud's would be easy to hold if such a claim were true; we hope that by the end of this book it will become clear how much needs to be overlooked and misread in the *Menexenus* to be able to say such a thing about it.

Positive argument from precedent

This book's introduction cited ancient references to the *Menexenus*: Cicero, Dionysius of Halicarnassus, Hermogenes of Tarsus, Plutarch. The dialogue's name did not appear in other ancient authors anywhere near as often as they referred to the *Timaeus* or *Theaetetus*, but now and then a mention does turn up, and it is notable that in those mentions no commentator takes the speech to have been humorously intended (even if acknowledging humour in the opening conversation).

It is even more worth noting that no ancient author speaks of anyone *else's* belief that the speech is a parody. The best place to find such a mention would have been the *Anonymous Prolegomena to Platonic Philosophy*, dating to the sixth century of our era, because that introductory set of lectures contains the only clear description of how others were reading the *Menexenus*. If the *Prolegomena* comes late, and to that degree is distanced from ancient intellectual trends, it is also well situated by virtue of its lateness to survey many predecessors, over roughly nine centuries of the dialogue's reception. And the author's words for that reception are clear.

> Negative criticism of anyone cannot be the purport of a dialogue either: this would be unworthy of the divine Plato, finding fault for its own sake. Thus we refute those who held that the object of the *Menexenus* is to criticize and rival Thucydides. They say that the funeral oration was written for that reason, in competition with the funeral oration of Thucydides, but this is untrue.[21]

The book mentions no other description of the *Menexenus*. In fact it does not mention the *Menexenus* again. So the one tendency in reading the dialogue that another work sees fit to reply to sounds much like the reading that *our* book is defending. The desire to "rival" Thucydides and the spirit of "competition" would call on Plato to write a funeral speech better than the one Pericles delivered, not a burlesque of that speech.

To be sure, the author would object to the conclusions we are pressing for. But those conclusions correspond to a known ancient reading of the *Menexenus*. The *Prolegomena*'s author does not respond to, and shows no sign of having heard about, the approach that reads the dialogue as mockery.

In the century before the *Prolegomena*, Proclus' commentary on the *Timaeus* includes a reference to the *Menexenus*. Proclus is discussing *Timaeus* 19c–d, at which Socrates says he wishes he could deliver a worthy encomium to the good city described in the *Republic*. Proclus rebukes unnamed earlier readers who said Socrates lacked the skill that such rhetoric called for. The Greek that follows is open to different translations, but on one reading Proclus says that those who say such a thing, denying Socrates' ability to make good speeches, are "questioning the authenticity of the *Menexenus*".[22] He means not that someone other than Plato might have written the dialogue, only that the dialogue might not represent Socrates accurately. And the charge of biographical inaccuracy apparently presupposes that the funeral speech is a good one, as it would take no exaggeration to believe that Socrates the dialectician could produce an unskilled speech.

To the extent that we can piece together ancient responses to the *Menexenus*, they are oblivious to the possibility that one reads the speech as a parody or joke, even when commentators diminish the dialogue in some other way. Only much later, a dozen centuries after the *Anonymous Prolegomena*, did modern ears hear the parody that had eluded Plato's ancient readers.[23]

In fact, although the parodic reading is the received view today, the earliest modern readers treated the *Menexenus* as earnest political rhetoric. And later evidence, down to around 1700, suggests this treatment to have remained a common one.

The obvious place to begin is with Marsilio Ficino, who wrote short summative commentaries to most of the dialogues when he produced the first complete translation of Plato into Latin in the last third of the fifteenth century. Ficino's pages on the *Menexenus* are disproportionately interested in Athenian autochthony. He acknowledges that oratory is not Socrates' *métier*: Aspasia's name is in the dialogue, according to him, to explain why Socrates should be speaking in such uncharacteristic ways. But for Ficino the dialogue reflects Plato's pious love for Athens more than it communicates anything else, and it seeks to arouse the same sentiment in its readers. Parody is not in question.[24]

It is equally hard to see parody as a live possibility one century after Ficino, when Thomas Thomas comes to light as printer for Cambridge University Press, possibly the first university printer at Cambridge who did print books there. Thomas was best known for the *Latin Dictionary* he published, but in 1587 the Press also issued a Greek text of the *Menexenus*. This was the first Greek text put out by Cambridge, apparently only its twenty-seventh volume overall.[25] The website for the Press calls Thomas' *Menexenus* "the first of any work by Plato in the original to emerge from an English press".[26] The scholarly consensus of the day must have been something very different from the interpretation of the dialogue as parody, or it would not have made the dramatically early appearance it did.

When the *Menexenus* first appeared in English translation, the context again makes clear that it was read as earnest oratory. Gilbert West published a collection of Pindar's odes and other Greek texts translated into English, among which the only Platonic work was the *Menexenus*. West's introduction takes Plato to task for asserting the absurd doctrine of Athenian autochthony, and he seems embarrassed by the dialogue's partiality to Athens; nevertheless both criticisms imply that Plato held those positions. And West calls the last part of the speech, which reports the thoughts of the slain soldiers to their families, "as beautifull a Piece of Oratory, as is to be met with in all Antiquity".[27]

Works on other subjects written in the seventeenth and eighteenth centuries sometimes use the *Menexenus* to substantiate claims. Louis Ellies Dupin's mammoth history of Christian thought, *Nouvelle Bibliothèque des auteurs ecclésiastiques*, sprawls over fifty-eight volumes, which appeared between 1686 and 1704; the first volume cites Plato as Mosaic religious thinker, but also once, quoting the *Menexenus*, for information about the Persian Emperor Darius.[28] A long essay by Jean Barbeyrac "An Historical and Critical Account of the Science of Morality" accompanied his translation of Samuel Pufendorf's *Of the Law of Nature and Nations* into French, and then was translated into English, together with that book, in 1729. Barbeyrac condemned Plato, with reference to the *Menexenus*, for speaking of non-Greeks indiscriminately as barbarians.[29] And the immensely popular *Dictionnaire Historique et Critique* of Peter Bayle's, which began appearing in 1696 in French, then in English in the 1730s, includes extensive discussion of Aspasia in its entry on Pericles. It is a sympathetic discussion, unpersuaded by the ancient slanders against Aspasia, that draws on the *Menexenus*.[30]

Bayle and Dupin treat the dialogue as a historical source, where Barbeyrac finds evidence for Plato's political opinions in it. Neither use would make sense if the dialogue's status as parody were considered a possibility.

Two last examples. Theophilus Gale, expounding his religious non-conformism in 1677, spends over fifty pages on Plato's philosophical debts to Hebrew Scripture. In this enterprise Gale uses the *Menexenus* funeral speech in support of his claim that good constitutions made their citizens good and bad ones the reverse. That thought appears within the funeral speech (238c) as a postulate of politics; and Gale lists the *Menexenus* with the *Republic*, *Laws* and other unambiguous examples as a work of Plato's political philosophy.[31]

James Geddes, writing a lifetime after Gale, devotes himself to most un-theological topics, what we call "style", in his *Essay on the Composition and Manner of Writing of the Antients, particularly Plato*. Geddes is almost quoting Ficino, and shares Ficino's appraisal of the *Menexenus*, when he describes the dialogue as an exhortation to patriotism, and for that reason part of the introductory reading before the *Republic* and *Laws*. More relevantly to the question of parody, Geddes compares the funeral speech to both its precedent in Thucydides and its successor in the oratory of Demosthenes. On the one hand he says that Plato imitates the sublime speech associated with Pericles' name; on the other hand, his extended analysis of the *Menexenus* makes it the model that Demosthenes was to imitate, expressing the same thoughts as Plato's.[32] Geddes locates the *Menexenus* so continuously in the history of Athenian rhetoric as to leave parody on either hand unimaginable: Demosthenes could not be mocking Plato any more than Plato mocks Thucydides.

Negative arguments: against the *Menexenus* speech as parody

Along with the positive arguments it may help to reply to some assumptions or arguments that readers sometimes use when they call the *Menexenus* a parody, and a speech that is meant to be worse than the speech of Pericles. *These are a minor part of the approach to this dialogue.* Arguments against other arguments, or against assumptions about what makes a work a parody, will never matter as much as a reading that finds, as this book's reading tries to do, worthy positive claims being made in the work.

First, anyway, there is the business of Aspasia. At one time readers might have assumed that crediting Aspasia with authorship of the speech was itself Plato's act of disavowal. How could a woman have taught Socrates rhetoric, and such a shady woman? Even allowing for the example of Diotima in the *Symposium* who is said to have taught philosophy to Socrates, there is Aspasia's reputation. But the difficulties in knowing anything sure about that reputation have been pointed out. It might be worth repeating that the reasoning about the *Menexenus* and Aspasia's reputation threatens to become circular. It is more likely that the *Menexenus* joins with the comic poets on record in mocking Aspasia if the funeral speech is a joke and she is one of its butts. Her questionable status cannot prove the satirical intent of the dialogue if its satirical intent is first posited in demonstrating Aspasia's questionable status.

Other assumptions enter more obliquely. Modernity's experience with literary works that quote and rewrite other works has encouraged the belief that such appropriation and reproduction is mocking and subversive critique. On this view, a work with multiple references to another work is engaged in deflating it and quite likely deflating itself in the process. That is a reliable expectation for reading *Thus Spoke Zarathustra* with its steady reuse of Luther's biblical German; also when navigating among the mock-heroic allusions that are woven into the texture of *Lolita*. But rivalry among ancient authors could be more direct than its modern varieties. An ancient work often incorporated its predecessor in order to best it. Homeric scenes and themes in Herodotus' *Histories* show how Herodotus is trying to fashion a new and better epic; they are not there to ridicule either Herodotus or Homer. Subversion has not always been the only tactic in literary competition.

A third consideration may be the most straightforward, and has frequently been advanced. The framing dialogue – those sections (1) and (6) of the *Menexenus* taken as a pair, according to our list – has a rib-elbowing tone that seems as unmistakable a signal of a joke as the formulas that introduce literal jokes ("Did you hear the one about … "; "How many cowboys does it take … "). This frame, but especially the dialogue's "prelude", the conversation before the funeral speech, sets the stage for Socrates to present the speech he attributes to Aspasia. It might sound counter-intuitive to downplay the import of this major clue – or it can sound like the wilful dogmatic approach to reading Plato (an approach now widely chided) in which the interpreter looks away from scene and setting, frame and metaphor, in search of thesis and argument.

But consider first the general question of what such a frame may and may not mean. Then we can ask the question specific to the *Menexenus*, what the tone of *this* frame is.

Why does the levity in a frame trump the gravity of the material inside? To give the framing dialogue a preponderating significance is often to do no more than pay disproportionate attention to what comes first. What interpretive theory justifies *that* practice? Some literary readings of stories, plays and poems do function by deciphering those works in accord with rules or examples laid down within those works. Such works are said to possess a particular kind of self-consciousness, to contain the instructions for reading them. Leopold Bloom takes apart Molly's wordplay "bass barreltone" in *Ulysses* as a nod to readers to go after the novel themselves. Within Plato's corpus, the reading of Simonides that Socrates develops in the *Protagoras* functions remarkably well as a demonstration of how philosophers read, and how they may read the *Protagoras*.[33] But such embedded tips to readers do not have to appear at the beginning of the work, as these do not. The frame does not achieve special status as master key to the work simply by virtue of being a frame. Rather, what the frame says has to be a fruitful way of reading the particular piece.

There is even something aprioristic about looking to the frame to learn the secret about what it is framing. How did frames function in ancient poetry? *That* question almost never comes up in readings of Plato. The *Odyssey* starts off with "Muse, tell me [*moi*] about the man", and committed attention to *that* narrative frame ought to turn the subsequent epic into a first-person report. But the "I" fades away as the poem goes on. Maybe it matters throughout that the Muse (knowing, with an excellent memory, perhaps also unreliable) spoke forth the story. To make the *Odyssey* as a whole significantly into a Homeric monologue or memoir calls for readings of specific passages in it. The *moi* "to me" in the opening line will not be enough. Similar remarks apply to Hesiod's *Theogony*, with its own invocation of explicit untrustworthy Muses.[34]

Later analogues from Plato's own time or just before him are less exact. Does a Euripidean prologue behave as a frame? What about the chorus's closing lines in a tragedy by Euripides? The chorus is more likely to be in the position of telling the story of the tragedy than the god who recites the prologue. The nearest analogy to a dialogue like the *Menexenus* might be the poem of Parmenides, who reports his argument about being as something the goddess told him. This goddess in his poetry underwrites what otherwise might sound like human pomposity, given Parmenides' oracular presentation. The frame brings credibility to the poem, somewhat (but not exactly) as Homer's and Hesiod's Muses explain how these two poets could know everything their poems say.

If contemporary framing devices endorsed important discourse more than they undermined that discourse, then Plato would have known the device as an invocation of authority. He may or may not have used any particular frame for that purpose. But the discussion that appeals to frames ought to begin here, with a historical approach to poetic and dramatic frames antedating Plato, rather than with fantasies about what the frame "must" mean.

This much of our point is negative. To criticize the act of privileging the opening dialogue is not to assert any theory of ancient literary frames. We are noting that readers who call the *Menexenus* a parody often base their assessment on the opening conversation. Against this procedure we begin simply by asking whether it has any justification, for instance in literary frames as they existed before Plato. The burden of proof lies on those who would argue, from the putative tone of the opening conversation, that what follows is parody.

But it is possible to say more of a specific nature about Platonic frames, if we again take Proclus for a guide to ancient interpretive practices. Writing close to 800 years after Plato did, and having immersed himself in the Platonist tradition, Proclus knew what methods his predecessors brought to bear on the dialogues. In his commentary on the *Parmenides* he distinguishes specifically among the ways that readers have taken the *prooimia* "preludes". There have been commentators who did not look closely into the openings of the dialogues at all – *oud' … kathientôn* "not stooping" to look, Proclus says – but of those who did trouble themselves to study the *prooimia*, some took the opening scenes morally, deriving instructive lessons from the behaviour of the participants in the first paragraphs of a dialogue. Others, the ones Proclus most agrees with, made that moral reading part of a larger interpretation of the dialogue, working to understand the philosophy of the whole work so that they can then see it pictured or exemplified in the opening words.[35]

Myles Burnyeat (2012) explicates this passage with an added word of warning for those who think they already read Plato this way. What Proclus recommends is not to be confused with the approach (Burnyeat calls it the Straussian approach) that takes the prelude as guide to the whole. "So far from the opening scene telling you how to read the philosophy that follows, it is the philosophy that tells you how to read the opening scene".[36] One who takes the prelude as the instruction may conclude that the *Menexenus* has to be a joke; but it is easier to argue this position if you have not read the funeral speech first. In keeping with Proclus' method, we would be better off studying the speech for its philosophical content, only subsequently asking how the framing conversation anticipates the themes in the speech.

For example, the reader who finds Part II of this book persuasive, on the subject of fresh emphases on education in the funeral speech, and on the specific manner of improvisation at work in the process of composing it, will then profit from returning to the preface in which Socrates speaks of education with Menexenus, and explains the improvisatory composition of funeral speeches.

But suppose you do insist on starting with the framing dialogue. How funny and mocking is it really? Trivigno says in support of his own reading that "Menexenus immediately recognizes Socrates' praise as ironic and accuses him of implicitly mocking and criticizing the orators in general".[37] Menexenus does make that accusation. Only Trivigno's "recognizes" – a success word – raises a red flag. Recognizing something requires that the thing be there. Menexenus does say, "You are ridiculing [*prospaizeis*] the orators"[38] – but why trust his description of what Socrates is doing? The reader has seen Menexenus being glib and ignorant about subjects that call for thoughtful expertise. To his face Socrates calls him incompletely educated. Indeed the only appearance of the word *philosophia* in the dialogue is here, in the conversation between them, and is here only because Socrates denies philosophy to Menexenus. Perhaps his incompletely philosophical nature explains why Menexenus hears Socrates' language of magic and incantation as pure mockery, when in fact it resembles the one concession that Socrates repeatedly makes to poetry.

Long reads more sensitively when he speaks of an "unwillingness to laugh" in Menexenus.[39] Unlike Trivigno, Long casts doubt on how well Menexenus appreciates the funeral speech; the least that Plato's reader ought to do is to learn more from the speech than Menexenus does. Menexenus hears this *tour de force* and still has his mind on who really wrote the thing, Socrates or Aspasia.[40] He bears more than a little resemblance to young Phaedrus in the *Phaedrus*: in that dialogue Socrates delivers a powerful critique of writing, the written word imperiled by its separation from its author, and Phaedrus congratulates Socrates on the stories he can make up, as if he hadn't heard the news of the disappearing author.[41] Menexenus too looks in the wrong place for what he will be enlightened about.

Contra Long, however, what makes Menexenus unreliable is not his unwillingness to laugh, but that he is the only one laughing. Socrates delivers sublime praise to Athens and Menexenus is pleased with himself for getting the joke, as if what mattered were not the worth of a city but who wrote the compliment. Socrates attributes magical power to Athenian funeral speeches, a power that overcomes the barrier between the living and the dead. His speech when winding down will do the same, returning the dead soldiers' voices to address their own relatives. All Menexenus hears is mockery.

If Menexenus is the only one laughing, the funeral speech becomes the opposite of a joke that falls flat. It is a serious speech presented in a light-toned conversation, and consequently mistaken for a joke. That light conversation might lead clumsy readers to conclude that the whole speech is a joke. More delicate sensibilities recognize Plato's reasons to be ambivalent, and want to look deeper into the speech to see what Platonic wishes it is releasing.

Notes

1 Clavaud (1980: 45–74) classifies modern readings of the *Menexenus* into three groups: those who take the speech as serious, those who find it comical (*"comique"*), and a third group that tries to find a compromise between the other two (*"les conciliateurs"*). This classification is of course limited by the book's publication date of 1980.

2 See, for example, Klagge and Smith (1992); Press (2000).

3 Characteristics shared by all or most dialogues include their author's absence from them; the interlocutors' actual political histories; framing dialogues, etc.

4 Trivigno (2009): "Adherents on both sides", 29; "serious purpose", 31; on would-be compromise readings, 48, 49n.3; on martial virtue, 44; on care for citizens, 45; on overpowering praise, 46; on imperialism, 47.

5 *Ibid.*: "working definition", 30; "intentionally broad", 50n.8.

6 *Ibid.*: 30; emphases in original.

7 Thucydides *History* 2.35.1; Plato *Menexenus* 236d–e.

8 For example by Kahn (1963: 222).

9 Trivigno (2009): "inversion", 36; "parodying Pericles", 34.

10 Salkever (1993): "the *Menexenus* as ironic", 134; "no clear political program", 134.

11 *Ibid.*: modest ethical life for individuals, 139–40; resistance to totalizing political formulas, 135; "the greatness of Athens", 137; "Plato's aspiration", 140.

12 Long (2003): 50–51.

13 *Ibid.*: "aura of authority", 51, cf. 66; resemblance to Loraux, 53n.10; "unwillingness to laugh", 53.

14 *Ibid.*: freedom against care and communal justice, 51, 64; Periclean citizens as lovers, 54–58; Aspasian citizens as children, 59–63; "the self-reflective path", 68.

15 Salkever (1993): 140.

16 There is some ambiguity in Salkever's conclusion that "Plato sets in motion a way of talking about political life that both recalls and challenges Thucydidean political discourse" (*ibid.*: 140) – ambiguity in that the *recalling* implies something other than utter rejection of Thucydides, as if he had set the right terms for a political conversation but did not examine them adequately.

17 Notably, all the other extant funeral speeches follow Pericles in calling their task difficult. See Ziolkowski (1981: 65); Salkever (1993: 137). That Socrates makes no such opening gesture to the challenge he faces may reflect, as Salkever says (*ibid.*: 142n.31), his earlier comment about the ease of praising Athens to the Athenians (*Menexenus* 236a), but it also implies that intelligent and pedagogically sound public speaking does not have to be unnatural and forced.

18 Salkever (1993: 140). Long (2003) works hard, with some success, to deny the Platonic sound in this passage.

19 See, for example, Henderson (1975); Morgan (1998).

20 Clavaud (1980: 15, 126).

21 Westerink (1962: 49).

22 Proclus *Commentary on the Timaeus* 62.13; in Tarrant (2007: 156); also *ibid.*: 156n.159 on the meaning of this "authenticity".

23 For a summary of modern views on *Menexenus* as parody, see Clavaud (1980: 45–74). In order not to let this section overgrow its proper bounds we have focused on early modern receptions in English.

24 Ficino (2006: 140–42).

25 S. C. Roberts (1921): Thomas Thomas printer, 22; *Menexenus* in the list of early titles, 154.

26 See "Ten Great Cambridge Authors" at www.cambridge.org/home/page/item 5695869/?site_locale=es_AR.

27 G. West (1753): absurd doctrine of autochthony, II.282; dialogue's partiality to Athens, II.283; "as beautifull a Piece of Oratory", II.283. For a similar sentiment from the same time see Antoine Léonard Thomas, *Oeuvres Diverses*, volume III, published in French in 1773. Regarding the speech's closing report from the war dead to their survivors, Thomas writes: "*je doute que l'on trouve rien chez les Grecs d'une éloquence plus noble*" (Thomas 1773: III.59). He considers the thought to come, without irony, from Plato, whom one glimpses hidden behind Aspasia (*ibid.*: III.58).

28 Dupin (1690): Plato as thinker in agreement with Moses, I.6, I.406; *Menexenus* containing evidence about the history of Persia, I.41.

29 Barbeyrac (1729: 56, with footnote labeled "jjj").

30 Bayle (1739): sympathetic discussion, VIII.295; draws on *Menexenus*, VIII.305.

31 Gale (1677: IV.158).

32 J. Geddes (1748): *Menexenus* an introductory work, 134–35; funeral speech imitates Pericles, 67; is imitated by Demosthenes, 325–29.

33 On this example see Pappas (1989).

34 See Ledbetter (2002: 40–61) for helpful discussion of Hesiod's Muses.

35 Proclus *Commentary on Plato's Parmenides* 658.34–659.23; quoted and discussed by Burnyeat (2012).

36 Burnyeat (2012: 308).

37 Trivigno (2009: 33).

38 *Menexenus* 235c.

39 Long (2003: 53).

40 *Menexenus* 249d–e.

41 Plato *Phaedrus* 275b–c.

Part II

EDUCATION AND RHETORIC

5

SCENES OF INSTRUCTION;
PERICLES' MISSED
OPPORTUNITIES

Education and rhetoric

Even a glance at the *Republic* suffices to show how broadly Plato understands education and how entirely education pervades the new city. Rhetoric on the other hand barely appears, except maybe in the form of the noble lie: Socrates proposes that the city's leaders repeatedly tell all citizens of their birth out of the ground, with metals in their souls that justify sorting them into different social classes.[1] Maybe the rulers would tell this story at public meetings, maybe in schools. Anyway, and this must be no coincidence, the noble lie shares more than one defining detail with the myth of autochthony that Socrates tells in the funeral speech.

It does not follow from resemblances between the noble lie and the autochthony story that the speech in the *Menexenus* is a speech told within the *Republic*'s beautiful city. Some passages in the funeral speech tempt its reader to see the Athens being described as an Athens already transformed by philosophy, but this interpretation will not hold for the speech as a whole. But even without claiming the *Republic* to be the theory whose practice is told of in the *Menexenus*, a reading of the funeral speech would profit from seeing it as compatible with the *Republic*'s pedagogical politics. Both the ends and the means of education in the *Menexenus* overlap with the ends and means of education as the *Republic* conceives that process.

The *Republic* obviously politicizes education. But it matters more (and requires something beyond simplistic talk about propaganda and the total state) to understand how far the *Republic* also seeks to educate politics. This aspect of Plato's reforms goes to the heart of his political enterprise. What human society has henceforth left to occur according to the promptings of instinct, an instinct that the same human society has corrupted, can be done much better with instruction and regular practice.

Sometimes the instruction that the *Republic* recommends is closer to habituation, meant to instil tendencies to good behaviour in the city's guardians, than to formal tutoring in bodies of knowledge. As children the guardians ride out to watch battles so as to inure themselves to war's sights and sounds. They fight bravely, ignore money, mourn only moderately and in private. The education becomes intellectualized after Socrates identifies the city's rulers with philosophers, and recommends courses of study in arithmetic, geometry and astronomy. And often enough the least theoretical virtuous behaviour – care for parents, reverence towards the gods' temples – is said to follow from the good ordering of the soul, which would make training in the soul's highest cognitive functions the real education from which all others follow.[2]

In the *Republic*'s city, institutions and methods combine to produce both ordinary and extraordinary types of excellence: gymnastics and mathematics, music and dialectic. Exposure to beauty leads the young warriors to prefer beautiful things to ugly ones, and a honed taste in beauty is supposed to foster a preference for fine actions and the avoidance of sordid ones.[3]

Modern audiences appreciate such "progressive" proposals in the *Republic*. These show Plato's imaginative powers at work, and they are indirect, shaping what the twenty-first century would call "the whole person". For Plato mathematics produces good commanders both because it lets them calculate battleground logistics and by bringing them to abstract thought as such, so that they will command virtuously.[4]

Nevertheless, inasmuch as the familiar virtues of social behaviour appear together with these more elusive phenomena that Plato calls harmony in the soul, the pedestrian means that bring those traits into existence deserve to be included together with the new and intellectualist techniques.

The fact is that the *Republic* does not give up on traditional moral education. Plato is as much a reformer about commonsense moral training as he is when introducing new ideas of training. From his point of view Athenian culture failed even at the unphilosophical task of making its children abstemious and loyal. So the new education extends to traditional storytelling, retaining the form of children's earliest learning about gods and heroes but reversing the values they had learned. In place of the self-aggrandizing behaviour associated with Achilles and other impetuous heroes, and instead of reports about soldiers' craving life and avoiding death, children in the new city will hear about Odysseus restraining himself. Out with the tales of gods who lie and change shape, commit adultery with their brothers' wives and castrate their fathers; in with statements of the gods' goodness, truthfulness and aid to pious humans.[5]

The outcome of these changes will be catechism in a religion that the ancient Greeks could scarcely recognize, and a legendary history cut off at the root from nearly all the history they had known. With all due respect to Plato's innovations in logical training and music appreciation, the old-fashioned teaching he imagines is more than revolutionary enough. He shows what even traditional acculturation could accomplish in a new state.

Education becomes a more complex business when Socrates abandons good and bad stories to speak of good and bad storytelling methods. The target of his argument *mimêsis* "imitation, emulation, enactment, representation" is a name for a process in which one enacts a character, either speaking as that person does or writing the words such a person would most likely say. And although Socrates speaks mostly negatively about *mimêsis*, his dominating argument finds a double edge in enactment. Acting the part of an inferior or vicious person makes the actor inferior and vicious; but there would be no harm (and by the logic of the argument there ought to be some good) in taking on the part of a virtuous man, especially when that man is shown to be acting virtuously, exhibiting his intelligence and good sense.[6]

Literature contains almost no such characters today. Nor did the poetry of Plato's time. In practice this loophole for the enactment of "positive role models" may be small. Still, even such acting might find its way into what the *Republic* recognizes as education and acculturation.

This description of education in the *Republic* already touches on the types of education that the *Menexenus* will talk about. In the *Menexenus* as in the *Republic*, education includes tutelage in political leadership; training in military practice; lessons from beneficent divinities; the *mimêsis* of good models. The speech does not politicize education, but it does try hard to educate politics – you could say that it dreams of educated politicians – as if to imply that when philosophers take over the writing of funeral speeches, their versions will confront the task of educating the public as non-philosophers' speeches had not.

In this sense funeral rhetoric becomes a microcosm. The Athens of the *Menexenus* is not the *Republic*'s city, but it does show philosophy bringing a pedagogical impulse to funeral rhetoric that the *Republic* says philosophical rulers would bring to all aspects of governing a city.

Pericles and moral education

Even if the kinds of education that appear in the *Menexenus* are recognizable to the *Republic*'s readers, they take the special form they do because of the reply the funeral speech is making to Pericles. Whether or not the speech attributed to Pericles faces the need to educate its audience – this has been a disputed point – Plato certainly *perceives* Pericles as having ducked pedagogical and acculturative responsibilities. In a critique that extends across several dialogues, Pericles is consistently one who had the opportunity to educate (his sons, his foster sons, the people of Athens) as well as the responsibility to do so, but who left all his charges worse than he found them.

When Thucydides speaks in his own voice to assess the political leadership of Pericles, he praises Pericles for controlling the moods of the Athenian public. Pericles possessed both the rhetorical skill to inspire courage – and, when necessary, prudence in the face of a rash populace – and the judgement to know which effect a situation called for.[7] Controlling fear and rashness in accord with knowledge of what should be felt would seem to be as good a job of educating the public as a political leader could accomplish. It is the task of directing the public's emotions in accord with a reliable standard. And, armed with Thucydides' verdict on Pericles, readers have argued that the funeral speech contains a philosophical conception of courage, nearly a Platonic conception, and one that enables Pericles to improve the Athenians' courage as he does.[8] But looking at the words that Thucydides gives Pericles to say produces a different impression from Thucydides' words about Pericles. The speaker he quotes does not speak like the leader he describes. The funeral speech sounds if anything like an abdication of the need to improve its listeners, and an expression of doubt that moral education is possible.

The first paragraph already announces a reason to despair at improving the public. High praise for the dead will make the hearers who did not know those dead envious. More generally "people respond envying [*phthonountes*]" to whatever exceeds an accomplishment they would be capable of.[9] Where envy is the most natural response, emulation is not likely to occur. So much for the good role models as means of moral education.

As he nears the end of his speech and its consolatory section Pericles does speak of the courage the soldiers exhibited, and uses their example to inspire his auditors. "Fall in love with Athens", he urges the Athenians who are listening to him. "Emulate [*zêlôsantes*] the fallen soldiers ... do not dwell on the dangers of war".[10] But before those words he has spoken of the Athenian *meletais* "training" for warfare as it were from a distance, describing the practice rather than engaging in it. The result is a speech that voices no faith in training. Athens is an open society with no secrets their enemies would profit from learning; by implication Athenian military practice contains nothing to be learned. "We trust in ... the courage that comes from our own selves [*tôi aph'hêmôn autôn ... eupsuchôi*]". The Athenians do not "exercise in pain" as the Spartans do. Their courage derives "not from laws [*nomôn*] but from ways of life [*tropôn*]".[11] The effect of this tribute to Athenian preparation for battle is to leave the preparation looking mysterious, unarticulated by Pericles and probably inarticulable in his opinion.

One famous sentence calls Athens *tês Hellados paideusin* "the school of Greece" (as this is most often translated). More broadly than the concrete word "school", *paideusis* implies a process of education, even a curriculum. Pericles has already said that the Athenian constitution does not *zêlousêi* "envy, emulate" the constitutions of other cities. "We are a model [*paradeigma*] for some rather than imitating [*mimoumenoi*] others". Such remarks make imitation and learning seem to be happening everywhere in the world[12] – *except in Athens*. To learn and to need to learn bespeaks inferiority. Pericles can hardly picture the Athenians' learning martial virtue if their having to do any such thing as learn implies a natural or default state of cowardice.

Perhaps the democratic spirit as such inhibits talk of learning and teaching. When teachers stand above their students, education in virtue implies that one citizen surpasses others in virtue. But Pericles does not set himself above his fellow Athenians, even if Thucydides will elevate him in the narration of the

History. The funeral speech is no place for setting one citizen apart from the rest. The funeral honours all the dead soldiers together, and the speaker although selected to address the crowd must not let himself stand out either.

Modern democracies voice suspicions about education often enough to make the attitude familiar. "I never had a lesson" is a musician's boast, not a lament.[13] For more than a generation, college admissions in the USA have relied on students' scores on tests for which one "does not have to study" and on which in theory one will not perform better after tutoring. Such tests reflect the hope of offsetting all the advantages some students gain from twelve years' worth of superior schooling, as it were espying the true aptitude behind artificial differences in education.

Other interpretations of the speech by Pericles see a positive attitude in it towards education in virtue; but such interpretations have some hard passages to explain away. The contrast between Sparta and Athens, for example, appears to associate training in courage quite consistently with the enemy not the people of Athens. And so Ryan Balot, who wants to find a motive to education in Pericles, has to concede that "Pericles does not offer much explanation of how the Athenians' national character has been produced". This "not much explanation" is what we have been calling Pericles' silence about the educational process, evidence that his speech does *not* articulate a positive view of education. Instead of an account of where the fine national character comes from, Balot goes on to say, "Pericles' emphasis is on the Athenians' relaxed lifestyle … in spite of which they are still naturally courageous". But courage *in spite of* culture must be courage with a natural source. It will be courage perhaps vulnerable to being corrupted by bad customs, but not produced by good ones.[14] It is courage without an origin in public education.[15]

The attitude in the speech of Pericles is of secondary interest here. Understanding the *Menexenus* requires not knowing how to read Pericles but knowing how Plato would have read him. The speech by Pericles, as transcribed, contains passages that shy away from moral education even if other passages lend themselves to a contrary reading. And Plato would have recognized the anti-educational passages as the ones that are characteristic of Pericles, given the tenor of his criticisms of Pericles in other dialogues.

Thus a passage in the *Meno* makes Pericles an anti-Socrates, the one who should have faced charges of corrupting the youth. Anytus is defending democracy, claiming that the private citizen passes virtue along to other citizens, while political leaders pass virtue along more and better than anyone else, such leaders being in Athens the best of a fine lot. Athenian political democracy is an ongoing process of reciprocal education. In response Socrates wonders why political leaders cannot instil virtue in their own charges. He names Pericles, whose sons Paralus and Xanthippus learned how to ride a horse but evidently not how to distinguish themselves ethically.[16] The example offends Anytus; Anytus will later join Meletus in prosecuting Socrates, and his offence now conjoins the charge of corrupting the youth with the prominent bad example of Pericles himself complicit in the degeneration of Athenian youth.

Other dialogues contain what feel like replies to Anytus. The *Symposium* makes Alcibiades a witness for the Socratic defence. As foster son to Pericles he ought to know what the great statesman had accomplished; and Plato makes Alcibiades say that Pericles never had the effect on him that Socrates did, of making him ashamed of himself.[17] Imagine how Alcibiades might have turned out if more Athenians resembled Socrates, especially if Pericles had.

The *Gorgias* takes the offensive, pressing graver charges. Pericles fails as a father, as the example of his sons shows. And in a grand version of the same thing, he failed to improve the Athenian people. The people wanted the treats of empire and Pericles fed them docks, city walls and shipyards until they were glutted and so depraved they convicted him of embezzlement.[18]

The *Protagoras* brings Plato's criticisms of Pericles closest to the *Menexenus*. Pericles' boys Paralus and Xanthippus are both present for this conversation, Alcibiades too. The household evidently chases Sophists around; which might explain why Socrates poses the central question of the dialogue, whether virtue can be taught, with special reference to Pericles. For all his wisdom Pericles neither educated his boys himself nor entrusted them to a capable tutor, but let them wander everywhere picking virtue up at random, *automatoi* "automatically, spontaneously". Socrates tells the story of Clinias, brother of Alcibiades and a known ne'er-do-well whom Pericles lacked either the skill or the will to reform.[19]

What gives the *Protagoras* its relevance to the *Menexenus* is the combination of criticisms it asserts, concerning both the kind of *educator* Pericles is and the *speaker* he is. About ten pages (in a standard modern edition of Plato) after the anecdote about Clinias, Socrates says that Pericles, that unimpressive father (and despite his reputation as the city's master orator), is not even much of an orator either. He talks like a book! After finishing a speech Pericles is incapable of responding to a question about what he just said, but goes on at length like a brass gong that sounds on after being struck.[20]

The dialogues are usually more generous about Pericles' oratorical skill.[21] The *Protagoras* finds explicit fault with him even as a speaker. The *Menexenus* presumably does the same, for it has to be an insult to Pericles the rhetorical expert to have Socrates claim that Aspasia wrote the most famous product of his expertise. Suddenly the man who moved the assembly and shaped public opinion resembles a stereotype out of modern politics, the candidate pretending to address the public while reading someone else's words as they scroll up an electronic screen.

If what Socrates says in the *Menexenus* is true, it would account for what he says in the *Protagoras*. If other people write the speeches of Pericles, it is no wonder he has no good answers to new questions. All he prepared to say was this speech; ask him about any point in it and he will have to recite the same speech again.

The *Suda*'s entry on Pericles is provocative on this point, for associating him with the general practice of speaking from a prepared text. It would be invaluable evidence if not for the *Suda*'s overall unreliability; and contrary testimony from (older, more trustworthy) antiquity does attribute skill at quick retorts to Pericles, skill that ought to have made him a good improviser.[22] Most peculiarly the *Suda* says nothing about Pericles' speeches at funerals or in the assembly, which were the most famous scenes of his oratory. Still the report that he recited previously written speeches while others were still extemporizing reinforces the Platonic criticism. Were Plato's and the *Suda*'s descriptions responses to artifice in the speeches of Pericles, and formality in his bearing; or did Pericles in fact stumble in unprepared settings and so rule himself out of the dialectical exchanges that Socrates considers essential to philosophy?

The specific pairing of accusations in the *Protagoras* raises a further question, not necessarily to be answered in the *Menexenus* but worth bearing in mind when reading it. The *Gorgias* combines Pericles the father who cannot make his sons virtuous with Pericles the political leader who presides over Athenian citizens declining into spoiled children; and those charges belong together plainly enough. But what does failure at improving one's children have to do with the inability to answer philosophical questions? Do both shortcomings show what an inattentive man Pericles is, oblivious at home to the influence Alcibiades had on Clinias and oblivious in conversation to a questioner's need to understand? That would be damning enough, and it could be Plato's purpose in the *Protagoras*.

But accusing Pericles of inattentiveness would not explain his failure to improvise. Not caring enough could be why someone does not improvise. Picture a jazz musician who plays the same instrumental parts every night. "Why did you get in that rut?" An answer could be: "I don't care about this band" or "about the music, the audience, the job". Socrates speaks as if Pericles would gladly improvise an answer but lacks the ability. Try as he might he can only bring those same sentences to mind that he had memorized, and he might as well run through all of them again. His failure is better understood as lack of expertise. Pericles does not know how to handle surprising questions any more than he knew how to handle his surprising children.

Getting clear on how Pericles falls short as educator will illuminate the contrary standard that the *Menexenus* is setting for itself. And – to repeat our guiding point – if the Socratic speech lives up to that standard, its success will contribute to a general assessment of the new speech as improvement over the old.

Scenes of instruction in the *Menexenus*

At first sight the occurrences of education in the *Menexenus* make up a list too varied to summarize. It is hard to see what single phenomenon these examples could all be instances *of*. Still one generalization emerges, even if it is a negative one: the end product of education is rarely confined to knowledge as knowledge is usually understood. Nor does the *Menexenus* describe a process of education like what is usually thought of as the transmission of knowledge. Instead this dialogue looks for *paideusis* where it might not have been spotted, where its difference from education in the literal sense made it hard to see.

Framing dialogue

The opening of the *Menexenus* casts everyone in the role of either teacher or student, starting with Menexenus himself and what Socrates considers his crazy proposal to speak at the next funeral. Has Menexenus completed the course of education in philosophy that it would take to qualify him to speak?[23]

"I will study more if you think I should", Menexenus says. He had not imagined that making a speech might require learning something. But Socrates insists on philosophy as equally the origin of good funeral rhetoric and the first step in enlightened rule. And even if the joking tone about rhetoric in these pages supports a reading of the speech as parody, Socrates' call for philosophical training should show that the speech to come was born of knowledge.

Not surprisingly for a Platonic dialogue, this first reference to education presents an education that has failed. Menexenus did not study philosophy to prepare for public speaking, and does not appear to have studied anything else. Indeed Socrates' opening talk of education has nowhere to begin; it is mostly empty talk. The educator who can take Menexenus through the course of study he needs is no one specific and nowhere in sight. Nor has Socrates explained what philosophical study he means.

Socrates shows what an education could be when he brings Aspasia's name up. He completed a course in rhetoric. Education now means formalized teaching, with a tutor and a series of lessons, and threats of beatings to punish the student's lapses. And whereas the anti-Sophistic scenes in Plato contrast the Athenian fad for lessons with Socratic conversation, direct and gentlemanly, here Socrates sounds like an informed consumer comparing his top-notch tutors to the inferior variety.

One of the tutors in question gave Socrates lessons in rhetoric. Plato's Socrates is normally the opposite of an expert in rhetoric. He prefaces his defence speech announcing that he will speak off the cuff, and delivers such an uningratiating speech that the jury convicts him. Book 1 of the *Republic* turns into a showdown between Socrates and the rhetorical master Thrasymachus cast as his antipode; and in the *Gorgias*, Socrates represents philosophy and metaphorical doctoring of the soul against Gorgias' rhetoric, the equivalent of pastry-cooking and pander to the public.[24] As far as the trial of Socrates goes, it is easy to imagine his friends' consternation when this man who had bent interlocutors to his will suddenly could not work his miracles with the jury. His way of speaking must be something other than rhetoric, even the opposite of rhetoric, for he dominates private conversations in which orators find themselves helpless, and then fails on those occasions of public speaking at which orators shine.

Now however this claim that Socrates studied rhetoric with Aspasia means both that Socrates knows what there is to know about rhetoric, *and* that there is something to be known. This is one respect in which the *Menexenus* lies closer to the *Phaedrus* than to the *Gorgias*, for in the *Phaedrus* philosophy's superiority over rhetoric does not turn rhetoric into some empty non-subject but leaves it a practice that philosophers can do better than non-philosophers.

Pericles studied rhetoric under Aspasia, too. This mention goes by quickly but invites a question. Where does Pericles stand on the subject of instruction and being instructed? If Menexenus failed to study what a putative city leader needs to know in order to speak well, while Socrates undertook the study and mastered the subject, then Pericles represents the remaining third possibility. He undertook the instruction but failed to learn.[25]

First of all, Socrates' claim about Pericles taking lessons from Aspasia transforms Pericles from master of rhetoric into mouthpiece. At best he learned the words that Aspasia wrote and delivered them aloud. The encapsulation of Athenian values that made the speech famous as his greatest oratorical achievement was someone else's work. This portrayal of Pericles fits with what the other dialogues say. Studying rhetoric with Aspasia cannot have sufficed to make Pericles a leader if he was the corrupt influence on the body politic that the *Gorgias* says he was, or even if (as the *Meno* and the *Protagoras* say) he possessed virtues himself but could not pass them along. His education must have failed.

But it is crude and inaccurate to declare Pericles a failure, considering the (occasional) compliments that Socrates pays him. Pericles learned philosophy through his friendship with Anaxagoras, in a way that improved his rhetorical skills (given that, as that dialogue says, rhetorical skills generally require philosophical knowledge).[26] It is still conceivable, or it is *just* conceivable, that both Pericles and Socrates are to be marked as educational successes for Aspasia.

So whether or not Pericles counts as educated will hinge on Socrates' explanation of where he heard the funeral speech he is about to recite:

> Even yesterday I was listening to Aspasia going through a funeral
> speech for these very ones. For she heard what you say, that the
> Athenians are going to choose the speaker; then she recounted for
> me what sorts of things one ought to say, some on the spot [*ek tou
> parachrêma*] and the others she had earlier prepared [*proteron*

eskemmenê], from when I think she composed the funeral speech that Pericles spoke, sticking together some leftover parts from that.[27]

That some of the speech was the work of a moment goes to the matter of improvisation; the ready-and-waiting parts of the speech may tell where Socrates stands relative to Pericles in Aspasia's estimation. The thought of her gluing together (*sugkollôsa*) pieces of a speech, maybe literally sticking one papyrus scrap to another, might sound casual enough to impugn this new speech.[28] But that those pieces are *perileimmata*, leftover fragments, could make things worse. Did Aspasia lavish her best rhetorical inventions on Pericles and then dig through the wastepaper basket for a speech to give Socrates? Or does the clause mean that she held something back from the first speech she wrote, saving those prize bits for the later ones? A third possibility is more likely than either of those: Pericles either intentionally or heedlessly left out parts of the speech that Aspasia had written for him. Maybe he forgot those parts and maybe they struck him as inappropriate. Whatever the explanation is for his omissions, the speech to come will include passages that shore up the crumbling parts of the speech that Pericles delivered. It will glue back in the crucial parts of the argument that he had not thought to include.

Mimêsis *of virtue in the funeral speech*

Pericles treated the funeral speech genre as an occasion for nothing but praise. His opening remarks about the difficulty of such speeches have to do with proper and improper praise and one's ability to deliver it. The speech in the *Menexenus* begins with the fine deeds of the dead, but it expands the task of the speech with respect to those deeds: to praise those who have died and "kindly exhort the living", where that exhortation combines consoling the grieving elders and "ordering their children and brothers to imitate [*mimeisthai*] their virtue". Not surprisingly, the speech approaches its conclusion with similar words, that the parents of dead soldiers *tharrein* "take courage" and the soldiers' children *mimeisthai* their parents.[29]

Consoling the survivors does not educate them. Moreover this part of the exhortation is present in Pericles, who does console the parents of dead soldiers. What Pericles glosses over in the process, what does not belong in his view of politics, is the praise that helps to make the surviving young citizens as brave as the citizens who have died. If anything, Pericles doubts that the fallen soldiers will earn such praise, thanks to the work of envy. He encourages the living in admiring the brave dead, but without any advice about how *they* should become brave.[30]

The occurrences of *mimeisthai* as the *Menexenus*'s speech begins and ends therefore signal another intrusion of pedagogy where Pericles left it out. In Plato's hands the verb *mimeisthai* "imitate, represent, etc.", together with its cognate noun *mimêsis*, usually collect pejorative implications. Most famously *mimêsis* lies at the heart of Plato's attacks on poets and poetry in Books 3 and 10 of the *Republic*, as well as helping to define the Sophist, in the dialogue *Sophist*, as someone distinct from the philosopher. In those works the verb *mimeisthai* describes what duplicitous poets and ignorant painters do, actors when they are taking on bad habits, and charlatans, posing as philosophers, who spin subtle webs of words that simulate truth and wisdom without imparting any such things. In the *Menexenus* the same verb names what young people *should do* to become braver, not quite contradicting what Plato's arguments against poetry had said but rather seizing on the exception he allows for in *Republic* 3 – that one may mimic the good man when he is exhibiting virtue – perhaps also showing in the process that the loophole is larger than its passing treatment in the *Republic* would suggest.

As the *Menexenus* conceives it, education in virtue has teachers, in the persons of the dead soldiers, and their sons as students; its subject matter is identified as "virtue", with battlefield courage thought of as the central example. Such education differs in another respect from the opening dialogue's examples of education, for the success or failure of the process remains indeterminate. Socrates calls for the young to imitate their parents, even as he represents the parents' speaking from beyond the grave to urge their sons to surpass them in virtue. Whether or not the boys will become brave in the end is not for Socrates or anyone else to know. And yet the essential character of this education in virtue is definite. For what Socrates calls on the people of Athens to do, when given the model that brave dead soldiers provide, is what he claims the other Greek cities have already done thanks to the model that Athens set for them. (See "Other cities follow Athens", below.)

The origin of Athens

Socrates begins his speech by praising Athens and Athenians. For both the land and its people, praise begins with this people's birth out of their native earth. The Athenians called themselves "autochthonous", usually meaning that their first ancestors had been born from the Attic ground, although perhaps in de-mythologized form this boiled down to the belief that they had always lived in the same place. (Chapter 7 says more about this myth.)

Pericles begins with the boiled-down version. A more extravagant national myth might have embarrassed his chronicler. Socrates calls the Athenians "autochthonous" and makes clear that he means this word in the fullest mythical sense. The earth of Attica was the Athenians' mother. As the best mothers do, the earth not only produced those first Athenians but also had food waiting for them, in the form of already-domesticated wheat and barley. Then, evidently when their infancy was over, she brought gods to teach them. These unnamed gods educated Athenians in the *technai* "skills, crafts, professions" and also provided their first military training in the making and use of weapons.[31]

107

The nearest story to this in Plato is the *Republic*'s noble lie, a story for the new city's people that mythically accounts for both their social status and their education. The noble lie accounts for education by turning education mythically into an act of creation. After their actual training has ended, the young citizens learn that their lives to that point – birth, death and schooling – had been a dream. In fact they sprang from the ground fully grown, with metals in their souls corresponding to the social classes they now find themselves in. The earth receives all credit for their education as well as for the city's political divisions.

In effect the noble lie denies the existence of the very educational process on which the city's continued existence depends. What the guardians took for schooling while it was happening turns out to have been a dream. In this sense the noble lie creates a kind of recollection for all people, for mythically speaking they took in everything they learned before they were born.

On the other hand human society calls for education. Other dialogues offer up myths of original acculturation to account for the possibility of human social existence. Plato puts some of these explanations in other characters' mouths. In the dialogue named after him Protagoras tells a creation myth in which gods fly down to earth to imbue human souls with shame and justice. Aristophanes, with his own origin story in the *Symposium*, pictures Zeus and other gods cutting the first humans in half in a way that makes possible both the interpersonal bond of love (among all people) and the city-wide bonds of political engagement (for homosexual men).[32] The acculturated condition of existing human beings is now their natural condition. Education is not artificial, certainly not in the sense of having been begun by humans.

The result of such stories is to render human *physis* "nature" indistinguishable from *nomos* "law, custom". Education does modify the original condition of the human, as Pericles saw that it imposed upon and modified the Spartans' natures. But as he did not see, education is natural to the condition of humans as known, not merely normal for Spartans; and thinking as he did that Athens might escape the need to undergo training is fantasy.

Another reason for Plato's creation stories to include scenes of instruction does not involve Pericles but harks back to Anaximander, who is sometimes credited with having invented the theory of evolution. According to the few reports of his views, human beings originated in the sea or moisture. Perhaps he says that the first humans were fish who came ashore to dry land and walked.[33] And there is one report of his evolutionary theory that adds an argument why humans must have come from other animals rather than generating spontaneously as those other animals do. Those other animals get food for themselves as soon as they are born; so there is no trouble in imagining them first wriggling out of the mud and going forth to survive. Human beings are born helpless. Sprung straight from earth or sea or any other element they would have died at once. Hence they must have descended from other species.[34]

Anaximander's theory is no proto-Darwinian hypothesis of the sort that Empedocles will propose in the century after him. Even so it contains an implied argument against autochthony. Infants scattered over the ground is an image of mass death, not of the first life; between only these two alternatives, autochthonous birth and evolution from fish, evolution has the advantage.

Plato's antipathy towards evolutionary theories is hinted at several times in his dialogues, explicit in the *Sophist*.[35] An unworkable hypothesis about earth-born humans would fall before Anaximander's objection, so Plato posits a mythic reply. In response to the specific claim about the newly sprung humans' needing food, he makes the land around Athens domesticate wheat and barley (and plant olive trees) before giving birth. Against the general claim of aboriginal human helplessness, he sends gods to train those first humans and show them how to defend themselves. "Thus I have no need of the evolutionary hypothesis", he may as well be saying. Athenians could have sprung from the earth, assuming they had access to an education that precedes all education.

The theory of recollection makes for an apt comparison, despite the obvious differences – above all that Plato's dialogues present recollection as a non-mythical claim for which one can offer arguments. But both recollection and these myths that incorporate education into creation try to show a way out of predicaments about knowledge. In each case a highly prized form of education presupposes some knowledge that could not have been acquired through ordinary education. Ordinary education presupposes an extraordinary pre-education.

One last remark about this first tutoring. The acquisition and use of weapons must include military training, down to organization in a phalanx and practice at charging without breaking ranks. The gods' tutorials must also make the first humans brave; otherwise the weaponry would be useless. Thus the myth begins to explain how human beings learn courage – male human beings, on any natural reading of this passage. The *Menexenus*'s version of autochthony is going out of its way to cover how both sexes learn; for apparently before any mention of education, the speech has justified its own act of calling Attica "mother". "The earth has not mimicked [*memimêtai*] woman in pregnancy and birth, but rather woman the earth".[36] Part of the remarkable enterprise in the speech's first page, of heaping praise on top of praise (on which see more below), this remark about *mimêsis* turns the female act most identified with a woman's nature[37] into learned behaviour. *Mimêsis* is now so powerful that it turns mere women into mothers; or, to put it less fancifully, *mimêsis* no longer restricts itself to conscious human behaviour, still less to the perverted behaviour that one finds in the theatre. It is a natural force.

The thought occurs elsewhere in Plato. The Eleatic Stranger in Plato's *Sophist* speaks of *mimêsis* as though it could go beyond intentional copying carried out by conscious beings. In that dialogue the word *mimêma* "copy"

109

applies to such naturally occurring images as shadows and reflections. The Stranger speaks of gods mimicking;[38] but what counts in this image-making is not that divine action is at work, rather that the process of *mimêsis* has a natural function apart from its manifestation in human arts. Shadows and reflections result from regular natural processes. The tree's reflection in the pond resembles the tree that it reflects for the reason that light from the tree bounces back from the pond's surface. The resemblance in cases of natural *mimêsis* is the sign of a causal relation. So too, as the *Menexenus* says, women are not merely like the earth when they reproduce, they are like the earth because earth led the way.

Jean-Pierre Vernant famously said regarding Greek myth and morals that marriage is for the girl what war is for the boy: her great civic task and the object in mind as she passes the initiation into adulthood.[39] In the mythic part of the speech accordingly male Athenians learn to make and wield weapons while female Athenians learn to be wives for the city's sake. Stretching beyond the myth to the first and last parts of the speech, this mimetic act by women (both in the past and in present-day Athens) parallels the mimetic act that young men are being called upon to practise. They mimic their brave fathers where woman mimics her fertile mother.

Other cities follow Athens

Pericles had both accused other cities' constitutions of copying the Athenian constitution and called Athens the educator of Greece. Socrates enlarges that image of Athens the teacher in the historical narrative that makes up most of his funeral speech.

The history is mostly a depressing tale, but early on it is hopeful. Athens leads the fight against Persia and then makes other cities its partners in the fight. Socrates reads this brightest moment in the history as a scene of education. The Athenian victories at Marathon and Salamis taught courage to Sparta and other cities. Socrates says the non-Athenian Greeks *paideuthênai* "were educated, acculturated" by those who "battled at Marathon and ship-battled at Salamis", those non-Athenian others *mathontas kai ethisthentas* "learning and accustoming themselves" not to fear the barbarians. The non-Athenians "dared to endanger themselves on behalf of salvation, having become students [*mathêtaí*] of those at Marathon".[40]

It sounds incredible to call Athens the source of the Spartans' courage, not to mention negligent of the story of Thermopylae, where without the benefit of any training from Athens the Spartans showed what they were capable of. Nevertheless these claims point to a contradiction in Pericles. He too made Athens the teacher of all Greece, but then he turned around and explained the Spartans' courage in terms of the military discipline they imposed on themselves. Did Athens as the school of Greece teach Sparta, or did Sparta thanks to its unending discipline teach itself? Pericles wants both, crediting

Athens with Greek leadership while freeing its citizens from having to undertake training and discipline themselves. The *Menexenus* at least attributes virtue to training in virtue, showing by contrast what is incredible about the portrayal of courage in Pericles.

Instruction as intrusion

Each of these references to education and training in the *Menexenus* appears within a passage that has its original in the speech of Pericles. But the passages in Pericles omit calls to education, or undermine the education they do speak of. The answering passages can be read as inserting talk of training and acculturation where it should have been all along, answering questions that no one had asked – in other words, improving on the original. It is because talk of education *intrudes* into the original, surprising the flow of thought as it had come from Pericles, but also crucially because it *corrects* that earlier thought, that we believe Plato must see these changes as improvements.

In Pericles, Athens is the school for all Greece, yet Spartans learn courage at home; Socrates corrects that error by making Sparta the student of Athenian courage. Pericles wants to call Athenian soldiers courageous, but he shrinks from holding up those who died as models for the survivors to emulate. Holding them up would invite *phthonos* "envy",[41] so Pericles foregoes the mention of training in virtue; Socrates makes the change in the speech as striking as he can, calling for *mimêsis* with the same confidence that other dialogues condemn that process.

As for the gods' training the first Athenians, that is intrusion within intrusion. Pericles contented himself with mentioning the Athenians' long history in their home, a nod at the legend of autochthony that his fellow citizens knew about, before going on to describe the city's military and cultural achievements. In the version that Socrates replaces that speech with, the long time of Athenians' lives in Attica becomes their aboriginal presence in the land. Evidently one of the *perileimmata* that Pericles dropped from his speech explained how the Athenians first appeared in their city. And then even that story calls for another bit to glue into the text, what is unmistakable as addition to it, namely the story of those first people's education. They learned how to practise both war and peace; so that now those exploits and achievements that Pericles detailed can find an explanation he had not given. What he left out of Aspasia's original composition, the parts that he cut off and threw aside and she had to glue back on, now re-enters to explain the brilliance of Athens as Pericles presented it, unaccounted for.

The forced appearances of education in the *Menexenus*, what Socrates is pleased to call their *re*-appearance from Aspasia's unseen first speech, connect education as it is spoken of within the funeral speech to the education ever-present in the opening dialogue. At first glance the two seem to be divergent phenomena. Conversing with Menexenus, Socrates speaks of the need for *paideusis* "education" that will prepare the young man for the role of funeral orator; he recalls the tutoring that had made (or could have made) him and Pericles into public speakers. This is directed individual instruction for making political leaders. But for all the variety among the forms of education mentioned *within* the funeral speech, those tend to be non-academic mass instruction – mass acculturation, really – that aims at producing rank-and-file citizens.

Even the claim that Athens taught courage to Sparta and other cities conceives that teaching as it improved "the Greeks", "those other Greeks", not the cities as some abstract individual entities but the collections of people who live in them. What can these two pedagogical processes have to do with one another? In the phalanx, courage consisted in remaining in place, literally in rank and file, rather than spectacular one-man heroics. What does collective preparation for cooperative behaviour have to do with a few men's solo preparations for elevation to the first rank?

Suppose that the leftovers from the speech of Pericles that Aspasia stuck together with other passages to make this speech had been left over because Pericles left them out. Maybe he forgot to include those bits when he spoke: Socrates tells how alert Aspasia was to his own lapses of memory, possibly because Pericles had disappointed her in that respect. Otherwise Pericles left these things out on purpose. Which parts would those deleted or forgotten parts have been? Just the parts that press in to *this* speech unexpected; all the references to education, to begin with.

Socrates minded his beatings and did not forget a word Aspasia told him, so this speech will be a complete one. Having been educated properly in rhetoric, Socrates will deliver rhetoric that attends properly to education. When the educated speak, their speeches educate.

The link between training for the speaker and training in the speech appears in Socrates' challenge to Menexenus. *You* in the council chambers? Have you completed your *paideuseôs kai philosophias* "education and philosophy"? And will you follow the older members of your family in providing the citizens of Athens with an *epimelêtên* "caretaker, nurturer"?[42] To care for citizens, as by leading them to moral improvement, one must have first completed one's own education, even if one's own is formalized preparation in rhetoric and the education one imparts or inspires is something different.

Similarly, one finds primary and secondary school teachers today qualifying themselves to teach history or mathematics not mainly by learning those subjects but through courses at schools of education, studying in the broadest and finest sense the rhetoric of the classroom. What they learn in order to be able to teach is not the same material they teach.

Lest the two kinds of training still seem too far apart, there is that insistent *mimêsis* bringing them together. In addition to the explicit references to mimicry within the funeral speech there is its most unprecedented element, the peroration in which the speech turns to "what your fathers said" and

112

"what they would tell you now if they could". "You should believe you are hearing those very men [the dead soldiers] in what I report".[43] This report of the soldiers' words should seem to give the audience the very same soldiers speaking. It can replace the soldiers. But that is to say that it functions as an imitation or a surrogate does.

The *Menexenus* depicts three kinds of *mimêsis*. Socrates performs one, though he does not call it by that name, in re-presenting the speech that Aspasia had taught him. The citizens of Athens learn by *mimêsis*, its men when they imitate their fathers' acts of courage and its women when giving birth. And it turns out that Aspasia had her own learning to do, composing a last inspirational message out of what the Athenian soldiers had said while still alive and writing it – to use the language of *Republic* 3 – making herself like the soldiers.

In short, Aspasia imitates the dead in writing that part of the speech; Socrates imitates her in repeating the speech; the men of Athens will imitate their fathers and take on their courage. As unexpected as this is bound to appear to readers familiar with Plato's other works, *mimêsis* runs through the otherwise disparate educations that make some people democratic leaders and the others into their loyal followers.

Notes

1 Plato *Republic* 3.414b–415d.
2 Plato *Republic*: guardian children watching battles, 5.467c–e; guardians ignoring money, 3.416e–417a; private and restrained mourning, 10.605d; mathematics and astronomy, 7.525a–530c; the highest soul-education, 442e–443b.
3 *Ibid.*: 3.402a.
4 *Ibid.*: 7.525b.
5 *Ibid.*: stories about gods, 2.377b–383c; about heroes, 3.386a–392c.
6 *Ibid.*: *mimêsis* defined, 3.392c–393c; corrupting effect of acting bad parts, 3.395c–396b; salutary effect of acting the part of a good man, 3.396c–e.
7 Thucydides *History* 2.65.9.
8 See most recently Balot (2001). Balot does not equate the Periclean conception of courage with the Platonic conception found in the *Laches* – for interpreters who do, see *ibid.*: 506nn.2–4 – but he does ascribe an educational effect to Pericles, a teaching through appeals to shame (*ibid.*: 513–15).
9 Thucydides *History* 2.35.2.
10 The relationship between this *zêlos*, the envy that inspires emulation, and *phthonos*, a malevolent envy, is left unexplored in Pericles. Chapter 8 will touch on the contrast the *Menexenus* draws between them.
11 Thucydides *History*: dead soldiers' courage, 2.42; "fall in love", 2.43.1; "emulate", 2.43.4; training for warfare, 2.39.1; "courage from our own selves", 2.39.1; no painful exercise, 2.39.1; way of life rather than law, 2.39.4.
12 *Ibid.*: "school of Greece", 2.41.1; "model for some", 2.37.1. Livy *History of the Roman Republic* 3.31 claims that in the mid-fifth century, a few decades before this speech was given, Rome sent envoys to Athens to study the legal reforms attributed to Solon.
13 In *Duck Soup* (dir. Leo McCarey, 1933), Chicolini (Chico Marx) kicks a lemonade vendor (Edgar Kennedy), who says in fury "I'll teach you to kick me".

Chicolini's reply: "You don't have to teach me, I know how", and kicks the man again. The vendor's "I'll teach you" is elliptical for "I'll teach you what happens when … " and is, significantly, meant as a threat. (One threatens to teach.) Chico's status as comic hero depends on his not having had to study.

14 Balot (2001): "not much explanation", 512; "relaxed lifestyle", 513.
15 For a less partisan look at moral education in the Periclean speech, as well as at the critique in the *Menexenus*, see J. T. Roberts (2012: 141–44).
16 Plato *Meno*: Anytus on teaching virtue, 92e; Socrates on Pericles and his sons, 94a–b.
17 Plato *Symposium* 215e.
18 Plato *Gorgias*: Pericles as father, 472b; corrupting the populace, 517.
19 Plato *Protagoras*: Paralus, Xanthippus present, 314e–315a; Alcibiades, 316a; Pericles a moral educator, 319e–320a.
20 Plato *Protagoras* 329a.
21 See especially *Phaedrus* 269e–70a.
22 Pericles and Alcibiades were both known for their quick wits: Thucydides *History* 6.16.6; Plutarch *Alcibiades* 2.2, *Pericles* 8.4.
23 *Menexenus* 234a–b.
24 Plato: Socrates speaking in court, *Apology* 17b–c; against Thrasymachus, *Republic* 1.336b–1.354a; about rhetoric, *Gorgias* 485c. McCoy (2008) is an excellent study of distinctions that Plato tries to draw between philosopher and sophist as two kinds of speakers. That book also informs much in the discussion of rhetoric later in this part.
25 Logically speaking there is also a fourth possibility that you learn without studying. Fertile as that possibility proves to be in other Platonic works, it is not explored here.
26 Plato *Phaedrus*: Pericles good at rhetoric, 269e; his friendship with Anaxagoras, 270a.
27 *Menexenus* 236b.
28 Clavaud (1980: 97–98) makes a great deal of this manual-labour image and the ignobility it implies.
29 Thucydides *History*: praise and how to deliver it, 2.35.2; compare 2.36.1–2. Plato *Menexenus*: praise and exhortation, 236e; advice to parents and children, 248c.
30 *Ibid.*: Pericles consoling parents, 2.44; considering envy, 2.45.1; encouraging the living, 2.43.4.
31 *Ibid.*: Pericles begins, 2.36.1. Plato *Menexenus*: Athens autochthonous, 237b; earth had food ready, 238a; gods to teach Athenians, 238b.
32 Plato: Protagoras' creation story, *Protagoras* 320c–322d; Aristophanes and first humans, *Symposium* 189c–193d.
33 Plutarch *Symposium* 8.730e.
34 "Plutarch" *Strom.* 2 = DK 12 A 10.
35 Plato *Sophist* 265c–d. Note that his resistance does not extend to theories in which animals slip into increasingly *worse* forms (e.g. *Timaeus* 91d–92b). As it will for Darwin's critics, the trouble lies with explanations for human origins. Fish may as well have developed from other organisms, even from humans. That is no insult to humans, nor to fish (as far as humans are concerned).
36 *Menexenus* 238a.
37 See *Republic* 5.453b–c, where the great objection Socrates entertains to making women full guardians is their childbearing, and specifically the claim that childbearing constitutes their nature.
38 *Sophist* 266b–c.

39 Vernant (1974: 38).
40 *Menexenus*: non-Athenians "were educated", 241a; "dared to endanger", 240e.
41 In her invaluable comments on a presentation of part of this material before the Ancient Philosophy Society (23 April 2009), Professor Heidi Northwood observed that "envy" remains too narrow as a translation of *phthonos*. Rather this emotion should be seen as the unhappy contemplation of another's good fortune and the delight at the other's misfortune. Chapter 8 will return to *phthonos*.
42 *Menexenus* 234a–b. On the place of caretaking in the dialogue see especially Salkever (1993: 136).
43 *Menexenus* 246c.

6

PHILOSOPHICAL RHETORIC

The *Menexenus* finds fault with Pericles as orator not merely as educator. Read this dialogue as a joke and it must be showing, by resembling the speech of Pericles, how absurd that statement of Athenian principles really sounds. Take the speech as earnest and intended for public performance, and its departures from its Periclean model just as clearly demonstrate the inferiority of the earlier speech.

The present chapter, more than any other part of this book, will read the *Menexenus* with reference to Pericles. The speech that Socrates delivers resists the tendency that Pericles' speech has to elevate *ergon* "deed, work, action" above *logos* "word, speech, reason". Then the speech by Socrates advocates praise of a sort that Pericles had shied away from – advocates such praise, and also delivers it. This is praise taken to a hyperbolic degree. The hyperbole of Socratic praise raises a question about improvisation, a topic that Socrates touches on in his opening conversation with Menexenus. If the suggestions about Pericles' inability to improvise reflect a failure in his rhetorical skills, improvisation works as a fitting last shot against him in Plato's enterprise to show how much better rhetoric can be when philosophers produce it.

Logos and *ergon*

Historians of rhetoric associate Gorgias with the oppositional construction that became a hallmark of Attic prose. Without deciding how much in the speech of Pericles reflects Gorgias' influence, or speculating how far Thucydides tried to represent the way Pericles spoke, the reader who wants to understand the thought of the speech and the manner of its thinking should approach it through the conceptual oppositions that shape it. Balanced sentences and balanced clauses within them, and balances between sections of the speech, point towards the speech's logic and help to clarify its intent; and the most visible opposition is the one between *logos* and *ergon*. To some degree this opposition organizes all six surviving funeral speeches. In the genre as a whole, and especially in Pericles, *logos* and *ergon* play too large a role in the

116

argument not to be talked about, even if the play of those terms in Pericles has long been a commonplace.

The commonplace observation holds that Pericles opposes *logos* to *ergon* throughout his speech, not so that the two are complements but with *ergon* in the superior position. Indeed, because *ergon* can mean both "deed", hence the brave deeds of the soldiers being buried, and "action" or "act", as in the sacred act of the funeral ritual that honours those soldiers,[1] Pericles is able to open his speech with an argument against all such speeches. These men distinguished themselves with their *erga*, he says, so only *erga* can honour them.[2] Ritual for battlefield behaviour becomes tautologically the right exchange, while *logos*, a funeral speech, is a gesture as empty and therefore as insulting as trying to settle a local debt with foreign money.

In that introductory argument the *logos* at stake is the speech Pericles has been asked to give. As his funeral oration proceeds, the word *logos* will take on more meanings and pick up travelling companions. For now Pericles tells how hard it will be to calibrate the *logos* just right, by which he means the praise that funeral speeches are known for. Not enough praise and the dead man's relatives grumble resentment; too much and the rest of the crowd is sore with envy.[3]

One eloquent passage does appear to set *logos* on a par with *ergon*. The passage formulates a Greek ideal, or a modern idealization of classical ideals, and as a slogan for Greek antiquity it has taken on disproportionate weight in the speech. *Philosophoumen aneu malakias* "we philosophize without softness". The well-known Athenian exercise of deliberating over every course of action does not stop the city from taking action. "We judge issues for ourselves ... believing that actions [*ergois*] are not harmed by words [*logous*], but by our not being taught in words [*logôi*] before coming to the time of action [*ergôi*]". The Athenian people go to the assembly and talk all day, but when the talking ends they vote on a bill, run their city and march into battle. The Athenians accomplish more and better deeds when they have first talked out their options. In these sentences talk and action seem to belong together. Athenian *logos* exchanges for Athenian *ergon* with no incommensurability of currency.[4]

But to read the passage as a variation on *mens sana in corpore sano* is to miss its patriotic and racialist force. Pericles is saying that talk as such does *not* go over into action as such; the fact that it does translate into action *in the Athenian assembly* only shows how differently both talk and action work when they have been minted in Athens. It is a tribute to the Athenians' natures that they are able to deliberate and then go ahead and fight a war or put up public buildings. The compliment and the Athenian exceptionalism would be lost if discussions did not typically weaken human action. "We differ [*diapherountes*] in this respect ... in others ignorance is boldness and deliberation [*logismos*] leads to hesitancy".[5] As a rule, and away from Athens, *logos* leaches the strength from *ergon*. In Athens *logos* and *ergon* succeed at co-existing because Athenians possess such great reserves of untutored natural strength, the same reserves that let Pericles look down on Spartan discipline and every other kind of education. Athenians act boldly despite their culture of debate, not because of it. Deliberation as such imperils action.[6]

Every foreign trait comes to be opposed to the spontaneous Athenian *ergon* even if Pericles has to contradict his own stereotyping of the enemy in the process. When introducing his contrast between Athenian life and Spartan life, Pericles opposes courage "in our actions" to any *mathêma* "learning, information" that might help win a war.[7] Learning is for non-Athenians to use in military preparations. And as the speech progresses it collects training, learning and acculturation together with *logos* – which is to say: all of them as examples of *logos* – on the side that is not the *ergon*. In one respect what is not action is speech and reasoning, while in another respect the not-*ergon* is training and habituation.

As a result, the alternative to *ergon* that is learning becomes a necessary supplement for action in the case of non-Athenians. They have to learn and practice in order to achieve what Athenians are able to achieve in their native condition. And yet the passage about deliberation and action, just noted, will make *logismos* – that other alternative to *ergon* – the thing that saps native energy. If you are a foreigner, only *logos* permits you to act; your action must begin with the necessary infusion of *logos* in the form of learning; and yet foreigners with a *logos* lose the power to act. A little *logos* undoes them. The contradiction, for there is no other word for it, bespeaks the drive in Pericles' speech to collect all Spartan traits into one contrary to *ergon*, even when those traits are incompatible with one another. Athens is so much the place of action that Sparta must be the anti-*ergon* even though anti-*ergon* is not a single thing. Let Sparta be both enhanced and enervated by *logos*, but make Athens the *ergon*.

Other parts of the speech elevate *ergon* above *logos* in more routine fashion. In those passages *logos* literally means "speech". Talk is for the enemies of Athens, who boast about a small win against the city and lie about their losses. Talk is empty talk. When it comes to wealth and poverty, again, actions matter more than talk does, whether this talk be a boasting *logos* about having money or the unimportant business of *homologein* "admitting" to being poor.[8] Even shame attaches more to acts than to speeches.

Most surprising, and a bad fit with the ostensible harmony of *ergon* and *logos*, is the grand boast with which Pericles concludes his praise of Athens, only one paragraph after celebrating the Athenian love of deliberation:

> We shall be marveled at by both people of the present and those who come later, having no need of Homer to praise us, nor any other poet, who will momentarily delight with verses [*epesi*]: The truth about our actions [*ergôn*] will outdo their own poetic meanings

[*hyponoia*] ... We have established eternal memorials of our own good and evil everywhere.[9]

Homer and other poets, a combined symbol of *speech* (because poetry is after all a species of words), *education* (because Homer and Hesiod taught the Greeks)[10] and *custom*, represent anything that is not Athenian action. The acts of the Athenians are causes of both good and evil but supremely effective in either case.

Pericles associates *logos* explicitly with *nomos* "law, custom, convention". He begins with a reference to the unknown person who "established this speech [*ton logon tonde*] in law [*tôi nomôi*]"; *nomos* is that which provides for *logos*. The grounding for the *logos* is the *nomos*. Spartan courage, a product of education and hence associated with *logos*, is also called the product of Spartan laws. This celebration of *ergon* connects obviously with Pericles' reticence about education. To the degree that Athenian action springs up spontaneously out of the people's natures, Athenians will have no need of education in virtue. Or to put it the other way, perhaps a cynical way (and quite possibly how Plato would put it), to the degree that Pericles wants to avoid talk of improving his democratic supporters, he has to portray Athenians as already fully prepared to act. Their activity is now independent of law and culture and even independent of stirring rhetoric.[11]

To identify these dismissals of *logos* in the speech is not to accuse Pericles or Athenian democracy of anti-intellectualism. Modern "anti-intellectualism" sometimes blurs the difference between native intelligence and education, and it looks suspiciously at both. But on our reading Pericles moves along several paths to equate *logos* with *nomos*, that is with the social, the legal and the unnatural. And the education at stake is closer to enculturation or moral habituation, not the lofty kind of schooling that famous friends of Pericles like Anaxagoras and Protagoras brought to Athens.

The funeral speech in the *Menexenus* is not structured around *logos* and *ergon* to the same degree that the speech by Pericles is. Specific allusions to Pericles in the *Menexenus*'s speech are plentiful in the opening sentences and then fade, as if to fix the speech's relationship to its precursor in mind before going on in ways that Pericles could not have imagined. But in a sense the answer to Pericles begins before Socrates embarks on the speech or mentions Aspasia as its alleged author. In the framing conversation, Menexenus has no sooner told Socrates about his desire to be the speaker at this year's funeral, than Socrates launches into a tribute to funeral speeches. Death on the battlefield assures every man a splendid funeral. The speakers praise the dead and the living alike. "When I hear them and I'm charmed [*kêloumenos*]", Socrates says:

> I believe that I've become greater and nobler and better looking on
> the spot ... And this majesty [*semnotês*] stays with me for three days.

> Both the speech [*logos*] and the speaker's voice remain in my ears
> with such resonance that only on the fourth or fifth day do I recollect
> myself and feel where on earth I am. Until then I think I'm living
> on the Isles of the Blessed.[12]

As Bronwen Wickkiser points out, this opening salute to funeral rhetoric
establishes the theme that Socrates will take up again in his speech's first
sentence, the power of *logos*.[13] A speech at the funeral does more than the
funeral rite can by itself to bridge the gulf between living and dead. The
worship leaves Socrates where he is; the speech sends him to the heroes'
heaven.

Wickkiser argues valuably that it would be a mistake to shrug Socrates'
words away as no better than a joke. Consider how closely this paean to
rhetoric anticipates the reorganization of *logos* and *ergon* within the
Menexenus's funeral speech. Socrates follows Pericles in casting the funeral
rite itself as *ergon*. He says the soldiers received the right tribute in deeds and
now the *nomos* calls for a speech. "For when actions have been well done
[*ergôn ... eu prachthentôn*] it is in a speech finely spoken [*logôi kalôs rhêthenti*]
that remembrance and tribute come to be among the hearers towards those
who have acted [*tois praxasi*]".[14] Socrates sets up the same vocabulary Pericles
used – the soldiers' deeds, the funeral to honour them, the law requiring a
speech – but welcomes the *logos* that Pericles viewed with suspicion.[15] The
Greek of Socrates' speech makes word accompany deed in a grammatical
parallel, noun-adverb-participle: actions well done, then speech finely
spoken.[16] Where Pericles alienated *logos* from the cycle of Athenian death
and tribute, the *Menexenus* envisions *ergon* and *logos* working in tandem to
bring the dead the honours they deserve.

Wickkiser concludes from these opening sentences of the speech that one
hierarchy inverts the other. "Socrates has established the primacy and potency
of words (*logoi*) over deeds and actions (*erga*)".[17] But while it is essential to
recognize, as she does, the power that words have for Socrates as a rejection
of what amounts to their exile from the Periclean city, that word "primacy"
burdens the Socratic speech with impossible expectations. The primacy of
words *over* deeds promises that soldiers' actions will no longer matter to the
city, even possibly that the coming history will downplay Athenian actions
on the international stage. The *Menexenus* speech does not make either of
those claims. It is both truer to the speech and more reasonable for Socrates
to be returning fine *logos* to Athenian politics without expelling or demoting
action. As far as funeral speeches themselves go, he does not need to claim
that the right kind of rhetoric counts for more than anything else; only that
now, with a philosopher writing it, an *epitaphios logos* can find its proper
place in the city.

The correction is gentler than if the speech in Plato had reversed the
priorities of the speech in Thucydides. The more moderate correction also

fits better with Plato's conceit that both speeches came from Aspasia, one of them in her youth and the other the work of maturity (or even the enhanced maturity of afterlife); the first speech jagged with excisions, whether because Pericles forgot certain passages or wilfully omitted them, the second speech delivered whole by a faithful student with a good memory. If Aspasia speaks through these two very different spokesmen at different times of her life, you might expect one speech to turn a balanced pair of concepts into a stark opposition and ranking while the next speech realigns them.

Even without the fiction of Aspasia's authorship to justify the realignment, it illustrates what becomes of rhetoric when philosophers practice it instead of politicians. A democratically selected leader or public representative speaks modestly about his own act of speaking in order not to elevate himself either above the deeds of the dead or the capacity for deeds in the living. The dead do not really need his praise; the living really do not need his counsel. The philosopher is free from having to pretend that *logos* is empty and education is otiose.

And finally this change from the politician's weighting of *logos* and *ergon*, to the weighting a philosopher gives, works better as amelioration of the original speech than as a mocking exaggeration of its faults. There is nothing parodic about turning an opposition that privileges action into a pairing of the same words that refuses to. It makes no sense as a joke, not even as an intended joke that fell flat. But as an improvement, it does very well.

Praise

There are three explicit allusions to the speech of Pericles in the opening paragraph from the speech of Socrates.[18] Besides the play of *ergon* against *logos* there is Socrates' first mention of education, as noted in Chapter 5. Pericles had spoken as if the function of a funeral speech were solely to praise the dead, but Socrates also identifies the speech's effects on the living (to console the dead soldiers' parents and inspire their sons and brothers).[19] Third is the matter of praise, this time not as an obvious feature of the funeral speech but as a problem needing to be resolved.

Pericles finds the praising function of funeral speeches discouraging. "It is hard to speak measuredly [*metriôs*]" on such an occasion. Praise resists measure. It will sound like too much or too little, and very often both. Those who know the people being spoken of will wish more had been said, but the same amount will seem excessive to others, whose envy makes them resent and disbelieve any claims about accomplishments that they couldn't match. "But I will have to try as well as I can to chance upon [*tuchein*] the will and opinion of each of you" – a lost cause, but his duty under the law.[20]

The thought that too much praise is dangerous reappeared two years later in a tragedy by Euripides. The idea must have resonated with its original audience. The *Heracleidae* was produced in 429, the year Pericles died, and contains a speech by Iolaus who interrupts his own address to Athens.

"That's enough to the city. Praising too much [*lian epainein*] makes one prone to be envied [*epiphthonon*, from *phthonos*]".[21] For Iolaus the danger threatens from one side, excessive praise. It is the excess that Pericles harps on too, with only a nod at the danger of not praising enough.

When Socrates prefaces his speech in the *Menexenus* by stating the purpose of all such speeches – to praise, exhort, console – he stops to question himself. "Who of us could discover such a *logos*? Or rather where would we begin to praise [*epainountes*] good men?" He is not insinuating that such praise is impossible, as Pericles had found it to be. For Socrates the question he poses has an answer. Begin at the beginning. Since they were good these men should be praised as good; but they were good by having been born of the good. "Therefore let us first praise [*egkômiazômen*] their good birth, second their care and education [*paideian*]", after which the speech can expound on *tên tôn ergon praxin* "the doing of their actions".[22] Pericles saw a reason not to speak at all, and contented himself with telling the public he would pander to their beliefs and desires. Socrates sees a plan for a speech that aims at the audience to improve the young hearers' courage and reawaken the old ones' patriotism and fortitude.

Indeed, if Socrates' question about how to proceed did envision a problem with speaking, it would be the problem of not saying enough in a tribute to the dead. The introduction to the *Menexenus* speech ignores the possibility of excess praise that Pericles had posed as the great problem. This is an argument from silence, but it finds support in the framing conversation, where Socrates dwells on the high praise that everyone hears at a public funeral, clearly describing superlative compliments, the speakers "praising [*egkômiazontes*] the city in all ways". The audience loves this high praise, and even the *xenoi* "foreigners" present look at Socrates as a more distinguished being than before. As an Athenian being honoured, Socrates likes what he hears; the strangers seem to be moved by the rhetoric too, neither envious nor incredulous but rather inclined to consider the city *thaumasiôteran* "more marvellous" than they had before.[23]

Socrates does say later in this conversation that speaking well of Athenians amid Peloponnesians, or vice versa, would take the skills of a good orator.[24] But this does not make high praise perilous. In some ways praise for the Spartans before an Athenian crowd would have to reach even higher than local praise for locals, if that praise hopes to win the Athenians over. This kind of speech might also need to rely on indirection and special pleading; but Socrates is not claiming that it would have to be an attenuated praise. When praise is very high he imagines strangers admiring the object of praise, not attacking it.

Praise in Plato

Because the glowing words with which Socrates is about to speak of Athens strike some readers as proof that this is a parody, it will help to ask what other Platonic works say about praise.

Andrea Nightingale uses the *Lysis* and *Symposium*, Plato's two major comments on praise outside the *Menexenus*, to argue that Plato finds the encomium as such philosophically wanting.[25] If her reading is right it would be incoherent for Plato to endorse the *Menexenus*'s effulgent praise of Athens: a telling consideration even if not decisive (for his dialogues often contradict one another). In any event the evidence in favour of Nightingale's reading is more limited than it first appears. The *Lysis* and the *Symposium* are special cases, containing encomia from (respectively) Hippothales and Alcibiades, non-philosophers speaking under the pressure of erotic desire. Hippothales has been chasing Lysis, to everyone's amusement, and Alcibiades still pines for homely Socrates. The two deliver encomia gone awry, as Nightingale is right to say; but their failures as encomiasts have more to do with what they choose to praise, and with how unphilosophical they were before setting out to praise, than with any tendency towards harmful overstatement that Plato is claiming to inhere in the encomium as such.

Nightingale reaches for broader statements. "Alcibiades' eulogy for Socrates ... beautifully evinces the folly of praise".[26] An unforgettable phrase, "the folly of praise", but it misfires as a generalization about Plato. Whether as a genre of writing or as a form of speech depicted within Platonic writings, praise carries positive associations in the dialogues. Works of praise are permitted even under censorious conditions. *Egkômia* "encomia" directed towards gods, spirits and heroes are *prepousi* "fitting". *Republic* 10 ejects every kind of poetry from the city except religious hymns and encomia to good men. And in general the encomium is an acknowledged poetic genre in Plato's work.[27]

The dialogues do not exempt praise from criticism. Some kinds of praise are misguided or morally suspect, and Socrates or another lead character condemns that praise explicitly.[28] At other times the criticism is muted or indirect.[29] On occasion Plato's characters cite actual and hypothetical encomia whose objects could not possibly deserve praise.[30] Praise for salt and asses is doing something wrong whether it understates or overreaches.

But in all these instances the praising goes wrong because the object deserves no praise of any kind. The passages critical of praise do not imply that tyranny, sophistry and musical innovation have received *excessive* praise, more than the correct amount (where there is some correct amount). Indeed, of the forty or more passages in Plato that find some fault with praise,[31] not one condemns an act of praise on the grounds that it is excessive. That is, no passage concedes that the object in question deserves *some* praise but ought to have received less than it did. Pericles saw excessive praise to praiseworthy objects as the constant danger threatening public speakers, but Socrates ignores that possibility in the *Menexenus* as Plato's characters regularly ignore it.

In this respect Plato agrees with the orator Isocrates. According to the *Encomium to Helen*, the risk for the encomiast is that of not speaking strongly enough about "what is commonly called good or fine, or exceeding virtuous [*diapherontôn ep'aretêi*]". In the same work Isocrates writes, "I am being reasonable [*eulogos*] in using such hyperboles [*têlikautais huperbolais*]" about Helen.[32] "Reasonable hyperbole" sounds like an oxymoron, but the phrase does attest to a willingness to sound excessive in one's praise. The oxymoron points to something paradoxical in praise as such, that it hits the right note when it has gone too far.

Indeed hyperbolic praise is honoured and even courted in the dialogues, as when Lysimachus says that the young speak the highest praise for Socrates, or when Socrates says that he never heard his friend Theodorus praise anyone as much as he praises Theaetetus. In another case Socrates promises to praise Euthyphro's wisdom "forever" if Euthyphro can prove a certain point about piety. Socrates no doubt expects he will never have to deliver on that pledge, but that does not deny the worthiness of effulgent praise when circumstances are right.[33]

When it comes to *erôs* "love, desirous love", Socrates says in the *Symposium* that he will *aei* "always" praise that god.[34] But Plato's other great dialogue about *erôs*, the *Phaedrus*, has more to say about praise and its limits than the passages that Nightingale finds in *Symposium* and *Lysis*. The *Phaedrus* contains three speeches on *erôs*, one by Lysias, one in the mode of Lysias' rhetoric by Socrates, and the final speech, again by Socrates, that repudiates the other two. Whatever the merits of the second speech may be – better than Lysias, but still problematic? As misguided as the speech of Lysias? – it is agreed that the last of the three is put forward as superior to the other two. The *Phaedrus* is also very much a dialogue about rhetoric, and this final speech is supposed to show what a philosopher can accomplish in a speech – how the philosopher outdoes the professional speechwriter. (Not coincidentally the *Phaedrus* sets up the closest parallel situation to the *Menexenus*, with Socrates improving on an existing speech for the benefit of a young man listening.)

The first of the three, the speech by Lysias, urges the young man who is its audience to give himself to the non-lover. Lovers treat their boys badly, among their faults being excessive praise of the one they love. The answering speech by Socrates, put forward as an improved version of that same misplaced anti-eroticism, amplifies the horror of the lover's excessive praise.[35]

While the final speech does not address the lover's tendency to praise, it stands as a rebuke to the portrayal of lovers developed in the first two speeches. As such it condemns the inferior rhetoric that disrespects praise. And when Socrates comes to sum up the two speeches he made, their willingness or unwillingness to praise is what distinguishes them. Twice he looks back on his own rhetorical experiment (unworthy speech followed by worthy one) as the movement from censure to praise.[36] He did wrong when speaking ill of praise and the impulse to praise, right when he praised. In this dialogue about philosophers making rhetoric, the best rhetoric turns out to be the kind that praises – and, it seems, that praises the (philosophical) inclination to praise.

In a way that Pericles seems unable to imagine, too much praise can be the right amount. It is too much compared with a factual description of the object and for that very reason the right amount as a register of value. So if the other dialogues are trustworthy guides, hyperbole in the *Menexenus* will not necessarily show that something has gone wrong with praise. Socrates' question of how to calibrate praise is not haunted, as Pericles' question had been, by the threat of too much praise.

Socrates has changed the terms for measuring praise in another respect too, which partly explains why he does not worry about praising too much. Pericles appealed to the people in the audience as the standard by which to measure praise. Praise could say too much or too little compared with *what his audience wanted to hear.* His promise to aim at what people want and believe reinforces his sense of the audience as the standard. When Socrates asks how to calibrate praise in his speech he makes no reference to the audience. Praise for these dead Athenians needs to do justice to their qualities. The assumption is that praise can do justice to its object, or fail to, independently of whether it pleases or rather overwhelms its listeners.[37]

The quality of praise

Given that Pericles accedes to the demand that he praise the Athenians despite his stated qualms, the Platonic speech will not differ from its predecessor by praising where the other refused to. So how can the two acts of praise best be distinguished? Does one of the speeches praise Athens *more enthusiastically* than the other? With *greater consistency*? It may not be possible to answer such questions without unverifiable appeals to one's "sense" of the two speeches. And there are differences in the way the two praise that can be set out more clearly than such perceptions of strength and weakness in a speech's compliments.

Beginning with his question how to praise the good soldiers, and continuing for about one Stephanus page of the speech, Socrates harps on the nature of praise, the grounds for praising, and the terms in which one registers praise. At least eleven remarks in this one page can be called observations about praise:

i   "How could we correctly [*orthôs*] begin praising [*epainountes*] good men?" (237a)

ii "It seems to me that by nature [*kata phusin*], as they were good, so too we should praise [*epainein*] them". (237a)

iii "But they became [*egenonto*] good by growing [*phunai*] from those who are good [*ex agathôn*]. So let us first praise [*egkômiazômen*] their good birth [*eugeneian*]". (237a)

iv "Their good birth first began [*hupêrxe*] with their ancestors' origin not being arrivals ... They were autochthonous [*autochthonas*], residing and living in their fatherland". (237b)

125

v   "[The Athenians' ancestors] were nurtured not by a stepmother [*mêtruias*] as others are but by a mother, the land [*chôras*] in which they lived". (237b–c)

vi   "It is most just to pay tribute to [*kosmêsai*] their mother herself [*tên mêtera autên*]". (237c)

vii   "The country [*chôra*] is worthy [*axia*] of being praised even by all humans, not only by us … first because she is loved by the gods [*theophilôs*]". (237c)

viii   "How could it not be right for all humans to praise [*epainesthai*] the one whom the gods praised [*epêinesan*]?" (237d)

ix   "Second, praise [*epainos*] is justly hers because … she chose and gave birth to humans out of all the animals, humans who alone are aware of justice and the gods". (237d)

x   "Our earth and mother presents sufficient proof that she gave birth to humans; for she produced wheat and barley" (food for humans, hence the food a mother would give). (237e–238a)

xi   "One should accept tokens [of motherhood] more [*mallon*] with respect to the earth than with respect to a woman; for the earth [*gê*] has not imitated [*memimêtai*] the woman in conceiving and giving birth but rather the woman the earth". (238a)

As noted, one judges the rightness of praise relative to its object (i) not relative to the audience's expectations. The good men who fell in battle were good by nature and therefore deserve a praise that speaks to their natural traits (ii). The men's natural goodness moreover begins with their *eugeneia* "good birth" and the "good ones" they grew from (iii, iv). In other contexts *eugeneia* can refer to aristocratic birth; here it is revealed to mean that these Athenians' ancestors were born of the Athenian land or *chôra*.[38]

Autochthonous birth turns up in Athenian funeral speeches,[39] and no wonder. Athenians would have found it natural for a funeral speech to recall their collective birth out of the Attic soil on the occasion of the collective return into that soil by a group of their fellow citizens.[40]

Autochthony trumps all other comparisons among cities by grounding the superiority of Athenians in nature, all the more dramatic considering that *this* nature is a divine earth capable of yielding up living human beings and domesticated crops. Supernatural autonomy supplies a superhuman basis for calling Athenians praiseworthy, and it sets them beyond comparison with other Greeks. Socrates appears ready to take his praise to extremes.

Autochthony silences comparisons with other cities inasmuch as the major other cities in Greece claimed to have been founded by foreigners. Socrates exploits this difference by reserving the trope of the parental city, the mother- or fatherland, for Athens's use alone. Only Athenians still live with their mother. Other Greeks are in a stepmother city, someone they live with who feeds them but did not give birth to them (v).

It should be obvious that the distinction does not accomplish everything that the speech wants to. Having been born of a place really only makes one praiseworthy if the motherland is also worth praising (vi). So Socrates redirects his attention to the land that mythically produced Athenians. Here too the praise begins by setting its object apart from all possible competitors as well as alleging a non-human basis for the praise. Poseidon and Athena quarrelled over which of them the city would be dedicated to (vii). Athens is "god-loved" and "praised by the gods" as no other city is (viii). What the gods praise deserves praise from "all human beings" too (viii).

Then in a surprising return to mundane fact Socrates sets myth aside and presents an *argument* for the surpassing praiseworthiness of Athens. Athens gave birth to human beings when every other place was issuing animals (ix). Like a true mother the land provided exactly the *trophê* "nourishment" that her newborns needed, not milk but wheat and barley and olives (x). As a matter of fact the land is the truest mother of all. Human mothers imitate the great mother earth and not the other way around (xi).

The strategy of praise becomes more oblique. Each argument in this passage reverses or undermines something that Socrates said a few sentences earlier. For example he commends Athens (ix) for having produced the autochthonous Athenians where other stretches of land gave only brutes to the world. And yet he has just commended Athenians as "well-born" by virtue of their origins in the Athenian ground (iii, iv, v). The result is circularity. The exceptional Athenians unlike all other people originated in the ground, and the ground they grew up in was exceptional, as witness its producing them.

Another reversal or undermining comes in (x). Socrates already called the people of other cities *trephomenous* "nourished" by their home countries, fed by the homeland as if by a stepmother (v). Now he claims that because the earth *trephetai* "nourishes" her people she shows herself to be a *true* mother. The verb is the same in both passages. The consolation that non-Athenians had had to satisfy themselves with – food alone, the token of living in one's step-motherland – now guarantees that Athenians reside in their true mother's bosom. To put it conversely, the food that the earth brings forth demonstrating her motherhood of Athenians runs the risk of showing that she is one more stepmother. How can he adduce the same act of feeding as evidence of legitimacy in one instance and evidence against legitimacy in the other?

The matter of the true mother becomes more vexed in (xi), which reads as a multiple improvisation on themes in Pericles. Pericles alluded to Athenian autochthony in his speech but also cast the superiority of Athens in the vocabulary of original and copy. "We are rather [*mallon*] a model [*paradeigma*] for some than imitators [*mimoumenoi*] of others".[41] Socrates incorporates that appeal to *mimêsis* or imitation, and the emphatic comparison, into his praise for the motherland. Human mothers have mimicked the homeland rather than the reverse. Proofs of true motherhood apply to the land *mallon* "rather than" to human mothers.

Socrates' differentiation between mother and stepmother distorts the Periclean praise of Athens to the brink of contradiction. When the *Menexenus* distinguished Athens from other Greek cities, it made Athens the mother to their stepmother; the present distinction between model and copy demotes the human mother who had metaphorically been the image of Athenian pre-eminence. That is: Athens is like a mother and nothing could be better than that. On the other hand Athens is something incomparably better than a mother. Mothers derive their excellence from their capacity to bear and also nourish their young. Socrates then acknowledges that capacity only to the degree that it derives from the earth's far superior virtue in those functions. The origin or cause of the Athenians' excellence is the great mother that it is only by exceeding (being as it is the model to be copied by) Athenian mothers.

Socrates' impossible overemphasis communicates the drive at work behind an unarticulable statement. But what is that statement that is incapable of being made? Why should it prove so difficult to adduce reasons for the splendour of Athens that the arguments fall into circularity and begged questions? It is as if Socrates courted failure by trying to supply earthly arguments for the high status that Athens enjoyed mythically. An argument of such ambition should not be surprised if it finds itself without an available vocabulary for comparison. The impossibilities in the rhetoric imply that the human beings made by Athens cannot suffice to prove the worth of the land (*contra* ix) when even the best humans derive their worth from having been land-made (iv). The nourishment that the land provides is impressive but (*contra* x) falls short of proving that Athens is the great mother, given that this same act of nourishing also defines stepmothering cities (v).

Socrates is putting more pressure on his arguments than they can bear, and they collapse. There is nothing degraded about the earthborn humans or about Attic crops. They only will not testify to the surpassing excellence of Athens when they belong to a more ordinary world that they lack the ability to surpass.

If (ix) and (x) fail by appealing to inadequate bases for demonstrating the city's excellence, (xi) specifies what makes these grounds inadequate. If the Athenian land is the true mother that human mothers imitate, no terms taken from the human realm could do justice to the city. It is no compliment to an original to compare it to its copy. "You look as nice as your reflection" sounds like a weak joke directed at someone primping in front of the mirror. As compliments go it only praises the mirror; likewise the effort to make Athens the true mother and all human mothers its copies. Athens now belongs to a different order of things from Athenian people, their food and their human mothers, and Socrates' arguments cannot achieve what he wants from them. Any comparison with the objects of ordinary experience would have to set the city impossibly above those objects, diminishing the tokens of Athenian superiority in the very act of basing an encomium to Athens on those tokens. The praise that Socrates has in mind for his city is excessive by nature: it exceeds what words of praise are capable of saying.

Crito

It is hardly surprising to say that other Platonic works also transfer affective responses away from an object of experience to an entity posited as that object's truer version and something that the object of experience imitates. But the specific ontological priority of Athens over Athenians, according to which a human mother becomes the likeness of the earth mother, finds a parallel in Plato's *Crito* that is close enough to be worth describing, given that Socrates rests his defence of his actions to Crito on an analogy in which the Athenian laws function as every citizen's parents.

Early in the dialogue, Crito is urging Socrates to cooperate with his friends and escape from jail. Among other considerations Crito points out that Socrates has young sons. If he escapes he can provide for the boys, who otherwise will have to fend for themselves. Socrates replies at length to Crito's arguments but not to that one. He almost completely ignores the father–son relation that Crito thought would carry the day, not even touching on this point until close to the end of the dialogue and then with a cursory reply. Socrates' role as the father to young boys appears not to carry emotional associations or imply any extraordinary duties.[42]

Strangely, therefore, when Socrates invokes the personified laws of Athens in the same dialogue, he makes them claim that they fulfil a parental role. In fact this is the most genuine parental role of all. Only thanks to the laws does Socrates enjoy the privilege of a free citizen's birth, a status for which one might vulgarly thank biological parents. The laws provided for young Socrates' education, as one expects parents to do. Athens's laws are like the Athenians' parents; in fact they are more completely parents to individual citizens than those citizens' parents are. Human parents account for the easy part of an Athenian's birth, what you could call a mere semblance of birth, considering that human babies turn up everywhere while Athenian citizens are the exception even within Athens and almost non-existent elsewhere. For real births you need city laws.[43]

The human parents' contribution becomes ancillary to the parental work done by the laws. Human parents are practically imitations of the laws.

Socrates' refusal to leave Athens for his own sons' sake, in other words, does not follow from his rejecting the value of being a parent. The personified laws make the case for a citizen's obedience to them precisely by virtue of being a citizen's parents. Far from slighting fatherhood Socrates depends on it – not as it applies to human parents though, only in this higher sense.

The *Crito*'s readers debate how far Socrates wants to take his own argument. Does he endorse every claim the laws make in this argument, or is there some difference between the loyalty they demand and the loyalty that he thinks is justified? Depending on how interpreters answer this question, they will find the parallel to the *Menexenus* either more or less exact.[44] Nevertheless both dialogues do present this striking Platonic innovation of the city as a metaphorical parent that supersedes the literal parent as more perfectly parental.

Excess in praise

The *Crito*'s transfer of parental relations from literal parents to what may have seemed to be a derivative metaphorical kind, who are the ones then said to be the primary parents, is only one example of an argumentative step that Plato's readers can find in many dialogues. In the *Symposium* beauty as such is supposed to work as an ultimate object of desire, individual human bodies becoming poor substitutes for that true *erôs*, no better than an early way station on the path towards beauty. Other examples will spring to mind.

The reason for bringing such examples up is not to review Plato's ontology or epistemology, only to take note of how his dialogues often see objects of praise, and how they address such objects. The transfer of loyalties to a new and truer object in the *Crito*, *Symposium* and other works testifies not to a uniform status for the higher objects of praise – no reason to equate Athenian laws with beauty as such, nor to put the Athens of the *Menexenus* into the same ontological heaven occupied by the Forms – but to a pattern in the activity of Platonic praising, whatever object that praise may choose on a given occasion. An excess in praise understood simply *as* excess, as "more praise than the thing warrants" or "more praise than the person praising really feels", might not lend itself to further description. If that excess follows a consistent pattern, that pattern will be worth spelling out.

Excessive praise cannot entirely follow a formula, for then it would lose the sense that it communicates of sailing into new waters. Nevertheless some classical samples of praise do suggest a general form.

Some time near the end of the fifth century Gorgias wrote his *Encomium to Helen*, a work that created a rhetorical genre, or added a new twist to a standing genre, characterized by the speaker's heaping praise on an object that had been abused or ignored until then. We have noted the examples of praise for the trivial referred to by Plato and Isocrates: tributes to salt, bumblebees, goats. Those encomia are merely unseemly in the way they squander resources on unworthy objects. Gorgias' *Helen*, the more perverse act of praise, sets out to exonerate Helen from blame for running away with Paris and triggering the Trojan War. If Plato looked to the *Encomium to Helen* as a springboard to his own praise-lavishing,[45] he would have found Gorgias saying that Helen "did no wrong" despite her bad reputation; was "the foremost of the foremost men and women", beyond compare in beauty; had inspired "the greatest erotic desires"; and owed her incomparable beauty to her divine parentage by Zeus, "tyrant over all".[46] In the *Encomium to Helen* excessive praise is (along with other things):

- *one-sided*, suppressing all negative traits of the object being praised, as when Helen is said to have done no wrong;

- *denying comparison*, declaring any other models faulty and unworthy of being compared with the object of praise, as when Gorgias calls Helen "foremost" and the inspiration to the greatest desires;[47] and
- *transcendentalizing*, appealing to nature or divinity to ground the praise in a source beyond the human, as in Helen's divine parentage.

When Plato's contemporary Isocrates wrote his own speech about Helen, forty or fifty years after Gorgias and some years after Plato's *Menexenus*,[48] he praised Helen according to the same principles. His praise is one-sided in that when Isocrates defends Paris at length for wanting to possess Helen, he only glances at the fact of her willing elopement. His encomium denies comparison in attributing "the greatest share of beauty" to Helen; he approves of Gorgias for claiming that Helen "surpassed all others". For Isocrates beauty itself is divine, so Helen's divine standing does not need mythic testimony. She warrants the exceeding praise she receives by virtue of being so beautiful, even though Isocrates does take note of her parentage.[49]

Isocrates is not the only inheritor of the encomiastic tradition, and not the only Athenian author one could look in for high praise. But unlike other authors of praise in Plato's time he defends the rhetoric of praise as well as exemplifying it. The *Encomium to Helen* announces its own excessiveness, saying that the true encomium is the one that exerts and extends itself to be worthy of its subject. Giving salt its due is no great achievement. But "all those who attempt to speak of such things as are admitted to be good and honourable ... have fallen far short of the truth". And: "It is difficult to rise to the importance of such things as deserve it".[50] As both an apology and a putative example, the *Encomium* invites its reader to take the one-sidedness and other such characteristics as paradigmatic attributes of its excessive praise.

The details about praise in the *Menexenus* should have already shown that its praise of Athens possesses the same characteristics. The funeral speech transcendentalizes by tracing the superiority of Athenians to their ancestors' divinely caused birth and divine first training. It interprets the myth of autochthony in a way that removes Athens from comparison with any other Greek city, those others (thanks to their barbarian founders) becoming no better than half-Greek. As for presenting its object as one-sided, if that is not obvious from the way Socrates talks about Athens during the first page of the speech, it cannot be doubted by the end of his historical summary.

These features of high praise that take the excess beyond mere exaggeration again resonate with other passages in Plato's dialogues. At the risk of generality, praise that possesses the characteristics listed above can be seen at work in many descriptions of the Forms. The Forms possess their properties one-sidedly; one has to omit negative traits in speaking of such entities, just as the orators omit Helen's misdeeds. Where beautiful individual things are both beautiful and ugly, "beauty itself" is only, and can only be, beautiful.[51]

This purified condition of the Forms constitutes part of what is called their *self-predication.*

Meanwhile that feature of the Forms that is sometimes called their *non-identity,* their distinctness from every particular visible being, posits a difference between each intelligible being and those objects of experience with which it shares its name. Justice as such is not identical with any individual just law, state or person. That is to say that the Form cannot be compared with the particular thing, better still that the Form cannot be confined to any such comparison. It stands apart from the many particulars as beautiful Helen stood apart from the many beautiful women of ordinary life.

Trying to decide how literally Plato means his references to the Forms as divine[52] would take this discussion of his rhetoric even further afield. But whether the Forms line up more truly among supernatural items or within a suitably expansive conception of nature, they are not part of the human order.

All this is to say that calling the Forms self-predicating, non-identical and either natural or divine is to speak of them in the language that praise rhetoric marks as hyperbolic or extreme. That is to say that the Forms have to be spoken of in praise that is inventive enough to overcome the pedestrian limitations inherent in language. One example might be uncharacteristic, but it makes the point. In *Republic* Book 6 Socrates praises the good, known to many English readers as the Form of the Good. "The good is not being [*ousia*] but exceeds being in power and dignity" – and Glaucon responds by calling this praise "divine hyperbole [*daimonias huperbolês*]".[53] The right language for the Forms is too much language, or rather too much *for* a language. The right language is experienced as more than the language can handle. In that case praise might have a useful role to play in philosophy as a deployment of language that evokes higher beings than those to be met in ordinary experience.

Improvisation

Either excess, or some other way of escaping formulaic language, might be a feature of praise in general. The proverbial *damning with faint praise* is grounded in the sense that praise that works, praise that does not damn, will threaten to be too much praise. Faint praise fails – it resembles a damning – if praising calls for some kind of enthusiasm to the point of invention.

The point may be put in J. L. Austin's terms, extending some of his observations about the formulas he called performatives; which is to say that Austin's analysis, however far from Plato in origin and purpose, provides modern terminology for understanding Plato's treatment of praise. In Austin the formulas "I congratulate you" and "I apologize" perform the tasks they name, respectively congratulating and apologizing,[54] but no such formula exists for insults. One can thank with the words "I thank you" (indeed that is often the best way), but to say "I insult you" is not to insult you. The words "I insult you" do often promise that something else will soon be said that *does* insult you, but the mention of insult will not do the job.

Similarly, although Austin does not discuss this case, "I praise you" alone does not make itself true. It does not accomplish the work of praising as "I apologize" does the work of apologizing. "I praise you" is a more natural-sounding sentence than "I insult you", as are such locutions as "I want to praise you" and "Let us now praise ... ". Such locutions tend to be followed by the praise, as in a reminder that speaking of the praise does not constitute praising in the same way that speaking of a promise is a promise. Said by itself, the formula "I praise you" threatens to be grudging praise and effectively no praise at all. Successful praising takes place with an openness not called for in its putative opposite, blaming.

In fact, and despite the common linking of praise with blame, the two are not quite opposites. Blaming is the opposite of crediting; the truest opposites to praise are probably abuse and insult; and they call for openness in expression as praise does. Such "openness" does not imply that any words at all can work as words of praise, nor that every act of praise calls for pure invention. One finds openness in the act of insulting in spite of the associations between insult and ritual phrases, or standard tropes. Insult and praise both pose the challenge, which never goes away, of finding the right degree. Say too little and there is no insult in one case, no praise in the other; say enough and you risk having gone too far. In the absence of a performative formula, the question "Did you praise or didn't you?" calls for an act of judgement of a sort that is not required for "Did you promise?" or "Did you apologize?" – these latter being questions that can be answered with appeals to fact and not interpretations of fact.

Where success is not assured by use of a formula, one finds the act of *trying*. Rarely does one have to try to promise. But Socrates is trying to praise Athens and its people.

One also finds improvisation where there are no formulas. Compare apologies and promises, both of which are better when not improvised. This may be because words that are merely tantamount to a promise, words that are *practically* a promise, are used by someone who wants to improvise *not* keeping the promise; and apologetic-sounding words that do not include "apologize" can be used to evade actual apologizing.[55]

In spite of giving the subject only passing treatment, the *Menexenus* nevertheless says more about improvisation than anything else Plato wrote, and connects improvisation with praise. The Greek verb that translates as "to improvise" is *autoschediazein*, which occurs only rarely in Plato and tends to be used pejoratively by him, as it is used by authors before Aristotle.[56] Plato too normally uses *autoschediazein* for the act of fabrication. "Tell us [about your motivations] so that we don't make something up", Socrates on trial imagines people asking him. Elsewhere "I had hoped to be able to tell Meletus that

I no longer had to make things up out of my ignorance"; and Hermogenes says to Socrates in the *Cratylus*, "I think you didn't make this up but heard it somewhere".[57]

But declaring that *autoschediazein* never means improvisation in the neutral sense that it carries today requires forcing the natural sense of some passages. It may prove to have been too hasty to see improvisation appearing for the first time only in Aristotle. In Plato's *Euthydemus*, for instance, Socrates speaks of putting forward a rough version of his argument. *Tolmêsô apautoschediasai* "I will dare to improvise". Socrates is not demeaning what he says but indicating the high stakes of the conversation. He braves the dangers of making up an argument because the argument needs to be given. In the *Phaedrus* Socrates introduces his first speech on love: "I will be ridiculous if I improvise something on the same topic as a professional poet". Again improvisation sounds like the clumsy result of ignorance, but the opprobrium attaches to Socrates the non-rhetorician rather than to the ad lib as such.[58] What Socrates fears will make him ridiculous is not that he *improvised*, but that *he* improvised. In such passages there is conceptual room permitting Plato to use *autoschediazein* to denote a respectable mode of composition.

In the *Menexenus*, it is Menexenus who first uses *autoschediazein*. He says that whoever is chosen to speak at the funeral will have to "make something up" on short notice. Socrates answers him that the potential speakers have their speeches *pareskeuasmenoi* "prepared", even though it is not hard to *autoschediazein* such talks either, if need be. He tells Menexenus how Aspasia made the speech he is about to recite, going through some parts *ek tou parachrêma* "on the spur of the moment" and attaching together other parts left over from the speech she had written for Pericles.[59] Socrates is apparently describing a technique of oratorical improvisation in which the speaker adds new remarks to prepared elements. This is what it means to invent a speech, that a general model is tailored to fit a particular occasion. On this view improvisation consists in adding details to the model, not in making something up out of whole cloth.[60] And not only poor orators put their speeches together this way, for Aspasia herself combined the ready-made and the newly invented in composing this funeral speech; this is what Socrates also describes as gluing additional parts into the existing speech, and it seems to be standard compositional practice.

The passage that inspired this consideration of rhetorical excess, the opening to the *Menexenus* speech, is itself improvisatory in the way that Socrates describes *autoschediazein*. The speech from 237d to 238a has been constructed out of elements taken over from Thucydides. The superiority of Athens and the long-running continuity of its population, for example, both come straight from the funeral speech of Pericles.[61]

Another improvisation takes up Pericles' personification of Athens, when he called on the men in his audience to be in love with the city.[62] The *Menexenus* speech de-eroticizes the attachment, making it a son's devotion, and turning the mistress into a mother. As Athens had been a *deserving* mistress for Pericles – presumably one who is true – so too Socrates feels the need to stress that he means a true mother and not a simulation.

Speaking of mistresses and mothers reminds us that Plato is presenting this speech as Aspasia's composition not Socrates' own. And in this instance her alleged authorship adds to the import of the improvisation at work. For if Plutarch is a reliable source, Pericles fell in love with Aspasia to a degree that Athenians found worthy of gossip. She was his beloved mistress.[63] Upon marrying Pericles she became his sons' stepmother, then soon the mother of his younger son Pericles. As someone who could move from one of these relations to the other and sometimes insisting on one role rather than another, Aspasia has the ability to picture the city of Athens as not just one of the three but interchangeably mistress, stepmother or mother. And passing from one available metaphor to another is a standard move in verbal improvisation.[64]

In yet another case, Plato responds improvisatorily to Pericles' mention of *mimêsis*. Pericles found words for elevating Athenian governance over the forms of government in other cities by making Athens the original, and turning those other cities' constitutions into its copies or imitations.[65] Socrates clinches his point with an appeal to *mimêsis* and, like Pericles, establishes the city's superiority by reason of its status as the mimicked object – though he uses the occasion of this speech to say more about how *mimêsis* can function within moral education, improvising on the theme of city and imitation to account for the citizens' moral improvement.

The impromptu variations are not limited to topics that Thucydides attributed to Pericles. The soil that Socrates apotheosizes (237e–238a) appeared in the *History of the Peloponnesian War*, though not in the funeral speech. Thucydides asks in his own disenchanted voice why a single population should have lived continuously in Attica. Other cities went through migrations and upheavals. The Spartan invasion of Laconia was a notorious case that made Athenians wonder why they had been spared such population movements; Athens luckily has always had the same people living in it. But what accounts for this good luck? Knowing that Athenians used autochthony to account for the difference, Thucydides proposes a different explanation. The thin soil of Attica cannot feed many people; therefore the land never attracted foreign plunderers.[66]

It is perverse of Thucydides to focus on the same earth that autochthony stories celebrated and to call the soil preternaturally barren where the myth made it impossibly fecund. But then – and here is the improvisation – Socrates perversely alludes back to Thucydides when he speaks of an Attica so fertile that it not only sprouted menfolk but even greeted them with divinely domesticated barley and wheat. He makes the rich farmland's yield the telling criterion by which Athens shows itself to be its people's true mother.

Incidentally Plato is improvising regardless of whether the *Menexenus* speech turns out to be playful or deadly earnest. With the speech of Pericles in hand Socrates extemporizes his patriotic praise, sometimes inverting or overstating elements of the original but consistently sorting those elements into a coherent new whole. This is how orators make something up, *autoschediazein*.

The magic of rhetoric

Socratic improvisation might be directed entirely against Pericles. If Pericles was a speaker who did not improvise, a more capable speechwriter who begins with philosophical insight may be one who can put speeches together in a new way.

That report from the *Suda* that Pericles spoke in public from prepared texts, where everyone before him had been known to *schediazein*, needs to be treated with suspicion. But even if the *Suda* is only repeating gossip, it invites the question of why anyone should have circulated such claims about Pericles. The positive assertion in Plutarch that Pericles wrote nothing but legislation implies a history of gossip and speculation to the contrary, concerning his preparing texts to speak from in public.

If Pericles did not improvise, and if by his own statement in Thucydides he preferred not to praise, this is one reason to see improvisation and open or potentially excessive praise in tandem. Both by improvising and by praising freely Socrates moves philosophical rhetoric away from the Periclean model.

But improvisation might also lead back to praise by another route, if it represents the negation of a kind of utterance that is not supposed to be improvised, namely the formula of magical ritual. This thought has to be put without insistence, if for no other reason than because the religious vision in Plato remains neglected by his contemporary readers.

When the *Menexenus* begins and Socrates first describes the preternatural effects of funeral rhetoric, he calls the speeches that so move the crowd *ek pollou chronou paraskeuasmenôn* "prepared a long time before", the speakers not praising *eikêi* "at random, without a plan". This speech contains vocabulary of magic. The orators *goêteuousin* "perform sorcery". Socrates is *kêloumenos* "charmed, bewitched", and seems *semnoteros* "more revered, more august" to the foreigners present.[67]

Spells, potions and other magical operations have to be prepared, often long in advance, and normally according to formulas. Modern information about Greek magic is limited – Plato himself is one of the earliest sources[68] about its practices – with much of what is known dating from Hellenistic Egypt a century or more after Plato's death. But curse tablets, those small sheets of thin lead inscribed with spells and buried where chthonic powers will get the message, appear in most parts of the Greek world and date from pre-Hellenistic antiquity. And the inscriptions on curse tablets fall into patterns that make it plausible to call their spells formulas or stock phrases.[69]

The point is not true of ancient Greece alone. However it is that magic is related to ritual in human culture, the two share a compunction for reiterating a practice in the same way on each occasion. But the iterability of magic puts a certain weight on Socrates' reference to funeral speeches' having been prepared. These speeches that send him flying to the Isles of the Blessed, speeches that control the movements to disembodied souls – in other words *spells* – are speeches prepared in advance and not delivered *eikêi*, without a plan, or freely.

The closing movement of the *Menexenus* speech, when the lessons of history are done, brings the voices of the dead to speak to Athens.[70] Call this the necromantic part of the speech, the part that can control the movements of dead souls. Therefore, it must be the part already long prepared, because it has to be delivered in exactly the same way each time. In that case the improvisations in the speech must occur in the sections that precede these closing words from the dead. Those improvised parts include the introduction to the speech, the mythical prehistory of Athens and the long account of Athenian history – all the parts of the speech that are involved in praising. If the speech both praises and conjures, it conjures insofar as it contains formulaic sections written long ago; but it praises, verging on over-praising, insofar as it leaves itself free to invent on the fly.

Notes

1 This characterization of the double sense of *ergon* is made elegantly by Wickkiser (1999: 66).
2 Compare a passage in the Gettysburg Address (e.g. at www.ourdocuments.gov/doc.php?flash=false&doc=36), here apparently appropriating Pericles: "In a larger sense, we cannot dedicate – we cannot consecrate – we cannot hallow – this ground. ... The world will little note, nor long remember what we say here, but it can never forget what they did here".
3 Thucydides *History* 2.35.2.
4 *Ibid.*: philosophize without softness, 2.40.1; judge issues, 2.40.2.
5 *Ibid.*: 2.40.3.
6 Compare a hypothetical statement of New York City's exceptionalism that could run like this: "Most people like to get a good night's sleep before going to work. We New Yorkers stay up doing our preparatory research for the next day's work, because we are able to work well without sleeping". Someone who argued this way would believe that skipping sleep is harmful to work in general, but that New Yorkers are exceptional in being able to do without it. Likewise Pericles thinks that deliberation is harmful to action as a rule.
7 Thucydides *History* 2.39.1.
8 *Ibid.*: boasting enemies of Athens, 2.39.3; talk and money, 2.40.1.
9 *Ibid.*: 2.40.4.
10 On poets teaching the Greeks see Herodotus *Histories* 2.53.2; Aeschines *Against Timarchus* 142; cf. the treatment of Homer as (problematic) informant about the Trojan War, Thucydides *History* 1.3.
11 Thucydides *History*: *nomos* that established funeral speeches, 2.35.1; Spartan courage the product of laws, 2.39.4.
12 *Menexenus* 235b–c.
13 Wickkiser (1999: 68–69).

14 *Menexenus* 236e.

15 Pericles is not alone. As a rule the surviving funeral speeches begin by depreciating themselves by comparison with the soldiers' actions: Lysias 2.1; Demosthenes 60.1; Hyperides 6.1–2.

16 Wickkiser (1999: 67).

17 *Ibid.*: 68.

18 Classical authors of course did not write paragraphs. Less anachronistically this paragraph may be called the first five Greek sentences, more or less *Menexenus* 236d–237a.

19 Pericles mentions praise alone, Thucydides *History* 2.35.1–2; Socrates adds consolation and exhortation, *Menexenus* 236e. Socrates names two functions of the speech before subdividing the second, which is aimed at the living auditors, into two purposes in turn. The speech should "praise [*epainesetai*] the dead and benevolently exhort [*parainesetai*] the living". These two verbs rhyme, both of them deriving from the root *aineô* "praise, recommend". The word play suggests that praise already contains a wider range of rhetorical actions than Pericles imagined.

20 Thucydides *History*: praise too little or too much, 2.35.2; Pericles appeals to wishes and desires of all, 2.35.3.

21 Euripides *Heracleidae* 202–3. Also see lines 303–6, 329–30, which echo the funeral speech's remark about laws to protect the oppressed (Thucydides *History* 2.37.3). For that matter the *Menexenus* alludes to the *Heracleidae* in turn, as if these three works were carrying on a political discussion among themselves (Aty 1982: 10nn.52–53).

22 *Menexenus*: the question how to praise, 237a; the answering plan for a speech, 237a–b. In what follows we will treat both the verbs *epainein* and *egkômiazein* as meaning "to praise", and their related nouns *epainos* and *egkômion* as corresponding acts of praise. Sometimes it will prove more appropriate to treat the last of these terms as literally referring to an encomium, a formal speech of praise. Similarly *epainos* literally can mean a poem or hymn of praise.

23 *Ibid.*: speakers praising Athens, 235a; foreigners present regarding the city as marvellous, 235b. The word *xenos* has both broad and narrow applications, but here it naturally reads as "non-Athenian". In all likelihood Socrates is referring to *Greek* non-Athenians, as Plato would (and this dialogue does) use the more pointed *barbaros* to refer to non-Greeks; but if *xenoi* at 235b were to include barbarians, that would change the sense of the sentence.

24 *Ibid.*: 235e. That Aristotle quotes this phrase twice but never engages with the *Menexenus* otherwise suggests that it became a free-floating proverb, again not tied specifically to any views about envy in the audience.

25 Nightingale (1993).

26 *Ibid.*: 127.

27 Plato: "encomia" are "fitting", *Laws* 7.801d–e and cf. 8.829e; poetry ejected except for hymns and encomia, *Republic* 10.607a (a position consistent with 3.397c–d, 5.459e, 5.468d); encomium an acknowledged genre, *Ion* 534c, *Laws* 12.957c, *Protagoras* 326a.

28 Plato: Callicles praises the wrong people, *Gorgias* 518e; praise from those who lack experience not valued, *Laws* 1.639c, and cf. *Crito* 518e; people should not praise innovations in music, *Republic* 4.424; wrongheaded praise that tragedy receives, *Republic* 10.605d–10.606b; the philosopher scornful of the praise that goes to kings and to a heroic genealogy, *Theaetetus* 174d–175a. See also *Gorgias* 519a; *Laws* 4.706c–d, 4.711b–c; *Phaedrus* 260c; *Protagoras* 346b; *Republic* 6.488c–d, 7.528e, 8.562d; *Symposium* 198d–e.

29 Plato: Sophists praised, *Euthydemus* 303b–c; victims of bad diet praise the people who made them ill, *Gorgias* 518d–e; Euripides and other poets praise tyranny, *Republic* 8.568b; cf. *Protagoras* 346b on Simonides and tyrants. Also see *Laws* 3.700c, *Phaedrus* 257e.

30 Someone has written an encomium to salt, Eryximachus says at *Symposium* 177b. This seems to be a historical statement, as Isocrates refers disparagingly to encomia to salt and bumblebees, *Encomium to Helen* 12. *Phaedrus* 260b imagines a praise-speech about an ass; the counterpart at *Laws* 1.639 is praise for a goat.

31 Because praise can be a vague phenomenon, vague enough to be talked about without using the word for it (in Greek, without using *epainein* or *egkômiazein* or related nouns), an exact count is impossible. Unscientifically it is possible to tally up at least 130 references to praise in the dialogues, of which forty are disapproving.

32 Isocrates *Encomium to Helen* 12, 54.

33 Plato: Lysimachus on the young, *Laches* 180e; Socrates on Theodorus, *Theaetetus* 145b; Socrates on Euthyphro's wisdom, *Euthyphro* 9b. See *Laws* 6.775b commending universal praise for obedience to wedding laws, *Timaeus* on the praise owed to Athens and Athenians ("I'll never be able to praise the city and its men adequately", 19d).

34 Plato *Symposium* 212b.

35 Plato *Phaedrus*: Lysias against excessive praise, 233a–b; Socrates against it, 240e.

36 *Ibid.*: 265c, 266b.

37 Isocrates again offers an apposite comparison. See *Panathenaecus* 36: "It is difficult for praise speeches [*epainous*] to equal actions of hyperbolic [*huperballousi*] greatness and beauty". For Isocrates, the desire to measure out praise properly becomes the desire to make the praise match its object.

38 Later in the fourth century, probably in the 340s, the speaker in the courtroom speech *Against Neaera* introduces Theogenes as *eugenês*, meaning that the man was a native Athenian, 59.72. Ober (2005: 11–12).

39 See Loraux (1986: 19, 90–91, 203–4, 210–11, 244–46). Direct references to autochthony in other funeral speeches include Demosthenes 60.4, Hyperides 7; an oblique reference in Thucydides *History* 2.36.1.

40 Socrates draws the connection between birth from the land and return to the land in death, Plato *Menexenus* 237b–c. The remark is a jab at Pericles for having denied that it matters where Athenians are buried, Thucydides *History* 2.43.2–3.

41 *Ibid.*: allusion to autochthony, "The same people have always dwelled in our land", 2.36.1; more a model than imitators, 2.37.1.

42 Plato *Crito*: Crito's argument about sons of Socrates, 45c–d; cursory reply from Socrates, 54a.

43 *Ibid.*: laws and education, 50d; laws like Athenians' parents, 50e; laws more parental than biological parents, see especially 51a–d, where Socrates makes his revaluation of filial values explicit.

44 For one take on this point of contact between the *Menexenus* and the *Crito* see Berges (2007).

45 Wickkiser compares *Helen* to the *Menexenus* speech along different lines. Wickkiser (1999: 67).

46 Gorgias, *Encomium*: Helen did no wrong, 15; was foremost of the foremost, 3; inspired greatest desires, 4; was daughter of Zeus the tyrant, 3.

47 Praise that denies comparisons appears in the *Symposium*, when Alcibiades is honouring Socrates. He says he knows of no model to compare the man with. For other Athenians, Homeric figures come to mind. The encomiast might

compare Pericles to Antenor the Trojan elder or Nestor the wise old Greek: Plato *Symposium* 221c. (Homer singles Antenor out as wise: *Iliad* 3.203, 7.347.) Socrates has no forebear.

48 The opening sections of the *Encomium to Helen* seem to represent certain followers of Socrates as still alive and Gorgias as dead. Such clues have led to a date of around 370 being assigned to the speech. If Plato wrote the *Menexenus* not long after 386, then it comes a decade and a half before the Isocratic *Encomium*.

49 Isocrates *Encomium to Helen*: on elopement with Paris, 49; greatest share of beauty, 54; Gorgias spoke rightly, 14; the divinity of beauty, 54; Helen's parentage, 16.

50 *Ibid.*: fallen short of truth, 12; difficult to rise, 13.

51 Plato *Symposium* 211a.

52 A striking passage occurs in *Republic* 10.597b: Socrates says there are three couches, "the one being the one in nature [*en tēi phusei*], which we would say, I believe, that a god made [*theon ergasasthai*]". How seriously he meant such a claim has been disputed since antiquity, though there is a good argument to be made that this entire stretch of Book 10 is a religious condemnation of artistic representation.

53 Plato *Republic* 6.509b–c.

54 Austin (1962: 30–31).

55 Such words do give the impression of being used for the purpose of evading a real apology. "I'm sorry you feel that way", says the telephone voice of the corporate representative in an improvised surrogate for apology designed to assuage in the way that apology does, but without apology's moral commitment.

56 Much of the material on improvisation in this section is indebted to Tobyn DeMarco's work on improvisation.

57 Plato: "Tell us", *Apology* 20d; "I had hoped", *Euthyphro* 16a; "I think you didn't", *Cratylus* 278c.

58 Plato: *Euthydemus* 278d, *Phaedrus* 236d.

59 *Menexenus*: to make something up, 235c; they have speeches prepared and make up the rest, 235d; Aspasia's composition method, 236b.

60 The dominant improvisatory art form today is jazz; and jazz soloists frequently describe improvisation along the same lines. If they do not write out and memorize a piece and play it back during a performance, they also do not invent blindly without much-practised phrases.

61 See Thucydides *History* 2.36.1, 2.41.1.

62 *Ibid.*: 2.43.1.

63 Plutarch *Pericles* 24; see Athenaeus *Deipnosophistai* 12.533.

64 Thus in the *Theaetetus*, the interlocutor Theodorus moves from one metaphor for philosophizing to another. Socrates compares their conversation to wrestling in Sparta, 162b; Theodorus later remarks that Socratic conversation is rather like the deadly wrestling practised by Antaeus and Skiron, 169a–b. Either could be the kind of grappling that takes place in philosophy, so Theodorus supplants one metaphor with the other.

65 Thucydides *History* 2.37.1.

66 *Ibid.*: 1.25.

67 *Menexenus*: speeches prepared, not at random, 234c; sorcery, Socrates bewitched, seeming more august, 235b.

68 Plato on sorcery: *Meno* 80b, *Republic* 2.364b, *Symposium* 202e. *Laws* speaks strongly against permitting sorcery in the good city, 10.909b. See Gellrich (1994). On magic in Greek and Roman antiquity see Graf (1997).

69 Graf (1997: 118–74).

70 *Menexenus* 246c–248d.

Part III
MYTH AND HISTORY

7

MYTH

Stories of Athens

Together, the *Menexenus*'s mythical prehistory of Athens and the chronicle that follows take up two-thirds of the funeral speech, over nine Stephanus pages out of the speech's thirteen.[1] More than it does anything else, the *Menexenus* tells a story of Athens that sets Athens above other Greek cities and far above the non-Greeks.[2]

But it distorts this stretch of text to categorize it all generically as "narrative that boasts about Athens". Such a description is insensitive to the difference between Plato's uses of myth and of history. By his time the two were seen as distinct. Historians differentiated between myth and history before the death of Socrates, even making "myth" an insult, as both Herodotus and Thucydides do.[3]

The *Menexenus* does not belittle the mythic, but it does use myth and history for different even opposed purposes; so this chapter and the next will look separately at the two narratives. The myth of autochthony shows Athens uplifted, established as "the good city" or as good enough, very possibly the best this world can hope to see. The subsequent history watches Athens disintegrate, consistently better than all the other places to live in the world but finally only the best of a bad bunch.

Maybe Plato thinks that it takes divine intrusion into the natural order to show how a city ever came into existence that stood so tall among other cities. Historical time on the other hand might run entropically from bad to worse, perhaps because natural psychological principles tend towards degeneration. In that case decline would be the natural subject for every historical narrative.

With both types of narrative Plato departs from the task of writing a speech that answers the speech of Pericles. Pericles could not have been less interested in charting Athens's decline, not even a decline in which the city's nobility gleams through the darkness. When he gave his speech the city had not yet experienced anything he would call decline, such as a significant loss in wealth or in number of allies, even if some Platonic dialogues see Periclean democracy itself as the city's moral decline. As for praising his city: Pericles makes a case for Athenian exceptionalism as the mythic parts of the *Menexenus* do, but grounding the city's superiority in myth seems as alien to his own sensibilities as it does to those of Thucydides.

Indeed, all that Pericles says about the past comes in one brief passage. A funeral speech needs to recognize the original ancestors of today's Athenians, who occupied Attica and bequeathed it as a free home to later generations; then the "fathers" of today's audience, those immediate ancestors who founded the Athenian empire; finally the adults of the present day living and dead, both the soldiers being buried and their surviving peers. These last-named troops enlarged the city's holdings and tightened its rule over them. The founding of Athens and expansion of its empire are subjects for a mythic prehistory of the city followed by historical narrative. But rather than relate either kind of story Pericles contents himself with identifying the topics that those stories would cover if someone *did* tell them. He will skip the details; everyone listening knows them. The Athenian past, although the first order of business for a speech like this one, does not need to be recalled.[4]

So in one sense the *Menexenus* rebukes Pericles by the mere fact of telling stories about Athens. It already surpasses its predecessor when it supplies information about the city that Pericles calls important but that he does not give his listeners. His omission is another missed educational opportunity that Plato will make up for. Good teachers err on the side of saying what goes without saying.

Recall that another feature of the *Menexenus* speech is its audacious, even excessive praise; and that strong praise is another feature of funeral speeches that Pericles leaves out of his own. The powerful praise, the myth of Athenians' origins and the history of Athens may all be seen as the parts that Pericles left out of the speech Aspasia wrote for him – the leftovers she glued together to produce this speech. The idea that "gluing together those leftover parts" is self-evidently an insulting description of the speech[5] does not survive a serious look at what those leftover parts are.

But beyond noting the fact of a rebuke there is not much to say about the *Menexenus*'s reply to Pericles about myth and history. A few passages read as specific replies, such as Socrates' mention of how well poets have treated the legendary past of Athens, against the line in Pericles that dismisses Homer and other poets as irrelevant to Athens (discussed in the next section of this chapter). Otherwise the idea of a reply to Pericles is too general to inform a reading of the *Menexenus*. Any words at all can contradict silence. Why should Plato have chosen these particular words when he wanted to tell Athens's story? Pericles does not provide the counter-text for the *Menexenus* to be read against.[6]

Clavaud makes much of the fact, a fact no one could deny, that nothing in Pericles corresponds to the *Menexenus*'s myth and history of Athens. For Clavaud these Periclean silences confirm what is implied by his book's title (in English: "The *Menexenus* of Plato and the rhetoric of his time"), namely that Plato's funeral speech is a sustained parody of Athenian oratory, especially the oratory found in funeral speeches. Not Thucydides, the real author at work behind Pericles, but Lysias and the later orators are the targets of Plato's criticism.[7]

What most weakens Clavaud's claim in connection with the *Menexenus*'s historical narrative is his tendency to equate Pericles with Thucydides. As a matter of scholarly caution he refers to the Periclean funeral speech in connection with Thucydides, not Pericles. It is true that the speech comes from Thucydides, whether lightly or heavily edited by him; but even if all the speech of Pericles is Thucydides, not all the relevant Thucydides is in the speech of Pericles. Plato may well have expanded his sights, in the historical section of the *Menexenus* – seeing Thucydides as his real target – to outdo the historian's version of history-writing in addition to his version of speech-writing. Aspasia the tutor of Socrates is responding on a grand level to Antiphon the tutor of Thucydides.

The next chapter will spell out this hypothesis as a plausible and concrete rival reading. Plato's version of how Athens spent the preceding century will emerge not as a response to Pericles but as an alternative to history-writing as Thucydides had redefined that practice.

As for Athenians' birth from the earth, the problem with Clavaud's approach is that aside from Pericles only Lysias has written a funeral speech dating to a time before the *Menexenus* – nowhere near enough to define the genre's treatment of autochthony.[8] Although the later speeches by Demosthenes and Hyperides might join with the speech of Lysias to define the parameters of a genre that the *Menexenus* parodies, it is at least as plausible (as we have said) that the *Menexenus* speaks without parody, and thereby helped to define the genre within which Demosthenes and Hyperides place themselves. Their speeches would then attest not to the causes of how Plato wrote a funeral speech but to the effects of his speech, the *Menexenus* contributing to the genre as moderns know it rather than responding to a genre that moderns can reconstruct independently of the *Menexenus*.[9]

Take away Hyperides and Demosthenes, and the so-called tradition of autochthony in the known funeral speech genre comes down to Lysias saying that Athenians have the land of Attica as both *mêtera kai patrida* "mother and fatherland". This phrase supports Loraux's reading of a degradation of the mother in Athenian rhetoric; but it is so far from being a story, and with its emphasis in such a different place from the *Menexenus*'s, that it cannot be taken to establish oratorical autochthony, or to define the limits within which Plato writes. (This is not to comment on the problem that Lysias was a non-citizen, one whose citizen status was much contested and widely known. Surely talk of a mother–fatherland from him cannot be taken at face value.)

None of this means that the myth in Plato bursts into existence out of nowhere. It means that the reader needs to look elsewhere for a context that explains what Plato's prehistory of Athens does assert, and also what it does *not* assert. Part of that context appears in other dialogues' mentions of Athenian birth from earth – the *Republic* and *Laws* indirectly, *Timaeus* and *Critias* positively. Without yielding a univocal meaning of the myth for Plato, these passages show its continuities with the traditional myth as Athenians knew it, and (to the extent that historians can establish such a thing) as they practised it. This is what Nicole Loraux calls the "auto-chthony of the Acropolis", a story or belief not nearly as far from the *Menexenus* as her categorization implies it to be.[10]

Showing Plato to be speaking with and about the religious tradition, not just speaking to the rhetorical tradition, permits a close look at the story that the Athenians told themselves about their origins. For all the importance of that story's play with femininities, it also problematizes its masculine element in ways that modern readings underestimate. Entering the traditional story through Hephaestus, whom contemporary interpretations equate with the masculine or the patriarchal, reveals a contradiction of attributes – especially a difficult set of attributes to accept in one's first forebear – that the story of Athenian beginnings seeks to resolve. But seeing the traditional story as resolving one question about Athenian culture will show how the Platonic story brings a new question to the myth and finds a new way to answer it.

Mythic passages in the *Menexenus*

Autochthony is one of several traditional stories, all of them glorifying Athens, that Socrates brings into the first part of his speech.

Gods competed over Athens, he says by way of proof that the city is worth praising. Socrates mentions no names, but he must mean the competition between Athena and Poseidon. Perhaps Kekrops ruled Athens then, for the dynasty of Erichthonius had not come to the throne. In one version of this story Athena narrowly won a plebiscite in which all the women voted for her. The men wanted Poseidon for their local god but were outnumbered by the women, and after losing the plebiscite they retaliated by depriving women of the vote. Gifts were at stake, according to the ancient sources. Poseidon made seawater burst magnificently into the heart of the city; Athena gave a humble but practical olive tree, the start of Athens's plentiful groves and oil.[11]

In this form the story belongs among those myths that Plato's dialogues are forever trying to silence. If Plato does not advocate monotheism he moves towards it by seeking to remove all mention of disagreement between gods. (The difference between a polytheism of like-minded gods and monotheism is theologically subtle and often invisible.) The *Republic*'s critique of myth takes any stories of divine quarrels out of the young guardians' earshot; in the *Euthyphro* Socrates declares those stories impossible to believe. In Plato's *Critias* this objection is explicit. Gods could not distribute their holdings with fights or disagreements. Athena must have been *assigned* to her city.[12]

Why does the *Menexenus* allude to the story without mentioning the gods' names? It may be that a taboo prohibited Athenians from calling upon the heavenly gods on an occasion of death; and Socrates is reciting a funeral speech, or purporting to. (He is not exactly pretending to recite one; but he is *pretending to be reciting*.[13]) Does Plato leave the gods unnamed in the interests of verisimilitude? He does not always hew to the fictional strictures of his dialogues that scrupulously, but the taboo might have been so powerful that no Athenian even pretended to be giving a funeral speech without omitting the gods' names.

Even so the omission could be over-determined. It is possible that Plato has other motives operating. He may well want to bowdlerize the patriotic myth whose full version would offend him. Socrates softens the image of a quarrel between gods by redescribing the event as their "praise" for Athens, as if what Poseidon and Athena had really wanted to do was pay the city a compliment; then softens the image further by leaving out the divine names that might call the unseemly scene to mind.

And Socrates could have another reason not to mention Athena's name. This suggestion will have to wait until later in the present chapter and the *Menexenus*'s myth of autochthony, which seems bent on excluding Athena from what had been her story. If the dialogue's myths are excluding her in particular, they will have to pass over the details of her competition against Poseidon.

Another reference to mythic matters, if more direct than this allusion to Athena and Poseidon, might puzzle the reader. Socrates says that legend attributes noble wars to Athens. The city fought against Amazons and Eumolphus of Eleusis, and against some Greek cities on behalf of others. The city's only cause for war has been pan-Hellenism. Socrates draws the customary moral from these stories but begs off elaborating. Poets told these tales much better already *en mousikêi humnêsantes* "celebrating [them] in music". Instead of repeating them, he will speak of things as no poet has. With that remark the myths give way to history and Socrates explains the beginnings of the Persian wars.[14]

This last remark is surprising both for what is true in it and for what is false. Poets had indeed told of the mythic wars in which Athenians drove off the Amazons, but Plato rarely takes the trouble to give due credit to poets. And then on the other hand, the contrast between mythic subjects the poets treated well already and the historical accomplishments left unsung, disregards the attention that Athenian literature paid to Marathon and other battles against Persia.[15] Poets did not do anything like neglect the Persian War. Most famously from today's perspective, and no doubt quite famously then, Aeschylus' *Persians* details the battle of Salamis, widely seen then and now as the decisive Greek victory.

Plato's dialogues usually find him both knowledgeable about the poets and contemptuous of their achievements. In this passage the funeral speech manages to sound neither knowledgeable nor scornful.

The next chapter ought to inform the question of poets' having told of battles against Persia. The shape that the *Menexenus* imparts to Athenian history will appear in that chapter as an unprecedented approach to historical narrative; in this sense what Socrates says in apparent ignorance will prove to be true. No one else has told the story *in these terms*, which are the right terms to tell it in.

The next chapter ought to show that, far from ignoring *Persians*, the historical narrative in the *Menexenus* replies to it. For if, as we have already suggested, the *Menexenus* stages a philosophical rejoinder to the *Persians* (perhaps even on the occasion of the play's revival), it is fitting that Plato should dismiss Aeschylus' account of the battle at Salamis as failing even to begin telling the history of Athens.

In any case, what the poets have already said covers a minor part of the past. The *Menexenus*'s history extends beyond the battles against Persia to events that poets truly did not tell of. As for the uncharacteristic respect being paid towards poetry about Athens and its legends, what seems surprising there contradicts not the actual Plato but a caricature of his arguments against the poets. The *Phaedrus* and *Republic* both approve of poetry that records and honours great achievements; and when they do, it barely comes up that such works were written in verse.[16]

There might be a rejoinder to Pericles buried in this acknowledgement of poetry's value to the city. Pericles sneered at the honour that a poet might bequeath upon Athens. The Athenians have no need for Homer nor for any other *epainetou* "admirer, one who praises", whose words bring passing enjoyment but "whose interpretation of our deeds [*ergôn*] the truth of the matter will outdo [*blapsei*]". This dismissal goes together with Pericles' devaluation of words compared with action, and with the warning about praise that begins his speech. It brings to mind what Thucydides the narrator says about his chronicle's superiority to fanciful tales that please for a moment.[17]

On the other hand Thucydides speaks of Homer with respect even when expressing scepticism about specific elements in the epics.[18] So the contrast between Athenian accomplishments and Homeric praise might have a more pointed reference. It is hard to say too much about the specifics of events dating back a century before Pericles, but (1) it is obvious to readers today and was noted in antiquity that Athens played a small role in the *Iliad* and *Odyssey*; (2) the Athenian tyrant Peisistratus and his dynasty were associated with some standardization of Homer's poems in the sixth century; and (3) also in the sixth century, probably during one of the Peisistratids' reigns, Athens quoted *Iliad* 2.558 to substantiate its right to the nearby island of Salamis. This last datum comes from Aristotle and sounds credible;[19] the diminutive place for Athens in Homer is immediately visible; and (1) and (3) together are enough to show that Homeric authority mattered concretely in the Greek world and Athens lacked the status that Athenians would have thought they deserved.

As for (2), the ancient testimony speaks confusingly about what Peisistratus and his sons did with Homer. The pseudo-Platonic dialogue *Hipparchus*, written in the fourth century, claims that this Hipparchus (son of Peisistratus, the most popular of his successors) both *ekomisen* "provided" the *Iliad* and *Odyssey* to Athens and established the rules for Athenian rhapsodes reciting the epics. Together with other evidence this passage has been taken to show that the clan of Peisistratus, the Peisistratids, established a "Panathenaic rule" that the rhapsodes must follow in adherence to a strictly ordered Homeric text. At the very least the Peisistratids encouraged the belief that they sponsored and controlled performances of Homer, as they were credited with having made tragedy available.[20]

According to later and less reliable sources, the family of Peisistratus accounted for more than the sequence in which to read Homer's epics. Strabo and Plutarch pass along the report of an interpolation: Athenians in the sixth century inserted the lines that made Salamis a long-time possession of their city. Strabo says that either Peisistratus or Solon inserted the lines, Plutarch and Diogenes insisting it was Solon and *not* Peisistratus, an insistence that implies an older tradition crediting Peisistratus. Other late authors speak of a complete "Homeric recension", again the work of Peisistratid Athens, that collected the fragments that were being recited in a hodgepodge by rhapsodes into a standard edition of Homer.[21]

Whichever story is closest to the truth, and whatever the Athenians believed, the story associates an appropriation of Homer, for patriotic purposes, with the tyranny that many in Athens looked back on as a golden age. Homer may have been the legacy of all Greeks but he also belonged to Peisistratus.[22] "We" however (Pericles is saying), Athenians living under democracy, no longer need the tyrants' subterfuge. The Athenians may have won territory on paper in the days of the Peisistratids; in the time of Pericles they won on land and sea.

If Pericles did cast Homer off not only because actions count for more than fancy words, but also because "Homer" signified an outmoded tyranny, then a rival funeral speaker who defers to the storytelling poets of old appears to be a speaker wedded to the city's traditions, and less committed to its democratic present. Then the *Menexenus* acknowledges the poets' testimony as a way of honouring the longstanding city of Athens, independent of its recent incarnation as a democracy.

There is a question at work here of whether to equate a state with its form of government. An Athens identified with its democratic constitution might feel the need to reject any tradition tainted by its association with tyrants. But Athens seen as a place and a legacy can embrace what Peisistratus accomplished on the city's behalf, for that city is only contingently – maybe only transitorily – a democracy. The *Menexenus* itself says that despite going by the name of "democracy" Athens is an aristocracy in vital respects, as if to keep the city distinct from its present form of government.[23]

It is fitting for another reason that Athenian identity should be at stake in Socrates' remark about poet-chroniclers. This theme – *what makes Athens the thing it is now* – runs through the sequence of mythic passages, from Athena's competition with Poseidon down to the military history; and, between these two, the main myth recounted in the *Menexenus*, the one this chapter is focusing on, this dialogue's version of the story that the first Athenians were first born from the Athenian earth.

In other ways the passage is a motley one. The opening and closing myths are spoken of, not told. They generate their lessons quickly and directly – they exist only in order to lead to those lessons. The competition between the gods proves the city's merit; its mythical military history demonstrates the altruistic pan-Hellenism of Athens. These are the morals that Athenians regularly drew from these stories. Indeed Socrates can cite the myths and their morals in such shorthand fashion exactly because they are customary tales and he takes them in the customary way. Neither content nor import needs revisiting.

But between the beginning and end of this myth-passage Socrates recounts a myth rather than just referring to it, and when he does he makes that myth a new story with new meaning. Ge (earth) brought forth the first people of Attica, ancestors of all subsequent Athenians.[24] True mother that she was, Ge nursed the babies she had borne. She fed them with spontaneous growths of wheat, barley and olives; then she saw to the first Athenians' education under the care of gods who taught them the *technai* "professions, skills" necessary for war and peace.

Some version of autochthony, as birth from the native land is commonly known, had been told in Athens before the birth of Socrates. Nevertheless the *Menexenus* does not draw a single familiar moral from autochthony but finds several implications in the story about Athens's place in the larger world. This speech does not even tell the old story in the old way. This alleged spoof that allegedly recycles clichés of previous speeches in fact departs from the tradition of Athenian autochthony. Who the Athenians' parents are, the circumstances under which they make their babies, and who cares for the first local people, are all transformed in this telling. The *Menexenus* puts autochthony to new work. This is the dialogue's true mythic subject. And together with the history of Athens that follows, this myth tells a new story about the city.

Plato's myths

This myth of autochthony operates within the context of the *Menexenus* but also against the backdrop of Platonic myths as a whole. Mythic passages occur in Plato's dialogues with enough regularity that the reader of any one of them needs to have some sense of the myths as a whole, with repeating features and certain persisting goals.[25]

The pages ahead might seem to interrupt this chapter's treatment of the *Menexenus*'s myth, but general comments about myth-writing in Plato are not gratuitous. There are numerous theories and pictures of the Platonic myths afield among his readers; it is surprising how many theories ignore the religion in the myths, which is to say ignore the lives and the import that a given myth had before Plato appropriated it for his own purposes. What follows is an attempt to reorient the discussion of Plato's myths before addressing the *Menexenus*, so that it becomes clear why we frame its autochthony strategy in the way we do, against the backdrop of autochthony myths in Athens.

There is no other way to say it. The myths make trouble. From observations about shoemaking or a geometrical proof, a dialogue swerves to tell what Zeus decided to do about virtue. Plato's dialogues labour at teaching their readers how to reason, then conversation gives way to mythologizing as if to throw that hard-won rationality to the wind. Should the reader swerve too and replace rational inquiry with pious appreciation? What becomes of reading when Platonic writing becomes something so different?

Earlier generations emphasized the difference between philosophy and myth in Plato's works. This is sometimes spoken of, in the dialogues' vocabulary, as the difference between *logos* "reason, speech, account, argument" and *muthos* "myth, tale, story". And an interpreter might say, as interpreters did say, that the myths in his dialogues let Plato explain what he could not know by other means or what he could not say by other means. The philosophical *logos* with its precision and logic suits one kind of truth but it cannot either grasp or communicate those other truths, possibly higher truths, that the myths concern themselves with: death and the afterlife, the origin of human beings or of organized society, or of the physical universe.

Such a scholarly approach has piety on its side, but it lends itself to excesses that obstruct interpretation. To say "These truths are ineffable" is a conclusion, not a guide. And most philosophers today avoid discussions of mystic insight and higher ways of knowing. It is not surprising that the philosophers who read Plato should want to avoid dwelling on the myths' mystic natures. Instead, the consensus today emphasizes the closeness between myth and philosophy for Plato. In the recent anthology that appears to have defined this consensus, the editor's introduction speaks of the philosophy and myth in the dialogues being "interwoven". One contributor, who explicitly denies old commonplaces about Platonic myth and the unsayable or the irrational, instead calls the myths "extended similes", no more "outside" the philosophical in the dialogues than any other simile is. Another author in the volume reads the *Timaeus*'s story of creation in a way that shows how – for that myth, anyway – an appropriate *muthos* becomes indistinguishable from appropriate *logos*.[26]

On this approach, the myths persuade and teach their readers.[27] This function explains why interpreters do not need to classify Platonic myth as radically different from Platonic argument. Not only do the myths continue the project of the arguments, this purpose that they have undercuts images of Plato the mystic seer, possessed by Muses as he releases some radically other type of discourse. Plato *can* always state his point in clear philosophical language, even if he sometimes *chooses* to state it in mythical language to reach audiences for whom philosophy's vocabulary is unattractive or foreign.

This way of understanding the myths in Plato makes them resemble the *Republic*'s noble lie, that falsehood to be promulgated inside the good city as religious propaganda. But reading the myths as persuasive does not commit you to the view that they aim *downwards*, whether towards the ignorant or just towards the chronically ill-behaved. And some adherents to this general theory of the myths distance themselves from condescending pictures of the persuasion they bring about. Christopher Rowe calls the myths a "bridge" connecting the dialogues' arguments with the concerns and values that Plato's non-philosopher readers might have. This horizontal metaphor (there may be a ladder from heaven to earth but never a bridge) reinforces what Rowe says in literal terms, that the myths may well bring equals to understand one another, not necessarily inferiors to understand their superior.[28]

David Sedley goes further. He interprets the myth of the afterlife that concludes the *Gorgias* as an allegory restating symbolically what that dialogue argued for with premises and logic. Certainly as allegory was practised in ancient Greece it was directed towards an audience of insiders. An allegory bypassed the ignorant, as riddles did, to inform the enlightened or the initiates. Now the myths seem to aim at equals, not at the unwashed crowd that is most often imagined as the audience for propaganda.[29]

But if the "persuasion and pedagogy" view of Plato's myths avoids the simplistic sense of them as propaganda, in another way the question "What does Plato mean to do with his myths?" still simplifies the reader's task. The question makes Plato's intention when writing myths the end of the inquiry. But one of the compelling features of most of the myths, as well as what makes them such trouble for Plato's readers, is that they lived a full existence outside his dialogues.

This point leads to the second way in which the noble lie differs from most mythic passages in Plato, which may matter more than the lie's being consciously designed propaganda. The audience for the noble lie, unlike Plato's readers and unlike Plato himself and every other Greek of antiquity, knows only a moralistically edited mythology. Growing up in the good city, children hear no stories about the gods' lusts, lies, form-changes or capricious infliction of misfortune on mortals. Because their acquaintance with the myths has been so restricted, when *these* people hear the noble lie it will say only and definitely what their elders mean it to say. In fact the lie's meaning will be all that the city's rulers *can* mean when they repeat it, because the rulers grew up learning the same expurgated mythology. It is as if the city's young people first learned an artificial language and then received instruction in that language, from teachers who knew only the same language. Under such circumstances words can indeed take their meaning from the intent with which they are spoken.

These audiences' condition contrasts with the condition of the audience that hears the other myths in the dialogues – the audience that hears those myths as opposed to *over*hearing them, as Plato's readers overhear the noble lie. As a rule the myths go out to characters inside the dialogues, and to readers outside them, who know a wealth of myths in excess of the catechism that Plato would have preferred people to have received. In just about every case except the noble lie, Plato has to use a mythic language he did not create or prune into shape.

Plato's scholarly commentators recognize the mythic raw material he works into "his" myths. In the same recent collection, Charles Kahn identifies the traditional antecedents to the *Statesman*'s myth of the age of Cronus; Malcolm Schofield shows what became of the mythic ingredients to the noble lie; for Catalin Partenie's overview of the volume it is essential to begin a general description with the traditional stories that Plato himself calls by the name *muthoi*. To similar effect G. R. F. Ferrari distinguishes the contrived stories that the Sophists used to illustrate their themes from the genuinely "religious" mythopoeia in Plato.[30] And yet acknowledging that traditional myths exist beneath the myths in Plato is only the first step in charting how the Platonic stories arose from the traditional ones, where they changed or did not change in the process, and to what effect. Because Plato's readers did not grow up in the *Republic*'s city, the stories and mythical characters they find in his dialogues will carry surpluses of associations. It is an open question, needing separate inquiry in each case, how these additional meanings amplify and deepen – or where they reverse, negate and pervert – the Platonically intended meanings of the myths.

In the *Phaedo* Socrates associates himself with Apollo, saying he composed a hymn to that god. Apollo brought lucid dreams like Socrates' own, and health and wise counsel. But Aeschylus' *Agamemnon* shows him to be a distant god unmoved by tears, and the *Iliad* begins with his plagues and help to the enemy.[31] As a figure devoted to Apollo Socrates offers insights worthy of an oracle and shows friends how they can heal their souls; but his peers might also find him Apollonian in his scorn for the tears of intimates, his fondness for the city's enemy Sparta, or the plague of anti-democratic sentiment he was suspected of having brought to Athens. As long as Apollo remains a complex character, which will remain the case for as long as Greek religion resists Plato's efforts to reform it, linking Socrates to him will potentially mean more than the comparison was intended to mean.

Something similar occurs in connection with David Sedley's reading of the myth in *Gorgias*, according to which that myth recapitulates the dialogue's ethical argument. Sedley proposes that Zeus represents Socrates; which means that Socrates is bringing a new soul-examining morality to Athens, as Zeus (in this myth) brought soul-examination to the last judgement that assigns human beings to eternal reward or punishment. Socrates as Zeus the

Saviour and guarantor of the moral order: all very well. But this myth refers to Zeus' "inheriting" his power from Cronus. The old stories make clear it was a sons' revolt against their fathers that brought the new order. Is Socrates another Zeus in this respect too? Meletus and Anytus could not have put their charges more strongly than if they too had called Socrates morality's "Zeus the upstart".[32]

To return to Rowe's description of Platonic myths as "extended similes": the difference between simile and metaphor nicely captures the difference between how the Platonic myths tend to be read, as if (simile-like) commanding the traditional materials that they invoke, and on the other hand an approach to reading them that finds indefinitely more suggestions for an interpretation in those traditional materials, as one can say indefinitely more in explicating metaphors.

The work of a simile comes to an end when you give the point of it; for this reason similes often appear together with a statement of their point. A new car is like a ticket to the moon. You will travel 250,000 miles but at an outlandish price. In a metaphor however one finds unspecifiably many resemblances. As Stanley Cavell says, paraphrases of metaphors imply "and so on",[33] the paraphrases having no definable conclusion. A car's front window is a shield (whence its name "windshield") in that you drive holding it out in front of you; and it protects you; and its forward face is convex; and cars resemble armoured soldiers; and they move in a phalanx; and so on. Even without rhapsodizing over the power of metaphor one can see metaphor and simile as two different figures that call for distinct ways of interpreting.

For Plato's reader, seeing the myth as a simile precises and constrains interpretation. There are many reasons to prefer interpretation under such conditions. But Greek myths make better metaphors than similes. The divine characters in them possess tangled and conflicting attributes, and the divine actions in the myths tend to be imbedded in larger complexes of story.

Plato's dialogues themselves seem to see myths this way, resisting exact interpretation rather than yielding to it. This point needs to be made in specific terms; as a general description of all the myth-filled passages in the dialogues it fails. The allegory of the cave, for one, loses nothing when it is translated into a ranking of cognitive states and their objects. There is nothing supernatural in this story. It is an extended simile as other Platonic inventions also are, comparable with the Sophists' stories that Ferrari speaks of. Again, in the *Symposium* Socrates says that *penia* "Poverty" seduced *poros* "Resourcefulness" and bore him the love-child Love. Entirely unlike the many-faceted particularities who inhabit traditional myths, these divine parents amount to a single abstract trait apiece; their Love is a two-splendoured thing. If *penia* and *poros* were anything but need and capability, the story would fail, which shows how barely it resembles a story to begin with.[34]

Stripping a myth off to see the assertion inside is easier when Plato stitched together the myth in the first place to fit that assertion. The dialogues also treat some traditional myths as no more than the lessons they can be translated into. Thus the eschatological myths cited in the *Laws*, familiar tales of afterlife reward and punishment that the characters acknowledge and do not tell;[35] also the myths that Socrates cites in the *Menexenus* that prove how good Athens is. Such stories become extended similes by virtue of being treated that way.

A different treatment is evident in the *Statesman*. The Stranger in that dialogue tells a story about alternating epochs, one in which a great providence governs the universe and the contrary type – of which the present age is an example – without divine rule, in which humans have to take care of themselves. Depending which way the universe spins, the world experiences either a golden age or the familiar circumstances of scarcity, labour and force.[36]

The story aims at a moral. An imperfect time like the present calls for pragmatic politics. There is no point in arriving at an idealized definition of a statesman when the world in which statesmen must operate is itself so far from ideal. But the Stranger's own remarks warn against over-emphasizing this assessment of the story. He reflects that he hoisted a *thaumaston ogkon tou muthou* "wondrous bulk of myth" and then used *meizoni* "a larger amount" of it than would have been necessary for making the point.[37] To rule out utopian thinking it would have sufficed to say that the people of the present do not live in a golden age. But to explain the present age one therefore has to explain golden ages, to make clear what is missing from this one. So the Stranger drew on an old story about Cronus to create a contrast with the present era, and under the spell of that story he shifted his attention from the known world to this unknowable one that lies both behind the present and ahead of it. The myth, meant to show up the imperfections of this age, created an age that purported to be something positive and more than "not now". The myth exceeded the purpose it was put to.

For example, the people in the golden age grow younger each year, and they may or may not spend their time philosophizing.[38] We do not know, the Stranger says. It is impossible to tell whether one philosophizes without aging, whether a youthful creature facing no decrepitude ahead would make the effort to practise dialectic. This is a deadly addendum to the myth's stated purpose, which had been to proscribe those quests for definitions that are suited to an ideal world. For it now seems possible that philosophy in some guises has no home anywhere, neither in the present godforsaken world where one *should* not seek the true (divine) statesman nor in the world that has god at the helm, where one could live contentedly without bothering to.

The myth gives more than a statement about philosophy's limits. It reveals a vision of the universe that yields up more than it might have been meant to. The myth can be elaborated or paraphrased indefinitely further.

When some dialogues advise against the allegorical interpretation of myths, it seems again that myths will not boil down into non-mythical statements. One famous example occurs early in the *Phaedrus*, when Socrates demurs from giving a naturalistic explanation for the myth about Boreas and Orethyia. Is this myth about the north-wind god's kidnapping a maiden just a way of saying – is it an extended simile that says – that a gust of wind blew the girl off a cliff? Socrates would rather examine his own soul than embark on speculations about myths. This contrast that he draws makes myth the domain of symbols that resist translation.[39]

The warning in *Republic* 2 is more direct. Socrates is reviewing the myths that attribute immoral behaviour to the gods. He recognizes that some people interpret these stories so that they say something quite different from what they seem to mean. Without denying the merits of such interpretations, without denying that they might say true things about the myths, Socrates says they do not offer enough protection. Young people won't know which part is the *huponoia* "hidden meaning". They will retain only the surface meaning that Hephaestus bound Hera to her throne and was thrown down by his father.[40] This caution begins with the thought that the myths do not disappear when they have been unriddled. Something in their stories persists despite having been interpreted.

A less attended-to passage from the *Theaetetus* returns to these issues. In the *Iliad* the god Ocean is called "the origin of all" and Socrates equates this claim with the Heraclitean doctrine of flux. Homer conceals the Ephesian philosophy in myth, apparently to his credit, because Socrates criticizes the Ephesians for delivering the same doctrine in open literal terms. On the view that Plato's myths are propaganda, the mythic form ought to popularize the doctrine, but here Socrates is saying the opposite.[41] Philosophers who tell their doctrine straight let every passer-by take it in. Mythic form resists widespread comprehension; something is lost when you render a myth in literal terms; the mythic form must contain something not accounted for in a non-mythic version of the same doctrine.

Philosophers have to become passive about myths. This seems to be the import of the passage in the *Phaedo* concerning Socrates and the command he dreamt of "practice music". Socrates thought the philosophical conversations that he fell or jumped into were music enough. Awaiting execution he decides to play it safe and write poetry; but a poem needs a *muthos*, and being incapable of inventing stories Socrates takes some from Aesop.[42]

This episode lets Plato put a contrast in Socrates' mouth that illuminates his own writing, between writing that begins by taking over known *muthoi* and the music that Socrates naturally composed, or Plato's variation on that tune, namely (spoken or written) philosophical conversation. If the purpose of philosophical exchange is saying what you mean just as you want it said, then adopting *muthoi* departs from that practice by relinquishing control over what is being said. Where writers draw their material from existing sources they cannot control what the *muthos* says and means.

What Plato means his myths to say is an inescapable question about them, but not the only question to ask. There is also: what would this myth be saying otherwise? What does it mean *but for Plato?* Like the Demiurge forced to make the world out of recalcitrant matter, Plato must begin with the wondrous bulks of myths that are already there before him. No doubt the persuasive power of myth recommends myth to him, but he remains wary of the mythic elements his readers have already learned, that he would have preferred them not to know.

So the myths, and certainly such stories as autochthony in the *Menexenus*, call for exploratory looking, first at traditional versions of the story being told and then at any variations that appear in other dialogues. Autochthony permits both kinds of exploration, for other versions of that story are known from sources independent of Plato, and Plato also speaks of autochthony elsewhere in his corpus. The *Republic*'s noble lie in part retells an autochthony story, and three other dialogues allude to it. Those passages are a natural second stop on the path back to the *Menexenus* and its story about where Athens came from.

Autochthony in Athens

It is tempting to analyse the autochthony tradition into distinct versions, for all the reasons one usually has for dividing a large field of data into smaller subjects. Readers have not resisted this temptation enough. Loraux identifies two genres of the story; she labels them "Acropolis" and "Kerameikos" to signify respectively autochthony as it was known in Athenian tragedies staged in the shadow of the Acropolis – the *Ion* of Euripides the pre-eminent example – and the kind that was promulgated by the Athenian funeral orations, whose speakers delivered them in the Kerameikos quarter, the area for graves and burials.[43]

Separating the myth into two varieties leaves the *Menexenus* commenting not on Athenian autochthony as such but only on a restricted variety of autochthony proper to the funeral speeches. The speech of Socrates speaks to the autochthony of the Kerameikos not to Acropolis autochthony. Socrates is addressing Athenian rhetoric and not broader manifestations of the belief in autochthony.

This restriction is already false. Other passages in Plato testify to the importance he attaches to autochthony as part of the civic religion, not just a feature of local speechmaking. The dialogues covered in the next section equate autochthony with the origin of all people, but nothing in those passages connects them with Athenian funeral rhetoric, as they would have to be connected if a robust Kerameikos tradition governed such stories of autochthony.

In any case, the taxonomy rests on slim evidence. To say that autochthony takes a particular form in the funeral speeches, a form that then explains the version of autochthony found in the *Menexenus*, one would need to cite references to autochthony found in the speeches before Plato's. This rules out

Hyperides and Demosthenes, whose funeral orations respond to a genre to which the *Menexenus* has contributed. For another reason it rules out Pericles, who is silent about the subject. Indeed the word *autochthôn* only appears in the *History of the Peloponnesian War* "to refer to the claim of the Sicilian Sicans to be autochthonous", and Thucydides denies that claim.[44]

The oratorical tradition of autochthony before the *Menexenus* therefore consists of one sentence. Lysias says that the Athenians, "unlike most people, were not gathered together from everywhere to inherit a strange land after having driven other people out; but, being autochthonous [*autochthones ontes*] held the same place as both mother and fatherland [*mêtera kai patrida*]".[45] This sentence is consistent with autochthony as the *Menexenus* presents it, but also consistent with any number of other stories. Athenians belong in Athens and the earth is their mother – this is not exactly going out on a limb or spinning a yarn. And recall that as a non-citizen Lysias would never have been allowed to deliver a funeral speech, nor encouraged to write a patriotic speech like this one for someone else to recite. His oration must have been a display-piece; and to the degree that Plato is indeed commenting on the tradition of public speeches that have been given in Athens, he will *not* be referring to Lysias.[46]

The allegedly sharp distinction between two great varieties of autochthony thus comes down to one variation that occurs within the tradition, that the stories sometimes credit Athenians *en masse* with having been born from Ge, and sometimes attribute autochthonous birth only to one or two members of the city's ruling family. The tradition includes stories about a first king Erechtheus; sometimes he is called Erichthonius, but elsewhere Erichthonius is the earthborn figure and is the father of Erechtheus. Yet other stories identify an even earlier king, Kekrops, also born from the earth. Euripides' *Ion* alludes to an autochthonous king, as the *Iliad* also does. But by Plato's time, and not just in Lysias, the earth had been claimed as the place of origin for all Athenians. This seems to be the implication of a line in Aristophanes' *Wasps*, for instance, a play from Plato's childhood whose chorus of old Athenian men claims to be autochthonous.[47]

In fact the two kinds of stories work in tandem and the difference between them is minor. In order to go from an ancient king's earthly origin to their own origin, people who tell these stories only need one additional premise, that they are descended from their founding king. And this is not a rare belief. When the first king blurs into the first ancestor, what makes the king also makes the king's people.

The best proof of this point may be found in the premier representative of the so-called "Acropolis tradition", the *Ion* of Euripides. This play explains the legitimacy of its title character Ion by fitting him into the family of Erichthonius. The political consequences of his genealogy are widely recognized; for the Athenians with their Attic dialect, so close to the Ionian version of Greek, often reinforced their closeness with the Ionians of the eastern Aegean islands and the coast of Asia Minor. After the events in this play, Ion – now established as part of the Athenian family – will go on to sire the Ionian people. But in order for this play to be commenting about Athenians as an ethnicity and Ionians as a related ethnicity, it must be assuming that *the origin of a people is the origin of their primordial king*. It could not fulfil its political purpose otherwise. So why the make-believe about crossing town to hear a completely different version of autochthony? Stories about the birth of the first king are one way of telling the beginning of the ethnicity. In Adam's birth we all share earth.

The main source available today for the complete story of Athenian autochthony dates to some centuries after Plato. The work by Apollodorus called *Library* multiplies the unique first Athenian births: Apollodorus calls Kekrops the first king and an *autochthôn*, and then tells how the later figure Erichthonius was also born from the earth. This latter story also contains elements not found in Euripides, beginning with the god Hephaestus. According to Apollodorus, Athena visited the workshop of Hephaestus seeking armour and he tried to rape her. She eluded his advances – evidently ardent advances, because Hephaestus *apespermênen* "ejaculated" onto Athena's thigh. She used a wad of wool to wipe the semen to the ground. Once on the ground, and possessed of the efficacy that the gods' seed had in Greek mythology, it impregnated Ge. After having given birth to the baby Erichthonius, Ge turned him over to Athena, who kept him in a basket.[48]

Despite the late date for the version in Apollodorus, many parts of this story are attested from an early time. Athenian vase paintings depict Erichthonius reaching up to Athena. The ritual re-enactment of this story at the annual festival the Panathenaea involved a basket commemorating the one that Athena kept the baby in, a container Euripides invokes in the *Ion*, which tells of Ion as an infant cradled in the style of Erichthonius.[49]

Given the antiquity of the tradition, it is noteworthy that the *Ion* fails to mention the part that Hephaestus plays. Ge and Athena bear and rear Erichthonius regardless of who his father must have been. The story seems fully capable of going on as it was without him. And that is odd in turn because the Athenian variety of autochthony has been interpreted as degrading women. Hephaestus the phallic patriarch creates a son through his efforts alone. "The first Athenian was not born from the union of the sexes, but from their disjunction". In this ultimate rape fantasy, male wilfulness suffices to make babies. Male babies suffice too, for that matter. There was no tradition in Athens of autochthonous women.[50]

The *Ion*'s use of autochthony suggests that the story moves along well without Hephaestus. Indeed something stronger is the case. The traditional myth itself removes and replaces him. The myth is about his removal and replacement. Hephaestus leaves his semen and the story never mentions him again. The real action concerns two goddesses and the child who passes from one to the other. This early king and founding father comes from Ge but learns from Athena, while the variation in the part that Hephaestus plays suggests some awkwardness about him as the king's father. If autochthony excludes the species woman, this myth also excludes a species of man.

This is not to pretend that the myth is denying or supplanting patriarchy, as if grounding Athens in proto-feminism. Quite the contrary, this myth poses no threat to Greek patriarchy, inasmuch as its father figure does not belong clearly in any category of idealized divine fatherhood. Zeus defines sky-god patriarchy, and other Olympians (Apollo, Hermes, Ares) resemble Zeus enough to count as model father-gods. Poseidon and Hades are genuine patriarchs, even if they draw their strength from the earth or the underworld. Hephaestus stands alone. For one thing he possesses none of the other gods' attractiveness. Despised by his mother Hera, cuckolded by his wife Aphrodite, and (in the autochthony story) refused by Athena, he stands at the opposite extreme from Paris, the exemplar of desirability whose approving judgement those three goddesses courted. The mythic tradition makes Hephaestus an outsider to the Olympians' company, ugly and lame where they are beautiful, hard-working (they would never dream of labour), a cuckold, and the one god the others all laugh at.

Not just a literalization of his otherness – though it is that too – but a fact presented to explain that otherness, is Hephaestus' repeated departure from Olympus. He does not have a stable place in the heavenly home of the sky gods but is the only one of them who gets thrown off Olympus and stays away in a pique. The *Iliad* recalls when Zeus hurled Hephaestus to earth, then adds a story of Hera's having done the same to him, perhaps as a consequence of the first hurling (for she is ashamed to have a disabled son). "Hephaestus is expelled from Olympus as if he did not really belong there", one commentator says. In a tradition outside Homer Hephaestus sends Hera a beautiful throne from down on earth; she sits down and it magically binds her. The gods plead with Hephaestus to return and release her from the throne but he refuses. Finally Dionysus, the only god that Hephaestus trusts, gets him drunk and puts him on a donkey to lead him back up to Mount Olympus.[51]

Hephaestus' distance from Olympus can be restated as his closeness to earth. He trusts the vegetation god Dionysus. As the lame god he hobbles bent to the ground; as god of the forge he works in cave-like smithies with metals taken from deep inside the earth. His original association may have been with fire and especially the volcanic (geothermic) kind.

Sources outside Homer make Hephaestus the son of Hera alone, therefore a counterpart to Athena the daughter of Zeus alone. As the product of Zeus and notably of his head, Athena enters life untouched by the feminine unpleasantries of reproduction. She belongs only in the sky. The origin of Hephaestus is nothing but parturition, feminine unpleasantry unrelieved by a masculine contribution. He even absorbs some of his mother's duties in connection with marriage and birth, and it is as a male god of childbirth rather than as the male Athena that Hephaestus splits Zeus' skull open so that she can be born.[52]

The other child that Hera produces alone is Typhone or Tuphaeon, himself practically a son of Ge and certainly a monster. If deformed Hephaestus is the cause of Hera's greatest rage against Zeus, the mighty effect of that rage is Typhon. Hera prays to Ge and to the Titans imprisoned inside the earth. She strikes the *chthona* "ground" and makes the new monster.[53] The nearest kin to Hephaestus is non-Olympian and all-earth, even if it is one who stands even further removed from the heavenly order.

In the *Odyssey* the physical distance between Hephaestus and Mount Olympus is linked to his wife's unfaithfulness. Ares slips into Hephaestus' bed telling Aphrodite that her husband has gone to the island of Lemnos to be with *Sintias agriophônous* "wild-talking Sintians". This adjective recalls the *Iliad*'s *barbarophônos* "foreign-tongued", said of the non-Greek Carians. The Sintians are not only uncouth but probably also foreign. Lemnos was a cultic centre for Hephaestus, another one being the nearby Samothrace, and both islands were said to have been settled by the Pelasgians of Attica. Herodotus says that when the Athenians drove these indigenous non-Greeks out of Attica they settled Lemnos and Samothrace, the ones in Samothrace introducing the cult of the hobbling Kabeiroi who might have been known as sons of Hephaestus.[54]

In other words, even among humans Hephaestus trafficks with outsiders. That movement no doubt explains his frequent border crossing among gods.

Along with his faults, Hephaestus possesses a keen intelligence and skilled hands. He makes beautiful objects, including emblems of civilization: the shield of Achilles, but also Zeus' sceptre and aegis and Hera's bedchamber.[55] Homer calls him *klutotechnês* "glorious craftsman", *polumêtis* "of much wisdom", *poluphrôn* "of much intelligence", and (in the *Homeric Hymn* to Hephaestus) *klutomêtis* "of glorious wisdom".[56]

Ancient creation stories could differ widely in the genus of creative power they attributed to gods. Some create by giving birth, as when Ge spawned Uranus, others by manufacturing. Hephaestus is fecund and earthy, bent on reproducing, but also intelligently productive, thereby combining both ways of creation in his person. Reproductive creation is aristocratic and natural, more characteristically Greek. Manufacture is intelligent but it can suggest servility; in any case the Greeks kept it segregated from reproductive creation. Besides Hephaestus the deity most associated with skilful production is the virgin Athena. The single name Hephaestus now represents a concatenation of traits that the Greeks would have seen in tension with one another or even contradictory.

Athenian autochthony as traditionally understood works to resolve the contradiction embodied in Hephaestus. (You do not have to read this as a problem with his non-Greek allegiances, but seeing Hephaestus as foreign does imply that autochthony tried to constitute Hellenic ethnicity even before Plato.) The story begins with the contradiction brought to the fore: Athena visits her brother's workshop in search of weapons, one skilled expert to another. His sexual arousal reasserts his phallic identity. Now he is both an intelligent artisan and a man of earth, and now the narrative sets about removing him from its action.

First is Athena's refusal. She will not touch the ejaculate, which does not belong on her. She wipes it off with wool, because Athena's defining technology is weaving, and she interposes that technology between herself and her brother's fertility. Her gesture says to his advance "I am a god of intelligence"; and the next move, throwing the bespermed wool to the ground, says "This part of you belongs with Ge".

Having issued his semen, Hephaestus disappears from the story, even before his son is conceived. Ge and Athena together take the father's place. Ge is fertile and magical; she contains ores and dark places and makes volcanic fires. Athena belongs on Olympus just as decidedly as the earth could not go up a mountain. Besides weaving she gave bridles and flutes to mortals. Thus, she and Ge can divide Hephaestus' attributes between them. As a god of skilled activity he resembles Athena, while as a chthonic god he is more like Ge.

The myth therefore separates *technê* from earthy fertility and magic, and continues to distinguish the two. The baby Erichthonius leaves Ge to go to Athena, and this move makes him Athenian. The vase paintings alluding to this myth focus on his movement from mother to nurse because the myth exists to mark the difference between those two, and the Athenians' progress from one to the other.

Once with Athena, Erichthonius lies in a basket. The basket is the closest thing to a uterus Athena uses, as the wool she wiped Hephaestus' semen with was the closest she would come to touching it. Basket and wool belong to her technology of weaving. The founding of Athens, and perhaps what makes Athens Greek rather than Pelasgian, depends on separating conscious intelligence from nature's magic. Speaking non-mythically: did those Pelasgian natives represented by Hephaestus actually father the first Athenians? It does not matter, because the Athenians' mothers define them now. They began in the magically nourishing earth, but then supplanted it with the powers of human intelligence. The Athenian dynasty can begin once governing intelligence separates from the land to be governed.

Autochthony in Plato

In the autochthony myths before Plato, variations in the roles that Hephaestus played served as a clue that his role was at issue for those myths; that their task consisted in ferrying Hephaestus away from the Athenian dynasty. For often enough what varies from one version of a tale to another is that tale's special concern.

Within Plato's dialogues there is no articulated genre of autochthony stories comparable with the genre of myths he tells about the afterlife, but multiple substantive references to autochthony still appear in his writings. The variations among these references suggest at least two points of Platonic interest in autochthony. His stories differ according to which ethnicity they take autochthony to account for, and also in the roles they assign to Athena. Both points of interest will turn out to matter to autochthony in the *Menexenus*. Looking for Athena in the *Menexenus* reveals something radical in this dialogue's portrayal of (Athenian) culture, while focusing on ethnicity leads us to a peculiarity in the way that the *Menexenus* sorts humanity; that peculiarity grounds the historical narrative and shows something about the Platonic structure beneath that narrative.

Besides references to autochthony in *Critias*, *Laws*, *Republic* and *Timaeus*,[57] there is a passage worth touching on in Plato's *Sophist*. That dialogue refers to materialist philosophers as both *autochthones* and *gêgeneis* "earthborn". This is not a joke about the philosophers of Athens. The clear example of local materialism would have been Anaxagoras, and he only lived in the city, having been born in Asia Minor, and did not have auto-chthonous ancestors.[58] Materialist philosophers come from earth in a bad metaphysical sense, being connected to the earthly domain rather than to that heavenly order that knows the Forms. They are earthborn in the same way that matter is, which explains why they study matter as assiduously as they do.

By interchanging the words *autochthôn* and *gêgeneis* in the *Sophist*, Plato equates the Greek word for autochthony with what "autochthony" means now, namely birth out of the earth. Etymologically the Greek word only means that one hails from the *auto* "same" *chthôn* "land, ground", always having lived in this place; being indigenous. It seems that Athenians believed themselves to have always been in Attica before they claimed to have sprung from its soil. Plato is therefore assuming the full-blown version of the myth. Athenians come from the land because out of the ground. And this means all Athenians, evidently committing Plato to the Kerameikos version of autochthony – but really it ought to provide a reason for rejecting that taxonomy, a taxonomy that would put Plato in a role he is not often accused of, as propagandist to the Athenian folk.[59]

Of the presentations of autochthony stories in other dialogues, two sound cynical about the stories' political uses, sceptical that birth from earth ever happened. These presentations occur in the *Republic* and *Laws*, where such stories are assessed as political discourse. The *Republic* has the noble lie, which Socrates calls "nothing new" and "something Phoenician-like". In the good city the elders of every generation will tell the young adults that their childhood had been a dream. Not only hatched underground, they grew to adulthood there too, dreaming of walking around in the open air and being educated, when in fact everything they learned was implanted in their souls through the earth. Because the earth put different metals in them the citizens belong to different classes of society. So the noble lie underwrites patriotism – the land is everyone's mother – but not egalitarian citizenship.[60]

As Malcolm Schofield observes, the *Republic* makes more of the lie's differentiation between citizens than of its implications for civic unity. What matters about this myth is that people have different metals in their souls, which is not part of traditional autochthony. It does not even require that far-fetched tale, which Glaucon tells Socrates he should be ashamed of proposing to tell. A wild tale about earthly gestation is tolerated because it helps to justify what Plato considers a metaphorical truth about social stratification.[61]

In calling his story "Phoenician", Socrates evokes the founding of Thebes by Cadmus, who came to mainland Greece from Phoenicia and sowed the ground with a dragon's teeth. The first generation of Thebans grew from this planting. The Athenian Stranger in Plato's *Laws* has the same story in mind when he says people are credulous. See how many believe the *Sidôniou muthologêma* "Sidonian fairy tale" about armed men emerging from the soil and founding a city. This must be the Theban tale: Sidon was a Phoenician city and home to Cadmus. The Stranger says people accepted the story "however implausible it is", not sharing the public's credulity though not lamenting it either, any more than Socrates in the *Republic* laments his future townspeople's willingness to believe the noble lie.[62]

The cynicism in these passages, if that is the best word regarding a story Plato wished were true, would account for the stories' being overheard in the *Laws* and *Republic* rather than told. Socrates does not recount the noble lie but describes the future telling of it; the Athenian Stranger in the *Laws* observes how willing audiences behave rather than addressing such an audience. The Theban origin of this story might account for the distancing. The autochthony in question is the Theban variety. The speakers in these passages might even use "Phoenician" as a euphemism that spares them from saying "Thebes". Thebes has been called the anti-Athens of tragic theatre,[63] and Theban autochthony could sound implausible to Athenians even if they believed something nearly identical about themselves. Thus when Plato shrinks from endorsing the truth of Theban autochthony he is more a loyal Athenian scoffing at an enemy city than a subversive scoffing at religious tales of origin.

As the version in the *Menexenus* does, autochthony in Plato's *Critias* and *Timaeus* evokes the Athenian tradition. Those two dialogues are so closely linked that the *Critias* takes up where the *Timaeus* ends. Socrates barely speaks in either dialogue, but the Athenian Critias plays a significant role in both, and in both he is the one who mentions autochthony.

In the second of the two dialogues, which Critias dominates, he identifies Athena and Hephaestus as parents of all Athenians. Besides having a father in common, these gods are united by their *philotechnia* "love of expertise" and *philosophia*. How natural that they should have cooperated to make the *andras ... agathous ... autochthonas* "good autochthonous men" of Athens, and then to establish the city's constitutional order *epi noun* "in their thought", in the minds of those good Athenians.[64]

Exactly *how* did Athena and Hephaestus make these good men? Plato generally prefers not to repeat ribald stories, and the *Critias* restrains itself even more than other dialogues do. Critias denies that Athena and Poseidon ever quarrelled over Athens; his pairing of the man-making siblings intellectualizes them beyond all personality. So it is not surprising to find him using vague verbs about the two gods' *pephukuian* "having grown, having brought about the birth of" and *empoiēsantes* "making" or possibly "inserting" the Athenians (inserting them into the soil).[65] The like-mindedness between Hephaestus and Athena rules out rape as the cause of Athenians, but then Plato replaces that explanation with one verb that says the men were *made* (as the reference to the gods' *philotechnia* also implies) and a second saying they grew or were *grown*.

It could be that the two verbs specify what the two gods did separately, combining their actions in one sentence to emphasize the concord between the siblings. Maybe Hephaestus made the first people and Athena tended them as they grew. Such specialization fits with what Critias said in the *Timaeus*, in his long story about Solon's visit to Egypt. An Egyptian priest tells Solon about Athena, who nurtured and educated "your land and ours". This priest makes the Egyptian city Sais a second Athens, perhaps in reply to Herodotus' *Histories* (which the *Timaeus* alludes to elsewhere). According to Herodotus the Egyptians identified all the gods, the worship of whom then spread to Greece; Plato reverses the order so that Athena cares for Athens first and Sais a thousand years later, having received *to sperma ... humōn* "the seed of you", and subsequently the seed for Sais, *ek Gēs te kai Hēphaistou* "from Ge and Hephaestus together".[66]

In this context *sperma* cannot refer to sperm or semen, even though the word has that sense elsewhere. Ge and Hephaestus together did not make semen. "Your seed" must mean "the beginnings of you", something that flowered into the Athenian people. This could amount to the old story about autochthony with the improper first part cut out, as well as explaining what the *Critias* means by "making". Hephaestus and Ge produced Athenians and Athena grew them with a nurse and tutor's care.

One discrepancy remains between the *Critias* and *Timaeus*, that in one story these gods make only Athenians and the other extends autochthony to Egyptians too. In general Plato's dialogues vary in their answers to "Who comes out of the earth?" Egyptians do it, Phoenicians do it (which also means, the Thebans), and sometimes the barbarians together with Athenians; in other places only Athenians.[67] Autochthony stories seem to be able to move anywhere on earth. This variation implies that for Plato a main task for these stories is that of endorsing a particular ethnicity's status.

One other variation involves Athena. In the noble lie she does nothing, while the *Timaeus* has her stepmothering the first Athenians, and the *Critias* somehow credits her with having brought the Athenian population into existence. Plato has put his finger on a puzzling aspect of Athenian autochthony. The patron deities of Greek cities tended to be female, and citizens might want their patroness to play the part of a mother. What to do when she was an avowed virgin? Whether the worry is widely Greek or only Plato's, it expresses itself in this variation among his versions of autochthony. To bring citizens out from the soil is to force the question of what role a protecting virgin warrior can play in mothering a city.

Autochthony in the *Menexenus* will comment on ethnicity. In fact the *Menexenus* strains the myth so much, in the interests of making it yield a ranking among nations, as to give away an important part of Plato's agenda for this dialogue. Athena is crucial too. The funeral speech offers an astonishing answer to the perennial worry about Athena and autochthony. This answer is worth looking at closely, because it lets Plato do nothing less than reverse the traditional logic of autochthony, a logic that had equated Athens with intelligent consciousness as opposed to – standing apart from; supplanting – a magical nature.

Autochthony and nature in the *Menexenus*

In his versions of autochthony Plato appears to be sensitive to the tradition that distinguished Ge from Athena, not because he follows the old pattern but in his focus on Athena. What is her place in autochthony stories, and what work does she do? And so looking for Athena in the *Menexenus*'s version of the myth is the quickest way to see a new moral Plato wants to draw from autochthony. It is still true that the *Menexenus* makes education come before human culture. But that conclusion now has something provisional about it, open to improvement in light of a deeper reading of the myth.

The place to begin is the most closely examined spot in the myth, where it praises the earth's maternity. The earth of Athens abounds in crops to feed Athenians. This proves what a mother she is. Women's bodies make food for babies only when they bore the children themselves, not when they take another mother's child.[68] Socrates uses the verb *hupoballomai* to describe the actions of non-mothers; this verb emphasizes not the taking-in or adopting that a foster mother or stepmother does, but rather the act of putting something forward, presenting something, as an imposter mother does when she announces that the babe in her arms is her own. As Loraux observes, *hupoballomai* "suggests substitution or deceit". What other cities do for their citizens is fraudulent. Specifically, it perpetrates the fraud that Athenian men feared most in their homes. A woman procures someone else's baby and presents it to her husband as hers (and his). Every Greek city other than Athens becomes not just the non-mother but a vivid species of bad mother.

Ion, in the play by Euripides named after him, remarks that "we suffer badly" from a *mêtruia* "stepmother", as if the ideal of autochthony required belittling every other kind of parental care. The *Menexenus* participates in this same differentiation between mothers.[69]

Surprisingly, the readers sensitive to gender politics have failed to remark on another implication of the passage. Separating good mother from bad against the backdrop of Athenian autochthony amounts to attaching this verb *hupoballomai* to Athena. The story had Athena substituting Ge's baby for her own; she becomes a pretender to motherhood, not despite her role as patron of Athens but in the act of fulfilling that role. The move from Ge to Athena would put all Athenians into the place of those unenvied other Greeks who live with stepmothers.

Whether for that reason or another, Ge takes over Athena's place in this version of the myth. She becomes first nurse and teacher to Athenians and Athena moves into a secondary role. Ge nurtures her new babes *pros hêbên* "until youthful prime; until puberty".[70] What would Plato consider that age to be? Eighteen? Fourteen? But even a twelve-year-old is too big to be laid in a basket and carried by girls. So Athena will not simulate a mother's early care in this story; that care reverts to Ge. Earth bears and also rears. Athena must content herself with educating adults.

When the education does begin, Ge has a group of gods available. Socrates refuses to name the gods whom Ge entrusts with teaching the first Athenians, but they must be more than one. Does Athena go from lone instructor to one of a pair? These unnamed deities impart both *technai* and– something different from *technai* – training in the *ktêsin* "manufacture" and *chrêsin* "use" of weapons.[71] This rhyming phrase probably includes Athena as warrior, though *making* weaponry was the domain of Hephaestus. As for the peacetime *technai*, Athena is one of those teachers, but essential skills were also credited to Apollo, Artemis and Hermes. Add in viticulture and agriculture, and Dionysus and Demeter go on the list. Athena might be one out of six or seven divine tutors, where once she had done all the teaching alone.

Ge claims other aspects of what had been Athena's cult. With Hephaestus gone she turns into a virgin mother. Plato does not even have to amend the tradition in this respect, for already in Hesiod's *Theogony*, early in that story of the world, the earth reproduced both sexually and parthenogenetically. She delivered Pontus and Uranus by herself, only later bred with Uranus.[72]

The last example of Ge's supplanting Athena might be the most convincing one just by being precise and small. In the contest between Athena and Poseidon that Socrates alludes to, the tradition attributes Athena's victory to the olive tree she gave the city. In the *Menexenus*, describing the care that Ge lavished on those first Athenians, Socrates tells of the wheat and barley that grew from the Attic earth – *and the olive tree too*. The great gift from Athena that had made Athens her city becomes one more gift from Ge.[73] The earth has absorbed Athena.

167

By assigning Athena's defining characteristics to Ge, the *Menexenus* recombines the female figures that the old autochthony story separated. Human civilization and its technologies no longer stand at a remove from the fertility and magic of nature, and potentially in opposition to it; now nature does the work of culture. For Athenians nature domesticates itself, bringing forth wheat and barley without any prior work by farmers, and providing for the first Athenians' education.

We observed that the *Menexenus* depicts education as a cultural process founded by an originally natural event. This significant feature of Ge's early care for humans shares a feature with other notable Platonic depictions of learning: for learning to be possible in ordinary life, some extraordinary learning must have taken place first. Some dialogues argue for recollection, according to which exposure to the Forms before birth lets you grasp them again in embodied life. The *Republic* offers a mythical interpretation of "first learning" in the noble lie, but also proposes the first educational act for revolutionary politics, in which the philosophers establishing their new regime cast adults out of the city walls and train the first batch of children.[74] It is in this spirit that the *Menexenus* depicts a team of gods teaching the skills of civilization to the new people of Athens. All later Athenians providing for their children's education are following Ge's example. Ordinary education takes place now because a miraculous first act of learning once took place. Human society began in the state of nurture.

Greek myths had spoken of divine education long before Plato. But the disputatiousness among gods that Plato finds objectionable infected this domain as well. Prometheus stands out as the figure who taught human beings to make fire and how to sacrifice to the gods. His willingness to subvert the divine order and deceive Zeus made this first education a trauma, and the cause of humans' estrangement from their first fellowship with the gods. Even what gods teach can separate human beings from their natural first condition, as the differentiation between Athena and Ge symbolically indicates in traditional Athenian autochthony. Human nature traces back to Ge and human culture to Athena.

The final significance of this new Platonic autochthony is therefore its optimism about education. Now nature generates the *technai* of nature: the metals on the ground and also the skill at working metal; wool on the sheep's back and the craft that turns it into clothing on human backs.

Loraux comments, on this aspect of the funeral speech, that Platonic autochthony blurs the line between nature and intelligent conscious activity. "The confusion between *physis* and *technê* is a systematic one in Plato". As an example Loraux cites the noble lie, in which "autochthony is accommodated to the artisanal production of the citizens".[75] Only the word "confusion" mars this description, which otherwise acknowledges the remarkable implication of autochthony as Plato reconceives it. Production (via human skill) does merge with (natural) reproduction, as Loraux says. But Plato is not making the earth do the work of human technicians. *That* description implies that the work of those technicians arises independently of nature. Plato sees the human work in the *technai* as the fruit of nature: he is restoring that work's natural status. Artisanal production too manifests nature's magic.

Autochthony and human difference in the *Menexenus*

The new myth's account of education will imply some things about Athenians that are relevant to the historical narrative that follows, for it makes Athens both naturally inclined towards learning and preternaturally situated to receive it. Pericles bragged that Athenians teach the world never explaining how they could have learned what they know. This myth fills in the gap: Athenians are both the world's finest minds and its luckiest students.

But the autochthony myth matters more to the coming history of Athens than as a description of Athenians considered by themselves. It participates in the speech's distinction among kinds of people, Greek and otherwise. The trouble here is that some of what Socrates claims to be shown by Athenian autochthony actually undermines autochthony.

By comparison with the noble lie, the autochthony myth in the *Menexenus* seems dedicated to human equality. Both stories make earthly birth a basis for patriotism. The city is the citizens' mother, and as brothers and sisters they are a unified group. But the noble lie distinguishes between unity and equality, insisting on the people's mutual loyalty even as it inscribes class structure into their souls. Civic unity for the silver-souled auxiliaries means obedience towards their golden siblings the rulers, not equal authority with them.[76]

Pericles had already spoken to the possibility of authority in democratic Athens. Democratic culture was one thing, democratized governance something else. The Athenians' equality in their private lives did not open public offices to all citizens indiscriminately. All Athenians received equal treatment under the law and yet those recognized for their merits had greater political authority assigned to them. Pericles does not argue for this paradoxical characteristic of Athenian society. He asserts that his city can enjoy all private benefits of equality without risking incompetent leadership.[77]

Here again the *Menexenus* makes more sense as improvement than as mockery. For in a clear allusion to the speech of Pericles, meditating on the city's being called a democracy, the *Menexenus* speech endorses a similar claim to the one by Thucydides but also argues for it. What Pericles asserted as fact, Socrates derives (if by somewhat perverse logic) from the Athenians' collective birth. Despite going by the name *dêmokratia* the constitution of Athens is an *aristokratia* "rule by the best". For example the city has always had a king, though that position is based on merit.

Pericles would not have dared to speak of *aristokratia* however one took that word, although the two speeches agree in contrasting the constitution's name with the fact of rule by the best citizens. But in the *Menexenus*, rule by the best takes place because of the citizens' equality rather than in spite of it. The Athenians' *isogonia* "equality of birth" causes them to honour *isonomia* "equality before the law", to such a degree that they are able to install their finest peers in office without courting tyranny. Their natural equality makes stratification possible because Athenians know it will not deliver them into slavery. What Pericles had boasted of the new speech accounts for.[78]

In their private lives, in a parallel to being free from even the threat of tyranny, the Athenians never fear slavery between citizens. Another motor of world history fails to operate inside the city. No slaves or masters when they all come from the same mother.[79]

Still, it would take a blinkered interpretation of the two passages to call the *Menexenus* egalitarian. Rather than deny differences among humans this passage projects them onto the world outside Athens, where the noble lie had collected human difference within the city. This is not hypocrisy. Egalitarianism tends to begin under conditions of inequality and at least at first it fosters those conditions. Equality within a group becomes possible when that group stands apart from another one, this internal equality heightening the difference in rank between that group's members and the outsiders. Sparta's land-owning citizens the Spartiates called themselves *homoioi* "equals, peers" while reducing the Helots to subhuman status, and for the purpose of uniting their members in endless war against their serfs.[80] (The English word "peer" makes this doubleness of meaning clear: parity within the group, disparity between it and others.) The *Menexenus* similarly denies differences among Athenians, but only in the context of enhancing differences between Athens and everyone else. It will transplant the *Republic*'s three classes from one city's interior to humanity at large.

Because egalitarianism in general is ambiguous, this stratification of humanity does not make conceptual trouble for the *Menexenus*'s use of autochthony. Autochthony signified Athenian superiority before Plato. The conceptual trouble comes in another way, when the funeral speech uses autochthony *both* to set Athens apart from Greece's other cities, *and also* to bind all the Greek cities together. This double implication will prove productive, permitting the *Menexenus* to find order in the events of international history. And inasmuch as autochthony has come to mean Ge's reabsorbing the role of Athena, so that the city's place among the peoples of the world is guaranteed by earthly nature rather than being imposed upon that nature, the history that Socrates tells will follow natural law. But the analysis depends on forcing autochthony into contradictory consequences. This is a measure of how powerfully Plato wants both implications of autochthony, that he insists on both despite their sitting uneasily with each other.

On one side is the superiority of Athens. This point appears early in the speech, as soon as Socrates mentions autochthony. These dead soldiers being honoured at the funeral began their lives with a good birth. Their ancestors' *genesis* "origin" was not *epêlus* "immigrant". Other Greek cities told stories of having been founded by heroes who came to their land from elsewhere, often enough from a place outside Greece. Cadmus the Phoenician founded Thebes; the *Menexenus* also mentions Danaus the Egyptian founder of Argos, and Pelops (after whom the Peloponnesus was named) who came from either Phrygia or Lydia.[81]

Both legend and recent memory also told of Greeks' peregrinations within Greek territory. Many Peloponnesian Greeks, very much including the Spartans, represented their ancestral arrival on that peninsula as the "return" of the descendants of Heracles. Socrates alludes to that legend of return in this very speech. Athens aided the descendants of Heracles when the people of Argos tried to stop them from settling nearby.[82]

Within the retrievable past many Greek cities had sent out citizens to found new cities. It is a distortion to call these cities "colonies" in the modern sense, but they were subordinate in rank and esteem and expected to defer to the mother city. Thucydides marks the beginning of the Peloponnesian War with a fight between Corinth and Corcyra, a *polis* that Corinth had founded and from which the Corinthians still demanded a subordinate's deference. This difference in prestige sometimes expressed itself in stories that embroiled the founders of the later cities in criminal violence, as it were compromising the cities before they came into existence.[83]

Socrates casts the difference among Greeks in terms that this chapter has already examined. Non-Athenians live with their *mêtruia* "stepmother" in a house other than the one they started out in. The lower status of cities founded in the archaic centuries transfers to the cities founded by non-Greek heroes. They all may as well be "colonies"; they all rank below Athenians with their good birth.[84]

But then Socrates lumps the Greek settlements together with cities founded by non-Greeks. A passage only a few lines long harangues the non-Athenian cities of Greece as not truly Greek. Athenians are *eilikrinôs* "purely" Greek and *amigeis* "not having been mixed" with barbarians. Other Greeks are *phusei men barbaroi ... nomôi de Hellênes* "barbarians by nature, Greeks by convention", attacking non-Athenians' ethnic identity with the Sophists' opposition between nature and custom. Finally, switching to the vocabulary of Platonic metaphysics, the speech says Athenians are *autoi Hellênes* "Greeks themselves, Greeks as such". Plato calls the Form of Beauty *auto to kalon* "beauty itself" using the same formula; and just as the dialogues contrast the beauty of beauty itself with visible objects that are both beautiful and ugly, so too the Athenians' being *Greeks as such* is a matter of their not being *meixobarbaroi* "part-barbarian", which is to say not being both Greek and not.[85]

Despite falsifying other cities' traditions, even falsifying traditions that this same speech acknowledges, at least it is consistent as a gesture of patriotism. Athens is the real thing as Greek cities go, hence the most Greek. The sentiment is not far from the audacious claim that Thucydides attributes to Pericles, "Athens is the school of Greece", picturing a Greece whose other cities have to learn how to be Greek cities from this defining example of the species.[86]

This high rank for Athens also appears in an epigram that has been attributed to Thucydides. According to a later source, he commemorated Euripides saying *patris d'Hellados Hellas Athênai* "his fatherland was the Greece of Greece, Athens". Simon Hornblower calls the verse "a fine four-line epigram … which I see no reason to deny him [i.e. Thucydides]"; but if Thucydides did write these lines, he is saying in his own voice what Pericles says obliquely, that by virtue of being *something less* than Athens the other cities are thereby *less Greek*.[87]

Modern analyses of tribalism and nationalism will find the disenfranchisement of non-Athenian cities a familiar trope, the strange assimilated to the absolutely strange. Plato takes up a Thucydidean theme and outdoes it, either in order to improve on the speech of Pericles with a more thorough statement of Athenian superiority, or to mock Pericles with an untenable patriotism that implicitly rebukes patriotism as such.

Unfortunately for the familiarity of such a reading, the *Menexenus* also uses autochthony in a way that requires the other cities to be Greek. This contrary implication of autochthony – unlike Athenian democracy, unlike Athenian superiority – does not correspond to anything Pericles says. It feels inserted into the funeral speech to serve a purpose. Socrates says that Athens acts on behalf of Greece as a whole. The Greeks ought to stand together against Persia, and sometimes they do, and when they unite against this common enemy they can count on the altruistic pan-Hellenism of Athens. The reason proffered is Athenian autochthony. Being born from native soil makes Athenians love Greece as such. It led them to fight on behalf of Boeotians, to war more gently against fellow Greeks than against foreigners, to release Greeks from slavery.

The core argument is reasonable, assuming the premises. Autochthonous birth means an origin free from external contributions, so the people of Athens must be full-blooded Greeks. Being purely Greek they would be the Greeks most concerned about the bloodline. But why should this concern make them behave altruistically towards cities that have adulterated the bloodline that Athenians love? Helping *those* cities only pollutes Hellenism further. Athenian superiority had just mandated that non-Athenians not count as truly Greek, but for the purpose of motivating Athenian foreign policy they now seem to be quite Greek enough, even fully Greek, and all of them as Greek as one another.[88]

Trying to defend pan-Hellenism, the speech appeals to both of the customary criteria for shared ethnicity, namely language and descent. Socrates says that Athenians endured their wars against Persia on behalf of themselves and *tôn allôn homophônôn* "the others speaking the same language". Less than a page later he urges that Greeks battle other Greeks with more restraint than they show against barbarians, calling the fellow Greek *homophulon* "one from the same tribe". The non-Athenians who had been marked for pan-Hellenist treatment for using the same language as Athenians now belong to the same tribe.[89]

Plato is not the only person to appeal to more than one criterion for ethnic identity. Birth and language both served that purpose. The word *phulê* "tribe" may have connoted something more conventional by Plato's day than it meant archaically; nevertheless membership in a *phulê* seems to have been a matter of birth alone. To be *homophulos* with someone else is to share ancestry with that person.[90] Kinship could transcend political differences even without uniting all Greece, as when Thucydides has the Ionians appeal to their near-relatives the Athenians for help against Persia.[91]

Meanwhile language is relevant to grounding ethnic identity perhaps as early as the *Iliad*, which calls the Carians *barbarophônoi* "foreign-tongued", the contradictory of *homophônos*. In Herodotus, the Athenians equate *to Hellênikon* "Greekness" with the combination of being *homaimon* "having the same blood", *homoglosson* "same tongue", and shared religious and other customs. Jonathan Hall argues that Isocrates, around the time of Plato's death, articulated the shift from a genealogical basis for descent to a "cultural" one in which language played a major role; Hall argues that this shift followed after a time during which culture and descent had been appealed to together. The *Menexenus* is therefore drawing on the signifiers of ethnic identity from its own time to construct a pan-Hellenic identity.[92]

But however compatible the two criteria for identity are, or were treated as being in Plato's time, neither one can justify the altruism of autochthonous Athenians. Sameness of language makes all Greeks equal to Athenians, or at least – what matters to this argument – equally Greek. Athens might still be the one city that nurses at its mother's bosom while the rest eat substitute food, but this difference cannot make Athens more Greek than the others if Greekness is linguistic.

If Greek identity as sameness of language renders autochthony irrelevant, speaking of tribal kinship with the other Greek cities makes it false. Kinship with other cities denies what the autochthony myth insisted on, that Athenians and other Greeks come from different stock. The flat-out contradiction becomes explicit when Socrates repeats this word *homophulos* later in his speech. First, pan-Hellenically, the word meant other Greek cities; then the historical narrative arrives at the Athenian battle between oligarchs and democrats and the gentle resolution the city made to that quarrel, the Athenian population being indisposed to civil war because (after all; remember autochthony!) the populace is *homophulos*.[93] Whatever sameness of tribe means, it cannot both unite Athenians with one another as joint descendants of the earth *and also* unite them with non-Athenian migratory Greeks elsewhere.

What follows is that the funeral speech can call those residents of other Greek cities fellow tribesmen or fellow Greek speakers, or both. What it cannot do is assert both Athenian superiority and Athenian pan-Hellenism. Pan-Hellenism must deny what autochthonous birth, the basis for Athenian superiority, asserts. For that matter, the speech's tripartition of humanity into Greek Athenians, non-Athenian near-Greeks, and barbarians fails together with its explanation for Athenian altruism. If autochthony determines ethnicity, then Athens alone counts as Greek in a world that is otherwise barbarian. There are two kinds of people in the world, not three: Athenians and others. And if autochthony does *not* imply ethnicity, the word "Greek" means what it had meant, but again the world has two groups in it, the Persian and other non-Greeks on one side and all Greeks on the other, Argive and Athenian alike. Whatever makes the Athenians Greek should produce a world with two ethnicities in it, and yet Plato demands three.

The meanings of autochthony

Even if Plato included talk of autochthony only because all funeral speeches did, he did not set the traditional story into his speech unaltered. The *Menexenus* resists the myth in its given form, not simply moralizing with the help of the story but rewriting the story, working against its traditional narrative, so as to be able to moralize in particular ways:

1 The traditional myth foregrounded Athena to celebrate the triumph of consciousness and *technê* over chthonic forces. Plato's version reabsorbs Athena into Ge, to suggest that Athenian culture is not a force distinct from nature but is nature itself.
2 The myth set Athens apart from all other Greek cities, which lack the same descent from local earth. Plato's version retains Athenian exceptionalism but reinterprets the city's superiority as the difference between Greek and barbarian.
3 The myth said nothing about the city's relations with other Greek cities. On Plato's version, Athenians' pure birth makes them solicitous of the welfare of other Greek cities, which are now understood as Athens's Greek peers.

The third change differs from the first two in that subverting the myth goes so far as to violate its basic assumptions. What does it mean to find a moral in the autochthony story that contradicts autochthony? Autochthony had meant an absolute distinction between locals and others but Plato wants to force it into pan-Hellenic duty. The conflict indicates the power of this intention, that it seeks to establish the Greek status of non-Athenian cities despite the doctrine of autochthony.

More specifically Plato's funeral speech seeks to divide the world into three populations. To discriminate among the three groups the speech puts pressure on the myth of autochthony that that myth cannot bear.

Of course the world has changed for Plato since Pericles spoke, when the Persian wars and subsequent battles against the empire were receding into the past. Periclean Athens could define itself as the Athens that was not at war with Persia, for Pericles justified the great building project on the Acropolis, which would include the Parthenon, on the grounds that Athens no longer had a quarrel with Persia.[94] Freed from focusing on the great non-Greek enemy, Pericles comprehends the world in Greek terms: Delian League and Peloponnesian League, Athens *contra* Sparta. His organizing pair of words *logos* and *ergon* suits that world: Athens does the work of winning wars while its enemies talk mere *logos*. There are two camps; perhaps attributing articulate speech to the other camp, even if that is empty verbiage, requires that the enemy be speaking Greek.

A generation and a half later, the *Menexenus* reflects a world in which Persia wielded increasing influence, having set the terms of the peace with which the *Menexenus*'s historiography concludes. The next chapter will consider this history at length; but already that much information suffices to show how differently the two funeral speeches conceptualized the world's great powers. Observers in Athens at the time of the *Menexenus*, who could not have foreseen Macedonia's rise to power, may be forgiven for organizing history around Persia and the Greek enemies of Athens. In retrospect Pericles would have struck them as parochial for imagining a world politics with only two players in the game. A sophisticated strategy for relating history now appears to need at least three elements.

If the three elements arise naturally, which is to say that natural forces can explain their existence, so much the better, for then history does not have to be seen as chancy. A historical narrative can follow a clear trajectory, even if the trajectory is the gloomy falling action that goes from Athenian triumph over Persia to Persian triumph over all Greece. The myth of autochthony as the *Menexenus* tells it (1) makes intelligence and education natural to Athens, so natural that the Attic earth created them; then (2) raises Athenians (naturally, again) so high above other Greeks as to put those others into a separate class of human beings; and then (3) establishes a bond (also natural) among all Greeks against their common barbarous enemy.

The desired implication of the myth is a reorganization of humanity, along natural lines, into three groups, in the interests of describing historical events. If the myth cannot ultimately deliver this combined implication, it is not for lack of effort on Plato's part. He inherited the story that his speech must tell and there is only so much he can force it to say.

Notes

1 Portions of this chapter previously appeared as Pappas (2011a, 2011b).
2 *Menexenus*: over nine pages of myth and history, 237b–246a; thirteen pages of speech, 236d–249d.

3 The only appearances of *muthos* "myth" as a word or root in Herodotus are pejorative: *Histories* 2.23, 2.45. Compare Thucydides *History* 1.22.4: Thucydides compares his own work to that of other historians granting that audience members might not enjoy his history because of *to mê muthôdes* "the non-fabulous quality".

4 Thucydides *History*: Pericles on recognizing ancestors, 2.36.1; fathers, 2.36.2; adults of the present, 2.36.3; omitting details, 2.36.4.

5 Clavaud (1980: 97).

6 In fairness to Pericles, there might be a simple reason why his speech omits the past. The events that Pericles skips over belong to the Pentekontaetia, the fifty years between the end of the Persian War and the start of all-out war against Sparta. Only a bit earlier in his *History* (1.89–1.118) Thucydides set out to detail what took place during those years. Given that special effort to account for the generation before the war against Sparta, it might not be surprising that Pericles says as little as he does.

7 The denial that Plato is criticizing Thucydides constitutes a running theme. Clavaud (1980): the alleged absence of references to Thucydides in *Menexenus*, 146–47; no mention of Thucydides in connection with Sicily, 150; the entire history a caricature of other orators, 166. "One will not be surprised that Plato … parodies Thucydides much less than you would expect … He was parodying other, more typical orations" (*ibid.*: 171; our translation).

8 Loraux falls into similar methodological problems in her treatments of auto-chthony, especially Loraux (1993) with its sweeping assertions about autochthony as portrayed "in the Kerameikos", the version of the myth found in Athenian funeral orations, which were delivered in the part of Athens called the Kerameikos (on this classification see "Autochthony in Athens" below). In her epilogue Loraux admits to one major regret about her book's argument: "As for my regret – its name is Plato" (*ibid.*: 240). But her return to the subject in Loraux (2000), while it may have assuaged her regret, does not undo the methodological problems with her argument.

9 Another possibility would be that Plato meant his speech as a parody, but all his original audience took it seriously; see Clavaud (1980: 34–35). Aside from its historical arrogance, this proposal defeats itself by admitting that orators after Plato destroyed the evidence for his parody by altering the genre he had putatively pilloried. If they thought Plato wanted to write a serious speech and followed his lead, then they turned the genre into a setting in which the *Menexenus* speech looks serious. This possibility leaves the *Menexenus*'s status as parody unknowable in principle.

10 Loraux (1993: 8).

11 Competition between gods, *Menexenus* 237c4–d2. The quarrel is depicted on the western pediment of the Parthenon. Athenian women voting for Athena and losing their vote: Augustine attributes this version to Varro, *City of God* 18.9. This version seems designed to explain something, such as the tightened criteria for Athenian citizenship that Pericles supported in 451/0.

12 Plato: against stories that tell of gods' quarrels, *Republic* 2.378b–d; quarrels and *peplos*, *Euthyphro* 6a–c; Critias on Athena and Athens, *Critias* 109b.

13 On this distinction see Austin (1958: 271).

14 *Menexenus*: mythical wars, 239b; poets' singing stories already, 239b; what no poet has spoken of, 239c.

15 Clavaud (1980: 137–38) presses this point.

16 See *Phaedrus* 245a; *Republic* 10.607a. The *Republic* speaks of *humnous* "songs, hymns", which accords well with the verb *humneô* at *Menexenus* 239b.

17 Thucydides *History*: Pericles on not needing poets, 2.41.4; rival histories with fanciful tales, 1.22.
18 *Ibid.*: speaking of Homer with respect, 1.3; scepticism regarding the epics, 1.11.
19 Aristotle *Rhetoric* 1.15, 1375b30.
20 "Plato" *Hipparchus* 228b. On evidence for a Panathenaic rule Davison (1955: 7); Isocrates *Panegyricus* 159, Lycurgus *In Leocratem* 102; Plutarch *Pericles* 13.6, Diogenes Laërtius *Lives of the Eminent Philosophers* 1.57. Boyd (1995) is sceptical, but Nagy (1992: 50) finds it plausible that some rule of performance existed consistent with the *Hipparchus*'s testimony.
21 Interpolation: Diogenes Laërtius *Lives of the Eminent Philosophers* 1.57; Plutarch *Solon* 10.1; Strabo *Geography* 9.394. See Davison (1955: 16). Recension: Cicero *de Oratore* 3.137; *Palatine Anthology* 11.442. On this evidence and how to appraise it see Boyd (1995: 35–36); Nagy (1992: 47–48). Boyd (1995: 42) calls the grounds for believing in a recension "shaky ancient evidence"; Nagy (1992: 42–52) implies as much when he reads the tradition as the metaphorical expression of a truth about epics' reaching fixed form. Parallel stories from Sparta attribute the Homeric texts to Lycurgus: Aelian *Varia Historia* 13.14; Plutarch *Lycurgus* 4.4; see Boyd (1995: 36n.3).
22 Zatta (2010) on Peisistratus and the golden age; see "Aristotle" *Constitution of Athens* chapter 16, "Plato" *Hipparchus* 229b.
23 *Menexenus* 238c–d.
24 The Greek *hê gê* translates as "Earth" the name of a personified being and also as the neutral physical object "the earth". Here the capitalized "Ge" will be used as a personified being's name.
25 For a synopsis of scholarly materials before 1986, see Smith (1986: 20n.1). Frutiger (1930) is still required reading. On the dominant genre – myths about reward and punishment after death – see Annas (1982), more recently Fussi (2001). But Partenie (2009a) promises to become the work standardly consulted, and this section will make special reference to some of the papers in that collection.
26 Partenie (2009c: 19); "extended simile", Rowe (2009: 135); *muthos* and *logos* in *Timaeus*, Burnyeat (2009: 178–80).
27 Also see Partenie (2009b), which advances this point more explicitly than any of the contributions to Partenie (2009a).
28 Rowe (2009: 144). See also Pappas (2011b).
29 Sedley (2009).
30 Platonic myths and traditional antecedents: Kahn (2009: 150–51); Schofield (2009: 106–9); Partenie (2009c: 2); Ferrari (2009: 128).
31 Apollo: Socrates and, Plato *Phaedo* 61a–b (cf. *Apology* 21b); distant god, Aeschylus *Agamemnon* 1075, 1079; plague and aid to enemy, Homer *Iliad* 1.43–52.
32 Sedley (2009).
33 Cavell (1969: 74–81).
34 Allegory of cave not supernatural, Kahn (2009: 148); birth of Love, *Symposium* 203b–c.
35 Plato *Laws* 10.903b–905d. See Stalley (2009).
36 Plato *Statesman* 269c–274d.
37 *Ibid.*: 277b.
38 *Ibid.*: growing younger, 270e; not known whether they philosophized, 272c–d.
39 Plato *Phaedrus* 229c–230a.
40 Plato *Republic* 2.378d.
41 Plato *Theaetetus*: Ocean origin of all, 152e (Homer *Iliad* 14.201); Ephesian philosophers reporting this doctrine openly, 180d.

42 Plato *Phaedo*: dream command to work at music, 60e; poetry needs *muthoi* and Socrates takes his from Aesop, 61b. Betegh (2009) comments on Socrates' putative inability to invent *muthoi*.

43 Loraux (1993: 8).

44 The word *autochthôn* in Thucydides, *History* 6.2.2; "the claim of the Sicilian Sicans", Pelling (2009: 471).

45 Lysias 17.

46 On Lysias and performance, Herrman (2004: 27).

47 Autochthony for Erechtheus, *Iliad* 2.547–48; for Erichthonius, Euripides *Ion* 267–68; for Kekrops, Apollodorus *Library* (below); for all Athenians, Aristophanes *Wasps* 1075–76. It should go without saying that comedy belongs as close to the Acropolis as tragedy does; but Loraux (1993), which contains a chapter titled "The Comic Acropolis", never mentions *Wasps*.

48 Apollodorus *Library*: Kekrops, 3.14.1; Erichthonius, 3.14.6. Guaranteed efficacy: no Greek myth reports a male god's sexual act without an ensuing pregnancy. The Greek gods were perfect in some respects, if not morally.

49 Thucydides *History* 6.56.1 speaks of a basket to be carried by a maiden *en pompêi tini* "in some procession", though this is not necessarily the Panathenaea. Euripides *Ion*: Ion had been placed in an *aggos* "vessel", 1398; covered with *mimêmata* "imitations" of Erichthonius, 1429.

50 Autochthony degrading women, Saxonhouse (1986: 258); Hephaestus makes a son, Loraux (1993: 128); "first Athenian", Loraux (2000: 24); no autochthonous women in Athens, Loraux (1993: 78–79, 115n.17). See Hesiod *Works and Days* 90 about the lives of human beings *prin* "before" the appearance of a woman.

51 Hephaestus: lame, *Iliad* 18.397, *Odyssey* 8.308; traps Ares and Aphrodite in his bed, *Odyssey* 8.266–366; thrown to earth by Zeus, *Iliad* 1.586–94; again by Hera, *Iliad* 18.395–405; "Hephaestus is expelled", Rinon (2006: 6). Rinon develops this picture of a suffering Hephaestus with human characteristics, though extrapolations to the god as "tragic" are less convincing. On visual evidence for Hephaestus' return to Olympus, see Pausanias *Description of Greece* 1.20.3; one literary allusion occurs in Pindar, fragment 283. Delcourt (1957: 78–79); also Hedreen (2004); Seeberg (1965).

52 Hera the only parent for Hephaestus, Hesiod *Theogony* 927, *Homeric Hymn* 3 to Pythian Apollo 317–18, Apollodorus *Library* 1.3.5. See Loraux (1993: 128); but she is too attracted to the parallelism between Athena and Hephaestus (*ibid*.: 25). Hephaestus and birth and marriage: Naxos and Samos both associated his birth "with rights of marriage or of progamia", Walton (1960: 287).

53 Typhon child of Ge, Hesiod *Theogony* 820–22. *Homeric Hymn* 3 to Pythian Apollo: Hera and Typhon, 307–55; Hera bears Typhon alone, 307; her anger toward Hephaestus, 317–18; prayer to Ge *et al*., 335–37; *chthona*, 340.

54 Ares about the Sintians, Homer *Odyssey* 8.294; *barbarophônos*, *Iliad* 2.867. Herodotus *Histories*: Pelasgians settling Lemnos, 6.137–40; settling Samothrace with Kabeiroi, 2.512. On Kabeiroi see Detienne and Vernant (1978: 269–72); Levin (1959: 332).

55 Homer *Iliad*: shield of Achilles, 8.469–613; sceptre of Zeus, 2.100–102; aegis of Zeus, 15.307–10; Hera's chambers, 14.166–67. Also see Hesiod: Pandora, *Theogony* 571–72, *Works and Days* 60–71; her head-dress decorated with lifelike animals, *Theogony* 584. See Rinon (2006: 10n.34). Rinon oversimplifies in saying "Hephaestus' artistic activity is … deeply connected to his fall" (*ibid*.: 19). The idea of redemption through fine artmaking eases the contradiction that Hephaestus represents, and which the myth of autochthony is wrestling with.

56 Homer: *klutotechnês, Iliad* 1.571, 18.143, *Odyssey* 8.286; *polumêtis, Iliad* 21.355; *poluphrôn, Iliad* 21.367, *Odyssey* 8.297; *klutomêtis, Homeric Hymn* 20, 1. For these epithets and for the god's cleverness of technique that extends beyond beautiful objects to technological marvels, see Holmberg (2003: 7).

57 Loraux comes to different conclusions about these passages: Loraux (2000: 116–21).

58 Anaxagoras from Clazomenae: Diogenes Laërtius *Lives of the Eminent Philosophers* 2.6, Plutarch *Pericles* 4.4.

59 Plato *Sophist*: matter-lovers *autochthones*, 247c; *gêgeneis*, 248c. On the changing meaning of *autochthôn* in Athens see Rosivach (1987). See Plato *Statesman* 271a–b, which speaks of all human beings in the age of Cronus being *gêgeneis* "earthborn". We pass over that passage here because (1) it does not mention "autochthony", (2) it removes birth from earth to an era radically separate from the present, and (3) within that other time all humans are born from earth, not just one city's people. But note the Stranger's comment that one should not disbelieve such stories (*ibid.*: 271b).

60 Plato *Republic*: the lie *mêden koinon* "nothing new" and *Phoinikikon ti* "something in the Phoenician manner", 3.414c; citizens grown in earth, 3.414d–415c.

61 The noble lie and its politics, Schofield (2009). Glaucon chides Socrates, *Republic* 3.414e.

62 Plato *Laws* 2.663e. The word *muthologêma* implies the speaker's disbelief as its root *muthos* does not have to.

63 Zeitlin (1990).

64 Plato *Critias*: Hephaestus and Athena having *koinên phusin* "shared nature", unified by *philotechnia* and *philosophia* as well as parentage, 109c; good autochthonous men, 109d. Note that *andras* refers to men in the gender-specific sense. These are male human beings Critias pictures having come out of the soil.

65 Plato *Critias*: no quarrels among gods, 109b; gods making and growing humans, 109d.

66 Plato *Timaeus*: Solon and Egyptian priest, 23d–e; *ethrepsen kai epaideusen* "she nurtured and educated" Athens and Sais, 23d; *sperma* from Ge and Hephaestus, 23e. On overtones of Herodotus in *Timaeus* see Herodotus on sameness of religion. Almost all the names of the gods went from Egypt to Greece, *Histories* 2.50. Other echoes include *erga ... megala kai thaumasta* "great and wondrous deeds", *Timaeus* 20e; cf. *Histories* 1.1. Węcowski (2004: 146n.22). The motif of Egyptian priests' educating the recently ascendant Greeks is also common to the two works: *Histories* 2.143, *Timaeus* 22b–23b.

67 Again Plato *Statesman* 271a–b, which posits all people of the golden age as earthborn, is relevant.

68 *Menexenus* 238a.

69 Loraux (2000: 90). Ion on stepmothers: Euripides *Ion* 1330.

70 *Menexenus* 238b.

71 *Ibid.*

72 Hesiod *Theogony*: Ge bearing Uranus alone, 126; making Pontus without *philotêtes* "love, friendship", 132; breeding with Uranus, 133.

73 *Menexenus* 238a.

74 Plato: recollection, see esp. *Phaedo* 72e–73a; revolutionary education, *Republic* 7.540e–7.541a.

75 Loraux (1993: 127n.76).

76 See especially Schofield (2009).

77 Thucydides *History* 2.37.1.

78 *Menexenus*: *aristokratia*, 238c–d; Athenian kings, 238d; *isogonia* and *isonomia*, 239a.

79 *Menexenus* 239a. The narrative ahead will associate several events with real or threatened enslavement.

80 Spartan *homoioi*: Xenophon, *Constitution of the Lacedaimonians* 10.7; cf. the implicit appeal to similarity among citizens in Herodotus *Histories* 3.55.1.

81 *Menexenus*: ancestors' *genesis*, 237b; Danaus and other city fathers, 245d. Some cities did claim to have also begun autochthonously. Herodotus calls Arcadians and Cynurians autochthonous, *Histories* 8.73; but they were no political competition for Athens. See Loraux (2000: 14–16).

82 *Menexenus* 239b. Lysias' funeral speech elaborates on this early Athenian contribution to Greeks' finding homelands: Lysias 2.11–16.

83 Thucydides, *History*: what started the war, 1.23.6; Corcyra and its own "colony" Epidamnus, 1.24; Corinth hating Corcyra for being disrespectful, 1.25.3–4; Corinthians saying "We did not establish [Corcyra] in order to be insulted", 1.38.2. Murderous city founders: Tlepolemus and Rhodes, *Iliad* 2.661–69, Pindar *Olympian Ode* 7.27–33; matricidal Alkmeon and Akarnania, Thucydides *History* 2.102.5–6, Plutarch *Moralia* 7723–73b, Pausanias *Description of Greece* 1.43.7. These citations all appear in Dougherty (1998).

84 *Menexenus* 237b.

85 *Ibid.*: 245d: Athenians *eilikrinôs* Greek and *amigeis*; other Greeks barbarians by nature; Athenians *autoi Hellênes* and not *meixobarbaroi*. On this *eilikrinôs* see Loraux (2000: 118–19). For this vocabulary in Plato's metaphysics see *Republic* 5.479a–b, *Symposium* 211a–b.

86 Thucydides *History* 2.41.1.

87 Thucydides on Euripides, Page (1981: 307); "a fine four-line epigram", Hornblower (2004: 24). Thanks go to Tad Brennan for this reference.

88 Perhaps to keep the number of categories at three, the *Menexenus* says nothing about ethnic divisions within Greek ethnicity. The Athenians sometimes played up their Ionian ethnicity, casting Ionians as the antipodes to the Peloponnesian Dorians. See Connor (1993). But Plato does not even nod at those concerns.

89 *Menexenus*: homophônos, 241e–242a; homophulos, 242d.

90 Many cities subdivided their population into *phulai*. Several names for *phulai* in Peloponnesian cities are the same from city to city, prompting speculations that these tribes represent archaic ethnic subdivisions; but the evidence about *phulai* is mostly classical, making such proposals hard to defend (Hall 2007: 47–48). Cleisthenes created the *phulai* of Athens, Herodotus *Histories* 6.131.1; this probably means that he replaced the traditional basis for membership with a new arbitrary one, and Athenians would not subsequently have seen their *phulai* as an age-old inheritance. Nevertheless, within the new tradition membership continued to be based on birth.

91 Thucydides *History* 1.95.1. The Ionians ask Athenians to lead the anti-Persian fight *kata to xungenes* "because of our kinship". On political uses of "kinship" (though many examples have to do with an *individual*'s ties to another political entity), see Jones (1999).

92 Carians, Homer *Iliad* 2.867; *to Hellênikon*, Herodotus *Histories* 8.144; fourth-century shift, Hall (2002: 172–211; cf. Hall 1997: xiii).

93 *Menexenus*: other cities homophuloi, 242d (already cited); Athenian populace homophulon, 244a.

94 The story is ancient but has also been disputed since antiquity. The Greeks allegedly swore, before the battle of Plataea in 479, not to rebuild the temples that the Persians had destroyed on the Acropolis of Athens. These would make a more fitting memorial to Persian aggression in their ruined state. Then in

mid-century, more than a decade before the war with Sparta, Pericles convinced the Athenians to approve the ambitious building project that would include the Parthenon and Propylaea, partly on the grounds that the oath no longer applied now that Athens and Persia had agreed to cease their hostilities. See Boedeker (2007: 53); Rhodes (2010: 17).

8

HISTORY

Philosophical history

As short as it is, the *Menexenus* would shrink to nothing without the historical section of the funeral speech.[1] The dialogue would also be livelier without this report on a century of Athenian history that has the dryness of a bad caricature of history teaching. Battle follows battle with sparse detail. Some events go together, but in many cases cause and effect are hard to make out amid improbably splendid Athenian motives on one side and inexplicable bad luck on the other.

Remarkably, the history manages to have a tedious "factual" tone without being factual. No one would call it objective. Socrates' narrative excuses Athenian actions while putting other states' actions in the worst light. The partisanship is ponderous. And yet readers are more likely to attribute playfulness to the *Menexenus*'s historiography than any other trait.[2] Sometimes they take the distortions of history to be satirizing Athenian patriotism, deflating its public rhetoric, or lampooning the very idea of historical inquiry. Plato cannot think that this garbled log of wars and the entities that fought them is a fruitful way to recount the Athenian role in the preceding century's events.[3] The only sequencing principle, to those readers' eyes, is the steady dissolution of the Greek world.[4]

Assessing the history in the narrative calls for consulting other historical writings of this time. If Plato is distorting the facts, the rival sources will best reveal his distortions. But Plato's readers need to examine his history from an internal perspective as well, seeing how it fits among his other dialogues and therefore how it represents Plato. This second approach, rare among commentators, may free Plato's history from a purely reactive interpretation that reads every phrase in the *Menexenus* as either denying Thucydides, or agreeing with him or parodying him. Such approaches risk turning Plato's narrative into a series of tangents to other historians' narratives.[5] A reactive interpretation tends not to seek an ordering principle within Plato's narrative or corpus, inasmuch as the ordering principle lies outside the *Menexenus* or the Platonic dialogues;[6] but this chapter will consider the historical order belonging to the world outside the *Menexenus* alongside the specifically Platonic order that turns up inside it.

Omissions and other distortions of history

Many commentators have pointed out omissions, rearrangements, distortions and errors in the historical section of the funeral speech. More than a century ago C. E. Graves gently noted the "veil" that Plato cast over "the weak places of Athenian history", as when the speech portrayed the Boeotian war as an act of liberation, or the Athenians' return of the Spartans at Sphacteria as a kindness.[7] Thanks to these many responses, the factual errors in the funeral speech have become familiar to all readers, even if the patterns behind those errors have been left under-examined.

The facts are least at issue when Socrates begins his history. After all he begins at the moment of greatest Athenian glory, when the city took the lead in rebuffing Persian invasions into Greece. There is nothing to deny here. Still the emphases, sometimes at odds with other accounts of the war, seem to aim at a particular purpose.

Socrates starts with the growth of Persia, which he casts in the role of an enslaving power. In the span of a few sentences the Persian throne is said to have enslaved (or to be enslaving) Europe, Asia, the Medes, the *gnômai* "thoughts" of all human beings, and many great and warlike peoples.[8] History begins with enslavement, and is kept moving along by the occasional countervailing noble force that liberates – here Athens.

Following Herodotus, Socrates traces the Persian invasion of Greece back to the support that Eretria and Athens provided to the Ionian rebels, those Greek-speaking cities along the coast of Asia Minor that revolted against Persian rule. To pay back the intruders Darius invaded Greece in 490, conquering Eretria but not Athens. Athens stood alone at Marathon. Sparta, Socrates adds, arrived a day too late. These elements of the story are in Herodotus too: Eretria and Athens burned down the Persian city of Sardis, and in Darius' avenging invasion Eretria fell, though under obscurely related circumstances that suggest that Athenian reinforcements abandoned the Eretrians. Anyway Athens called on Sparta for help, though for religious reasons the Spartans did arrive late; and the small Boeotian city Plataea fought with Athens.[9]

To the prevailing *cause* of the world's events, slavery and the fight for freedom, the funeral speech adds its first itemization of history's *participants*. In the *Menexenus* unlike Herodotus' *Histories* Athenians are not present at the fall of Eretria, nor Plataeans at Marathon. The speech seems to require that Athens acted alone.

When the fighting with Persia takes up again a decade later, it still seems imperative to specify which battles count and which do not. Socrates orders them: the naval battles at Salamis and Artemisium – Socrates speaks of *tôn andrôn tôn tote naumachêsantôn* "those men then battling at sea" – then the last stand on land, at Plataea, where Athenians and Lacedaimonians united to defeat the Persian juggernaut.[10] Socrates insists on the proper ranking among these although nothing else in his version of history depends on it. Salamis and Artemisium belong after Marathon and before the joint Greek land battle at Plataea.

Some readers find history being rewritten in the slighting reference to the Spartans at Marathon, when in truth the Spartans' imminent arrival may have goaded the Persians into beginning the fight before they were ready. But this is a small nit to pick when the facts are as the speech presents them. Surely the *Menexenus* should not be obligated to interpret all the data it reports with the greatest charity towards Sparta. Even failing to mention Plataea is forgivable, in light of the small troop size that city represented on the field. Athens effectively did fight alone at Marathon.[11]

Thermopylae is another story. According to legend, that battle took place the same day as the sea fight at Artemisium; in any case it was before Salamis. The Spartans distinguished themselves at Thermopylae, or rather immortalized themselves, and inspired other Greeks to rally against Persia, but Plato does not even include this occasion on the list of battles. Yet he acknowledges the Spartan presence at Plataea. If he wanted to leave Sparta out of the war, why mention them by name at one battle and omit the other battle's name?

Salamis hints at an answer. Herodotus reports the fight at Salamis as the decisive battle that ruined the Persians; Aeschylus implies as much in his *Persians*, when Xerxes' herald arrives to tell of the catastrophe in Greece and does not mention Thermopylae. But the compresence of different Greek navies in that fleet is such a significant feature of the battle that Herodotus explains at length how and why a Spartan, representing a city with no navy, should have become admiral of the combined fleet.[12] The battle also combined land and sea fighting. Aeschylus' messenger dwells on one scene of a slaughter on dry land: Greek troops landed on the small island of Psyttalea where Persian soldiers were waiting to join the battle, and killed those choice troops.[13] For Aeschylus that infantry battle is the "other half" of Persia's loss at Salamis; so Salamis is a mixed fight won by mixed Greeks; yet here is Socrates emphasizing both its status as a sea battle and as a solo effort by Athens. The narrative is already drawing attention to its classifications of military engagements according to *where* they are fought and *who* fights in them.

After disposing of Xerxes the *Menexenus* puts special weight on the years after Plataea, which it depicts as a time of consolidation among Greek cities and a final clean-up against Persia – which amounted to the same thing, Persia having to be put to flight before some Greek cities could overcome their fear. Athenian soldiers drove the whole barbarian force "from the sea". These were the men, Socrates says, who *naumachêsantes* "sea-battling" at Eurymedon, *strateusantes* "warring, mobilizing" in Cyprus, and *pleusantes* "sailing" against Egypt and others, caused the Persian king to attend to his own security rather than continue making designs on Greece.[14]

Except for *strateusantes*, a general verb describing the actions of an army that can apply equally to infantry movements or a fleet's mobilization, this passage speaks exclusively of naval action. Socrates is continuing to draw attention to the types of military engagements that Athens is involved in. The tide did turn against Persia at Eurymedon, whether or not Athens's ulterior motive there was to intimidate and dominate its Greek allies (a process that Socrates sees as unifying Greece), and despite the reversal in Egypt, for the immediate success that the Athenians achieved there was followed by complete defeat.[15]

By all accounts Cimon led the Athenians at Eurymedon, a battle fought in the middle 460s. (The campaign in Egypt, which lasted for six years, began not right afterwards as the funeral speech implies, but in 460 or 459.) Thucydides calls Eurymedon *pezomachia kai naumachia* "land-battle and sea-battle". Versions told in later antiquity, which go into detail about the battle's tactics and may be informed by a different source, depict Cimon arriving with a fleet for a naval engagement that turns into a fight on land. Victory took place on dry land, according to Diodorus Siculus' *Library of History*. The terminology in the *Menexenus* is positively insisting on the contrary of what other histories report.[16]

The *Menexenus* follows Thucydides in dating the first dissent among Greek cities to the years after Eurymedon, but the terms of its explanation depart from Thucydides in a way that will prove significant. Socrates says that Athens "received that which human beings direct towards those who do well: *zêlos* first and then *phthonos*". As a rule *zêlos* and *phthonos* are both translated "jealousy" or "envy", but this would make the sentence a riddle instead of an explanation.

The charged term is *phthonos*, often more malevolent than envy alone and more akin to *Schadenfreude*. Plato's *Philebus* says that *phthonos* accounts for an audience's enjoyment of comedy; the emotion is pleasure at the *kaka* "ills" befalling others. Socrates on trial blames the *phthonos* of the populace for his coming conviction, although they have no reason to envy him.[17] As a response to superiors, which would seem to be the situation at hand, *phthonos* is resentful. The study of these Greek emotions by Ed Sanders calls it "begrudging envy" inasmuch as *phthonos* can describe the act of begrudging someone else honour, praise and position.[18] Thus Plato's *Timaeus* says the creator-god feels no *phthonos*, being not merely without envy but "ungrudging". The *Phaedrus* excludes *phthonos* from the divine realm for similar reasons.[19]

As for *zêlos*, it might have carried a sense of destructive envy or covetousness in archaic Greek. The word is unstable in Hesiod's *Works and Days*, sometimes resembling the Good Strife that Hesiod contrasts with Bad Strife, then also coming close to *phthonos* in meaning. But later authors used *zêlos* as the positive alternative to *phthonos*, sometimes as what turns into *phthonos*. Of these later authors the closest to our purposes is Thucydides, in the last speech he attributes to Pericles. Pericles evokes the spectacle of the Athenian empire. The man who wants to accomplish something himself *zêlôsei* "will want to emulate" the Athenian achievement, while the one who has gotten nothing for himself *phthonêsei* "will envy it". Socrates is voicing much the same sentiment. The allies turned from a positive response to another's good fortune to a negative one, resenting Athenian success.[20]

Thucydides traces the differences among the former allies to a specific event. Faced with a revolt by their subject Helots, the Spartans asked Athens for help. Cimon sent troops to Sparta, but the Spartans did not trust them: they saw the Athenians as *allophulous* "members of a different tribe" or non-kin. The Spartans sent the Athenian soldiers home, offending Athens and leading Athens to give up the *xummachia* "alliance" that the two cities had maintained since the Persian invasion.[21]

Whatever the cause may have been, the proof of hostility was the pair of battles the two cities fought at Tanagra and Oenophytae. According to Thucydides, the Spartan army entered the Greek mainland for other reasons and then lingered near Attica, perhaps with the intention of attacking the Athenian democracy. Both suspicious and seizing the occasion of Sparta's vulnerability, the Athenian army marched out to engage the Spartans, losing amid much *phonos* "killing" on both sides. Two months later the Athenians returned (after the Spartans had gone home) to confront the Boeotians alone at Oenophytae, where they took 100 hostages.[22]

When Socrates recounts the same events he softens the bad news. Tanagra had no clear victor, but the Athenians came back to decide the issue at Oenophytae. On this telling their motives have been ennobled. Twice the *Menexenus* says that the Athenians fought on behalf of the Boeotians' freedom. Plato's readers rebuke him for attributing this best of all motives to the Athenians when they actually fought for reasons of the opposite extreme, for the sake of conquest.[23] Against this charge of distortion it is worth noting that although Thucydides does not speak of Athenian altruism, he makes clear that the Athenians were right to suspect the Spartans' motives. Even on his interpretation the Athenians over-reacted to a fear of attack; hardly the same as aiming at conquest.

History accelerates, Socrates skipping to events that Thucydides reaches only volumes later. The Peloponnesian War is under way, or more specifically the Archidamian War, as the first phase of the fighting is sometimes called. Thucydides cannot imagine an event more important to human history than the war between Sparta and Athens, and he claims to have surmised its significance as soon as the fighting began; Socrates simply speaks of *pollou polemou* "much war". He chooses one battle from this phase to identify by name, the fight at Sphacteria, in southwestern Peloponnesus, that Athens won. It is another *naumachia* "sea-battle". Plato's speech emphasizes the clemency with which Athens fought, taking Spartan prisoners rather than slaughtering them. Thus a single battle demonstrated both Athenian military superiority over other Greeks and the city's commitment to a kind of pan-Hellenism.[24]

It would take pages just to list the events that Thucydides includes between Oenophytae and Sphacteria. That Plato recounts history with at least the distortion of selective memory, compared with Thucydides, ought to be granted without argument. As for Sphacteria itself, Thucydides includes an element of luck in his story. The general Demosthenes was supposed to sail to Corcyra but stopped at Pylos first, where bad weather *kata tuchên* "by chance" drove the ships to shore. The Athenians moored and decided to build a wall, so luckily they were ready when the fight came against Sparta. Commending Athens for this victory would have compelled Thucydides to speak highly of Demosthenes, whom the *History* scorns, as well as the demagogue Cleon. In the present context Thucydides portrays Cleon as ruining an excellent opportunity for negotiation, refusing to bargain for a mutually desirable peace with Sparta after this lucky win.[25]

Thucydides probably overstates his case. Diodorus Siculus reads Athenian success at Sphacteria as the product of forethought and wise strategy, suggesting that Socrates is right to say the battle proved Athenian military superiority. Among modern historians, George Cawkwell takes Thucydides to task for not recognizing Demosthenes' merits as general. The Athenian strategy at Sphacteria must have been canny, Cawkwell says, and a reflection on Demosthenes' expertise.[26] Again, the *Menexenus* for all its brevity might contain the more accurate representation of this battle.

Despite their differences, Thucydides and Diodorus Siculus agree that the fighting at Sphacteria took place on both land and sea. In fact they use nearly identical language to make this point, both of them registering surprise at what must have surprised all Greece at the time, that Sparta the land power fought at sea while Athens the naval force fought on land.[27] This reversal must have become part of the lore surrounding this battle; and the evidence goes clearly against Socrates' simplistic reference to Sphacteria as a naval battle. His choice of the word *naumachia* feels insistent, again as if he were compelled to sort the battles into their categories.

Next comes another jump in the chronicle, to the war that recommenced after the truce of Nicias. In 415 Athens sent a huge fleet to invade Sicily, renewing hostilities that would not end until the Athenian surrender a decade later. Socrates' summary of this war includes the Sicilian Expedition, "the sea-battles at the Hellespont", negotiations between Athens's Greek enemies and Persia, and then another naval battle at Arginusae.[28]

In Thucydides, the Sicilian Expedition is a slowly grinding climax to his history, begun in Athens's imperial ambitions and visibly leading towards disaster, even if Thucydides did not live to bring his story to its wretched finish. The idea for the invasion originates with appeals from Leontini and Egesta, but the desire for power and wealth draw the Athenians to undertake the invasion, and political infighting among the Athenians accounts for the size of the force that sails, with generals who have no use for each other. As for why the Expedition met with crushing defeat, the narrative in Thucydides offers a cluster of explanations, from the desertion of Alcibiades to Nicias' superstitious timorousness, to the "national character" explanation that the Syracusans possessed the same quick and bold temperament as the Athenians.[29]

Socrates replaces this entire painstaking analysis with a remark about the distance between Athens and Sicily, plus the all-purpose *edustuchêsan* "they had bad luck".[30] His reference to the trophies that the Athenians raised in Syracuse (i.e. the battles they won) even suggests that victory had been closer than it was.[31] As for why Athens ever restarted the war, Socrates returns to the Athenians' constant willingness to free other Greeks. But while Plato may well be pressing an explanation at odds with the type found in Thucydides, modern readers should not rush to call the historian a realist and the philosopher's speech a distortion, whether the result of Plato's naivety or of his satirical impulse. Cynics can distort reality too. Donald Kagan has represented Thucydides as tendentious in his claims about Athenian motives, which are the very claims that Plato's critics accept credulously when they take issue with the *Menexenus*'s history. In particular Kagan calls simplistic the claim in Thucydides that Athens invaded Sicily for material or imperial reasons. The wish to help a threatened ally makes better sense of the assembly's deliberations than a quest for domination would, even assuming Thucydides' own report of what people said at that meeting.[32]

Socrates surely does simplify, and thereby distorts, when he blames the Athenian loss on the distance from Athens to Sicily. As Thucydides tells the story, the reasons for the Athenian loss come to more than travelling distance. And yet Thucydides might reinforce the *Menexenus*; he might even be the source for Socrates' claim. According to Thucydides one Syracusan, Hermocrates, predicts that Athens will find itself too far removed from Sicily to respond flexibly to warfare there. If Syracuse prepares a fleet it will have an advantage at sea.[33] Meanwhile Hermocrates makes the same claims about Athenian *motives* that Thucydides puts forward in his own voice, that Athens coveted Syracuse and so pretended to want to aid the Sicilian cities. In other words Thucydides is presenting Hermocrates as a reliable interpreter of events.[34] And later sources report that long after the Athenians had been slaughtered at Sicily, their fellow citizens back home had still not heard the news. Socrates is not obviously wrong to blame the Athenian loss on the distance to Sicily.[35]

From the infantry battles on Sicily[36] Socrates proceeds to multiple naval battles at the Hellespont, a vague reference – Athens both lost and won major battles in that area – that apparently refers to engagements fought in 411/410, among the last events Thucydides tells of: one battle off Cynossema, another at Abydus and a third at Cyzicus. The funeral speech says the Athenians captured all the enemy's ships in one day, though the reports of smaller numbers in Thucydides sound more plausible. The first battle netted the Athenians twenty-one ships and they took another eight a few days later; the *History* does add that a trireme sped back to Athens with the *anelpiston* "unexpected" good news, which rumor may well have puffed up into more than those twenty-nine ships.[37]

The greater distortion lies not in how Socrates reports this set of battles but in his choice to report this one out of all the war's fights, selectively presenting a victory that the Athenians found meaningful, omitting (among others) the immediately preceding losses on Euboea that brought the Spartans within striking distance of Athens and its harbour.[38] Then Socrates reports the enemy's ethnic betrayal, the mutual-aid treaty between Sparta and the Persian governor Tissaphernes in the year before the Athenian naval ventures. As Thucydides also does, the *Menexenus* represents the last phase of war as unnecessary; but where the *History* finds the Athenian itch for conquest and hasty policy at fault, the funeral speech locates what was truly *anelpistos kai deinos* "unforeseeable and terrible" – Socrates uses that phrase twice within a few lines – in the other Greeks' alliance with barbarians. Here is the surprise that made the war turn out as it did. For although Socrates is loath to admit to any bad news for Athens, he is soon saying "we defeated ourselves" – a euphemism, but one that concedes defeat.[39]

Thucydides reports the conditions of the treaty much earlier in Book 8; and well before coming to those terms he tells why the treaty took place to begin with. Tissaphernes owed the king back taxes, and hoped that by neutralizing the Athenians he could collect tribute from the Greek cities under his jurisdiction. The Persians, the Spartans and the weaker Greek cities had begun to plot against Athens with renewed encouragement in the wake of the disaster in Sicily, for now their victory seemed within reach.[40]

By ignoring the Persians' motives as Thucydides reports them, Socrates can pin the blame for the treaty on the other Greek cities. The motivating impulse behind history shifts from one imperial governor's anxiety over his budget to the non-Athenians' character. And what is that character? In Thucydides the Persians and Spartans are pouncing on a weakened Athens. Their actions are rational even if not splendid. But according to the *Menexenus*'s version of history they are moved by *philonikia*,[41] whose literal etymology means "love of victory" but more often, as actually used, was an unattractive motive, contentiousness or resentful quarrelsomeness – something akin to the spiteful *phthonos* with which lesser Greek cities contemplate Athens's pre-eminence. The other cities look more rivalrous if a proof of Athenian virtue and might sent them scurrying to deal with Persia, than they would look if the sight of Athens weakened by Sicily led them to seize an opportunity for victory.

To protest that the Platonic speech misrepresents the pact between Sparta and Persia[42] is not false, but is sometimes put forward incuriously, without the question *why* Socrates should insert the treaty in the narrative where he does, and why he should assign it the significance that he does. There are at least three explanations, and they are compatible with one another.

1 First is *philonikia*: the other Greeks suffer from a character flaw, not the worst flaw (Socrates does not call them money-grubbing or lustful), but bad enough to differentiate their souls from the soul of Athens. Later in this chapter *philonikia* and *phthonos* (the malice glimpsed among non-Athenians after the Persian War) will point towards a deep structure in history. Moving the treaty to the time after an Athenian victory brings out the contentiousness in the other Greek cities.
2 The stress that Socrates places on this moment shows how much it matters that alliances with barbarians are now part of Athenian history. Who makes peace with the King, and when, becomes a recurring question in the remainder of the chronicle, as it had not been before. From now on Greeks are making common cause with Persia, to everyone's detriment.
3 The third consideration comes back to the two texts' relationship with one another. Thucydides himself follows the successful naval battles around the Hellespont with a shift back to Tissaphernes, whose action closes Book 8 and as much of the *History* as was written. Alcibiades claims to have made Tissaphernes "more of a friend" than he had been, although Thucydides portrays the Persians jockeying for influence with Sparta. Anyway, everyone wants to know what the Persians will do next. The *History* ends with Tissaphernes sacrificing to Artemis; if Plato were writing this part of the *Menexenus* while consulting Thucydides, this closing sequence could have been the cause of his own displacement of events – or if not the cause then the excuse, Plato seizing on the *History*'s turn to Greek–Persian relations to complete and correct Thucydides. As Thucydides writes history, the Persian alliance plays a secondary role in the war. An accurate history, from Plato's point of view, would note the international intrigue that Thucydides acknowledges, then amplify its significance as Thucydides does not.[43]

One more battle remains before Athenian defeat and civil war. Out of all the events of the next six years Socrates chooses Arginusae, the last significant engagement of the war, fought in 406. Athens won brilliantly, with eleventh-hour reinforcements arriving just in time to reverse what could have been a massacre. Even in Xenophon's *Hellenica*, which tells the story from Sparta's perspective, the Athenians are valiant. Sparta may chafe at playing the courtier to Persia, but Persian money subsidizes the Spartan fleet. The Athenian general Conon loses thirty ships when Sparta's fleet of 170 reaches him at Mytilene. Athens sends out a fleet and wins decisively. Misfortune prevents the surviving Athenians from collecting their shipwrecked fellows, according to the *Menexenus*; Xenophon specifies that the wind was the cause.[44]

But while Socrates concludes that Arginusae demonstrated Athenian power, most ancient accounts emphasize the battle's depressing aftermath, in which satisfaction at victory was eclipsed by the officers' blaming one another for not having retrieved the shipwrecked survivors. In the end Athens executed six generals *en masse*, among them the young Pericles, son of Pericles and Aspasia. (See comments on this case in Chapter 3, on Socrates.) Socrates evidently used his powers as executive officer of the day to block this illegal suspension of judiciary procedure, but whether because another officer succeeded him the next day, or for some other reason, his veto did not prevail. It is poignant to imagine Socrates defending the son of the political figure he once mocked; even more poignant to think Aspasia might have written a speech, and Socrates then recited it, with no special emphasis on these events from either of them. "We defeated ourselves", and not least by throwing even the victorious generals into a pit;[45] but the speech does not stoop to particulars about losing a son or standing alone against the assembly.[46]

Self-defeat implies a city that is not one. Division within the city can become civil war, as it did in Athens when the Thirty Tyrants tried to hold on to power despite increasing opposition from the democratic faction. The *Menexenus* recalls the return to democracy as harmonious. That the reality was bitter and bloody is too well known to need arguing: Socrates himself acknowledges that reality at his trial, referring to the Tyrants' not only slaughtering their enemies but also spreading the blame around for those arrests. Xenophon and Lysias make the extent of this terror clear.[47]The funeral speech understates the civil war. And no doubt the understatement furthers the general propagandistic effect. But note that it also serves the purpose of reintroducing ethnic unity into history, right after those other cities affronted Hellenic unity by cozying up to Persia. The Athenians quickly settled such civil war as they had because they were a *homophulos* populace, members of the same tribe or stock. If only such motives applied to the other Greeks!

Strictly speaking, the chronicle continues for another two full pages after the defeat of Athens (and largely after the death of Socrates). But the distortions in those pages are harder to catalogue. Socrates spends more of the remaining narrative interpreting world events and their participants' motives than he does telling what happened. These are recent events, as he says – and in fact the way the speech passes over them is one more reason to date the *Menexenus* close after the last incidents it relates. It tells of these final incidents with a tone suited to that which goes without saying.[48] Athens forgave its barbarian enemies but not its Greek erstwhile friends. (The ignominious end to the Peloponnesian War, elided over in the actual chronology, is tacitly admitted to here. The other Greeks had taken Athens's ships away and torn down its walls.) With Athens absconded from the responsibility of keeping other cities free, Sparta soon enslaved them. Greeks and Persians alike pleaded for help. Athens showed its one culpable impulse, its pity, liberating fellow Greeks once more and looking the other way while Athenian citizens, acting privately, gave aid to Persia.[49]

The speech restates the cause for the city's actions, its Hellenic purity. No barbarian ancestry mingles in Athenian bodies, so Athens refused to let Persians hold the Ionian Greek cities of Asia Minor. This decision, which the speech mentions twice, organizes the few specific references to military events that remain: Athens fighting with Persia against Sparta, then fighting at Corinth and Lechaeum. Socrates comes back to the Athenian alliance with Persia *after* his mention of Corinth and Lechaeum, making the alliance the act of clearing the sea of Spartan ships. He apparently means the actions of the Persian fleet under Conon's command.[50]

When it reaches the Corinthian War the speech comes as close to a confession of failure as it ever does. "In this war as well *esterêthêmen* 'we were deprived of' good men, who dealt with *duschôria* 'bad ground' in Corinth and *prodosia* 'betrayal' at Lechaeum". But Athens fought alongside and against other Greeks at Corinth; Socrates turns elusive when Persia enters the story. He makes Athenian cooperation with Persia the private work of lone Athenians, not the city's collective action. This is false. Conon may have commanded the Persian fleet on his own initiative and answering to Persian rulers, but he worked on behalf of Athens. It was Sparta that Conon chased from the sea. More than one source says he brought Persian money to his hometown to rebuild the strategic long walls that connected Athens with its port Piraeus. Socrates says proudly that Athens built up its navy and walls and again proudly that it kept them after the Corinthian War. He only does not admit who paid for them.[51]

Most obscure of all is the way this speech treats the King's Peace. That treaty ended the Corinthian War in 386, so by rights it should be the final event in the *Menexenus* speech's history. In a way the peace treaty does appear in the speech, but transposed and negated, as an unwelcome thought would be in a Freudian dream. Socrates negates the bargain that Persia struck with the major Greek cities and turns it from an *effect* of warfare into a *cause*. Xenophon and Diodorus Siculus, whose narratives differ in other essentials, both assert that:

1 Athens formed an alliance with other Greek cities, principally Thebes (395).
2 The alliance fought Sparta.
3 Sparta, stuck in two wars at once, approached Persia seeking peace.
4 Persia declared that it had the right to rule all Greek cities in Asia Minor.
5 Sparta and the other Greeks agreed, and the Peace established the new status quo for the eastern Mediterranean.[52]

Athens probably disliked the Peace.[53] It meant that the Ionian cities that had risen up against Persia more than a century earlier – Athens had supported that rebellion, and Persia's invasion of Greece had been the reply – after all this fighting, would belong to Persia again. The Persian Wars proved to have been not a decisive war after all, only a preliminary battle that the old King lost en route to the new King's finally winning the war by other means.

Losing Ionia was not merely a sentimental affair and not even a symbol. It meant that Athens could no longer imagine re-establishing its old empire. Sparta governed Greece, with Persia behind the throne. (The Spartans themselves might not like to acknowledge that Persia determined the new political landscape, but their reluctance must have been the symptom of general Greek contempt for deals with the Persians.[54])

Given the unacceptability of this new reality, which in turn makes the King's Peace unacceptable, presenting the events of recent history in their raw state is impossible; nor just because this is a funeral speech and therefore propagandistic. It would pain Athenians to be reminded of history's final dispensation (or what promised to be the final dispensation at the time, to Athenians unprepared for Macedonia's rise). Plato does not have to be seeking dramatic verisimilitude to speak obliquely of the King's Peace; it is enough for him to be Athenian and sharing in his city's humiliation.

To see the obliqueness in the *Menexenus*, consider what the funeral speech does to the events attested to by historians, which in that form constitute a sequence of cause and effect:

$$(1) \to (2) \to (3) \to (4) \to (5)$$

For example, *because* (2) the other cities fight Sparta, *therefore* (3) Sparta seeks peace, and so (4) Persia stipulates that it keep the Ionian cities. But the last stretch of the *Menexenus*'s historical narrative may be schematized:

$$(1) \to (4) \to \sim(5) \to (2)$$

The negation in front of (5) refers to Socrates' denial that Athens ever agreed to Persian control over the cities in Asia Minor.[55] Athens did sign the Peace, but Socrates denies the fact twice. And then, instead of making the negotiation with Persia a consequence of warfare, as it seems to have been, Socrates inverts the causal sequence so that Athens appears to have fought and lost because of its principled stand on behalf of Ionia. The fundamental information is all here, but rearranged to hide the forbidden thought that Athens formed an agreement with Persia contrary to those Greek cities' freedom. This retelling softens the hard news, which is nevertheless too important to leave out altogether, that Persia now controls Greece. The cycle that began with Athens's first principled opposition to Persia – before Marathon and consequently *at* Marathon – reaches its ignominious finish with the Peace. The speech can disguise that last fact as if in a dream, because every Athenian listening or reading knew what had happened and understood what it meant.

Apart from the distortions that are most visible concerning the events that Socrates reports, there are the unreported incidents and relationships that Plato's readers have drawn attention to. Some commentators focus on longer lists of omissions, others on shorter ones, but a few turn up on more than one list. Of three significant distortions cited in Kahn's treatment of the *Menexenus*, two are the dialogue's silence about Athens's empire (before and during the Peloponnesian War) and its silence about its times of amicable relations with Persia (especially around the Corinthian War). These are two of the three significant distortions that Trivigno finds in the *Menexenus* as well.[56] These steady misrepresentations of history do not have to prove that the speech is a parody, but they do demand some explanation.[57]

This chapter will offer an interpretation that accounts for Plato's emphasis on Persia. The interpretation begins with the undeniable fact that recent commentators have been right to press, which is that Plato must have a reason for showing Athens steadfastly at odds with Persia despite all the other changes in international relations, and (as in connection with the King's Peace) at odds with reality. The *Menexenus* aims at expounding a universal history, one with a schema that accounts for the entire known world and illustrates basic principles of motivation and action.[58] Patriotism aside, the constraints of such a history will call for Athens to function as a solo and *sui generis* participant in world events, as well as a state that (for reasons to be explained) refuses to make alliances with Persia.

The speech's silence about "empire" is a harder business. Everyone knew that Athens had brought its allies together into a league of putative equals that it came to dominate and even tyrannize. In his last speech in Thucydides, Pericles tries to rally an assembly full of dispirited plague survivors to continue the war against Sparta. He appeals to their pride in Athenian military successes. Athenian *archê* "rule" does not extend merely over *xummachôn* "allies"; it is greater than that. It will be remembered that *êrxamen* "we ruled" more Greeks than any other Greeks did. What Athenians risk at this turning point in the war is not just enslavement but loss of *archê*. To make clear the imperial nature of this rule Pericles even says that Athens is now *hôs turannida* "like a tyranny" among the other Greek states.[59] Why should Socrates' anti-Periclean speech ignore the international relation that defines Periclean Athens? Does his silence serve to conceal Athens's ugly past and implicitly to condemn Pericles' policy of conquest? Or is Plato refraining from saying anything where he had nothing nice to say?[60]

But maybe proposals about the political purpose of eliding over the empire are looking in the wrong place, presuming that the historical narrative of the *Menexenus* could hold such an entity as the Athenian empire and wondering why it failed to mention it. A different hypothesis should be open to consideration, that the story being told in this dialogue presupposes a different political ontology. Whether the empire was a good or bad thing, or the cause of Athenian bullying and cruelty, speaking of empire forces the historian to redescribe the dynamic of international relations, so that Athens is not an individual participant in those affairs but part of a larger body. It is easier to visualize a state's actions on the world stage as if the state were an individual and acted as one; and the universal history that this chapter finds in the funeral speech will consistently treat Athens as such a unit.

The *Menexenus* and the historians

Besides differing from other historical accounts in the facts it includes, the *Menexenus* also seems novel in its methods of historical narrative and historical explanation. It is practically impossible to say at this remove what historical works were available in Plato's day and which of them he would have read; still, orienting the funeral speech among the historians whose works survive might help to focus what if anything is new about Plato's historiography.

What Plato read

No events mentioned in the funeral speech would require Plato to have read or listened to any works of history written in his time. Most of those that were not important incidents had taken place after his birth, and the rest (e.g. Salamis) would have been familiar to everyone. Nevertheless it is almost beyond doubt that Plato read other historians. There were local histories, lost today, that chronicled individual cities in isolation from all other world events; he likely also read *Gês Periodos*, "World Survey" by Hecataeus of Miletus, the author Herodotus treats as a predecessor.

The local histories of Athens are known collectively as "Atthidography". Although only fragments remain from this genre that began before Thucydides and continued after the death of Aristotle, those surviving parts suggest that the Atthidography available to Plato would not have influenced the *Menexenus*. From what we can tell, aetiologies, etymologies, genealogies and the explanations of religious ritual seem to be common elements in the local histories; they are all absent from the history that Socrates tells in the *Menexenus*.[61]

As for Herodotus, he does not tell of many events that also appear in the *Menexenus*. The *Histories* ends with the Persian Wars, about where the funeral speech begins. Plato seems to have read Herodotus, at least by the time he wrote the *Timaeus*, which contains several allusions to the *Histories*, including what is close to a direct quote from its first sentence;[62] and in another context it would be worth developing points of correspondence between Plato's *Theaetetus* and Herodotus' work. But Herodotus will not inform the specifics of history as told in the *Menexenus*.

Xenophon's *Hellenica* is less relevant than the *Histories*. Nothing in the *Menexenus* depends on Plato's having read the *Hellenica;* and because of the late date of that work it is possible that Plato never saw it, or had not seen it by the time he wrote his own chronicle. The *Hellenica* will probably not inform historical method in the *Menexenus*, whatever its intrinsic historical worth might be.

Thucydides is another matter. Scholars in the past sometimes denied that Plato read the *History*, or denied that he paid attention to what he did read.[63] Given the numerous ways in which Plato's history diverges from Thucydides', this judgement is understandable. On the other hand the *Menexenus* funeral speech is closely attentive to the speech of Pericles as structured in the *History*. There is no evidence that the famous funeral oration existed in any other context or other written form. Plato must have known the version as it appeared in Thucydides, and he must have read much of the rest of the *History*. Can we imagine a Plato so uninquisitive that he read the speech and set out to reply to it but did not bother reading the rest?

As for all the divergences between Plato and Thucydides: there is a third obvious possibility besides his reading then disregarding the *History* and never having read it at all. Plato could have been disregarding Thucydides actively and deliberately, taking a stand against a number of points of Thucydidean history and historiography. The stand involves Plato's own answers to why one writes history in the first place; which events a historical account should include; whether those events come together in a grand overall shape or lead to a definitive conclusion; and how any one event brings about the one after it.

Why write history?

Thucydides' motives have integrity even if he does betray biases and personal grudges along the way. Setting down a lasting record of events, adding to the store of human knowledge, have become standard for historical practice, along with the unconcern for immediate effects that those motives imply; and perhaps also (though it would not be cordial to impute this to historians at large) unconcern about the immediate delight that a work of history brings its audience.

Socrates announces a different set of motives as he begins his funeral speech. One tells the history of Athens in order to praise the dead and improve their survivors, and presumably to do both right away. Thucydides has left out what his *History* might have included if it *had* ever been recited to a crowd, which is to say a function in the culture that produced it.

The *Menexenus* might even be eschewing the ambition to produce historical knowledge for its own sake (assuming that Plato believes there is any such thing as historical knowledge). As if to stress the unimportance of historiography's record-keeping function, Socrates asks as his speech approaches very recent events whether he needs to tell those stories. Everyone present knows them. It is like something that Critias says in the *Timaeus*, not about recent events but about a story so old that everyone has forgotten it. Retelling the tale will be a "hymn of praise" suitable to the goddess on the occasion of her festival. As different as the *Menexenus*'s history is from the stories of legendary Athens that Critias speaks of in the *Timaeus*, both contexts seem to call for some instrumental value to justify the telling of history; and praise is at least one of those instrumental values.[64]

If you attribute motives to ancient historians according to what they declare their motives to be, then history for praise's sake aligns the *Menexenus* more with Herodotean than Thucydidean history. The *Histories* begins by announcing three purposes:

1 It will preserve otherwise-forgotten actions – but then every historical account preserves some version of the past.
2 It will tell why the Persian War took place – another unobjectionable motive for historians, and one that does not distinguish Herodotus much from Thucydides.
3 Herodotus also speaks of the *kleos* "glory" that great men and great events deserve. To recognize the *kleos* of the great is to praise them. Herodotus may praise less than Socrates does in the funeral speech, and Thucydides may praise his favourite figures, such as Themistocles and Pericles, more than his official image of history-writing would imply; but if the *Menexenus* wants a spiritual predecessor among the historians of its time, that would more likely be the one who announces praise as a task for history.

Universal history

Whatever the reason for writing about history's incidents, the story that results will have to *select* and *organize* the events that it tells of, and also in some way *explain* them, if not explaining the totality of facts then at least accounting for many of them taken separately.

Plato's predecessors and contemporaries will not account for the selectiveness in the funeral speech's history. The readers of Herodotus sometimes wonder what criterion he could have used for excluding stories from his book, in light of the impression he gives of welcoming every character and wild tale. Of course this first impression does not last. To a greater degree as the *Histories* continues, it focuses on facts germane to the war against Persia, the event that Herodotus must have grown up hearing about as unsurpassed in importance. And so, broadly speaking, he may be described as selecting the most noteworthy historical incidents to include in his work.

Thucydides makes the criterion explicit. He writes about the Peloponnesian War because it exceeded the Persian and even the Trojan wars in importance; for the same reason Thucydides rarely pauses to talk about anything but Athenian activity pertaining to that war. Xenophon behaves as heir to the historical tradition in his attempt – even if it is only a professed attempt – to tell of what he found "noteworthy".[65]

Plato does not seem to be fishing for important events the way the historians do. This is not to say he is unselective in his choices, only that he is rejecting the idea that history should be about the greatest battles, and should detail the most notable events. He replaces that standard with a philosophical conception of history, in deference to which he both omits some facts that every other historian would include, and includes what the others pass over.

After the selection of events comes the work of arranging and explaining them. Those tasks have a way of blurring into each other, depending on what you take the dominant sign or effect of "universal history" to be. Sometimes a history of all things everywhere shows its ambition *diagnostically*, finding the same cause or few causes (e.g. class struggle) at work in all historical events. Then history exhibits a uniform texture, and it speaks universally insofar as the explanatory theory finds the same specific sequences everywhere.

A history may also present itself as universal *teleologically*, if it finds all events tending in a single direction, towards the end of days or the end of history. Then history enacts a uniform text, a story that no matter how multifarious is bound to reach a single conclusion.

Either, or neither, kind of universal history may be called "determinist". Neither one can claim that title exclusively, and although the two approaches to history might overlap they do not have to. The same force might determine each step in a sequence without the total sequence's ever arriving anywhere. Conversely, history might be heading for a single *telos* by means of countless different causal sequences.

Thucydides, for example, emphasizes prevailing causes in history but rarely speaks of large-scale patterns of historical narrative. What stands out is his pronouncement about the cause of the Peloponnesian War that superseded all others. The *alêthestatê* "truest" explanation lies in the Athenians' becoming *megalous* "great" and causing *phobon* "fear, terror" in the Spartans. Wars begin when a state has military reasons to feel threatened.[66]

Thucydidean thinking has such a seductive unsentimentality that modern readers may forget Thucydides is offering one diagnosis among many. As J. E. Lendon has recently argued, many ancients assessed international relations in the quite different vocabulary of prestige, deference and insult; moreover Lendon says they were right to do so. Lendon's first claim stands regardless of whether the second one does. Whatever the truth of the matter about the causes at work in Greek history, the classical sources that Diodorus Siculus would later draw on, as well as the man in the Athenian street, found it more natural to assess the relations among cities in terms of genuine and perceived insult. Even if Thucydides is right and other classical observers are wrong, his analysis strikes the other ancients as foreign and counter-intuitive.[67]

Diagnostically, then, Plato might follow a vision of history as rigorous as the one Thucydides adheres to, without committing himself to Thucydidean calculations of force and fear. Indeed the *philonikia* or competitiveness that this chapter will find at work among Athens's rivals (what the *Menexenus* calls the half-Greek cities) fits congenially with assessments of leadership and demonstrations of respect. As Lendon says, the Greek cities themselves assessed the political landscape in terms of which city was *hêgemôn* and which others had to defer to that one. These will be close to the terms the *Menexenus* appeals to.

By comparison, that bottom-line motive in Thucydides, *phobos*, is not a candidate for generating history as Plato sees it. The speech never ascribes fear to Athens. Other Greeks are afraid of Athens, otherwise of Persia; the King of Persia fears Athens too; but Athenians act from different motives.[68]

Herodotus does not diagnose all historical change in terms of a single force or commonest cause of action. The *Histories* is full of causal explanations, but they cover a range of motives.[69] Any determinism in Herodotus must be a very soft variety, in which many of the greatest events are notable for their contingency. They could well have turned out otherwise: as one commentator writes, "Herodotus took every opportunity to show that the Persian War had not been inevitable".[70]

Even so, such universality as history does possess for Herodotus derives from its total text as opposed to any continuity in texture. Something like mega-history is visible in the great cycles that Herodotus announces at the start of Book 1. "I will go forward and tell the story of small and great cities and people alike. For of those that were great in the past, many became small, and those that were great in my time were previously small". The change does not come by chance. Smallness means poverty, and poor nations become tough; meanwhile riches make men soft, hence vulnerable, and the great subsequently fall into smallness. Herodotus brings his grand narrative to a finish with the Persian king Cyrus espousing exactly this causal mechanism at work in history, a succinct explanation at the end of Book 9 for the phenomenon that Book 1 began by observing.[71]

Plato's dialogues are fond of cyclical visions of history in other contexts.[72] The funeral speech refuses to read repetitions and cycles in the passage of time (as the next section will argue); in this respect it contradicts Herodotus. But it replaces the pendulum of Herodotus not with a chaos of unintelligible small events, as if that were the only alternative to cyclical repetitions, but with a steady story. Herodotus will turn out to have been right to see a general pattern in history. He only did not look closely enough to see what that pattern really was.

Order in history

To see what Plato's history lesson purports to teach[73] perhaps as other historians of his time did not try to do, it may be worth leaving aside the omissions and inclusions and ask, as few readers have asked, what internal logic might drive the resulting narrative. What sense does this story make to Plato? Consider the sequence:

1   Marathon. Athens wins a land victory over Persia (240c–d).
2   Artemisium and Salamis. Athens wins a sea victory over Persia (240e–241b).
3   Plataea. Athens and Sparta together win a land victory over Persia (241c).
4   Eurymedon, followed by expeditions to Cyprus and Crete. Athens and Greek allies defeat Persia (and its subject Egypt) decisively at sea (241e).

Now other Greek cities begin to envy the honour that Athens has earned for itself. The Peloponnesian War begins:

5   Tanagra and Oenophytae. Fighting over freedom for Greeks in Boeotia, Athens defeats Sparta (242a–b).
6   Sphagia (= Sphacteria). Athens defeats Sparta in a sea battle but spares the Spartans present (242c).
7   Sicily. Treacherous Greek cities impose heavy losses on Athens in land battles (242e–243a).
8   Hellespont. Athens wins a ruinous sea battle over allied Greek cities (243a–b).

At this point the enemy cities join forces with Persia (243b).

9   Mytilene/Arginusae. Athens defeats Sparta and Persia at sea in a disastrous battle (243c).
10   Corinthian War (I). Corinth and Lechaeum. Athens joins with Persia to battle Sparta on behalf of other Greek cities. Athens loses a difficult battle on rough ground at Corinth (245e).
11   Corinthian War (II). Athens and Persia drive Sparta from the sea (246a).

The battles alternate between land and sea, falling into pairs or triplets (1, 2), (3, 4), (5, 6), (7, 8, 9), (10, 11), as determined by who Athens's allies and enemies are. Athens fights alone against Persia at Marathon and again in the naval confrontations of 479. Then Athens fights together with Sparta and other Greek cities, first by land at Plataea and then at sea.

Part of the sculpting of history has the effect of putting army and navy on equal or close to equal footing. In the *Menexenus* the two win together and lose together. This is to say that neither force is more effective than the other, also to say that they aim at the same targets. Accordingly the *Menexenus*'s language repeatedly pairs army and navy.[74] Thus Athens returns to warfare *teichisamenê … kai naupêgesamenê* "having built walls and ships".[75] Army and navy do not represent distinct foreign policies. But describing army and navy this way amounts to a remarkable concession, given how many

Athenians had come to see their navy as a symbol of decline. Especially after the debacle at Arginusae, when Athens won the battle but left its shipwrecked sailors to drown, "navy" seemed to equal radical democracy and the chaos that democracy produced.[76]

The navy's second billing in the *Menexenus* is not meant as an insult to ships. Rather it makes the difference between army and navy a difference in degree. The ranking simply puts Athens's army ahead of its navy, and not nearly far enough by comparison with some dialogues. The *Republic* makes no provision for a navy despite its recognition that even the first most primitive city will ship goods in and out by sea and despite its ship-of-state metaphor for the disorderly city.[77] The *Laws* positively condemns the effect a navy has on citizens. People who fight by rowing instead of by meeting the enemy on dry land only learn to be cowards. Much better to give up the benefits of maritime commerce than to endure the corrupting consequences of sea travel.[78] Moreover a navy empowers the most impoverished segment of the population, which Plato saw as the constituency most favouring military expansion.[79]

The other dialogue that contains something like a history of real-life Athens, the *Critias*, pictures a beautiful Athens of legendary past without either ships or walls. It is Atlantis, the infamous enemy, that packs hundreds of thousands of sailors into its fleet of 1,200 ships.[80]

But the *Critias* might also show why the Athens of history *ought to* have been depicted with a navy. That is the only dialogue that Plato abandoned unfinished. Maybe he did so because the all-infantry Athens it imagines could not have defeated the island nation and its thousand ships. Cities that isolate themselves from world politics can maintain only marching regiments to defend themselves with, but a city engaged in alliances and power politics in the world as it exists will have to sail into that world. The navy in the *Menexenus* is a sign that the Athens it tells of will be embedded in larger politics. Somewhat as *Republic* Book 8 attends to economic activities, not because Plato values money but because citizens acting as economic agents bring about constitutional changes, so too Plato does not have to like navies to include them in his history of the world beyond Athens.

Soul, city, world

In addition to alternating land and sea forces the *Menexenus* rigs its chronicle to finesse the order of participants, making that order: Athens fights alone; Athens fights alongside other Greek cities; then Athens against those cities; lastly Athens fights together with Persia.

Barbarians literally threaten in this history, even if Plato does neglect to mention the warm gates they stormed through. But as our discussion of autochthony emphasized, Socrates' talk of *barbaroi* distracts from the rigorous division of peoples that is at work: not a division in two as ethnocentricity alone would have it, but three. World history now involves real Greeks

(Athenians), barbarians (paradigmatically the Persians) and half-Greek people from the cities outside Athens. Psychodynamic relations among these three determine whether the best of them preserves a healthy harmony in the whole or the lower elements rebel to destabilize that harmony.

Education is part of the relationship. The good birth that sets the uppermost group apart does not release them from the need for good training. When gods tutored the first Athenians, they included the instruction necessary *pros tên huper tês chôras phulakên* "for the guardianship of their territory". So another word for Athenians might be *phulakas* "guardians".

Having been so finely educated, these finest people exercise their leadership by training those below them. Athenian victories at Marathon and Salamis taught Sparta and the other Greeks the virtue of courage. "The other Greeks were educated [*paideuthênai*] by those who fought at Marathon and Salamis, learning and accustoming themselves [*mathontas kai ethisthentas*] ... not to fear the barbarians". The mixed Greeks later "dared [*etolmêsan*] to risk endangering themselves, having become students [*mathêtai*] of the Marathon soldiers".[81]

Talk of wars and barbarian enemies recalls the *Republic*'s proposals for a new warfare that favours fellow Greeks.[82] But something else in the *Republic* is more to the point. Socrates says he wants the city's divisions to correspond to aspects of human nature; so as a first heuristic he identifies actual appearances of (1) *to thumoeides* "the spirited element", (2) *to philomathes* "knowledge-love" and (3) *to philochrêmaton* "money-love", the motive impulses behind the city's classes and roughly the names of the motives he will find in human souls.[83] In this passage the three motives are said to be found among (respectively) (1) Thracians, Scythians and other people to the north, (2) Athenians,[84] and (3) Egyptians and Phoenicians.

The Hippocratic treatise *Airs, Waters, Places* had already associated ethnicities with character traits before Plato's birth, most notably the Europeans with courage and people of "Asia" (whatever area the author means by that word) with cowardice.[85] The *Republic* does not take the line of thought further, but leaves Socrates' analogy standing as a possible mapping between parts of the soul and nations of the world. The *Menexenus*'s explanation of history can be read as the development of this suggestion. One ethnicity guards and teaches, the next is its auxiliary and the third generally threatens. Sparta's reputation for warrior courage most approximates to that of the northerners in Thrace and Scythia, so on this reckoning Sparta functions within the world as the *thumoeides* does in the individual human being.

Certainly the *Republic*'s classification of Egyptians and Phoenicians transfers to Persia, which the *Menexenus* calls wealthy and numerous. And it is relevant that the *Menexenus* refers to Egypt as an enemy, thus linking Egyptians with their fellow barbarians the Persians. The *Menexenus* funeral speech also acknowledges the multiplicity of the nationalities contained within the Persian Empire. Persia may go by a single name but it is a grab bag of ethnicities, much as the *Republic* calls the soul's desiring element *poikilon* "manifold".[86]

Aligning the *Menexenus*'s ethnic categories with the three parts of the soul is a logical extension of the *Republic*'s city/soul analogy. Thanks to this alignment, psychological principles can be invoked in accounting for historical phenomena. The *Menexenus* strives to tell an orderly story of the Athenian century, indeed to order the existing story by identifying the dominant motives that move history along.[87] Where *Republic* 8 confines itself to the doings within one city, holding the rest of Greece fixed, the *Menexenus* speech situates Athens amid neighbouring and domestic powers largely holding internal politics constant.[88]

And so during happy times justice within the city and pan-Hellenic harmony abroad are both ensured by the respective top groups' wise governance. A small power that recognizes what is best for the larger body it belongs to educates the less perfect members of its own kind; the training partly consists in bringing out the next group's courage so that the amorphous third con-catenation of humanity surrenders to their alliance. The small governing power is a peacemaker, restraining its *orgê* "anger" in the interests of *to koinon* "the common", what is common to all Greeks. This is a city that lets shame govern its behaviour, as if to say that measure is built into the Athenian nature.[89]

The three parties of the *Menexenus* all fit into these categories. This way of looking at justice in the world now makes sense of apparent Athenian altruism to other Greeks – the Athenians are the *guardians* of the world – and at the same time explains their superiority – the *Athenians* are the guardians of the world. In the *Republic* guardianship is a function of breeding and birth that comes with responsibilities of altruistic service to the lower classes.

Not only the parties to history but their motives and destiny recall the *Republic*.[90] For the cooperativeness and the moral instruction that characterized Greece during the Persian Wars prove not to survive the subsequent peace. International harmony begins to decline along a trajectory familiar from the *Republic*. This is the meaning of the order in the *Menexenus*'s list of battles. Warfare reduplicates relations among the city's classes and the soul's parts.

In Greece as in the *Republic*'s city the first step is momentous. What could undo a well-functioning system? The fault lies with that problematic middle group whose imperfections turn it away from the great alliance.[91] The middle group comes under the influence of *phthonos*, the grudging envy or malice already noticed in the *Menexenus*'s history. In *Republic* Book 8, the chronicle of worsening souls pictures a good man moving from the first rank to the second, becoming timocratic. This man hears his mother complaining about the advantages that other women have. *Her* husband, the best kind of man, does not give his family the possessions and honours they would like to have. So the soul's turn to the worse begins with resentment, or what can fairly be called grudging envy, at the advantages that other people possess.

Later in the story of souls' declines the word *phthonos* is explicitly associated with the second-best person (as well as with worse types). Socrates says that in the timocratic type of man the spirited part of the soul has gone wrong. Such a man satisfies his *philotimian* "desire for honour" not with the honours that come of behaving virtuously but rather by *phthonos.*[92]

The *Menexenus* finds the same wish for domination operating in Greek cities considered as individuals. After the wars against Persia, Socrates says Athens was honoured at first by those so-called compatriots. But "she received that which human beings direct toward those who do well: *zêlos* first and then *phthonos*". The Peloponnesian War followed. Other Greeks admired Athens, but the wish to emulate gave way to resentment. As already seen, the contrast between *zêlos* and *phthonos* sets an admiring respect for superiors against the resentful wish to see them brought low. And as in the late books of the *Republic*, the element that should have been an aide to the natural leader becomes the cause of the first decline.[93]

The *Menexenus* also applies the word *philonikia* "contentiousness" to the non-Athenian cities of Greece,[94] reinforcing the parallel to the *Republic*'s psychology. The context makes clear that Socrates is not using that word in a positive or even neutral sense, meaning (for instance) "competitiveness". The other cities see Athens ascendant and the thought pains them, and they seek victory in an unacceptable manner, through a treaty with Persia. Plato does sometimes use *philonikia* without negative connotations, but more often the word implies something disagreeable. The dialogues sometimes pair this contentiousness with a baser motive, implicitly contrasting the two but only by way of distinguishing bad from worse. The penalty for spurious prosecution in the *Laws* depends on whether *philonikia* or *philochrêmatia* "love of money" is the cause – worse to sue in hopes of gain than for the purpose of ruining a rival – but still the difference comes to death in one case, in the other case death after the second offence.[95]

More broadly the *Timaeus* calls *philonikia* and *epithumia* "desire" two human motives that feed one's bodily nature, making a soul more mortal, as opposed to the intellectual pursuits that feed the soul's immortal yearnings. This *epithumia* is the *Republic*'s word for desire, understood as the soul's third part, and the passage in the *Timaeus* comes close to recapitulating the *Republic*'s psychology, with *philonikia* in the place of that second-ranked part of the soul the *thumos*. As a matter of fact the *Republic* itself puts *philonikia* into that same place; *philonikia* is evident in the second-best regime, early in the good city's decline, because of the prominence of the *thumos* "spirit, anger" in a timocratic regime. Where *thumos* is at work, *philonikia* is the sign.[96]

It is telling that centuries later, when Polybius self-consciously undertakes to produce a universal history that will bring Greece and Rome together in a grand story of the world, he appeals to *phthonos* as the *Republic* and *Menexenus* do. For Polybius the number two's wish to supplant number one is a constant in world history. It is hard not to see Plato as his inspiration, especially given that no one else from classical Greece had spoken of history in those terms.[97]

As for the lowest of the world's three forces, the *Menexenus* portrays it re-entering history for tactical reasons. The second-best element seeks to cement its own place by joining in an alliance with the third; the third now asserts its own pre-eminence. And even here a psychological explanation might be at work that the *Republic* would recognize.[98] Socrates says that Athens had a reason to ally itself with the Persians. At first blush he is only piling on the praise. If you wanted to criticize Athens *dikaiôs* "justly" and *orthôs* "rightly", he says, you would have to say that the city "has always been excessively prone to pity". In this instance Athens could not stand to watch even Persia suffering and allied itself with the King. Athens is *philoiktirmôn* "fond of pitying".

Socrates might seem to be *pretending* to criticize Athens, saying, "Our flaw is that we care too much about world justice"; as people pretend to criticize themselves when they call themselves perfectionists. But suppose that the funeral speech calls this accusation "right" and "just" not as a joke, but with the purpose of distinguishing what right justice commands from the surrender to pitying passions. After all, the *Republic* envisions a city whose rulers do not let compassion stop them from assigning bronze souls to the third rank, according to Socrates' explication of the noble lie. Pity that contravenes the demands of rational rule would amount to the soul's lowest part governing when it ought to be obeying.

For that matter it is pity, not one of the high-profile desires like lust and hunger, that *Republic* 10 condemns in connection with tragedy. Socrates urges a ban on mimetic poetry in order that the good citizens not be encouraged to enjoy lamenting people's misfortunes.

In both of the relevant passages from the *Republic*, the words for pity come from the root *eleos*; the *Menexenus*'s description of Athens as prone to pity, *philoiktirmôn*, is built on the root *oiktos*. Some Greek authors show a definite preference for one of the two words (*eleos* or *oiktos*) over the other, but they seem to overlap considerably in meaning and psychological force.[99] If the *Republic* sees no joke in curbing pity in the interests of justice, this passage in the *Menexenus* can be read as a diagnosis of the world's final deterioration. The worst political element returns to power in coincidence with the worst psychological element's sway over Athens.

The proof that history reached its terminus in 386 is the progress of enslavement. In the *Republic* slavery provides the occasion for seeing power in a perverse or distorted form;[100] along similar lines the *Menexenus* charts the sombre spread of slavery. The funeral speech discovers the beginning of history within Persia, when Cyrus frees the Persians and enslaves the Medes. Slavery is not merely physical, which is why Socrates insisted that the Athenians cannot be one another's slaves or masters. Non-Athenian Greeks are not attached to natural liberty in the same way: Athens releases them from *douleia* but they enslave themselves again.[101] At last, as the tyrant finally comes into power in *Republic* 9 and makes slaves of all citizens, the Corinthian War re-establishes Persia's dominance over the eastern Mediterranean; and the Greeks had no better model for a tyrant than the one who sat on Persia's throne.

A parody of history?

Previous commentaries have not noticed the importance to Plato of a tripartition of peoples, a division he cared about enough (as the previous chapter argued) to force it upon the dichotomy implied by autochthony. Nor have other treatments of the *Menexenus* observed that the tripartition lets Plato find an order in world history that resembles the orderly if dispiriting sequence that befalls the good city in *Republic* 8 and 9.

That the two themes work together implies more coherence to the funeral speech than it might first appear to have. It also must be said that an analysis of this complexity hardly makes sense as a parody of Pericles, whose speech says next to nothing about either non-Greeks or Athenian history. Much more probably Plato is offering an account of history of a kind that he believes other orators ought to have given (maybe other historians too). Psychological principles can now explain international alliances and their dissolution in meaningful Platonic terms – which is to say again that the narrative seems intended as a better work than its predecessors, not a mockery of them.

Notes

1 One part of this chapter, together with sections of the preceding chapter, previously appeared in Pappas and Zelcer (2013), although the sections combine in that article in a way that they do not here.

2 L. Mérider is one exception. On his reading the problem is simple error: "*Omissions délibérées, partialité des interprétations, grossisments systématiques ne sont pas les seuls défauts à relever dans l'exposé historique du Ménexène. On peut signaler des altérations manifestes et des mensonges grossiers*" (quoted in Zürcher 1954: 28).

3 Thus Collins and Stauffer (1999a: 89–90) say the speech "proves to contain its fair share of comedy or ridiculousness, including a long history of Athenian actions in war riddled with distortions". Also see Salkever (1993); Vlastos (1964).

4 Clavaud (1980: 173).

5 Interpreting the *Menexenus* as a response to other thinkers appears to have been common in the ancient world; at least enough to have incited the reply from the *Anonymous Prolegomena to Platonic Philosophy* noted in Chapter 4.

6 For example, Clavaud (1980: 137). Clavaud's analysis is based on a negative reading of the chronicle: facts omitted, others misstated. He offers no positive description of the narration.

7 Graves (1896: vii).

8 *Menexenus* 239–40a. Five forms of verbs containing the root *doul* "slave" occur within the span of 125 Greek words: *douloumenous, edouleue, edoulôsato, dedoulômenai, katadedoulômenê.*

9 *Menexenus* 240a–c. No other source recounts the story, told here, of the Persian army walking across Eretria holding hands, although it is plausible enough. Herodotus *Histories* 6.31 describes this "dragnet" practice and claims that the Persians used it whenever practicable, as it was on Chios, Lesbos and Tenedos. Herodotus *Histories*: Athens and Eretria supporting rebel cities, burning Sardis, 5.99.1–5.102.1; Eretria falling because of internal division, 6.100.1–6.101.3; Athenian reinforcements fleeing, 6.101.1; Spartans waiting for full moon, 6.106; arriving late, 6.120.1; Plataeans the only allies to Athens, 6.108. Plato repeats the handholding story in *Laws* 3.698d, though the Athenian Stranger sounds sceptical. In further contrast with the *Menexenus*, he claims that whether the story was true or not it terrified all the Greeks who heard it, *but especially the Athenians.*

10 *Menexenus*: Salamis and Artemisium ranked second after Marathon, 240e–241a; "those men then battling", 241a; Plataea with Athens and Sparta together ranked third, 241c.

11 Walters (1981) shows that the claim of solo Athenian effort at Marathon was common in local rhetoric, even becoming one official version of history co-existing with the version that called the Plataeans loyal allies. For Vlastos (1964: 190) the "error was so encrusted in the Athenian image of its own past that Plato may have been honestly mistaken on this point". Collins and Stauffer (1999b: 41–42) propose that simply by marching towards Marathon the Spartans boosted Athenian morale and caused the Persians to make hasty decisions.

12 Herodotus *Histories*: roster of cities in the Greek fleet (127 Athenian ships out of 271 total), 8.1.1; Eurybiades the Spartan admiral of joint naval forces, 8.2.2; Sparta convened the council of war because other Greek generals did not trust Themistocles, 8.58.

13 Aeschylus *Persians*: messenger's report on Salamis, 249–471; Salamis the ruination of Persia, 273, 284; Xerxes' best troops at Psyttalea where Greek infantrymen slaughtered them, 447–71; sea battle only half of the misfortune, 435–37. See Strauss (2004).

14 *Menexenus*: driving Persia from the sea, 241d; "sea–battling", 241d; "warring", 241e; "sailing", 241e.

15 Thucydides *History*: Athens consolidating its own *archê* "rule, empire" at Eurymedon, 1.97.2; initial success in Egypt, 1.104.2; later failure, 1.109–10.

16 Thucydides *History* 1.100; cf. Diodorus Siculus *Library* 11.61, Plutarch *Cimon* 12.5.6.

17 Plato: allies' *zêlos* and *phthonos*, *Menexenus* 242a; *phthonos* and comedy, *Philebus* 47e–50c; pleasure at *kaka* going to others, *Philebus* 48b; public's *phthonos* toward Socrates, *Apology* 28a. Harte (2010) writes about *phthonos* in comedy; the word is significant in Pindar, as in *Pythian* 7.18–19, for example: "I grieve that *phthonos* is the repayment for fine actions". On the Greek vocabulary for varieties of envy, grudging and malice, see Sanders (2014: 33–57).

18 *Ibid.*: 38–39. *Phthonos* begrudging honour, etc.: Aeschylus *Agamemnon* 833, 904; Aristophanes *Knights* 1051; Thucydides *History* 2.35.2; Xenophon *Anabasis* 5.7.10.

19 Plato: creator without *phthonos*, *Timaeus* 29e; divine realm, *Phaedrus* 247a. See Stevens (1948); see Burnyeat (2009: 182n.33) on *phthonos* in the *Timaeus*; Burnyeat says "without grudging", diagnoses *phthonos* as "the wish to keep all good to oneself", criticizes the words "jealousy" and "envy" in other translations of *Timaeus* 29e.

20 *Zêlos* versus *phthonos*: Sanders (2014: 46–49); distinction almost prefigured in Hesiod *Works and Days* 20–26; *zêlos* as positive alternative, Demosthenes 20.141; turning into *phthonos*, Sophocles *Oedipus Tyrannus* 381–82; Pericles on Athens and other Greeks, Thucydides *History* 2.64.4. See Sanders (2014: 48).

21 Thucydides *History*: Spartans ask for aid, 1.102.1; see Athenians as *allophulous*, 1.102.3; end of alliance, 1.102.4.

22 *Ibid.*: Spartans in Boeotia, 1.107.4; Athenian mobilization, 1.107.5; Athenian suspicions, 1.107.6; Spartan victory amid losses, 1.108.1; Spartans returning home, 1.108.2; Athenian victory at Oenophytae, 1.108.3.

23 *Menexenus*: Tanagra and Oenophytae, Boeotians' freedom, 242a–b. Modern readers: Collins and Stauffer (1999b: 44n.20); cf. Walters (1981), who reads Tanagra as an attempt to break up the Boeotian league.

24 *Menexenus* 242c–d. Thucydides on the significance of the war, *History* 1.1.

25 Thucydides *History*: all the events between Oenophytae and Sphacteria, 1.108–4.3; Sphacteria, 4.1–39; Athenians landing by chance, 4.3.1; Cleon's refusal to negotiate, 4.21.3.

26 Diodorus Siculus *Library* 12.61–63; Cawkwell (1997: 73–74).

27 Thucydides *History* 4.14.3; Diodorus Siculus *Library* 12.62.7.

28 *Menexenus* 242e–243c.

29 Thucydides *History*: appeal from Egesta, 6.8.1; political infighting, 6.8–25; departure of Alcibiades, 6.61; Nicias superstitious, 7.50; Syracusan temperament, 7.40.2, 8.96.5.

30 *Menexenus*: *dia de mêkos tou plou* "on account of the length of the voyage", 243a; "bad luck", 243a.

31 The trophies on Sicily have been called a "pathetic gesture" to prop up Athenian morale (Kagan 2003: 312). But it is worth bearing in mind that as the *Menexenus* appraises world events, victory and defeat come down to whether or not a state is enslaved. Athens failed to carry the day on Sicily but was not enslaved; therefore this was no defeat.

32 Kagan (2009: 164–86). Some of Kagan's remarks are worth quoting: "Thucydides' interpretation does not in fact accord well with the Athenians' behaviour as reported in his own narrative" (*ibid.*: 167); "Apart from Thucydides' characterization, we have no reason to believe that the Athenians who received the Segestan request for aid in 416/15 were planning to use it as an excuse to conquer Sicily" (*ibid.*: 167–68); "[Thucydides'] first reference to the expedition of 415 assumes a goal of conquest from the start … Before presenting an account of how the decision was made – indeed, omitting a description of the debate in the assembly – he has established his view of the motive for the action, which is unsupported by his own narrative and contradicted by the evidence" (*ibid.*: 185).

33 Thucydides *History*: speech by Hermocrates, 6.33–34; *plou mêkos* "great distance" between Athens and Sicily, 6.34.4. Note that Socrates is effectively quoting Hermocrates' prediction as after-the-fact explanation.

34 Thucydides *History*: Hermocrates on Athenian motives, 6.33. What complicates this use of Hermocrates is his appearance in the dialogues *Timaeus* and *Critias*, which were evidently planned as instalments in a trilogy whose last member would be the *Hermocrates*. On the original plan, Hermocrates would have delivered the third long speech about Athens and its place in world history. Because Plato never finished the trilogy it is impossible to be sure of his stance toward the man; but he and Thucydides might both have made him a credible mouthpiece.

35 On the long delay before Athens heard of the defeat see Plutarch *Nicias* 30. A stranger came to town, stopped into a barbershop, and commented on the calamity that he assumed all Athens knew about. For failures of communication

across much smaller distances see Plato *Phaedo* 57a–b. Echecrates in Phlius, a town that is barely a walk from the Isthmus of Corinth, says he hears very little news from Athens.

36 The speech says *epleusan* "they sailed" to Sicily, but does not speak of the expedition as a naval action. Indeed setting up *tropaia* "trophies" implies dry land, and most of the fighting in Sicily did take place on land: *Menexenus* 242e–243a.

37 Thucydides *History*: naval battles, 8.104–7; ships captured at Cynossema, 8.106.1–3; ships at Cyzicus, 8.107.1; "unexpected" good news, 8.106.5.

38 See Thucydides *History* 8.94–96.

39 *Menexenus*: *anelpistos kai deinos*, 242e–243b; other Greeks' alliance with Persia, 243b; "we defeated ourselves", 243d. Note that the *Menexenus* reiterates this *anelpistos*, meaning something unforeseeable *in the bad sense*, right after its reference to the naval battles near the Hellespont, which is when Thucydides uses the word in a positive sense to mean an outcome *better* than anything the Athenians hoped for. The word *anelpistos* occurs twenty-one times in Thucydides but is rare for Plato, which suggests that he would have needed a reason to use it twice in a single passage as he does here. This might be a point at which Plato wanted to correct Thucydides, making the unforeseeable event that followed the Hellespont the Spartans' treaty with Persia. This thought goes with the possibility that Socrates reasons from Hellespont to Persia in the following sentence; see point 3 below.

40 Thucydides *History*: the treaty, 8.18; Tissaphernes' motives, 8.5.4–5; encouragement of plots against Athens, 8.2.

41 Plato *Menexenus* 243b.

42 Thus Collins and Stauffer (1999b: 46n.26).

43 Thucydides *History*: return to Tissaphernes, 8.108–9; Alcibiades made him "more of a friend", 8.108.1; Persians jockeying for influence, 8.109; Tissaphernes sacrificing, 8.109.

44 *Menexenus*: Athenian ships cut off at Mytilene, fresh ships sent, misfortune keeping bodies from being collected, 243c. Xenophon *Hellenica*: Sparta chafes at being Persia's courtier, 1.6.6–7; Persia funds Sparta, 1.6.18; Conon trapped at Mytilene, 1.6.16–17; Athens sends 110 ships (as opposed to Plato's sixty), 1.6.24; Athens wins, 1.6.33–34; but wind prevents Athenians from gathering the dead, 1.6.35.

45 This passage follows Socrates' reference to Arginusae. Rahn (1971: 504–5) reads Xenophon as making a similar point. He argues that Arginusae is a turning point for Xenophon, who emphasizes that the Athenians defeated themselves by succumbing to mob rule, ignoring their own laws even in the face of victory. See Euryptolemus' speech in *Hellenica*, 1.7.33. The Athenians were behaving like a defeated city. Thucydides too has Athens surrendering because it defeated itself through internal strife, *History* 2.65.

46 On the turns of the trial see Xenophon *Hellenica* 1.7; perhaps more objective is Diodorus Siculus *Library* 13.101–2, where Socrates is not mentioned. Socrates as lone opponent to illegal procedure: *Hellenica* 1.7.15, and *Memorabilia* 1.1 and 4.4; also see Plato *Apology* 32b–c; *Gorgias* 473e.

47 The Thirty Tyrants: Plato *Apology* 32c–d; Xenophon *Hellenica* Book 3; Lysias 12 *Against Eratosthenes*.

48 *Menexenus*: chronicle continues, 244b–246a; these recent events, 244d.

49 *Ibid.*: Athens forgave barbarians not Greeks, 244b–c; had lost ships and walls to Greeks, 244c; absconded to form power vacuum that Sparta exploited, 244c–d; was begged for help, 244d; is guilty of pity for the oppressed, 244e; freed Greeks and let Athenians help Persia, 245a.

50 *Ibid.*: Athenians free of barbarian admixture, 245c–e; refused Persian demand for Asian cities, 245c, e; fought with Persia against Sparta, 245b; at Corinth and Lechaeum, 245e; drove Sparta from sea, 246a. The acts of the Persian fleet under Conon are chronicled by Diodorus Siculus, who has Persia imprisoning Conon before the events that Diodorus calls the Corinthian War: *Library* 14.79, 14.85 (Conon and the fleet), 14.86 (Corinthian War). Xenophon might put the imprisonment later: see *Hellenica* 4.4.5–13 for fighting at Corinth, Conon's imprisonment at 4.8.16. But it is hard to match the battles Xenophon testifies to with events reported in the *Menexenus.*

51 *Menexenus*: "In this war", 245e–246a; private citizens helping Persia, 245a; Athens building walls and ships, 245a; keeping them, 245e. On Athenian friendliness with Persia at this time see Diodorus Siculus *Library* 14.81.4; Conon commanding Persian fleet, 14.79.5; fighting Sparta, 14.79.6. For Conon's using his position to help rebuild the walls see Diodorus *Library* 14.85.3, Xenophon *Hellenica* 4.8.9–10.

52 These points occur in both Xenophon *Hellenica* and Diodorus Siculus *Library*: (1) *Hellenica* 3.5.7–17, *Library* 14.82.1–3; (2) *Hellenica* 4.4, *Library* 14.86; (3) *Hellenica* 5.1.29, *Library* 14.110.2; (4) *Hellenica* 5.1.31, *Library* 14.110.3; (5) *Hellenica* 5.1.35, *Library* 14.110.4. Regarding (1), Xenophon presents the alliance as Thebes' idea (*Hellenica* 3.5.7–16), but his hatred for Thebes may colour his report. Diodorus makes the agreement seem mutual; Lysias *Pro Mantitheus* at least does not ascribe the treaty to Theban instigation (Lysias 16.13). By the way, *Hellenica* calls this agreement the "first peace", looking ahead eleven years to renewal of the treaty in 375. The *Menexenus* shows no awareness of a second treaty; so even if Plato was not writing it exactly in 386 he did not wait long either. The two treaties have been called similar: Cawkwell (1981: 73).

53 Diodorus Siculus *Library* 14.110.4. In Xenophon Athens is more eager to agree to terms: *Hellenica* 5.1.29.

54 Cawkwell (1981: 80) argues that Xenophon systematically understates the intrusion into Greek affairs that the Peace constituted. The Spartan power that grew stronger after the Peace depended on the King's authority, but Xenophon felt compelled to treat the arrangement as less important than it was.

55 *Menexenus* 245b–c, d–e.

56 Kahn (1963: 225); Trivigno (2009: 38).

57 Trivigno (2009) uses the combination of these distortions to show that the dialogue is satirical; also see Henderson (1975: 34). But Kahn (1963: 225) excuses the distortions by arguing that the public did not expect much accuracy in their oratory, and generally allowed for lapses in memory.

58 See Liddel (2010) for a discussion of "universal historiography".

59 Thucydides *History*: speech to the assembly by Pericles (his last), 2.60–64; Athenian rule not merely over allies, 2.62.2; "we ruled" more Greeks, 2.64.3; Athenians now risk loss of rule, 2.63.1; Athens a tyranny, 2.63.2.

60 Silence to conceal past, Collins and Stauffer (1999b: 9). To say nothing where there is nothing nice to say, Kahn (1963: 225).

61 Pearson (1942) is still a good overview and first guide to Atthidography.

62 See *Timaeus* 20e on *erga megala kai thaumasta* "great and wondrous deeds", which fade from memory in time. The first sentence of *Histories* announces that it intends to preserve *erga megala kai thômasta* from eventual obscurity (Węcowski 2004: 146n.22). For a philosophical look at Plato and Herodotus together see Sharp (2006).

63 Thus Grote (1865: 3:410–11) says that Plato never read the *History* or read and then disregarded it.

64 Plato: recent events, *Menexenus* 244d; "hymn of praise", *Timaeus* 21a.
65 See Rahn (1971).
66 Thucydides *History* 1.23.6.
67 See Lendon (2006, 2007); also sections of a book in progress on the Peloponnesian War that he graciously showed us. Lendon does not discuss Plato's way of practising historical narration, but his sketch of ancient alternatives to Thucydides made it possible to situate the *Menexenus* among those alternatives.
68 *Menexenus*: non-Athenians fearing Persia, 240c, 241b–c; fearing Athens, 244d; King tends to his safety, 241e; finds himself in *aporia*, bafflement, 244d; fears, 245b. The King's fear is always of Athens. The non-Athenian Greeks are also said, twice, to be *katapeplēgmenoi* "overwhelmed, stunned" presumably by fear; but *phobos* and cognate words are absent from those passages.
69 See, for example, Derow (1994).
70 Van Wees (2002: 343).
71 Herodotus *Histories*: "I will go forward", 1.5.3–4; words of Cyrus, 9.122.3–4.
72 Plato on cycles in history: myth of Cronus, *Statesman* 268d–277b; cf. *Timaeus* 23a–b.
73 Kahn too focuses on the *Menexenus*'s history as the key to its overall import. He too alludes to the navy and to Pericles' role in Athenian history (Kahn 1963: 223–24). But he does not look at the history as an illustration of historical and psychological causal principles. His orientation towards the dialogue prohibits that approach, for he dismisses inaccuracy as a by-product of the genre it belongs to. No one expects historical fact in a funeral speech. Right or wrong, this premise predisposes a reader not to look for significance in the way Plato has organized his list of Athenian battles. As for Pownall, he emphasizes the historical inaccuracies in the *Menexenus*, but with too much stress on demonstrating that the dialogue as a whole is parodic; see Pownall (2004: 49).
74 *Menexenus* 241c, 244c, 245a, 245e.
75 *Ibid.*: 245a. The pairing of walls and ships seems to have been a common expression in Greek writing. The orator Andocides pairs them in his speech arguing for a peace with Sparta: *On the Peace* 3.37. Aristophanes pairs them in *Birds* 379: "Cities learn, not from their allies, but from their enemies, how to build high walls and assemble fleets of ships". Walls and ships are paired in Euripides' *Rhesus*, Sophocles *Antigone* 1010 and Thucydides *History* 3.2.
76 See Strauss (2004), who considers not only what obvious anti-democrats like Xenophon said, but also assesses Arginusae as a focus for anxiety over the democratic navy.
77 Plato *Republic*: most primitive city, 2.371a–b; ship of state, 6.488a–489c. Describing the activities of the first city, Socrates says, "If some trade takes place by sea [*kata thalattan*] ... ", 2.371e. Athenians knew that commercial shipping invited piracy, so that no seafaring trade could take place until after someone possessed a navy strong enough to quash pirates. See Thucydides *History* 1.4–5. The ship-of-state image does not contradict the dialogues' usual contempt for ships and sailors. The ship of state is badly managed precisely because of its irrational, ungovernable crew, because it resembles a democracy.
78 *Laws* 4.704d–4.705e; Klosko (1986: 9–11). The *Laws*' condemnation of navies goes with the Athenian Stranger's denial that Salamis and Artemisium mattered to victory over Persia. Plataea won the war, says *Laws* 4.707c, as *Menexenus* 241c also implies, and as the most reliable sources from that time – Aeschylus and Herodotus – do not.
79 The modern reader needs to remember that wealthy Athenians would feel less allegiance towards the navy because they had to pay for it. A trireme was a

big-ticket item, funded until late in the Peloponnesian war by one rich man per ship. The concrete benefits of imperialism flowed to the Athenian public in the form of jury-duty pay and assembly pay, these and other expenditures made possible by the tribute Athens collected from the subject-states of the Delian League. Thus see a passage in Aristophanes' *Assemblywomen*, a play that Plato knew well, in which the Athenian assembly considers a motion to launch ships, the poor citizens voting "yes" and the rich voting "no" (197).

80 Plato *Critias*: ancient Athens forested (maybe because Plato links deforestation to timber for ships), 111c; Atlantis with fleet, 119a–b. On reading *Critias* for political and historical import see Naddaf (1994); Vidal-Naquet (1998).

81 *Menexenus*: Athenians educated to be guardians, 238b; other Greeks educated by Athenians, 241c; students of Marathoners, 240e.

82 Plato *Republic*: Greek cities should fight other Greeks with restraint, 5.469b–471b; internecine Greek war *stasis* "civil strife", 5.470a–b.

83 Plato *Republic* 4.435e–436a. In his comment on 436a, Shorey (1959) calls *philochrêmatikon* "a virtual synonym" for *epithumêtikon* "desire", citing *Republic* 580e and *Phaedo* 68c, 82c in support of this identification.

84 Herodotus *Histories* 1.60.3 as an example of Greek thinking about Athenians: "the Greek nation has of old been thought of as cleverer [*dexiôteron*] than the barbarians", while Athenians in turn are said to be first among Greeks in *sophiên* "wisdom etc.".

85 Hippocrates *Airs, Waters, Places*: cowardice of Asians, ch. 16; courage of Europeans, ch. 23.

86 *Menexenus*: Persia wealthy and numerous, 240d, 241b; Egyptians enemies of Athens, 241e; multiplicity of nations in the Persian Empire, 239d–e. The desiring part of the soul *poikilon*, *Republic* 9.588c.

87 Liddel, discussing the relevance of constitutional change to universal history among ancient historians, writes, "The *Republic*'s analysis of constitutional transformation was carried out without historical reference", contrasting this with the discussion of Persian and Athenian constitutions in the *Laws* (Liddel 2010: 22). The rich history in the *Menexenus* partly satisfies Liddel's wish for a Platonic universal history.

88 Internal constancy of Athens is another implication of the claim (238c–e) that Athens has always had the same form of government.

89 *Menexenus*: small power recognizing what is best, 239b, 242d, 244e, 245e; bringing out courage, 240e–241c; restrains its anger, 242d; serves the common as peacemaker, 242c–d; restrained by shame, 245a, e.

90 The several paragraphs that follow are especially indebted to the generosity and scholarly accomplishment of Heidi Northwood's comments at a meeting of the Ancient Philosophy Society, Baltimore, MD, in April 2009.

91 *Menexenus*: imperfections in the second-best group, 237b; that group leaves the alliance, 245d.

92 Plato *Republic*: timocratic man's complaining mother, 8.549b; his *phthonos*, 9.586c; *phthonos* in tyrannical souls, 9.579c, 580a; philosophical soul does not experience *phthonos*, 7.500c. For a precise distinction between *philotimia* and *phthonos* that makes a good gloss on *Republic* 586c, see Aristotle *Rhetoric* 2.10 (e.g. 1387b32, 1388a1–3).

93 Other cities' *zêlos* and *phthonos*, *Menexenus* 242a. Northwood writes in elucidation of this point: "as in the *Republic*, the 'fall' from the best in the *Menexenus* also involves a perversion of a proper love of honour and love of the best", a summation it would be hard to improve upon.

94 *Menexenus* 243b.

95 Plato on *philonikia*: the word used without negative connotations, *Laws* 8.834c; with disagreeable sense, *Gorgias* 515b, *Laches* 194a, *Laws* 9.860d, *Timaeus* 88a; two motives behind spurious prosecution, *Laws* 11.938b–c.

96 Plato: *philonikia* and *epithumia*, *Timaeus* 90b; and *thumos*, *Republic* 8.548c.

97 Polybius *Histories*: *phthonos*, 6.7.8, 6.9.1. See Liddel (2010) on Polybius and regime change as they figure in the history of universal history. For *phthonos* in other historians see Herodotus *Histories* 7.236 (but there it is merely a general description of all Greeks), Thucydides *History* 3.82.8, 3.84.2. Thucydides acknowledges *phthonos* as a contributory motive in history, but it does not belong among his "truest causes".

98 We owe this point to Heidi Northwood.

99 Plato: Athens made alliance with Persia out of pity, *Menexenus* 244e; rulers' not pitying lower souls in the good city, *Republic* 3.415c; tragedy and pity, *Republic* 10.606b–c. On *eleos* and *oiktos*, see Sternberg (2005: 22–24). Perhaps *eleos* connotes mercy in addition to pity, while *oiktos* specifies the emotional strength of the feeling. But Sternberg makes clear how difficult it is to distinguish between them sharply. The funeral oration of Lysias specifies that the men fighting at Salamis felt *eleos* for their children and *oiktos* for their aging parents; Lysias 2.39. Both are apt objects of pity, strong pity in both cases.

100 Plato's historical passages present slavery as an emblem of other forms of authority. One should expect to find authority threatened when people who should be free are slaves and vice versa. Thus in the *Republic* the first degeneration follows from preoccupation with property and with holding "as slaves those they once guarded as free friends … and occupying themselves with guarding against those they have enslaved": 8.547b. The freedom of people who ought to be slaves is just as bad a sign. Tyranny comes naturally into existence in a city where "male and female slaves are no less free than the persons who bought them": 8.563b.

101 *Menexenus*: Cyrus enslaves Medes, 239d–e; Athenians not one another's slaves or masters, 239a; non-Athenian Greeks when freed enslave themselves again, 245a.

CONCLUSION
Buried in philosophy

At every turn, this book has argued, the speech in the *Menexenus* puts itself forward as something better than the famous funeral oration of Pericles. Because a parody distorts the original or otherwise amplifies its faults, this effort to improve on the speech of Pericles prevents the *Menexenus* speech from having been meant as parody.

The *Menexenus*'s improvements to the funeral speech

On our reading the will to improve on Pericles appears everywhere. For one thing the speech surpasses the original in its emphasis on *education*. Where Pericles vaunted the virtue of Athenians, their courage above all, he omitted explaining how to educate his fellow citizens. The *Menexenus* speech forces education into each Periclean lacuna, specifically with talk of imitating the excellent fallen soldiers as the process by which one achieves the same excellence they had.

As rhetoric of *praise*, the new speech improves on the original by honouring the act of praising, and practising praise, where Pericles shied away from praising in practice and theorized about its dangers. He feared that high praise might excite envy in his audience; but Socrates, gluing the parts back into Aspasia's speech that Pericles had evidently cut out of it, lets the language of praise suit its objects: the earth of Attica, the city of Athens, the Athenian people's virtues.

The speech in the *Menexenus* most clearly improves on the speech that Pericles gave, or so Plato would have to see things, in its uses of *myth* and *history*. Pericles glided over the traditional Athenian story of autochthony despite its obvious popularity to Athenians. In place of his silence Socrates tells the story in its most patriotic terms, revising it as he does. When Earth alone has borne the Athenian people, they face no conflict between the two characteristics that the traditional myth had left them with, their natures from Ge and their intelligent *technai* from Athena. The *Menexenus* assigns Athena's traits to Ge and so lets nature do the work of culture. As Chapter 7 says, nature now generates the *technai* that had once been thought of as impositions upon nature.

214

Finally there is a new *history*, to be set against the chronicle that Thucydides had offered his readers as the serious way of writing the past. In this case we found the speech's well-known omissions, distortions and outright falsehoods playing a role of previously unsuspected precision, shaping the events of the preceding century so that international history (what an Athenian of the classical age would have seen as the world at large) fits the same patterns of decline that *Republic* 8 and 9 found at work in the city and the individual soul. Where Thucydides can only explain events in terms of bad luck, intractable human conflict and irrational fears contemplating irrational restlessness, the *Menexenus* describes a world of rational order that malicious envy sets on a downward path, until the forces of desire have taken over reason's role.

The book's overriding question "Was this intended as an improvement?" avoids debates that are incapable of resolving, in which one side hears merriment or smells an arcane joke, the other sees straight-ahead assertions and feels no humour. It seems plain to us that if the rewriting of some work issues in a new work *of the same kind*, one that is intended to be *a better example of the same form or genre*, then the new work is not a parody. It does not, in the words of a recent handbook of literary terms, "mock the style and stance of particular authors, works, or genres". Those who want to call a would-be better example of the same form or genre a parody according to some fresh and unorthodox conception of parody are welcome to that fresh conception as long as they agree that the *Menexenus* speech is meant to be superior to the speech we know as Pericles'. Literary terms change; after all, "parody" originally referred to musical antiphony.[1] But they will have to say that the New Testament parodied the Hebrew Bible and Einstein parodied Newton.

The *Menexenus* and other dialogues

Because reading through even a short dialogue takes time and many pages, and more than usual in the case of a work that has been less examined by scholars, the preceding chapters mainly looked into the claims and arguments of the funeral speech itself. To elaborate at every step about the view in Pericles that is being rebutted would have bloated this book and blurred its central arguments. We have pointed out where certain ideas in Pericles find themselves replaced by Socratic ideas: Athens as educator to other cities (which becomes Athens educating its own), Athens as mistress (improvised into Athens the mother), even the fundamental idea of a burial, the act of saying goodbye to Athenian soldiers, in Pericles close to a resolution to speak of them no more, in Socrates an occasion for them to give their own last speech.

As for the man behind the words of Pericles: Thucydides produced such a monumental history that it would be hopeless to try juxtaposing our reading of the history in the *Menexenus* to the overall story told in Thucydides. The complete account of what makes Plato's funeral speech philosophically better than the one Pericles delivered would require a complete account of both Pericles and Thucydides.

Even so it may be worth reading the *Menexenus* alongside other works, and especially alongside other Platonic dialogues. We have noted some connections along the way, but there is more to say. Regarding the progressive decline in history, experienced readers of the *Republic* will see other similarities between those two dialogues: the species of disunion that appears when a rational order crumbles, the persisting image of not just rationality within the dominant element but even philosophical rationality. As history, the *Menexenus* belongs close together with the *Republic*.

But there are also histories, after a fashion, in the *Timaeus* and *Critias*. The legendary Athens that those dialogues tell of is a city that had its origin in its people's autochthonous birth, then grew with wisdom and virtue until it halted a mammoth enslaving power. It is simpler to cast Plato as nothing but antagonistic towards Athens, and understandable; but the balanced story of how he saw his native city would put the *Timaeus* and *Critias* together with the *Menexenus*, and with passages in other dialogues, to bring forward a strain of patriotism, and Plato's sense of Athens as he would like to be able to love it – Athens as it would have to be for him to feel justified in loving it.

The *Menexenus*'s ripostes to Pericles on the subject of education might be the most specific. Every time Pericles slips past the idea of making his fellow citizens better, Socrates (or Aspasia) glues a comment back in about education. As a call to education in virtue the *Menexenus* harmonizes well with the *Republic* as a whole, of course, and with passages in the *Statesman* and *Laws*. But there are also the *Gorgias*, the *Meno* and the *Protagoras* to think of. In all these dialogues, every well-run city is said to need an education in virtue overseen by philosophy, but that is one element left out of democracy's civic culture. Again what Socrates does to the speech of Pericles looks like what Plato would call an improvement.

But even supposing that the speech by Socrates is *better* than the one it answers, and even if you call it *better by Platonic standards* on the grounds that it supports moral or political claims to be found in other dialogues; even so that does not make it *better rhetoric by Platonic standards*. The sceptic might not grant that Plato sees this speech as an example of rhetoric superior to the speech that Pericles made. On what grounds would Plato call the *Menexenus* superior rhetoric? We need a word here, even if it is no more than a closing word, about Plato's understanding of rhetoric, and if possible with reference to a less controversial source than the *Menexenus* itself.

Rhetoric dominates two dialogues, the *Gorgias* and the *Phaedrus*, although the two put forward different claims about the value that rhetoric *might* have, which is to say about whether it is open to philosophical redemption. At least at first sight the two dialogues' assessments are incompatible. The *Gorgias* lets Socrates voice such harsh judgements towards rhetoric that looking to it for the promise of good rhetoric feels desperate. It should not be the dialogue to bring into this parting look at Platonic rhetoric, when rhetoric on its analysis amounts to no more than practical canniness. Socrates calls rhetoric an *empeiria*, a word that translators render as "knack" or "empirical know-how"; a good ordinary single word might be "practice", and rhetoric is part of the more general practice that Socrates calls *kolakeia* "flattery, fawning, currying favour". Rhetoric belongs with cooking, standing against justice as cooking does against medical science. It is something you do and that you might even get better at doing, with time, but not because you come to know something in the process. After all teaching differs from rhetoric in that the former persuades by supplying knowledge, the latter by bringing belief without knowledge.[2]

Where practical tricks suffice in the realm of knack and know-how, philosophical knowledge could not accomplish more, even if a philosopher should think to attempt a rhetorical exercise. The very attempt would resemble a modern statistician's buying lottery tickets. Winning the lottery is a matter of chance; understanding statistics would not make you better at that chancy pursuit, except in the sense that seeing how bad the odds are would prevent you from buying a ticket. Likewise, knowing philosophy could only help you at rhetoric by steering you away from it. So much for a philosophically guided funeral speech. If this is the only conception of rhetoric to be found in Plato, then it almost follows that the *Menexenus* speech must be a parody.

The middle section of the *Theaetetus* contrasts philosopher with public speaker in similar terms. The man who speaks effectively in courtrooms appears to have genuine skill. And surely, whatever this ability to move a jury is, the philosopher does not possess it. But then the philosopher, a gentleman of the soul compared with the slavish orator, inquires into general truths as the orator could not hope to. As in the *Gorgias*, philosophically informed rhetoric is, if not an oxymoron, an absurdity by some other measure. (The *Gorgias* imagines a doctor having to debate a pastry chef; in the *Theaetetus* the philosopher is a gentleman while the courtroom speaker resembles a slave in the kitchen sweetening the sauce.[3])

Despite being associated with rhetoric, the *Gorgias* only spends about a quarter of its length on the subject, twenty Stephanus pages out of eighty. That first quarter attacks rhetoric without mercy, closing with a remark by Socrates that orators work without *nous* "intelligence", and that he does not expect to be disabused of that opinion. After this, rhetoric only returns to the conversation briefly, a couple of times; and in one of those returns to the subject Socrates says one thing that might be construed as a concession. Rhetoric could exist that improved its audience, though he does not think that Callicles (to whom he is talking) has ever seen an example of this nobler variety.[4]

Can Socrates be holding out the prospect of a new rhetoric composed and delivered by philosophers? The dialogue's subsequent conversation does not explore the question, but it is not hard to read such a promise in this passage. On the contrary the problem is that it is too easy; trivial really; and trivially easy to show that the *Menexenus* meets this one open standard. As long as the *Menexenus* speech is seen as somehow able to educate, the lone criterion in the *Gorgias* is satisfied. The speech contains true claims, as this book has argued. It seems to aim at keeping its audience moderate and thinking reasonably. The *Gorgias*'s Socrates would have to call it better rhetoric than the speech of Pericles.

The *Phaedrus*

According to most accounts of Plato on rhetoric it is the *Phaedrus* that suggests anything resembling a compromise. The same Socrates who scoffs at long speeches in other dialogues now calls himself a lover of rhetoric. He praises Pericles and nods at such rivals as Isocrates. To be sure, philosophy sets the terms for reconciliation with rhetoric. In the *Phaedrus* rhetoric is said to require an understanding of its subject matter, an understanding that calls for rigorous definition using the division-and-collection method. First narrow the large genera into smaller species, then be ready to talk. This is the philosopher's method. What professional speechwriters instead *believe* they need to know, what they find in manuals that distinguish the parts of every speech, is too little too late. A manual provides vague descriptions of speeches without regard for the knowledge that makes them work.[5]

Besides defining the item to be talked about, Socrates says, the practitioners of rhetoric must master a taxonomy of human souls. They need to identify the souls in their audience and tailor each speech to the type of soul that is hearing it. The *Phaedrus* makes clear that this knowledge comes from philosophy too. So you will be able to produce good rhetoric if you learn your subject as philosophers do and then communicate it according to principles of philosophical psychology. And not otherwise.[6]

The game is rigged in philosophy's favour, but at least the *Phaedrus* shows how it might be played. And the main speech that Socrates delivers, the one he treats as a case of successful rhetoric, appears to follow the dialogue's rules. This account of *erôs* praises the passion and the god who is called by the same name; even praises them to excess, as Socrates will praise Athens in the *Menexenus*.

One can always praise without knowledge. But if we make knowledge the Platonic touchstone for successful philosophical rhetoric, the *Menexenus* speech again passes the test. Every aspect of the speech that this book has investigated finds Socrates replacing Periclean propaganda with Platonic knowledge-claims – about education in the most pointed way, but also about rhetoric, and about the running of the city.

Even division and collection appears in the *Menexenus*, when Socrates separates Athens from all other Greek cities on the grounds that its people are indigenous to Attica while the people in other cities migrated to their present homes. Those who migrate have step-maternal cities where Athenians have a true motherland: the differentiation echoes the passage in the *Phaedrus* that separates good *erôs* from its bad variety (putting, as Socrates says there, the bad one on the left).[7] A god is at work in cases of good *erôs*, as the great goddess Ge lies behind the good city that is Athens and not, or not in the same way, behind other Greek cities.

What about the *Phaedrus*'s demand that philosophical rhetoric begin with what philosophy has to teach about souls? First notice how closely the *Menexenus*'s myth of autochthony is made to reflect what other dialogues say about the soul. As we argue, this myth that served other purposes in its traditional manifestations is made to say in the *Menexenus*, as it does nowhere else, that there are three types of human beings: Athenians, other Greeks and non-Greeks. In light of the fact that the *Menexenus* portrays those three types as behaving according to (respectively) reason, high-spiritedness that is capable of courage, and the desire for sex and other bodily pleasures, they embody the three parts of the soul as given in the *Republic*, but also in the *Phaedrus* and *Timaeus*. Surely this specificity about human motivations imbues the funeral speech with psychological content.

Of course, one can see the most famous sentence from the *Menexenus* as a nod to the *Phaedrus* and a sign that it meets the *Phaedrus*'s criteria for better rhetoric. When Socrates says "It is not hard to praise Athens among the Athenians"[8] he is already tipping Menexenus off (and the alert reader) that besides understanding the centrality of praise to the speech he is about to give, he understands the souls of the people who will hear it.

If this much soul-knowledge does not suffice, the great speech in the *Phaedrus* points to another way of understanding the subject. That speech clearly contains and seeks to demonstrate knowledge about human souls. Socrates ranks souls: this seems to be a central part of the knowledge available (even if the dialogue leaves open the possibility that there are other taxonomies available for sorting souls). Depending on the philosophical insight each soul achieved in its life before taking on a body, it will find itself in one of the following lives:

1 **philosopher** or beauty-lover or musical and erotic man;
2 legitimate king or **warrior**;
3 politician or **household manager** or *chrêmatistikos* "**financier**";
4 trainer or doctor;
5 prophet or priest;
6 poet or mimetic artist;
7 worker or farmer;
8 **sophist** or *dêmokopikos* "**demagogue**"; and
9 **tyrant**, tyrannical type.[9]

The point of writing out this ranking is that soul-knowledge, as this must be, contains knowledge of the degradations to which souls are subject. Readers

219

do not always connect this passage from the *Phaedrus* with the *Republic*'s tale of decline, the one that our previous chapter drew on, but the two fit together surprisingly well. The soul types in bold type on this list correspond respectively to (1) the Kallipolis or best city; (2) the honour-loving timocracy; (3) money-chasing oligarchy; then to (8) democracy, which makes a welcome home for sophists and elevates public speakers to powerful positions; finally to (9) tyranny.[10]

These are not extreme claims. The complete theory of the human soul will include a theory of how some souls are better than others and for what reasons. But if the argument of Chapter 8 is plausible, that the historical narrative in the *Menexenus* organizes events from recent history to match the stages of individual and political history one finds in *Republic* Books 8 and 9, that narrative too seems to contain some theory of soul, or is not ignorant of such a theory. By the standards that Socrates proposes in the *Phaedrus* for rhetoric a philosopher can respect, the speech in the *Menexenus* succeeds.

There is no other way to say it. Philosophizing pervades the funeral speech. We trust that by now it no longer seems like mock-philosophizing. The thought in the *Menexenus* gives this speech the status it has as serious rhetoric, fitting Plato's idea of how rhetoric might look if someone serious thought to practise it. If philosophers cannot govern the city yet, they might still help it along by coming forward on a sombre day to guide its mourning and give the survivors hope. The fallen soldiers may well find themselves waking on the Isles of the Blessed; at least (what also counts) their families will believe such a thing; for the soldiers are being, they will have been, buried in philosophy.

Notes

1 Parodies "mock the style"; the word meant antiphony (Mickics 2007: 224). As we said in the introduction, the proviso that the new work is meant as a better version *of the same genre* is meant to ward off a counter-example in which, say, a travel book is tedious but the parody of it is brilliant parody. "Galway Bay" is undistinguished as nostalgic song of home, but the parody is an excellent drinking song. In such instances the parody is a better example *of its kind* than the original had been, but is not, nor was intended to be, a better example of the same genre.

2 Plato *Gorgias*: rhetoric an *empeiria*, 462c; part of *kolakeia*, 463b; is to justice as cooking is to medicine, 465c; differs from teaching, 454e.

3 Plato *Theaetetus*: contrasts philosopher with orator, 172c–175e; speaker's appearance of skill, 173a–b; philosopher lacks it, 174c; philosopher surpasses orator in abstract inquiry, 175c–d; is to orator as gentleman to kitchen slave, 175e; cf. *Gorgias* 464e on doctor and chef.

4 Plato *Gorgias*: orators lack *nous*, 467a; noble rhetoric might exist though Callicles hasn't seen it, 503a–b.

5 Plato *Phaedrus*: Socrates lover of speeches, 236e; praises Pericles, 269e; acknowledges Isocrates, 278e–279a; rhetoric requires division and collection, 264e–266c; manuals of rhetoric inadequate, 266d–268d.

6 Plato *Phaedrus* 270e–272a.

7 *Ibid.*: 266a–b.
8 *Menexenus* 235d.
9 Plato *Phaedrus* 248d–e.
10 Why the four other types at ranks (4)–(7)? This is not the place to interpret the
   Phaedrus, but a few words are worth adding. First, the speech in the *Phaedrus*
   aims at completeness, accounting for all (free, male, Greek) souls. Second, Plato
   may well have observed what Aristotle would say after him: that actual
   constitutions combine oligarchical and democratic elements; therefore, if you
   want to find the greatest number of actual examples of humanity you should
   look between (3) and (8). Third, within (4)–(7) you find first the higher *technai*
   and then the lower ones: (4) higher rational professions, (5) higher irrational or
   "manic" professions, (6) lower irrational or manic professions, (7) lower rational
   professions.

BIBLIOGRAPHY

Annas, J. 1982. "Plato's Myths of Judgment". *Phronesis* 27(2): 119–43.

Aty, J. 1982. "Dorians and Ionians". *Journal of Hellenic Studies* 102: 1–14.

Austin, J. L. 1958. "Pretending". *Proceedings of the Aristotelian Society* 32(Suppl.): 261–78.

——1962. *How to Do Things with Words*. Oxford: Oxford University Press.

Avery, H. C. 1982. "One Antiphon or Two?". *Hermes* 110(2): 145–58.

Balot, R. 1999. Review of Podlecki, *Perikles and his Circle. Bryn Mawr Classical Review* 1999.1.14, http://bmcr.brynmawr.edu/1999/1999-01-14.html (accessed March 2014).

——2001. "Pericles' Anatomy of Democratic Courage". *American Journal of Philology* 122(4): 505–25.

Barbeyrac, J. 1729. "An Historical and Critical Account of the Science of Morality". Preface in S. Pufendorf, *Of the Law of Nature and Nations*, G. Carew (trans.). London: Walthoe *et al.*

Bauman, R. A. 1990. *Political Trials in Ancient Greece*. London: Routledge.

Bayle, P. 1739. *A General Dictionary, Historical and Critical*, vol. VIII, J. P. Bernard *et al.* (trans.). London: James Bettenham.

Berges, S. 2007. "Virtue Ethics, Politics, and the Function of Laws: The Parent Analogy in Plato's *Menexenus*". *Dialogue* 46(2): 211–30.

Betegh, G. 2009. "Tale, Theology, and Teleology in the Phaedo". See Partenie (2009a), 77–100.

Bicknell, P. J. 1982. "Axiochus Alkibiadou, Aspasia and Aspasios". *Acta Classica* 51: 240–50.

Blank, D. 1985. "Socratics versus Sophists on Payment for Teaching". *Classical Antiquity* 4(1): 1–49.

Bloedow, E. F. 1975. "Aspasia and the 'Mystery' of the Menexenos". *Wiener Studien* n.s. 9: 32–48.

Boedeker, D. 2007. "Athenian Religion in the Age of Pericles". In *The Cambridge Companion to the Age of Pericles*, L. J. Samons II (ed.), 46–69. Cambridge: Cambridge University Press.

Borthwick, E. K. 2001. "The Cynic and the Statue". *Classical Quarterly* 51(2): 494–98.

Boyd, T. W. 1995. "Libri Confusi". *Classical Journal* 91(1): 35–45.

Brandwood, L. 1992. "Stylometry and Chronology". In *The Cambridge Companion to Plato*, R. Kraut (ed.), 90–120. Cambridge: Cambridge University Press.

Burnyeat, M. 1977. "Socratic Midwifery, Platonic Inspiration". *British Institute of Classical Studies* 24: 7–16.

——2009. "*Eikôs Muthos*". See Partenie (2009a), 167–86.

——2012. "First Words: A Valedictory Lecture". In his *Explorations in Ancient and Modern Philosophy*, vol. 2, 305–25. Cambridge: Cambridge University Press.

Carson, A. 1992. "How Not to Read a Poem: Unmixing Simonides from *Protagoras*". *Classical Philology* 87(4): 110–30.

Cavell, S. 1969. "Aesthetic Problems of Modern Philosophy". In his *Must We Mean What We Say?*, 73–96. Cambridge: Cambridge University Press.

——2005. *Philosophy the Day After Tomorrow*. Cambridge, MA: Harvard University Press.

Cawkwell, G. L. 1968. Review of I. A. F. Bruce, *An Historical Commentary on the "Hellenica Oxyrhynchia"*. *Classical Review* 18(3): 288–90.

——1981. "The King's Peace". *Classical Quarterly* n.s. 31(1): 69–83.

——1997. *Thucydides and the Peloponnesian War*. London: Routledge.

Clavaud, R. 1980. *Le Ménexène de Platon et la rhétorique de son temps*. Paris: Société d'Édition "Les Belles Lettres".

Cohen, E. E. 2006. "Free and Unfree Sexual Work". In *Prostitutes and Courtesans in the Ancient World*, C. A. Faraone & L. K. McClure (eds), 95–124. Madison, WI: University of Wisconsin Press.

Colakis, M. 1998. Review of Henry, *Prisoner of History*. *Classical World* 91: 299.

Collins, S. D. & D. Stauffer 1999a. "The Challenge of Plato's *Menexenus*". *Review of Politics* 61(1): 85–115.

——1999b. *Empire and the Ends of Politics: Plato's "Menexenus" and Pericles' Funeral Oration: Translation, Introduction, and Notes*. Newburyport, MA: Focus Publishing.

Connor, W. R. 1993. "The Ionian Era of Athenian Civic Identity". *Proceedings of the American Philosophical Society* 137(2): 194–206.

Cooper, J. (ed.) 1997. *Plato: Complete Works*. Indianapolis, IN: Hackett.

Coventry, L. 1989. "Philosophy and Rhetoric in the *Menexenus*". *Journal of Hellenic Studies* 109: 1–15.

Davison, J. A. 1955. "Peisistratus and Homer". *Transactions and Proceedings of the American Philological Association* 86(1): 1–21.

Dean-Jones, L. 1995. "Menexenus – Son of Socrates". *Classical Quarterly* n.s. 45(1): 51–57.

Delcourt, M. 1957. *Héphaïstos ou la légende du magicien*. Paris: Société d'Édition "Les Belles Lettres".

Derow, P. 1994. "Historical Explanation: Polybius and his Predecessors". In *Greek Historiography*, S. Hornblower (ed.), 73–90. New York: Oxford University Press.

Destrée, P. & N. D. Smith (eds) 2005. *Socrates' Divine Sign: Religion, Practice and Value in Socratic Philosophy*. Kelowna, BC: Academic Printing & Publishing.

Detienne, M. & J.-P. Vernant 1978. *Cunning Intelligence in Greek Culture and Society*, J. Lloyd (trans.). Atlantic Highlands, NJ: Humanities Press.

Dillery, J. 2005. "Greek Sacred History". *American Journal of Philology* 126(4): 505–26.

Dombrowski, D. A. 1981. *Plato's Philosophy of History*. Washington, DC: University Press of America.

Dougherty, C. 1998. "It's Murder to Found a Colony". In *Cultural Poetics in Archaic Greece: Cult, Performance, Politics*, C. Dougherty & L. Kurke (eds), 179–98. New York: Oxford University Press.

Drews, R. 1986. Review of Fornara, *The Nature of History in Ancient Greece and Rome*. *Classical Philology* 81(2): 164–69.

Dupin, L. E. 1690. *Nouvelle Bibliothèque des auteurs ecclésiastiques*, vol. I. Paris: André Pralard.

Ehlers, B. 1966. *Eine vorplatonische Deutung des sokratischen Eros: Der Dialog Aspasia des Sorkatikers Aischines*. Munich: Beck.

Ferrari, G. R. F. 2009. "Glaucon's Reward, Philosophy's Debt: The Myth of Er". See Partenie (2009a), 116–33.

Ficino, M. 2006. *Gardens of Philosophy: Ficino on Plato*, A. Farndell (trans.). London: Shepheard-Walwyn.

Finley, M. I. 1973. *Democracy Ancient and Modern*. New Brunswick, NJ: Rutgers University Press.

Frangeskou, V. 1999. "Tradition and Originality in Some Attic Funeral Orations". *Classical World* 92(4): 315–36.

Frutiger, P. 1930. *Les Mythes de Platon*. Paris: Felix Alcan.

Fussi, A. 2001. "The Myth of the Last Judgement in the *Gorgias*". *Review of Metaphysics* 54(3): 529–52.

Gagarin, M. 2002. *Antiphon the Athenian: Oratory, Law, and Justice in the Age of the Sophists*. Austin, TX: University of Texas Press.

Gaiser, K. 1980. "Plato's Enigmatic Lecture: 'On the Good'". *Phronesis* 25(1): 5–37.

Gale, T. 1677. *The Court of the Gentiles, or, A Discourse Touching the Original of Human Literature*. Oxford: Oxford University Press.

Geddes, A. G. 1987. "Rags and Riches: The Costume of Athenian Men in the Fifth Century". *Classical Quarterly* 37(2): 307–31.

Geddes, J. 1748. *Essay on the Composition and Manner of Writing of the Antients, Particularly Plato*. Glasgow: Robert Foulis.

Gehrke, H.-J. 2001. "Myth, History, and Collective Identity: Uses of the Past in Ancient Greece and Beyond". In *The Historian's Craft in the Age of Herodotus*, N. Luraghi (ed.), 286–313. Oxford: Oxford University Press.

Gellrich, M. 1994. "Socratic Magic: Enchantment, Irony, and Persuasion in Plato's Dialogues". *Classical World* 87(4): 275–307.

Ginsburg, J. 1997. Review of Henry, *Prisoner of History*. *Classical Philology* 92(2): 189–93.

Graf, F. 1997. *Magic in the Ancient World*, F. Phillip (trans.). Cambridge, MA: Harvard University Press.

Graves, C. E. 1896. *The "Euthyphro" and "Menexenus" of Plato*. London: Macmillan.

Gray, V. J. 1981. "Dialogue in Xenophon's *Hellenica*". *Classical Quarterly* 31(2): 321–34.

——1987. "*Mimesis* in Greek Historical Theory". *American Journal of Philology* 108(3): 467–86.

——1991. "Continuous History and Xenophon, *Hellenica* 1–2.3.10". *American Journal of Philology* 112(2): 201–28.

——1997. "Reading the Rise of Pisistratus: Herodotus 1.56–68". *Histos* 1, www.dur.ac.uk/Classics/histos/1997/gray.html (accessed September 2013).

Greckol, A. 1999. "A Commentary on Plato's *Menexenus*". MA thesis, University of Alberta.

Grote, G. 1865. *Plato and the Other Companions of Sokrates*, vol. III. London: John Murray.

Hale, J. R. 2009. *Lords of the Sea: The Epic Story of the Athenian Navy and the Birth of Democracy.* New York: Viking.

Hall, J. M. 1997. *Ethnic Identity in Greek Antiquity.* Cambridge: Cambridge University Press.

——2002. *Hellenicity: Between Ethnicity and Culture.* Chicago, IL: University of Chicago Press.

——2007. *A History of the Archaic Greek World, ca. 1200–478 BCE.* Malden, MA: Blackwell.

Halperin, D. 1990. "Why is Diotima a Woman?" In his *One Hundred Years of Homosexuality*, 113–52. New York: Routledge.

Hanson, V. D. 1995. *The Other Greeks: The Family Farm and the Agrarian Roots of Western Civilization.* New York: The Free Press.

Harte, V. 2010. "Mixed Emotions about Comedy: *Philebus* 48a–50b". Paper presented at the Conference on Art and Morality in Plato, Leuven, 6–7 May.

Hedreen, G. 2004. "The Return of Hephaistos, Dionysiac Processional Ritual and the Creation of a Visual Narrative". *Journal of Hellenic Studies* 124: 38–64.

Henderson, M. M. 1975. "Plato's *Menexenus* and the Distortion of History". *Acta Classica* 18: 25–46.

Henry, M. M. 1995. *Prisoner of History: Aspasia of Miletus and her Biographical Tradition.* New York: Oxford University Press.

Herrman, J. 2004. *Athenian Funeral Orations: Translation, Introduction, and Notes.* Newburyport, MA: Focus Publishing.

Holmberg, I. E. 2003. "Hephaistos and Spiders' Webs". *Phoenix* 57(1–2): 1–17.

Hornblower, S. 1995. "The Fourth-Century and Hellenistic Reception of Thucydides". *Journal of Hellenic Studies* 115: 48–68.

——2004. *Thucydides and Pindar: Historical Narrative and the World of Epinikian Poetry.* New York: Oxford University Press.

Huby, P. M. 1957. "The *Menexenus* Reconsidered". *Phronesis* 2(2): 104–14.

Irwin, T. 2000. *Nicomachean Ethics*, 2nd edn. Indianapolis, IN: Hackett.

Isherwood, C. 2007. "Checking in with Glimmer Twins, Plato and Aristotle". *New York Times* (18 June), www.nytimes.com/2007/06/18/theater/reviews/18targ.html?pagewanted=all&_r=0 (accessed March 2014).

Jones, C. P. 1999. *Kinship Diplomacy in the Ancient World.* Cambridge, MA: Harvard University Press.

Kagan, D. 1991. *Pericles of Athens and the Birth of Democracy.* New York: Free Press.

——2003. *The Peloponnesian War.* New York: Viking.

——2009. *Thucydides: The Reinvention of History.* New York: Viking.

Kahn, C. 1963. "Plato's Funeral Oration: The Motive of the *Menexenus*". *Classical Philology* 58(4): 220–34.

——2009. "The Myth of the *Statesman*". See Partenie (2009a), 148–66.

Kassel, R. & C. Austin (eds) 1998. *Poetae Comici Graeci.* Berlin: de Gruyter.

Keefer, D. 2011. "Speaking Well of the Dead: On the Aesthetics of Eulogies". *Sophia* 50(2): 303–11.

Kerch, T. M. 2008. "Plato's *Menexenus:* A Paradigm of Rhetorical Flattery". *Polis* 25(1): 94–114.

Klagge, J. C. & N. D. Smith (eds) 1992. *Methods of Interpreting Plato and His Dialogues.* Oxford: Clarendon Press.

Klosko, G. 1986. *The Development of Plato's Political Theory*. New York: Methuen & Co.

Kyle, D. 2003. "'The Only Woman in All Greece': Kyniska, Agesilaus, Alcibiades and Olympia". *Journal of Sport History* 30(2): 183–203.

Ledbetter, G. M. 2002. *Poetics Before Plato: Interpretation and Authority in Early Greek Theories of Poetry*. Princeton, NJ: Princeton University Press.

Lendon, J. E. 2006. "Xenophon and the Alternative to Realist Foreign Policy: *Cyropaedia* 3.1.14–31". *Journal of Hellenic Studies* 126: 82–98.

——2007. "Athens and Sparta and the Coming of the Peloponnesian War". In *The Cambridge Companion to the Age of Pericles*, L. J. Samons II (ed.), 258–81. Cambridge: Cambridge University Press.

Levin, S. 1959. Review of Delcourt, *Héphaïstos ou la légende du magicien*. *Classical Review* 54(7): 332–34.

Levine, J. 1990. "*Ulysses*". In *The Cambridge Companion to James Joyce*, D. Attridge (ed.), 122–48. Cambridge: Cambridge University Press.

Liddel, P. 2010. "*Metabole Politeion* as Universal Historiography". In *Historiae Mundi: Studies in Universal Historiography*, P. Liddel & A. Fear (eds), 15–29. London: Duckworth.

Long, C. P. 2003. "Dancing Naked with Socrates: Pericles, Aspasia and Socrates at Play with Politics, Rhetoric and Philosophy". *Ancient Philosophy* 23(1) 49–69.

Loraux, N. 1986. *The Invention of Athens: The Funeral Oration in the Classical City*, A. Sheridan (trans.). Cambridge, MA: Harvard University Press.

——1990. "Kreousa the Autochthon: A Study of Euripides' *Ion*". In *Nothing to Do with Dionysos?*, J. J. Winkler & F. I. Zeitlin (eds), 168–206. Princeton, NJ: Princeton University Press.

——1993. *The Children of Athena: Athenian Ideas about Citizenship and the Division between the Sexes*, C. Levine (trans.). Princeton, NJ: Princeton University Press.

——2000. *Born of the Earth: Myth and Politics in Athens*, S. Stewart (trans.). Ithaca, NY: Cornell University Press.

Mahoney, P. O. 2010. "The Origin of the Olive: On the Dynamics of Plato's *Menexenus*". *Polis* 27(1): 38–57.

McCoy, M. 2008. *Plato on the Rhetoric of Philosophers and Sophists*. Cambridge: Cambridge University Press.

McPherran, M. L. 1996. *The Religion of Socrates*. University Park, PA: Pennsylvania State University Press.

Mickics, D. 2007. *A New Handbook of Literary Terms*. New Haven, CT: Yale University Press.

Moles, J. 1996. "Herodotus Warns the Athenians". *Papers of the Leeds International Latin Seminar* 9: 259–84.

Monoson, S. S. 1992. "Remembering Pericles: The Political and Theoretical Import of Plato's *Menexenus*". *Political Theory* 26(4): 489–513.

——2000. *Plato's Democratic Entanglements: Athenian Politics and the Practice of Philosophy*. Princeton, NJ: Princeton University Press.

Morgan, K. A. 1998. "Designer History: Plato's Atlantis Story and Fourth-Century Ideology". *Journal of Hellenic Studies* 118: 101–18.

Morrison, J. V. 1994. "A Key Topos in Thucydides: The Comparison of Cities and Individuals". *American Journal of Philology* 115(4): 525–41.

Naddaf, G. 1994. "The Atlantis Myth: An Introduction to Plato's Later Philosophy of History". *Phoenix* 48(3): 189–209.

Nagy, G. 1992. "Homeric Questions". *Transactions of the American Philological Association* 122: 17–60.

Nails, D. 2002. *The People of Plato: A Prosopography of Plato and Other Socratics.* Indianapolis, IN: Hackett.

Nehamas, A. 1982. "Plato on Imitation and Poetry in *Republic* X". In *Plato on Beauty, Wisdom and the Arts*, J. Moravcsik & P. Temko (eds), 47–78. Totowa, NJ: Rowman & Littlefield.

Nightingale, A. W. 1993. "The Folly of Praise: Plato's Critique of Encomiastic Discourse in the *Lysis* and *Symposium*". *Classical Quarterly* 43(1): 112–30.

Nussbaum, M. 1980. "Aristophanes and Socrates on Learning Practical Wisdom". *Yale Classical Studies* 26: 43–97.

Ober, J. 2000. Review of Wilson, *The Athenian Institution of the Khoregia. Bryn Mawr Classical Review*, http://bmcr.brynmawr.edu/2000/2000-10-02.html (accessed March 2014).

——2005. *Athenian Legacies: Essays on the Politics of Going on Together.* Princeton, NJ: Princeton University Press.

Olson, S. D. 2007. *Broken Laughter: Select Fragments of Greek Comedy.* Oxford: Oxford University Press.

Ophir, A. 1991. *Plato's Invisible Cities: Discourse and Power in the "Republic".* Savage, MD: Barnes & Noble.

Page, D. L. 1981. *Further Greek Epigrams.* Cambridge: Cambridge University Press.

Pallas, T. E. 1976. "Reflections on Plato's *Menexenus*". PhD thesis, University of California at Santa Barbara.

Pappas, N. 1989. "Socrates' Charitable Treatment of Poetry". *Philosophy and Literature* 13(2): 248–61.

——2011a. "Autochthony in Plato's *Menexenus*". *Philosophical Inquiry* 34: 66–80.

——2011b. Review of Partenie, *Plato's Myths. Philosophical Inquiry* 34: 101–6.

Pappas, N. & M. Zelcer 2013. "Plato's *Menexenus* as a History that Falls into Patterns". *Ancient Philosophy* 33(1): 19–31.

Partenie, C. (ed.) 2009a. *Plato's Myths.* Cambridge: Cambridge University Press.

Partenie, C. 2009b. "Plato's Myths". *Stanford Encyclopedia of Philosophy* (23 July), http://plato.stanford.edu/entries/plato-myths (accessed March 2014).

——2009c. "Introduction". See Partenie (2009a), 1–27.

Pearson, L. 1942. *The Local Historians of Attica.* Philadelphia, PA: Lancaster Press.

Pelling, C. 2009. "Bringing Autochthony Up-to-Date: Herodotus and Thucydides". *Classical World* 102(4): 471–83.

Pendrick, G. 1987. "Once Again Antiphon the Sophist and Antiphon of Rhamnus". *Hermes* 115(1): 47–60.

Petre, Z. 2009. "Revenants et Sauveurs: Le *Ménexène* de Platon et le Drame Attique". In *Memory, Humanity, and Meaning*, M. Neamțu & B. Tătaru-Cazaban (eds), 149–62. Bucharest: Zeta Books.

Pickard-Cambridge, A. W., J. Gould & D. M. Lewis 1988. *The Dramatic Festivals of Athens*, 2nd edn. Oxford: Oxford University Press.

Podlecki, A. J. 1998. *Perikles and his Circle.* London: Routledge.

Pomeroy, S. 1996. Review of Henry, *Prisoner of History. American Journal of Philology* 117(4): 648–51.

Poulakos, T. 1990. "Historiographies of the Tradition of Rhetoric: A Brief History of Classical Funeral Orations". *Western Journal of Speech Communication* 54(2): 172–88.

Pownall, F. 1998. "Condemnation of the Impious in Xenophon's *Hellenica*". *Harvard Theological Review* 91(3): 251–77.

——2004. *Lessons from the Past: The Moral Use of History in Fourth-Century Prose*. Ann Arbor, MI: University of Michigan Press.

Press, G. (ed.) 2000. *Who Speaks for Plato?* Lanham, MD: Rowman & Littlefield.

Rahn, P. J. 1971. "Xenophon's Developing Historiography". *Transactions and Proceedings of the American Philological Association* 102: 497–508.

Raubitschek, A. E. 1941. "The Heroes of Phyle". *Hesperia* 10(3): 284–95.

Rhodes, P. J. 2010. *A History of the Classical Greek World 478–323 BC*, 2nd edn. Oxford: Blackwell.

Rinon, Y. 2006. "Tragic Hephaestus: The Humanized God in the *Iliad* and the *Odyssey*". *Phoenix* 60(1–2): 1–20.

Roberts, J. T. 2012. "Mourning and Democracy: The Periclean *Epitaphios* and its Afterlife". In *Thucydides and the Modern World: Reception, Reinterpretation and Influence from the Renaissance to the Present*, K. Harloe & N. Morley (eds), 140–56. Cambridge: Cambridge University Press.

Roberts, S. C. 1921. *A History of the Cambridge University Press 1521–1921*. Cambridge: Cambridge University Press.

Romero, M. R. 2009. "'Without the Least Tremor': Ritual Sacrifice as Background in the *Phaedo*". *Epoché* 13(2): 241–48.

Rosenstock, B. 1994. "Socrates as Revenant: A Reading of the *Menexenus*". *Phoenix* 48(4): 331–48.

Rosivach, V. J. 1987. "Autochthony and the Athenians". *Classical Quarterly* 37(2): 294–306.

Roth, P. 1984. "Teiresias as Mantis and Intellectual in Euripides' *Bacchae*". *Transactions of the American Philological Association* 114: 59–69.

Rowe, C. 2009. "The Charioteer and his Horses: An Example of Platonic Myth-Making". See Partenie (2009a), 134–47.

Roy, J. 1997. "An Alternative Sexual Morality for Classical Athenians". *Greece and Rome* 44(1): 11–22.

Sage, P. W. 1989. Review of Loraux, *The Invention of Athens. Classical World* 83(1): 67–68.

Salkever, S. G. 1993. "Socrates' Aspasian Oration: The Play of Philosophy and Politics in Plato's *Menexenus*". *American Political Science Review* 87(1): 133–43.

Sanders, E. 2014. *Envy and Jealousy in Classical Athens: A Socio-psychological Approach*. Oxford: Oxford University Press.

Sandys, J. E. 1885. *M. Tulli Ciceronis: Ad M. Brutum Orator*. Cambridge: Cambridge University Press.

Sansone, D. 1985. "The Date of Herodotus' Publication". *Illinois Classical Studies* 10: 1–9.

Saxonhouse, A. 1986. "Myths and the Origin of Cities: Reflections on the Autochthony Theme in Euripides' *Ion*". In *Greek Tragedy and Political Theory*, J. P. Euben (ed.), 252–73. Berkeley, CA: University of California Press.

Schofield, M. 2009. "*Fraternité, Inégalité, la Parole de Dieu:* Plato's Authoritarian Myth of Political Legitimation". See Partenie (2009a), 101–15.

Sedley, D. 2008. *Creationism and its Critics in Antiquity.* Berkeley, CA: University of California Press.

——2009. "Myth, Punishment, and Politics in the *Gorgias*". See Partenie (2009a), 51–76.

Seeberg, A. 1965. "Hephaestus Rides Again". *Journal of Hellenic Studies* 85: 102–9.

Sharp, K. 2006. "From Solon to Socrates: Proto-Socratic Dialogues in Herodotus". In *La costruzione del discorso filosofico nell'età dei Presocratici* [*The Construction of Philosophical Discourse in the Age of the Presocratics*], M. M. Sassi (ed.), 81–102. Pisa: Edixioni della Normale.

Shorey, P. 1959. *Plato in Twelve Volumes.* Cambridge, MA: Harvard University Press.

Smith, J. E. 1986. "Plato's Use of Myth in the Education of Philosophic Man". *Phoenix* 40(1): 20–34.

Stalley, R. 2009. "Myth and Eschatology in the *Laws*". See Partenie (2009a), 187–205.

Stern, H. S. 1974. "Plato's Funeral Oration". *New Scholasticism* 48: 503–8.

Sternberg, R. H. 2005. "The Nature of Pity". In *Pity and Power in Ancient Athens*, R. H. Sternberg (ed.), 15–47. Cambridge: Cambridge University Press.

Stevens, E. B. 1948. "Envy and Pity in Greek Philosophy". *American Journal of Philology* 69(2): 171–89.

Strauss, B. 2004. "The Dead at Arginusae and the Debate over the Athenian Navy". *Nautiki Epithewrisi* [*Naval Review*] 545.160s: 40–67.

Tarrant, H. 2007. *Proclus, Commentary on Plato's Timaeus*, vol. I, book 1. Cambridge: Cambridge University Press.

Thomas, A. L. 1773. *Oeuvres Diverses*, vol. III. Amsterdam: E. van Harrevelt.

Tompkins, D. P. 1988. Review of Loraux, *The Invention of Athens. History and Theory* 27(3): 306–12.

Tracy, S. V. 2009. *Pericles: A Sourcebook and Reader.* Berkeley, CA: University of California Press.

Tritle, L. A. 2007. "'Laughing for Joy': War and Peace Among the Greeks". In *War and Peace in the Ancient World*, K. A. Raaflaub (ed.), 172–90. Oxford: Blackwell.

Trivigno, F. V. 2009. "The Rhetoric of Parody in Plato's *Menexenus*". *Philosophy and Rhetoric* 42(1): 29–58.

Tsitsiridis, S. 1998. *Platons Menexenos: Einleitung, Text und Kommentar.* Stuttgart: Teubner.

Tulin, A. 2000. Review of Tsitsiridis, *Platons Menexenus. Classical World* 93(3): 305–6.

Van Wees, H. 2002. "Herodotus and the Past". In *Brill's Companion to Herodotus*, E. J. Bakker, I. J. F. de Jong & H. van Wees (eds), 321–49. Leiden: Brill.

Vernant, J.-P. 1974. *Mythe et société en Grèce ancienne.* Paris: Maspero.

Vidal-Naquet, P. 1998. "Athens and Atlantis: Structure and Meaning of a Platonic Myth". In his *The Black Hunter: Forms of Thought and Forms of Society in the Greek World*, A. Szegedy-Maszak (trans.), 263–84. Baltimore, MD: Johns Hopkins University Press.

Vlastos, G. 1964. "*Isonomia Politikê*". In *Isonomia: Studien zur Gleichheitsvorstellung im Griechischen Denken*, J. Mau & E. G. Schmidt (eds), 1–35. Berlin: Akademie-Verlag.

Walsh, G. 1978. "The Rhetoric of Birthright and Race in Euripides' *Ion*". *Hermes* 106(2): 302–15.

Walters, K. R. 1981. "'We Fought Alone at Marathon': Historical Falsification in the Attic Funeral Oration". *Rheinisches Museum für Philologie* 124(3–4): 204–11.

Walton, F. R. 1960. Review of Delcourt, *Héphaïstos ou la légende du magicien*. *Classical Philology* 55(4): 286–89.

Węcowski, M. 2004. "The Hedgehog and the Fox: Form and Meaning in the Prologue of Herodotus' *Histories*". *Journal of Hellenic Studies* 124: 143–64.

West, G. 1753. *Odes of Pindar, with several other Pieces in Prose and Verse, Translated from the Greek*, 2nd edn. London: R. Dodsley.

West, W. C. 1988. Review of Loraux, *The Invention of Athens*. *American Historical Review* 93(2): 396–97.

Westerink, L. G. (ed., trans.) 1962. *Anonymous Prolegomena to Platonic Philosophy*. Amsterdam: North-Holland.

Wickkiser, B. L. 1999. "Speech in Context: Plato's *Menexenus* and the Ritual of Athenian Public Burial". *Rhetoric Society Quarterly* 29(2): 65–74.

Williams, B. 1993. *Shame and Necessity*. Berkeley, CA: University of California Press.

Wilson, P. 2000. *The Athenian Institution of the Khoregia: The Chorus, the City and the Stage*. Cambridge: Cambridge University Press.

Wooten, C. W. 1987. *Hermogenes' On Types of Style*. Chapel Hill, NC: University of North Carolina Press.

Worthington, I. (ed.) 1994a. *Persuasion: Greek Rhetoric in Action*. London: Routledge.

Worthington, I. 1994b. "History and Oratorical Exploitation". *Persuasion: Greek Rhetoric in Action*, I. Worthington (ed.), 109–29. London: Routledge.

Yunis, H. 1996. *Taming Democracy: Models of Political Rhetoric in Classical Athens*. Ithaca, NY: Cornell University Press.

Zatta, C. 2010. "Making History Mythical: The Golden Age of Peisistratus". *Arethusa* 43(1): 21–62.

Zeitlin, F. 1990. "Theater and Self and Society in Athenian Drama". In *Nothing to Do with Dionysos?*, J. J. Winkler & F. I. Zeitlin (eds), 130–67. Princeton, NJ: Princeton University Press.

Ziolkowski, J. E. 1981. *Thucydides and the Tradition of Funeral Speeches at Athens*. New York: Monographs in Classical Studies.

Zürcher, J. 1954. *Das Corpus Academicum*. Paderborn: Schöningh.

INDEX

Acropolis 49, 175, 180n94; as story genre 146, 157–58, 178n47

Aeschines (Attic Orator): *Against Timarchus* 137n10

Aeschines of Sphettus: *Aspasia* 34–36, 54n47, n50, n53

Aeschylus: *Agamemnon* 153, 177n31, 207n18

Aeschylus: *Persians* 44–45, 48, 50, 56n95, 57n118, 147–48, 184, 207n13

Aesop 156, 178n42

Alcibiades 24, 25, 39, 53n38, 54n52, 102–3, 114n22, 123, 139n47, 188, 190

Alcmaeonid family 47

Ameipsias: *Connus* 38

anachronism 21, 25, 26–29, 33, 37

Anaxagoras 3, 10n10, 24, 25, 48, 51n12, 57n114, 117, 105, 114n26, 119, 163, 179n58

Anaximander 108, 109

Andocides 211n75

Anonymous Prolegomena to Platonic Philosophy 85, 206n5

Antiphon of Cephisia 55n64, 90

Antiphon of Rhamnus 37–39, 55n64, n68, n69, n71

Anytus 101, 102, 154

Anytus of Euonymon 41

Apollo 153, 160, 167

Apollodorus 159; *Library* 178n48, n52

Archidamian War 186

Arginusae 17, 25, 33, 187, 190–91, 200–201, 209n45, 211n76

aristocracy 16, 55n66, 70, 72, 149

Aristophanes 3, 24, 32–33, 46, 53n35, 108; *Acharnians* 32, 52n33, 53n34; *Birds* 24, 51n11, 211n75; *Clouds* 24, 55n60, 56n90; *Ecclesiazusae* (*The Assemblywomen*) 53n35, 212n79; *Frogs* 3, 24, 51n11, 78; *Knights* 38, 55n61, 207n18; *Lysistrata* 53n35, 54n46; *Wasps* 38, 53n36, 55n62, 57n115, 158, 178n47

Aristotle 1, 7, 11n22, n24, 38, 46, 51n7, 52n30, 133, 134, 138n24, 148, 221n10; *Constitution of Athens* 40, 46, 56n78, n82, 57n104, n109, 177n22; *Eudemian Ethics* 55n65; *Nicomachean Ethics* 52n30; *Poetics* 74n1; *Politics* 51n7; *Rhetoric* 177n19, 212n92

Aristoxenus: *Harmonics* 52n25

Artemisium 17, 183, 184, 200, 207n10, 211n78

Aspasia 1–2, 5, 9, 10n7, 11n17, 15, 19, 20–23, 25–27, 31–37, 38–39, 40, 42–45, 46, 47, 51n2, n3, 52n26, 53n35, n38, n45, 54n46, n47, n49, n50, n52, n53, 59, 61, 65, 66, 67, 74n7, 81, 82, 87, 88, 91, 93, 93n27, 95, 102, 104, 105, 106, 107, 111–13, 119, 121, 134–35, 140, 144–45, 191, 214, 216

Athenaeus 53n40, 54n52, 55n60, 140n63

Athenian Stranger 3, 164, 207n9, 211n78

Athens: as educator 35–36, 215; as mistress 135, 215

Atthidography 195, 210n61

Attica 107, 109, 111, 135, 144, 145, 150, 161, 163, 214, 218

Augustine 176n11

Austin, J. L. 132–33

autochthony 30, 35, 54n51, 55n54, 83, 86, 97, 107, 109, 111, 125–27, 131, 135, 139n39, 143, 145–47, 150, 151, 157–75, 176n8, 178n55, 179n59, 180n81, 206, 214, 216, 219

Balot, Ryan 101
barbarian 17–18, 28, 39, 70, 87, 110, 131, 138n23, 165, 171–72, 174, 180n85, 184, 189–92, 201, 202, 212n84
battles: land and sea 149, 184, 187, 200, 201
Bayle, Peter: *Dictionnaire Historique et Critique* 87
beauty 18, 98, 130–31, 139n37, 171
Beauty, Form of 171
birth from the earth *see* autochthony
Boreas and Orethyia, myth of 156
boulê 43, 45, 74n9

Cadmus 164, 171
Callicles 217
cave, allegory of 9, 154
Cavell, Stanley 10n13, 154
Chaeronea, Battle of 28, 63, 64
Cicero 6–7, 11n19, 34, 54n53; *De Inventione* 54n48, n53; *De Oratore* 75n16, 177n16; *Orator ad M. Brutum* 11n19
Cimon 47–48, 59, 185–86
city/soul analogy 8, 71, 201–3, 215
Clavaud, Robert 7, 10n14, 11n18, n19, 51n6, 56n95, 84, 92n1, 114n28, 144–45, 176n9, 206n6
Cleisthenes 180n90
Connus 22, 37–38, 42, 50n1, 51n2, 55n59, n61, n62
Conon (Athenian general) 190, 192, 210n50
Corinthian War 6, 28, 29, 44, 63, 171, 192, 194, 200, 206, 210n50
courage 18, 35, 55n55, 83, 99–101, 106, 107, 109–13, 113n8, 118, 119, 122, 202, 203, 214, 219
Cousin, Victor 73
Critias 2, 164, 165, 179n64, 196, 197
custom 71, 83, 108, 119, 171
Cyrus the Great 16, 199, 205

dancing naked 42, 43
Darius 17, 45, 87, 183
Dean-Jones, Leslie 42–44, 50
Delian League 49, 175, 212n79
Demiurge 157
democracy 16, 40, 48, 49, 55n66, 62, 68, 70, 72, 73, 75n18, 80, 101, 144, 149, 191, 201, 211n77, 216, 220

Demosthenes (general) 187
Demosthenes (orator) 11n20, 28, 31, 40, 63–65, 67–71, 75n22, 76n35, 87, 139n39, 145, 158
Diodorus Siculus 185, 187, 192, 198, 210n50
Diogenes Laërtius: *Lives of the Eminent Philosophers* 4
Dionysus 3, 4, 160, 167
Dionysius of Halicarnassus 7, 85
Diotima 2, 10n7, 37, 88
dragnet practice 207n9
Duck Soup 113n13

earth, as mother 16, 35, 107, 109, 110, 126–29, 135, 145, 158, 162, 164, 166–67, 169, 170, 171, 215, 219
education 8, 16, 20, 30, 35, 37, 49, 55n54, n66, 56n87, 69–71, 76n28, 82, 83, 91, 97–101, 103–13, 113n8, 114n15, 119, 122, 129, 144, 150, 166–69, 175, 202, 214, 216, 218; moral 8, 34, 37, 68, 82, 98, 99–101, 114n15, 135
Egypt 17, 136, 165, 179, 185, 200, 202
Egyptians and Phoenicians 202
Ehlers, Barbara 34, 54n47
Eleatic Stranger 77, 109
Eleusis 40, 147
empeiria 22, 217
encomia to salt and bumblebees 123, 130, 131, 139n30
envy *see phthonos*
Ephesian philosophers 156, 177n41
Ephialtes 47, 48
Erechtheus (Erichthonius) 146, 158, 159, 162
ergon 71, 78, 82, 83, 116, 117–22, 137n1, 148, 175,
erôs 2, 35, 54n50, n51, 124, 130, 218, 219
Esther 19n1
Eupolis 32, 52n31
Euripides: *Heracleidae* 3, 89, 121; *Ion* 157–59, 167, 178n47, n49, 179n69
Eurymedon 17, 47, 184, 185, 200
Euthyphro 43, 124
evolution, theory of 108–9
exceptionalism, Athenian 117, 144, 174
explanation, historical 195

Ferrari, G. R. F. 153, 154
Ficino, Marsilio 86, 87

flux, doctrine of 156
foreigners 41, 118, 122, 126, 136, 172
Forms 130–32, 163, 168

Gale, Theophilus 87
Ge *see* earth as mother
generals, execution of 25, 33, 191
Gettysburg Address 137n2
Glaucon 132, 164
Good, Form of 132
Gorgias 61–63, 65, 70, 116, 130, 131, 140n48; *Encomium to Helen* 62, 123, 130, 131
Graves, C. E. 183
guardian, Athenians as 202–3

Hades 44, 76n27, 160
Hall, Jonathan 173
Hecataeus of Miletus: *Gês Periodos* 195
Helen 62, 124, 130–32
Hellespont, battle at 17, 187, 188, 190, 200, 209n39
Helots 170, 186
Henry, Madeleine 31, 35, 53n35, n39, 54n47, n49, n50
Hephaestus 54n51, 146, 156, 159–67, 178n51, n52, n55
Hermippus 32
Hermocrates 2, 188, 208n34
Hermogenes 7, 39, 134
Herodotus: *Histories* 31, 46, 53n34, 54n46, 57n100, 74n11, 88, 143, 161, 165, 173, 176n3, 179n66, 180n80, n90, 183, 184, 195, 197, 199, 211n78
Herskovits, David 51n4
Hesiod 90, 119, 185; *Theogony* 89, 167; *Works and Days* 178n50, n55, 185
Hipparchus, son of Peisistratus 149
Hippocrates: *Airs, Waters, Places* 202
Hippothales 123
historiography: Plato 82, 84, 182, 196; Thucydidean 57n106, 196; universal 194–95, 197–99, 204, 210n58
Homer: *Iliad* 148, 149, 153, 156, 158, 160, 161, 173; *Odyssey* 89, 148, 149, 161
Homeric Hymn 161
hoplite 24, 49
Hornblower, Simon 172
Hyperides 63–65, 67, 68, 69, 71, 75, 145, 158

improvisation 59, 60, 74n8, n9, 91, 103, 106, 116, 127, 132–37, 140n55, n56, n60
intertextuality 2
Ion 43, 44, 158, 167
Isles of the Blessed 27, 120, 137, 220
Isocrates 123, 124, 131, 139n30, n37, 173, 218

Kagan, Donald 188, 208n32
Kahn, Charles 1, 153, 194, 210n57, 211n73
Kallipolis 36, 220
Kekrops 146, 158, 159
Kerameikos, as story genre 157, 163, 176n8
Kierkegaard, S. 4
King's Peace (Common Peace) 25, 41, 44, 56n86, 63, 192, 193, 194
knowledge 15, 18, 21, 51n7, 71, 97, 99, 104, 105, 109, 196, 202, 217, 218, 219

Lamprus 37
Lechaeum 18, 192, 200
Lendon, J. E. 198–99, 211n67
Leontini 187
Libya 17
Livy: *History of Roman Republic* 113n12
logos 71, 74n2, 78, 82, 83, 116–22, 151, 175
Loraux, Nicole 71–73, 75n19, 76n39, n41, n46, 80, 145, 146, 157, 166, 168, 176n8, 178n47, 179n57
Lycurgus: *In Leocratem* 177n20
Lysias (orator), son of Cephalus 2, 61, 62, 63, 65, 67, 70, 75n16, n17, n18, 124, 145, 158, 191, 213n99; speech in the *Phaedrus* 44
Lysimachus 124

Marathon, battle of 5, 17, 29, 44, 110, 147, 183, 184, 193, 200, 202, 207n11
matchmaking 34, 53–54n45
mathematics 98, 112
Medes 16, 19n1, 183, 205
Megarian Decree 32–33, 53n33
Meletus 101, 133, 154
Menexenus, character: as son of Socrates 44, 50, 57n95
metals in soul 97, 108, 163, 164
midwife 22, 51n5, 53n45

mimeisthai 106–7
minêsis 5, 61, 99, 106–7, 109–13, 127, 135
mixed Greeks 171, 184, 202
mother 16, 107, 109, 119, 126–29, 135, 145, 150, 158, 162, 164, 166–67, 169, 170, 171, 215
Muses 89–90, 152
muthos 151, 156, 176n3, 179n62
myth 109, 110, 127, 131, 135, 143–75, 214, 219
Mytilene/Arginusae, battle at 17, 190, 200

Nails, Debra 28–29, 53n38
national character, as explanation 188–90, 202
Nestor 140n47
Nietzsche, F. 4
noble lie 83, 97, 108, 152–53, 157, 163–64, 166, 168, 169, 170, 205
nomos 71, 83, 108, 119, 120

Ocean (god) 156
Oenophytae 186, 187, 200

pan-Hellenism 147, 150, 172–74, 187, 203
Paralus and Xanthippus 25, 47, 101, 102
Parmenides 3, 89
parody, *Menexenus* as 4–9, 11, 23, 43, 44, 54n46, 65–68, 72, 73, 77–91, 104, 122, 145, 176n7, n9, 182, 194, 206, 214, 215, 217, 220n1
Partenie, Catalin 153, 177n25, n27
Parthenon 49, 175, 176n11, 181n94
Pausanias: *Description of Greece* 178n51
Peisistratus 148–49
Pelasgians of Attica 161
Peloponnesian League 175
Peloponnesian War 1, 23, 25, 29, 49, 60, 63, 70, 75, 79n19, 186, 191, 194, 197–201, 204, 212n79
Pentekontaetia 176n6
Pericles the Younger 25, 33, 52n31, 191
perileimmata 106, 111
Persia 6, 16–18, 29, 41, 44, 45, 47, 52n23, 56n86, 64, 110, 147, 148, 172, 175, 181n94, 185, 186, 187, 189, 190–94, 199, 200, 201, 202, 205–6; King of 17, 18, 45, 185, 190, 193, 199, 205; war against 5, 16, 17, 25, 44, 48, 50, 63, 147, 172, 175, 183, 186, 190, 193, 195, 197, 200, 204

Phaedrus 91
Philip of Macedon 28, 63
philonikia 189, 190, 198, 204
phthonos 111, 113n10, 115n41, 122, 185, 189, 190, 203, 204, 207n17, 213n97
Pindar 86, 178n51, 207n17
Piraeus 56n81, 192
pity 18, 191, 205, 213n99
Plataea 17, 180n94, 183, 184, 200, 207n11
Plato: *Apology* 2, 4, 9, 10n11, 24, 25, 27, 30, 51n10, n12, 52n14, n19, 55n64, n67, 56n83, 57n96, 76n27, 114n24, 131, 140n57, 149, 177n31, 207n17, 209n46, n47; *Charmides* 55n67; *Cratylus* 134, 140n57; *Critias* 2, 29, 146, 163, 164, 165, 166, 176n12, 179n64, n65, 201, 208n34, 212n80, 216; *Crito* 129–30, 138n28, 139n42, n44; *Euthydemus* 37, 50n1, 55n59, 134, 139n29, 140n58; *Euthyphro* 9, 21, 139n33, 140n57, 146, 176n12; *Gorgias* 21, 24, 47, 51n3, n6, n10, n12, 74n6, 102, 103, 104, 105, 114n18, n24, 138n28, 139n29, 152, 153, 209n46, 213n95, 216–18, 220n2, n3, n4; *Ion* 21, 138n27, 157, 158, 159, 178, 179; *Laches* 113n8, 139n33, 213n95; *Laws* 87, 138n27, n28, 139n29, n30, n33, 140n68, 146, 155, 163, 164, 177n35, 179n62, 201, 204, 207n9, 211n78, 212n87, 213n95; *Lysis* 10n9, 42, 56n89, 123, 124; *Meno* 57n107, n108, 101, 105, 114n16, 140n68, 216; "On the Good" 30; *Parmenides* 55n64, 90; *Phaedo* 10n10, 26, 42, 51n5, n12, 52n16, 57n117, 153, 156, 177n31, 178n42, 179n74, 209n35, 212n83; *Phaedrus* 2, 11n16, 22, 44, 51n3, 57n107, n114, 63, 75n16, 91, 93n41, 105, 114n21, n26, 124, 134, 138n28, 139n29, n30, n35, 140n58, 148, 155, 176n16, 177n39, 185, 207n19, 216, 218–21; *Philebus* 185, 207n17; *Protagoras* 2, 10n11, 25, 47, 51n9, n12, n13, 57n108, n117, 89, 102, 103, 105, 114n19, n32, 138n27, n28, 139n29, 216; *Republic* 3, 8, 9, 11n16, 29, 30, 36, 54n45, 63, 71, 84, 85, 87, 97, 98, 99, 104, 107, 113n1, n2, n12, 114n24, n37, 123, 132, 138n27, n28, 139n29, 140n52, n53,

n68, 146, 148, 156, 163, 164, 168, 176n12, n16, 177n40, 178, 179n60, n61, n74, 180n85, 201, 202, 203, 204, 205, 206, 211, 212, 213, 215, 216, 219, 220; *Sophist* 11n16, 107, 109, 114n35, n38, 163, 179n59; *Statesman* 155, 177n36, 179n59, n67, 211n72, 216; *Symposium* 2, 9, 37, 51n4, n9, 12, 55n67, 57n107, 88, 102, 114n17, n32, n33, 123, 124, 130, 138n28, 139n30, n34, n47, 140n47, n51, n68, 154, 177n54, 180n85; *Theaetetus* 10n9, 22, 51n5, 53n45, 57n117, 85, 138n28, 139n33, 140n64, 156, 177n41, 195, 217, 220n3; *Timaeus* 2, 11n16, 29, 30, 84, 85, 92n22, 114n35, 146, 151, 163–66, 177n26, 179n66, 185, 195, 196, 197, 204, 207n19, 208n34, 210n62, 211n64, n72, 213n95, n96, 216, 219

Plutarch: *Laconian Apophthegms* 11n18; *Life of Agesilaus* 55n56; *Life of Alcibiades* 114n22; *Life of Cimon* 46; *Life of Lycurgus* 177n21 *Life of Nicias* 208n35; *Life of Pericles* 11n15, 33, 46, 53n39, 57n100, 74n7; *Life of Solon* 177n21; *Moralia* 180n83

Polybius 204, 213n97

Poseidon 127, 146–47, 150, 160, 165, 167

praise 1, 7, 8, 9, 15, 16–18, 34, 35–37, 47, 67–70, 78, 83, 91, 99, 106, 107, 109, 119, 121–25, 125–29, 130–33, 136–37, 138n19, n22, 28, 139n31, n33, n37, 144, 147, 148, 166, 185, 196, 197, 205, 214, 218–19

Proclus: *Commentary on Plato's Parmenides* 90, 93n35; *Commentary on Plato's Timeaus* 85–86

Protagoras 3, 25, 48, 108, 119

pseudo-Demosthenes *see* Demosthenes

pseudo-Longinus: *On the Sublime* 62, 75n14

pseudo-Plato: *Hipparchus* 149

pseudo-Plutarch: *Lives of the Ten Orators* 39

Pufendorf, Samuel: *Of the Law of Nature and Nations* 87

Pylos 187

recollection, theory of 109, 168

revenant, Socrates as 26, 27, 44

revivals of tragedy 44

rhetoric 1, 5, 6, 7, 9, 11n23, 15, 20, 21, 22, 23, 27, 28, 33, 36, 37–40, 43, 44, 45–47, 50, 54n46, n49, 60–62, 68, 72–73, 75n16, 77–80, 82, 83, 86, 87, 97–99, 104–6, 112, 116–40, 145–46, 157, 182, 207n11, 214, 216–20; magic of 136–37

Rosenstock, Bruce 26, 27, 28, 44, 50

Rousseau, J. J. 4

Rowe, Christopher 152, 154

Sage, Paula Winsor 76n46

Salamis 17, 45, 50, 110, 147, 148, 149, 183, 184, 195, 200, 202, 211n78, 213n99

Samos 178n52

Sanders, Ed 185

Sardis 17, 183, 207n9

Schofield, Malcom 153, 164

Scythia 17, 202

Sedley, David 152–53

Segestan request for aid 208n32

sex, god's 159, 162, 167, 178n48

shame 32, 52n30, 102, 108, 113n8, 118, 203

ship-of-state metaphor 201, 211n77

Sicily 17, 187, 188–89, 200, 208n31, n32, 209n36

Simonides 3, 89

Sintians, wild-talking 161

Skiron 140n64

slavery 16, 17, 18, 33, 170, 172, 183, 191, 194, 205–6, 207n8, 208n31, 213n100

Solon 113n12, 149, 165

Sophist 21, 25, 38, 39, 48, 55n68, n69, 102, 107, 114n24, 153, 154, 171, 219–20

Sophocles 8, 11n24; *Antigone* 211n75; *Oedipus Tyrannus* 208n20

soul 8, 22, 26, 27, 38, 53n45, 71, 76n27, 97–98, 104, 108, 137, 153, 156, 163, 164, 169, 190, 201–5, 215, 218–20, 221n10

Sparta/Spartans 8, 17, 18, 24, 32, 49, 52n23, 55n55, 68, 70, 75n26, 100, 101, 108, 110, 111–12, 118–19, 135, 140, 153, 170, 171, 175, 176n6, 181n94, 183, 184, 186–87, 189–94, 198, 200, 202, 207n9, n10, n11, n12, 209n39, 210n50, n54, 211n75

Sphagia (Sphacteria), battle of 17, 183, 186, 187, 200

stepmother 70, 126–28, 135, 166, 167, 171
Strabo: *Geography* 149
stylometric analysis 30, 52n27
Suda 46, 59–60, 74n4, n8, 103, 136

Tanagra and Oenophyta, battle of 17, 186, 200
Thebes, founding of by Cadmus 164, 171
Themistocles 50, 57n118, 197, 207n12
Thermopylae, battle of 110, 184
Thirty Tyrants 39, 40, 41, 55n67, 63, 75n18, 191
Thucydides: *History of the Peloponnesian War* 4, 6, 8, 9, 10n6, 24, 31, 47, 49, 60, 61, 66, 87, 101, 120, 135, 136, 158, 176n3, n6, 187–89, 190, 194, 196, 199, 210n63, 215
thumos 204
Timaeus 2, 3
timocracy 220
Tissaphernes 189, 190
training 70, 71, 100, 108, 109, 110, 111, 112, 118, 167, 202, 203; of a wife 34; Socrates' 15, 23; Spartan 8, 70, 101
tripartition of humanity 70, 174, 201–6
Trivigno, Franco 78–79, 91, 194

Trojan War 53n35, 62, 130, 137n10, 197
Typhon, child of Ge 161
Typhone (Tuphaeon) 161
tyrant 149, 206, 219

Ulysses (James Joyce) 89

Varro 176n11
Vernant, Jean-Pierre 110
virtue 8, 15, 18, 31, 34, 35, 67, 69, 70, 81, 100, 101, 102, 105, 106–7, 111, 119, 151, 189, 214, 216

walls and ships 200, 211n75
Wickkiser, Bronwen 120
Wilamowitz-Moellendorff, Ulrich von 23, 51n6
Williams, Bernard 8, 11n24

Xenophon 21, 24, 25, 34, 35, 36, 38, 39, 41, 53n45, 54n46, n47, 55n68, 56n86, 190, 191, 192, 195, 197, 209n45, 210n50, n52, n53, n54, 211n76
Xerxes 45, 62, 75n14, 184

Zeno 48
Zeus 62, 75, 108, 130, 151, 153–54, 160–61, 168